INDOOR PLANTS

INDOOR PLANTS

THE ESSENTIAL GUIDE TO CHOOSING AND CARING FOR HOUSEPLANTS

JANE COURTIER & GRAHAM CLARKE

CONSULTANT ANNE HALPIN

Reader's Digest

A Reader's Digest Book
Conceived, edited, and designed by
Marshall Editions

PROJECT EDITOR Gwen Rigby
ART EDITOR Frances de Rees
PICTURE EDITOR Zilda Tandy
DTP EDITORS Mary Pickles, Kate Waghorn, Lesley Gilbert
COPY EDITORS Jolika Feszt, Maggi McCormick
MANAGING EDITOR Lindsay McTeague
PRODUCTION EDITOR Emma Dixon
EDITORIAL DIRECTOR Sophie Collins
ART DIRECTOR Sean Keogh
PRODUCTION Bob Christie

Library of Congress Cataloging in Publication Data

Courtier, Jane
    Indoor plants : the essential guide to choosing and caring for
houseplants / Jane Courtier and Graham Clarke.
        p. cm.
    Includes index
    ISBN 0-89577-921-8
    1. House plants. 2. Indoor gardening. I. Clarke, Graham.
    II. Title.
    SB419.C63 1997
    635.9'65—dc20   96-42046

Printed and bound in Italy

CONTENTS

INTRODUCTION 6
HOW TO USE THIS BOOK 8

Chapter 1
DECORATING WITH PLANTS 10

FOLIAGE PLANTS 12
FLOWERING PLANTS 14
CHOOSING THE RIGHT PLACE 16
DISPLAYING PLANTS 20
CHOOSING PLANTS FOR GROUPINGS 22
CONTAINERS 24
BOTTLE GARDENS AND TERRARIUMS 26

Chapter 2
THE PLANT DIRECTORY 28

SECONDARY PLANT LIST 146

Chapter 3
CARING FOR PLANTS 188

PLANT ANATOMY 190
THE IMPORTANCE OF LIGHT 192
TEMPERATURE AND HUMIDITY 194
WATERING 196
FEEDING 198
REPOTTING 200
TRAINING 204
PROPAGATION METHODS 206
SPECIALIST GROWING METHODS 210
PESTS AND DISEASES 212
BUYER'S GUIDE 216

GLOSSARY 232
INDEX 234
ACKNOWLEDGMENTS 240

INTRODUCTION

PLANTS HAVE A VERY SPECIAL PLACE IN OUR homes. They are living ornaments that grow and develop; they undergo subtle changes through the seasons, presenting an ever-varying display. They respond to and repay our care and attention. A thriving plant is a source of pride to its owner, and it imparts a feeling of well-being to any room. And for those who spend a lot of time indoors, houseplants provide a wonderful and all-important link with nature and the world outdoors.

You don't need to be a horticultural expert in order to derive pleasure from houseplants, but some knowledge of a plant's preferences for its growing conditions and the requirements for its maintenance will help it to thrive. And that is where you will find this book of immeasurable help. Here you will learn what it takes to ensure that your plants prosper: the ideal temperature and humidity and light conditions, their natural growth cycle, and whether or not they must have a rest period.

The more you know about your houseplants, the more you will appreciate them.

Not only can this book help you to keep the plants you already have in good health, it is an invaluable guide to finding new plants that will suit the conditions in your home as well. The information in this book will alert you to the basic needs of a wide range of plants—from the familiar foliage and flowering plants to exotic orchids. Armed with this book, you will have a better chance of success with any plant. In addition, you'll be wise enough to resist those (often disappointing) impulse buys. And you'll be able to appraise a plant that has eye-catching color, a sweet scent, or an unusual appearance with a knowledgeable eye.

A final word of advice and encouragement: If you find a plant that you want very badly, but feel cautious about it in terms of its specific needs, by all means take a chance and buy it—unless it is prohibitively expensive. Compare the price of a potted

Small cacti are mostly inexpensive to buy, so it is easy to make a collection. But the problem is how to display the little plants to advantage—a difficulty attractively solved here by massing them in a wire basket.

Orchids are the epitome of glamour and the exotic to most people. They are quite challenging to bring into bloom, but given the right conditions, orchids produce exquisite flowers. The pride and delight that these blooms inspire will far outweigh the care and attention they demand.

plant with that of a bouquet of cut flowers. Chances are, the plant will give you your money's worth even if it lasts for only a few months.

You can never be certain in advance how well a plant will do; you have to try it. Some plants are wonderfully (and unpredictably) cooperative. They do not seem to understand the rules, and they appear to be determined to thrive in the most unexpected places and under the least auspicious of growing conditions.

However, if a plant is failing, consider moving it to another location. For example, a plant that does not like drafts can be moved from, say, an entry hall to an area that has similar light but is more protected. You will be either pleasantly surprised by a dramatic recovery, or you will have to try yet another spot; you may even, eventually, have to admit defeat. But whether you are adventurous or not with your indoor gardening, take pride in your efforts and, above all, enjoy your houseplants.

Miniature cyclamens, primulas, and ivies, planted together in a ceramic trough, can bring the color and scent of spring into the home long before it arrives outdoors.

A more unusual plant, for a person who wants something different, is Clianthus formosus, *Sturt's desert pea, which produces spectacular scarlet flowers with a purple-black central blotch. It needs a cool bright room or greenhouse in order to flourish.*

Crocuses (left) *are another welcome, easy-to-grow reminder of spring. Plant a handful of corms in a small pot for a splash of color.*

HOW TO USE THIS BOOK

THE FIRST CHAPTER OF THIS BOOK TELLS YOU how to decorate your home with houseplants, how to take advantage of their shapes and special features, such as flowers and foliage. You will learn how to choose the right plant for every room in your house, and you will find ideas for the many different kinds of containers that can be used, plus information on supports for plants that vine and climb.

Chapter 2, The Plant Directory, is an exhaustive reference guide to more than 300 houseplants. It gives details of each plant's requirements—temperature, humidity, lighting conditions, repotting, origin, and more. The first part of the Directory covers the most popular houseplants; the second part deals with some of the more unusual plants and illustrates each specimen in full-color.

CHAPTER 1
Decorating with Plants

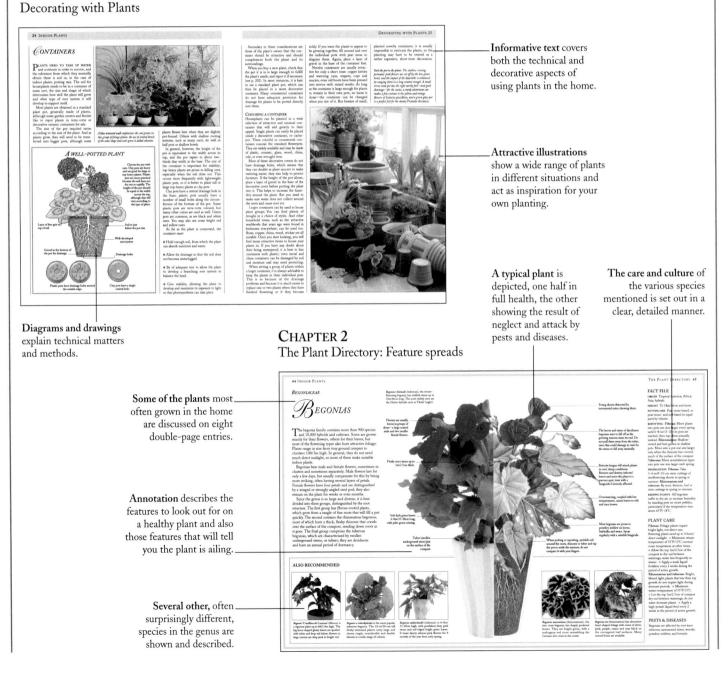

Informative text covers both the technical and decorative aspects of using plants in the home.

Attractive illustrations show a wide range of plants in different situations and act as inspiration for your own planting.

Diagrams and drawings explain technical matters and methods.

CHAPTER 2
The Plant Directory: Feature spreads

Some of the plants most often grown in the home are discussed on eight double-page entries.

Annotation describes the features to look out for on a healthy plant and also those features that will tell you the plant is ailing.

Several other, often surprisingly different, species in the genus are shown and described.

A typical plant is depicted, one half in full health, the other showing the result of neglect and attack by pests and diseases.

The care and culture of the various species mentioned is set out in a clear, detailed manner.

All you need to know about caring for plants is clearly set forth in Chapter 3. It begins with a simple explanation of how plants function, and goes on to point out how light, temperature, and humidity affect them. You will find the necessary information about feeding, watering, training, and potting, as well as some more-unusual techniques, such as growing plants hydroponically and under supplementary lighting.

Propagation by a wide variety of means is fully covered. And there is a wealth of valuable illustrated instruction about plant pests and diseases and how to combat them. A series of easy-reference charts summarizes the relevant information about all the individual plants that are profiled in The Plant Directory. And a concise glossary explains some of the less familiar technical terms used throughout the book.

Chapter 2
The Plant Directory

Plants are listed alphabetically under their scientific names, and the family names and most frequently used common names are also given.

The introductory text describes the plant and, in some instances, varieties and related species.

On full-page entries there is a second photograph, which is either a detail of the plant or shows another variety or related species.

Annotation around the plant gives tips for growing or information about possible pests and diseases.

Some other varieties of the plant or related species that you might like to grow are listed.

Photographs show a wide range of healthy plants; those that flower are displayed in bloom.

Chapter 3
Caring for Plants

Simple, straightforward, authoritative text covers all aspects of plant care. Charts give all the information about every plant in the Directory at a glance.

Annotated photographs show and describe some of the equipment you can use for specific jobs.

Easy-to-follow, step-by-step illustrations demonstrate the correct way to care for your plants.

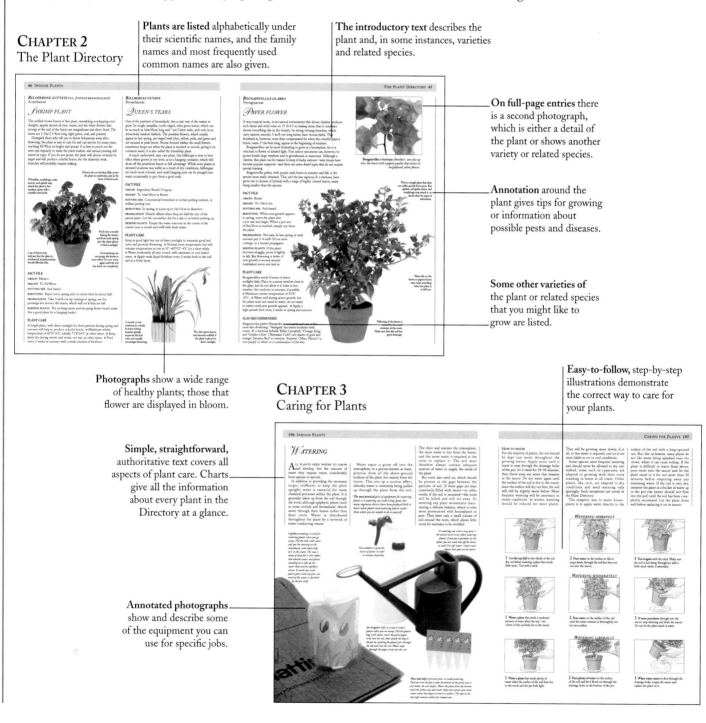

Decorating with Plants

Walk into any garden center or store with a reasonable selection of houseplants, and you will see evidence of the huge diversity of plant shapes and forms that exist. Among these shapes you will find some that are more appealing to you than others, but you will also need to bear in mind how suitable they are for the specific locations you wish to enhance in your house.

A tall, striking, "architectural" plant may be called for to provide a dramatic feature in a prominent position in a large, simply furnished living room. A smaller, more crowded room may be better served by low-growing foliage and flowering plants grouped together on a windowsill or table. No matter how attractive a particular specimen appears in the store, always try to imagine it in your own home before buying it.

Plant shapes fall into six principal groups, but there is some overlap among the groups.

Upright
A plant such as *Sansevieria trifasciata*, mother-in-law's tongue or snake plant, would be defined as upright, with its dramatic tall, sharp spikes. Such plants have no hint of spreading or trailing stems to soften the outline, even after several years' growth.

Bushy
Many indoor plants are classified as bushy. They may have several stems or just one main stem, which divides low down into a number of branches. The branches spread out to form a more or less rounded, bushy shape, which is well furnished with foliage. *Dieffenbachia maculata*, dumb cane, has a bushy habit, as do pot chrysanthemums. But with the latter, it is the way the raisers treat the plants, rather than their natural habit of growth, that gives them their form.

Trailing
Soft stems cascade down, sometimes concealing the plant's pot entirely. In some

Plants give a room an inviting air. Here a bushy fern and round-headed standard azalea lead the eye to the staircase wall, which is lightly clothed with a lax-stemmed creeper.

PLANT SHAPES

Dieffenbachia maculata

Ficus pumila

Chamaerops humilis

Ficus benjamina

Monstera deliciosa

Sansevieria trifasciata

instances, the stems are prostrate, such as those of *Zebrina pendula*, wandering Jew, or *Ficus pumila*, the creeping fig.

The stems of other plants strike out upward to begin with, then bend over gracefully as they develop, giving the effect of a fountain. The ever-popular *Chlorophytum comosum*, spider plant, has this appearance, although it is not just the grassy foliage that produces the effect. As plants start to mature, they produce lots of "baby" plants on the ends of long, pliable stems; these cascade down to make the plant a true trailer.

Climbing
A climber generally has lax stems, which will trail if they are not supplied with supports, but which will scramble eagerly upward when they are able to. Sometimes these plants need encouragement to start climbing; often nothing will stop them.

They may have twining stems, clinging tendrils, or aerial roots to support them in their upward quest.

Standard
Standards are treelike plants that have a main stem and a branching head. *Ficus benjamina*, a popular example, also has an attractive weeping habit, hence its common name of weeping fig.

Architectural
The term "architectural" applies to forms that are unusual and dramatic. The shape and outline of such plants is bold and eye-catching, and architectural plants are usually grown as stand-alone specimens. They are always large plants, tending to be tall rather than spreading, such as *Chamaerops humilis*, the European fan palm, which has big, boldly cut, fan-shaped leaves and sturdy, hairy stems.

FOLIAGE PLANTS

GROWN MAINLY FOR THEIR LEAVES, foliage plants may also produce flowers. Sometimes these flowers are an added short-term attraction. Sometimes they are insignificant. Occasionally they detract from the appearance of the plant and are best pinched off while in bud.

Foliage plants may be valuable for the shape, texture, or color of their leaves. They are normally of year-round value in the home, although a few, such as caladiums, die back in winter.

LEAF SHAPE
There are literally dozens of different leaf shapes, some of which are particularly attractive and striking. Leaf size, too, varies widely and, together with the shape, plays an important part in the overall effect created by the plant.

Among the many shapes to be found are the bold, handlike leaves of *Fatsia japonica*, Japanese aralia; the deeply incised leaf fans of *Howea belmoreana*, the curly palm; the heart-shaped foliage of *Philodendron scandens*, the heartleaf philodendron; and the sharp spikes of *Yucca elephantipes*, the spineless yucca.

The huge leaves of *Monstera deliciosa* develop slits and holes that give the plant its common name, Swiss cheese plant; and the foliage of *Syngonium podophyllum* is responsible for the names of goosefoot and arrowhead vine. The needlelike leaves of *Asparagus densiflorus* 'Sprengeri' make it look like a fern.

Many leaves are divided into leaflets, such as the narrow, scalloped fingers of *Dizygotheca elegantissima* and the umbrella-rib leaves of *Schefflera arboricola*, the umbrella tree.

The margins of leaves may be waved, crenulated, serrated, or toothed; the bases and tips of each leaf differ in their shapes and patterns. The size of leaves can range from the tiny, bright green pinheads of *Nertera granadensis*, the bead plant, to the extravagant foliage of *Monstera deliciosa* and *Ficus lyrata*, the fiddle leaf fig.

LEAF TEXTURE
Glossy, leathery, corrugated, downy, velvety, spiny, waxy—the texture of leaves can differ as much as their shape and color and can give fascinating visual, as well as tactile, effects. The boldly marked foliage of *Begonia rex*, painted-leaf begonia, has short, stiff hairs all over the surface, which gives it a rough, sandpaper texture. In contrast, the hairs on the foliage of *Gynura* 'Purple Passion,' the purple passion vine, are soft, producing a plush effect that gives the plant the common name of velvet plant.

The veins stand out prominently on the backs of the leaves of *Begonia rex*, whereas the raised veins of *Maranta leuconeura*, the prayer plant, appear on the top surface of the leaf. In

Chamaedorea elegans

Asparagus densiflorus 'Sprengeri'

Saintpaulia spp.

Pelargonium crispum

Jasminum polyanthemum

Kalanchoe blossfeldiana

Impatiens walleriana

Syngonium podophyllum

Dracaena marginata 'Tricolor'

Cyclamen persicum

Spathyphyllum wallisii

Camellia japonica

Nerium oleande

between the raised veins, tiny hairs give the maranta leaf a satiny look and feel.

Peperomias have deeply corrugated, wrinkled leaf surfaces, as do many pileas, including *Pilea cadieri*, the aluminum plant. The leaves of the rubber plant, *Ficus elastica*, are thick, glossy, and leathery. At the other end of the scale, the delicate, paper-thin, translucent foliage of *Caladium* x *hortulanum* has given it the common name of angel wings.

LEAF COLOR

If asked what color leaves are, most people would unhesitatingly reply "green." The majority of leaves may be predominantly green, but that is by no means the whole story. Even among plants with completely green foliage, there are many different shades and subtleties of color. Some greens are so dark as to be almost black – as in the rubber plant *Ficus elastica* 'Black Prince' – while the delicate foliage of *Adiantum raddianum*, the delta maidenhair fern, is the fresh, pale green of springtime.

Leaves can be variegated with gold, cream, or white, sometimes around the margin of the leaf, sometimes over its entire surface. These markings may take the form of irregular splashes or mottling, or they may occur in a distinctive pattern. The leaf veins are often highlighted by a contrasting color, and sometimes the leaves are so strongly variegated that they appear to be yellow or white with green markings. Many ivies are attractively variegated: *Hedera helix* 'Little Diamond' has small leaves with silvery edges, and the much larger leaves of *H. algeriensis* 'Gloire de Marengo' are mottled all over with several shades of green, gray, cream, and white.

Variegation in shades of pink and red may also occur: *Dracaena marginata* 'Tricolor' has long slender leaves picked out with fine cream lines and a bright pink edge. In *Maranta leuconeura erythroneura*, the herringbone plant, the leaves are fascinatingly marked, with bright red veins and an irregular backing of pale green or yellow on the central rib.

The green coloring in leaves is chlorophyll, which is essential for plants to be able to make their food satisfactorily. However, some plants seem to be able to survive with very little chlorophyll, which gives rise to interesting and unusual leaf colors. *Iresine herbstii*, the beefsteak plant, for example, is so called because its foliage and stems are a bright red. And some varieties of *Begonia rex* have leaves of pink, red, silver, and purple, with no green to be seen.

The delicate, paper-thin leaves of caladium are often white or cream with a pink central flush and perhaps just a fine margin of green or green veins. Easier to grow are *Coleus blumei*, the cheerful flame nettle, and *Codiaeum variegatum pictum*, known with good reason as Joseph's coat. Both of these can be found with leaves vividly patterned in a wide range of brilliant—and often gaudy—shades of red, yellow, orange, and brown. The chlorophyll in these nongreen plants is present, but it is well masked by the other pigments.

Begonia rex

Hypoestes phyllostachya

Schlumbergera x *buckleyi*

Ficus benjamina

Peperomia caperata

Hedera helix

Abutilon striatum 'Thompsonii'

Iresine herbstii

Gynura 'Purple Passion'

Clivia miniata

Dieffenbachia maculata

Dracaena sanderiana

Dracaena fragrans 'Massangeana'

FLOWERING PLANTS

JUST AS THERE IS AN ENORMOUS choice of leaf types, shapes, and colors among foliage plants, so the number of flowering plants is immense. Flowers appear in all colors of the spectrum. They may be small individually but carried in large numbers to produce their effect, or they may be large and bold enough for a single flower stem to be the center of attention. There is, too, a vast array of shapes from the simple, five-petaled trumpets of jasmine or daisylike cinerarias to the curious appearance of some members of the orchid family. Double, single, pendant, star-shaped, trumpet-shaped, pouched, or rosette-forming—the choices are endless.

Spring provides enchanting and colorful plants for the house. Pots of bulbs with miniature cyclamens, African violets, and primroses make a heartwarming display.

Sometimes a plant is not grown for its flowers but for the leafy, flowerlike bracts that may be far more colorful and eye-catching than the true flowers. *Euphorbia pulcherrima*, poinsettia, for example, has small yellow flowers in the center of showy red, cream, or pink bracts. And the scrambling bougainvillea also relies on papery, brightly colored bracts for its charm. Insignificant flowers may be

followed by interesting fruits, as is the case with *Solanum capsicastrum*, the false Jerusalem cherry.

Most flowers are grown for their color and appearance, but some are enjoyed mainly for their scent. Twining white jasmine can perfume a whole room, and the sweet scent of the waxy cream trumpets of stephanotis is almost over-powering. Gardenias are not easy plants to bring into bloom, but the white-to-cream, double or semidouble blooms are intensely fragrant.

Many spring bulbs—narcissi, hyacinths, and crocuses among them—can be flowered indoors, where their delicate perfume can be more easily appreciated than when they are grown in the garden. *Narcissus tazetta* 'Paperwhite' is a particularly good choice for fragrance and is simple to grow, flowering four to six weeks after planting (no cold, dark period is necessary).

By their nature, flowering plants tend to have a limited season of interest. The length of the flowering period can vary considerably. Some plants, such as orchids, have very long-lasting flowers; others have flowers whose individual lives are brief, but because new flowers are

constantly opening to replace them the period of interest is prolonged.

Many plants have attractive foliage, which makes them good to look at even when the flowers are over. The pineapple-like blooms of *Aphelandra squarrosa*, the zebra plant, last for several weeks; but when they die, the dark green leaves with their herringbone pattern of white veins make the plant still highly decorative.

Yellow and orange calceolarias, slipper flowers (right), *complement the glowing golden wood of an antique chest of drawers and mirror.*

A striking clivia (left) *with its fan of leaves and head of orange flowers is bold enough to stand alone.*

BUYING PLANTS

Indoor plants are available from a wide range of outlets, including supermarkets, florists, discount stores, and mail-order nurseries as well as garden centers. Always buy from an outlet where the plants are regularly and well cared for; otherwise, you are asking for disappointment. As a general rule, garden centers and nurseries will give you the widest choice and the most reliable plants.

In winter, protect the plant from cold weather on its journey home, preferably enclosing it entirely in a plastic sleeve or cardboard box made for the purpose. Once home, settle the plant in the location you have selected for it and avoid the temptation to keep moving it from place to place. Be prepared for it to look a little unhappy for a short spell as it adjusts to the different environment of your house; it is not unusual for a few leaves to fall or flower buds to drop off. As long as you have chosen a position that provides a suitable temperature, humidity, and light level for the particular species, it will soon recover and start to grow happily.

When buying plants, pick medium-size, robust, healthy plants with no obvious signs of damage, pests, or disease.

Test the soil surface with your finger: it should be just moist. Reject specimens that are bone-dry or sodden.

Look at the base of the pot to see whether roots are protruding from the drainage holes. A lot of visible root means the plant should have been repotted and its growth is likely to have been checked.

Flowering plants should have plenty of developing buds and not too many fully open flowers.

Avoid plants from display units near doorways. They are likely to have been subjected to fluctuating temperatures.

CHOOSING THE RIGHT PLACE

EVERY HOME WILL PROVIDE A surprisingly wide variation of environments, and it is important to select the right plant for the right place. This does not only mean choosing the plant that looks best in a particular location; it also means finding plants that will be happy in the conditions provided. The major variables are light levels and temperature; these are dealt with in more detail in Chapter 3.

Living rooms are probably the most popular areas for plant displays, since they are the rooms in which we tend to relax and enjoy our surroundings. Many plant lovers, though, like to have decorative plants in virtually every room of the house. Of course, each house will be different, but there are some general points that apply to most homes.

HALLS

The hall is often the first part of your home a visitor sees, and plants help to create a pleasant, welcoming atmosphere. It can be a difficult location for plants, however, since it is often narrow, restricting the room for plant displays, and receives little natural light. Halls are usually cooler than the living areas of the house. Opening and closing the front door causes drafts and temperature fluctuations, and if the stairway is situated in the hall, warm air will tend to rise, causing an updraft. The front door is often used only by visitors, so plants near it tend to be forgotten.

LIVING ROOMS

These rooms are generally fairly light, with plenty of windows, and they often face the sun. They are usually fairly large rooms, where taller, architectural plants can be most easily accommodated. They

A bedside table is the ideal place for an exotic orchid (above). *What better way to greet the morning than by gazing at the perfect blooms?*

Nothing could be more inviting than the prospect of a meal under a leafy vine in a sunroom (left) *full of colorful plants such as abutilon and campanula, which love the light.*

are usually comfortably warm while the family is at home, but the temperature may drop considerably at night and if the house is empty during working hours. Time-controlled central heating can also cause wide fluctuations in temperature.

Central heating also provides a dry atmosphere, and most plants will appreciate some extra humidity. See p. 197 for more details on how to provide this.

KITCHENS

Many families spend a lot of time in the kitchen. And while you are likely to be busy there peparing meals and cleaning up, plants help to create a welcoming, pleasant environment. A large kitchen may also be used for eating and as a general family room where many activities take place. This sort of kitchen tends to be kept evenly warm and is often reasonably light; it is therefore suitable for many types of plants.

Older houses or apartments may have small, cramped kitchens, which often face away from the sun and have small windows. Temperatures there tend to fluctuate widely, rising considerably during cooking but cooling down quickly afterward. Humidity levels in kitchens are often high, due to steam from cooking, washing, and so on. So plant leaves can quickly become coated with greasy, sticky deposits and thus need frequent cleaning. Consequently tough, glossy-leafed specimens may do better than those with soft, delicate foliage.

The kitchen is primarily a working area. Plants must not get in the way and should never compromise safety when people are working around hot surfaces.

Wicker pot covers tie in with the wicker furniture in this living room. Foliage plants, which need less light, stand at the back of the room, while the pelargonium enjoys a bright spot near the window.

Bright light, warm colors, and plants such as bamboo, orchid, and bromeliad, which thrive in a warm, humid atmosphere (below), *make this a bathroom to luxuriate in and enjoy.*

SUNROOMS

Increasing numbers of houses now have sunrooms, not just for growing plants, as was the case years ago, but to provide extra living space. Most modern sunrooms are fully heated and furnished, but the high light levels they enjoy still make them excellent places for a wide selection of plants.

Temperatures can become extremely high in summer, and ventilation and blinds or some other form of shading is

nearly always necessary to prevent leaf scorch and to lower the temperature to a more comfortable level. Unheated sunrooms will obviously be cold in winter and are unlikely to be suitable for many houseplants, although some warmth will be obtained from adjoining rooms.

BEDROOMS

Although the bedroom may be the room in the house where we spend most hours, we are asleep and unappreciative of the

delights of plants for much of the time. Many bedrooms face east, and the bedroom windowsill is a popular place for a few undemanding plants. A special effort needs to be made to remember to water them, however, since they can easily be forgotten in the family's often-rushed morning routine.

BATHROOMS

Although many bathrooms receive little sun, modern bathrooms have the advantage of being evenly warm throughout the day, with high levels of humidity, providing good conditions for plant growth. Light levels are often good, with frosted or obscured glass giving the bright, diffused light favored by many plants.

But beware: the temperature will rise rapidly when a bathtub or shower is in use, then it will fall quickly, leading to the cool, moist conditions that make plants prone to fungal disease.

CHOOSING THE RIGHT PLACE

NOTES FOR ROOM PLAN
The rooms in every house differ in their aspect, their size, how well they are heated, the lighting, and so on, and this will affect your choice of plants. This plan gives you a few ideas for plants that are likely to suit particular rooms.

BEDROOM
Cool to moderately warm; good light. Choose easy-to-care-for plants that can put up with a little neglect.

Cyclamen persicum
Fatshedera lizei
Fuchsia hybrids
Jasminum polyanthum
Maranta leuconeura erythroneura
Pelargonium × *hortorum*
Saintpaulia spp.
Spathiphyllum wallisii

BATHROOM
Moderate warmth; good diffuse light; periods of high humidity.

Adiantum raddianum
Asplenium nidus
Calathea makoyana
Carex morrowii 'Variegata'
Chamaedorea elegans
Chlorophytum comosum 'Vittatum'
Cissus antarctica
Cyperus alternifolius
Epipremnum aureum
Ficus pumila
Maranta leuconeura erythroneura
Nephrolepis exaltata
Peperomia scandens
Philodendron scandens

ENTRANCE HALL
Fairly cool; poor to moderate light. Plants must not be fragile.

Aglaonema commutatum
Aspidistra elatior
Chlorophytum comosum 'Vittatum'
Cissus antarctica
Clivia miniata
Fatsia japonica
Hedera helix
Tradescantia fluminensis

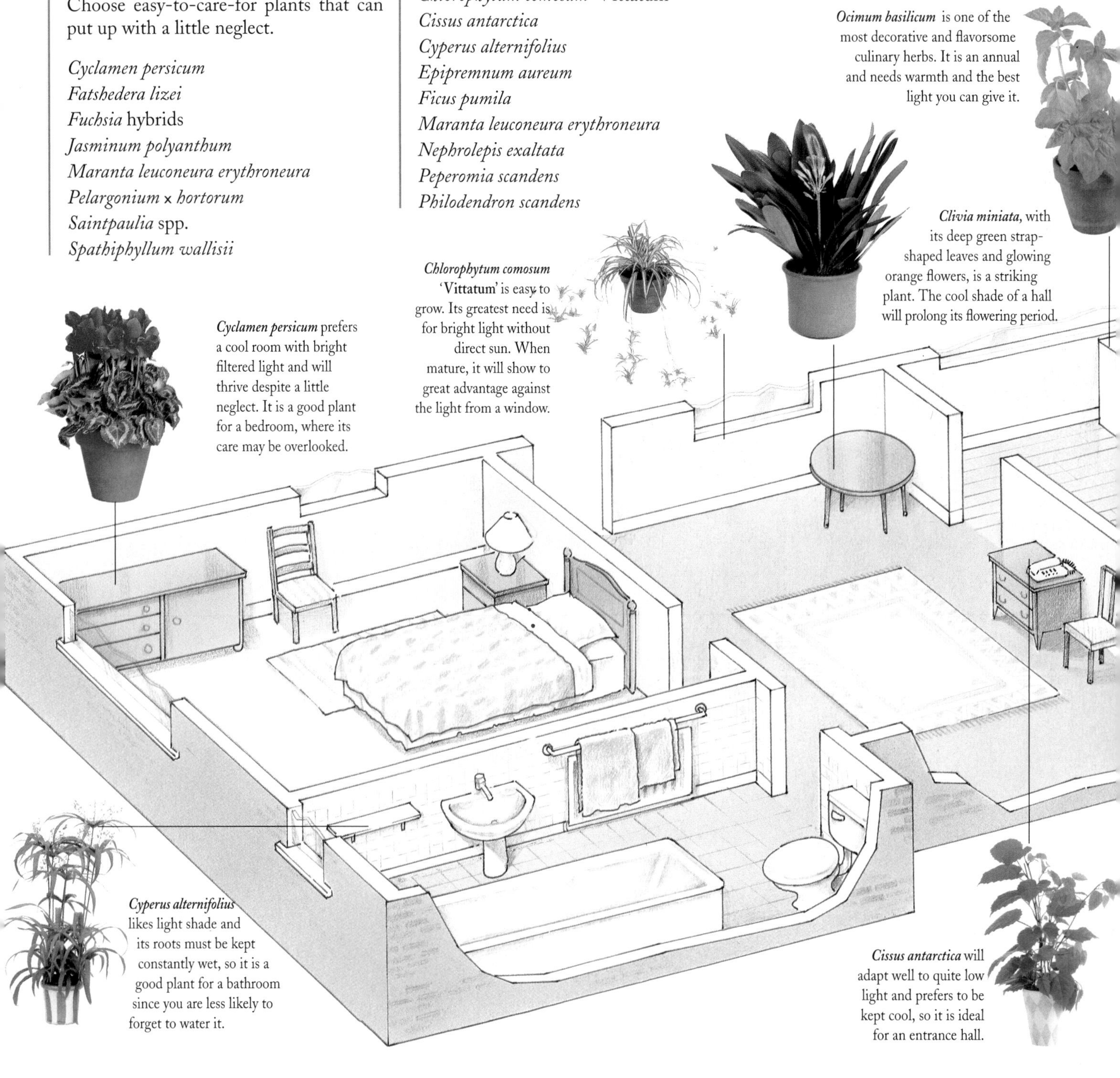

Ocimum basilicum is one of the most decorative and flavorsome culinary herbs. It is an annual and needs warmth and the best light you can give it.

Clivia miniata, with its deep green strap-shaped leaves and glowing orange flowers, is a striking plant. The cool shade of a hall will prolong its flowering period.

Chlorophytum comosum 'Vittatum' is easy to grow. Its greatest need is for bright light without direct sun. When mature, it will show to great advantage against the light from a window.

Cyclamen persicum prefers a cool room with bright filtered light and will thrive despite a little neglect. It is a good plant for a bedroom, where its care may be overlooked.

Cyperus alternifolius likes light shade and its roots must be kept constantly wet, so it is a good plant for a bathroom since you are less likely to forget to water it.

Cissus antarctica will adapt well to quite low light and prefers to be kept cool, so it is ideal for an entrance hall.

KITCHEN

Warm; humid; poor to moderate light; best to use temporary plants that can be replaced regularly.

Begonia rex
Chrysanthemum x *morifolium*
Coleus blumei
Epipremnum aureum
Hedera helix
Herbs
Impatiens walleriana
Saintpaulia spp.
Tradescantia fluminensis 'Variegata'
Zebrina pendula

LIVING ROOM

Warm; good light; adequate space for specimen plants and groups.

Begonia rex
Codiaeum variegatum pictum
Dieffenbachia maculata
Dracaena marginata
Euphorbia pulcherrima
Ficus benjamina
Ficus elastica 'Robusta'
Ficus lyrata
Hydrangea macrophylla
Kalanchoe blossfeldiana
Monstera deliciosa
Philodendron bipinnatifidum
Rhododendron simsii
Yucca elephantipes

GREENHOUSE OR SUNROOM

Heated all year; bright light. Take advantage of the good conditions to grow some more exotic specimens.

Abutilon pictum 'Thompsonii'
Aechmea fasciata
Aeschynanthus speciosus
Allamanda cathartica
Anthurium scherzerianum
Bougainvillea glabra
Caladium x *hortulanum*
x *Citrofortunella microcarpus*
Columnea x *banksii*
Datura x *candida*
Gloriosa superba 'Rothschildiana'
Orchids
Passiflora caerulea
Peperomia scandens
Philodendron scandens
Strelitzia reginae

Impatiens walleriana is a cheerful, free-flowering temporary plant. Set on a kitchen table at which the family has its meals, it brings the summer indoors.

Columnea x *banksii* enjoys bright light but not direct sun. It flowers profusely in winter and early spring, and is good in a hanging basket.

Bougainvillea glabra will thrive in the warmth and bright light of a sunroom, and will bloom throughout summer and fall.

Dracaena marginata is an excellent plant for a living room. It will tolerate a fairly wide variation in temperature and needs bright filtered light.

Hydrangea macrophylla provides a welcome temporary splash of color among the more permanent plants. When flowering is over, the plant can be put on the patio or planted outdoors.

Ficus elastica 'Robusta' with its sturdy straight stems and big shiny leaves will grow into a tall specimen plant in time. It will thrive in a wide variety of conditions and is largely trouble-free.

DISPLAYING PLANTS

THE MOST MAGNIFICENT PLANT CAN lose its impact if it is positioned wrongly. Choose a place that provides the conditions it likes and it will thrive. But you should also choose a place where it will be shown to its best advantage.

SPECIMEN PLANTS

Many plants can be successful when displayed on their own, as single specimens. These are normally fairly large subjects, with a bold outline or dramatic foliage, the so-called architectural plants. Such plants can make an excellent focal point, particularly if spotlights are used for highlighting.

Ficus elastica, the rubber plant, is perhaps less popular than it once was, but its relative, *Ficus benjamina*, the weeping fig, makes a splendid specimen plant. *Ficus lyrata*, the fiddle leaf fig, has a less elegant shape, but its large, boldly curved leaves provide a point of interest.

A well-grown *Dracaena marginata*, the Madagascar dragon tree, with its tree-like form and spiky foliage, looks especially good in a simply furnished, modern room. So do many of the palms, such as *Howea belmoreana*, the curly palm, or *Chamaedorea elegans*, the parlor palm. In older-style houses, plants with softer, more rounded, and less aggressive outlines are often more appropriate.

Climbing plants, trained up supports, can also make excellent specimen plants, and their eventual height can be controlled. *Monstera deliciosa*, *Philodendron scandens*, and *Epipremnum aureum* will all make large and statuesque specimens.

Specimen plants are best displayed where they do not have to compete for attention with elaborate furnishings: give them some space to themselves. Plain walls allow the foliage and outline of the plant to be properly appreciated; patterned wallpaper tends to create a confused effect unless the pattern is very subtle. Light-colored walls display most plants well, although pale and variegated leaves may show up better against darker backgrounds.

Use lighting to complement the plant and give it a new dimension after dark. Completely different effects can be achieved with low-level and high-level spotlights, and backlighting can give dramatic results when used with boldly cut foliage. Glossy-leafed plants are given extra sparkle with artificial lighting, but the foliage must be kept clean and bright.

Specimen plants are normally placed on the floor for the most satisfactory effect, although smaller plants can be set on low tables. Choose a decorative pot that will balance the height and width of the plant so that it does not appear to be top-heavy.

PLANT GROUPS

Grouping a number of different plants together has several advantages. It allows you to create a satisfying display with

Large architectural plants need large modern uncluttered spaces to show to greatest advantage (left). *This fine* Ficus benjamina *is well placed; it is the focus of attention at the entrance to the two minimally furnished and neutral-colored rooms, and at the same time it draws them together.*

A wide windowsill in a more traditional type of house (right) *calls for completely different treatment, with several plants grouped together. The grouping is not, however, random. The busy patterning of the pots and pitchers is given unity by their coloring and is offset by the block of red of the cyclamen and the strong color accent provided by the purple African violets.*

contrasting or complementary foliage types; short-term flowering plants can add welcome color and interest, since they can be removed or replaced when their blooms die back. Plants with ungainly shapes or leggy stems can more easily be disguised. And a plain-leafed plant that would look dull alone makes its own valuable contribution when set among other foliage or flowering plants.

Not only do plant groups often look better, they tend to grow better too, for a humid microclimate that provides excellent growing conditions is created within the group. It is also easier to look after plants when they are together than when they are dotted around the room: you are less likely to overlook them, and watering is less of a chore. Plants that are grouped together should all enjoy roughly similar conditions of warmth and humidity. Light is less important because it is easier to accommodate varying needs by strategic positioning.

The easiest way to create a group is simply to bring together plants in their individual pots and arrange them on a

HANDLE WITH CARE

Some houseplants need to be treated with caution, especially if there are children or pets in the home. A number of species are poisonous if eaten, and others can cause skin irritation or scratches. Children are probably unlikely to eat many houseplants, but brightly colored berries are tempting. Cats, particularly, and some dogs may chew a wide variety of plants, though they rarely seem to come to any harm.

Unpleasant skin rashes can be experienced after handling a number of plants, such as *Primula obconica,* by people who are allergic to them, but you do not need to have an allergy to suffer from the spines of cacti—even the silky-seeming hairs of *Cephalocereus senilis,* old-man cactus, hide vicious barbs. The tips of sharp, spiky leaves, such as those of some aloes, which may also bear spines, can also injure people. Be particularly careful not to position such plants at eye level, and remember that the eye level of children and animals is lower than your own.

COMMON POISONOUS PLANTS

Capsicum annuum	Ornamental chili pepper: poisonous berries
Datura candida	Angel's trumpet: all parts poisonous
Dieffenbachia **spp.**	Dumb cane: sap causes painful swelling of mouth and throat
Euphorbia pulcherrima	Poinsettia: poisonous sap
Nerium oleander	Oleander: all parts extremely poisonous
Solanum capsicastrum	False Jerusalem cherry: poisonous berries

windowsill or tabletop. The pots should be similar: plain terra-cotta ones are usually more pleasing than a variety of different-colored or patterned containers.

Saucers are necessary for effective watering and to prevent furniture from being spoiled by drips. If you do not want individual saucers, the plants can be placed together on a large tray.

If the tray is half-filled with pebbles or gravel, you can easily increase the humidity around the group by pouring water into the tray to just below the top of the gravel. Or you can put the plants in a deeper, ornamental container that will cover the individual pots entirely (see p. 25).

Already-planted groups in decorative containers can be found in many stores and garden centers. Do not expect these plants to have a long life, however. They are planted closely in small containers for instant effect and are chosen more for their appearance than for their similarity of needs. They should be regarded as short-term decoration, although individual plants can usually be saved if the group is dismantled and replanted once it begins to look jaded.

CHOOSING PLANTS FOR GROUPINGS

PLANT GROUPS USUALLY WORK BEST IF they have some sort of theme—color, texture, or shape—rather than being a haphazard mixture. Groups of plants from within the same family are often successful: cacti, for example, or air plants or spring bulbs. One advantage of this method is that all the plants will enjoy the same growing conditions. You may wish to compose your group entirely of the same species of plant, perhaps contrasting varieties and a range of flower or leaf colors, such as are found among *Saintpaulias* (African violets) or *Coleus blumei* (flame nettles.) Or you may prefer the massed effect of three identical poinsettia plants or florists' chrysanthemums.

With foliage plants, using a range of different shades of green can be effective, and a strongly variegated form is emphasized by displaying it among plants with plain leaves. The color of the variegation can be echoed by flowering plants, with the white markings of the weeping fig *Ficus benjamina* 'Starlight,' for example, being picked up by a white chrysanthemum or white campanula. Colors in the plant group can also be used to reinforce the color scheme of the room itself, or of a particular ornament or painting. Contrasts can be used effectively, with pale green walls forming a background for a group of dark green foliage plants enlivened with a brilliant scarlet poinsettia or a striking yellow kalanchoe, for instance.

Different-textured leaves also make interesting companions. Several species and varieties of peperomia and pilea have rippled or corrugated foliage, and some have variegation and stripes as well. *Asparagus densiflorus* 'Sprengeri' makes a bright green haze to contrast with the sharply upright spikes of the pineapple, *Ananas comosus*, or the leathery straplike leaves of a clivia.

The softly furry leaves of *Columnea gloriosa* and *Gynura* 'Purple Passion' seem to be just asking to be stroked, but spiky dracaenas and cordylines warn off would-be touchers.

One of the most pleasing ways to arrange a group of plants with different forms is to create a triangular shape, with one or two tall plants and a number of lower, more spreading types below them. The apex of the triangle can be in the center of the group or to one side of it. If all the plants are much the same height, it is sometimes a good idea to raise one of the pots to vary the level of the group.

FINDING THE RIGHT PLACE

The windowsill is probably the most popular place for any houseplant, but some, especially plant groups, deserve a more prominent position. A large group, with one or two tall specimens, is ideal for a place on the floor near patio doors, where the plants help to link the house with the garden outside and will enjoy good light. Smaller groups may occupy a display table or take the central position on a dining table.

A fireplace is often the focal point of a room, and in summer the hearth can house an attractive collection of indoor plants. A color theme of reds, yellows, and oranges, which mimic the flames, or

Plants with several different leaf shapes in shades of white, green, and cream are harmoniously combined in this arrangement for a hall. The tall, pale orchid provides the focus of attention, with the other, lower-growing plants grouped at its base.

cool blues, greens, and white emphasizing the summer season both work well. In summer the mantelpiece is also a good location for plants, particularly trailing varieties. A mirror behind the display doubles the effect, but extra care must be taken with the arrangement of the plants in this instance.

Always take the plants' needs, as well as their esthetic effect, into account when choosing their location. A group of plants may well brighten up a dark corner, but they will not stay in good condition for long unless supplementary lighting is used.

Do not position plants where people walking past will continually brush against them. The brushing is very likely to damage the plants, and it is annoying as well. And make sure that plants are safe and secure—not likely to topple over or drip water onto expensive furniture or carpets or electrical equipment.

A rough-textured sunny wall and brilliantly colored pots form a pleasing setting for this group of various cacti, a partridge-breast aloe, and a succulent, all of which look quite different but have similar growing requirements—an important consideration when you are grouping plants.

African violets, massed in a shallow china bowl and ranging from pale to deep mauve and pink to ruby red, are the ideal choice of plants here. They echo both the colors and the old-fashioned charm of the antique porcelain figurine, drawing the eye to it and at the same time providing a glowing pool of color among the otherwise cool neutrals of the room.

CONTAINERS

PLANTS NEED TO TAKE UP WATER and nutrients in order to survive, and the substance from which they normally obtain these is soil or, in the case of indoor plants, potting mix. The soil for houseplants needs to be in a container of some sort, the size and shape of which determines how well the plant will grow and what type of root system it will develop to support itself.

Most plants are obtained in a standard plant pot, generally made of plastic, although some garden centers and florists like to repot plants in terra-cotta or decorative ceramic containers for sale.

The size of the pot required varies according to the size of the plant. And as plants grow, they will need to be transferred into bigger pots, although some

A blue textured wall emphasizes the cool greens in this group of foliage plants; the use of several bowls of the same shape and color gives it added cohesion.

plants flower best when they are slightly pot-bound. Others with shallow rooting systems, such as many cacti, do well in half pots or shallow bowls.

In general, however, the height of the pot is equivalent to the width across its top, and the pot tapers to about two-thirds that width at the base. The size of the container is important for stability; top-heavy plants are prone to falling over, especially when the soil dries out. This occurs more frequently with lightweight plastic pots, so it is better to plant tall or large top-heavy plants in clay pots.

Clay pots have a central drainage hole in the base; plastic pots usually have a number of small holes along the circumference of the bottom of the pot. Some plastic pots are terra-cotta colored, but many other colors are used as well. Green pots are common, as are black and white ones. You may also see some bright red and yellow ones.

As far as the plant is concerned, the container must

● Hold enough soil, from which the plant can absorb nutrients and water.

● Allow for drainage so that the soil does not become waterlogged.

● Be of adequate size to allow the plant to develop a branching root system to balance the head.

● Give stability, allowing the plant to develop and maximize its exposure to light so that photosynthesis can take place.

A WELL-POTTED PLANT

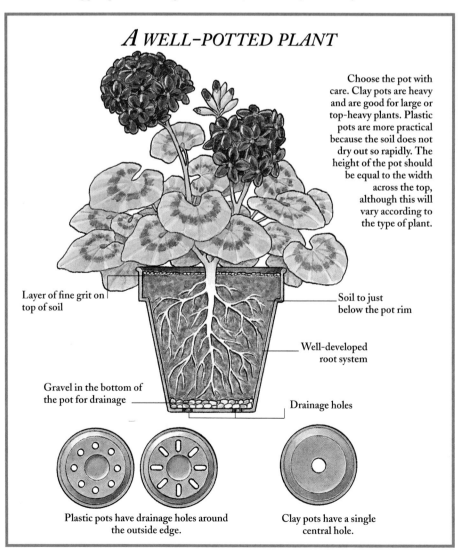

Choose the pot with care. Clay pots are heavy and are good for large or top-heavy plants. Plastic pots are more practical because the soil does not dry out so rapidly. The height of the pot should be equal to the width across the top, although this will vary according to the type of plant.

Layer of fine grit on top of soil

Soil to just below the pot rim

Well-developed root system

Gravel in the bottom of the pot for drainage

Drainage holes

Plastic pots have drainage holes around the outside edge.

Clay pots have a single central hole.

Secondary to these considerations are those of the plant's owner that the container should be attractive and should complement both the plant and its surroundings.

When you buy a new plant, check that the pot it is in is large enough to fulfill the plant's needs, and repot it if necessary (see p. 202). In most instances, it is best to use a standard plant pot, which can then be placed in a more decorative container. Many ornamental containers do not have adequate provision for drainage for plants to be potted directly into them.

CHOOSING A CONTAINER

Houseplants can be planted in a wide selection of attractive and unusual containers that will add greatly to their appeal. Single plants can easily be placed inside a decorative container, or cachepot. These colorful or ornamental containers conceal the standard flowerpots. They are widely available and may be made of plastic, ceramic, glass, wood, china, tole, or even wrought iron.

Most of these decorative covers do not have drainage holes, which means that they can double as plant saucers to make watering easier; they also help to protect furniture. If the height of the pot allows, place a layer of gravel in the base of the decorative cover before putting the plant into it. This helps to increase the humidity around the plant. But you need to make sure water does not collect around the roots and cause root rot.

Larger containers can be used to house plant groups. You can find plenty of troughs in a choice of styles. And other household items, such as the attractive washbowls that years ago were found in bedrooms everywhere, can be used too. Brass, copper, china, wood, wicker are all suitable. Once you start looking, you will find many attractive items to house your plants in. If you have any doubt about their being waterproof, it is best to line containers with plastic; even metal and china containers can be damaged by soil and moisture and may need protecting.

When setting a group of plants within a larger container, it is always advisable to keep the plants in their individual pots. This is so because of the drainage problems and because it is much easier to replace one or two plants when they have finished flowering or if they become sickly. If you want the plants to appear to be growing together, fill around and over the individual pots with peat moss to disguise them. Again, place a layer of gravel in the base of the container first.

Novelty containers are usually attractive for only a short time: copper kettles and watering cans, teapots, cups and saucers, even old boots have been pressed into service with mixed results. As long as the container is large enough for plants to remain in their own pots, no harm is done—the container can be changed when you tire of it. But beware of small, planted novelty containers; it is usually impossible to extricate the plants, so the planting may have to be treated as a rather expensive, short-term decoration.

Suit the pot to the plant. The shallow-rooting primulas' pink flowers are set off by the low green bowl, and the impact of the hyacinths is enhanced by ranging them in a long ceramic trough. A small terra-cotta pot has the right earthy feel—and good drainage—for the cactus, a sturdy aluminum can makes a fine contrast to the yellow and orange flowers of Justicia pauciflora, *and a green glass pot is a perfect foil for the dainty* Primula obconica.

BOTTLE GARDENS AND TERRARIUMS

PLANTS GROWN IN A SEALED GLASS container create their own, separate, virtually self-sustaining environment. A well-planted bottle garden or terrarium is attractive and easy to look after, but both the container and the plants must be chosen with care.

A wide range of containers is suitable, including candy jars, goldfish bowls, fish tanks, and even large brandy glasses. Try to choose one with a stopper so that it can be sealed, although clear plastic or plastic food wrap can be stretched tightly over the top of some glasses and jars. Specially made bottles are available for planting, but they are sometimes tinted green, which interferes with the growth of the plants. Choose clear glass or the lightest tint you can find. Terrariums like miniature old-fashioned greenhouses in

A terrarium shaped like an old-fashioned greenhouse with open sides is easier to plant and water than a bottle. It is also easier to care for plants and replace them when they become too large.

appearance are easier to plant and extremely attractive, although they tend to be expensive. Plastic versions are cheaper, but they may not have the same appeal as glass ones.

PLANTS FOR THE BOTTLE GARDEN

Bottle gardens and terrariums are ideal for delicate plants that like high humidity and will thrive away from the drafts and dry air of open rooms. The plants need to be slow-growing or your container will soon be swamped. Flowering plants should, on the whole, be avoided, since dead flowers may be difficult to remove and will soon rot.

Buy small specimens and check them carefully for any signs of pests or diseases before planting; remove any damaged stems or foliage cleanly.

Suitable plants include:
Adiantum raddianum and *A. hispidulum,* maidenhair ferns
Begonia bowerii, miniature eyelash begonia
Cryptanthus spp., earth stars
Ficus pumila minima, miniature creeping fig
Fittonia verschaffeltii and *F. v. argyroneura,* painted and silver net leaf
Pellaea rotundifolia, button fern
Peperomia caperata 'Little Fantasy,' emerald ripple
Pilea nummularifolia, creeping Charlie
Selaginella kraussiana and *S. martensii,* spreading clubmosses

PLANTING A BOTTLE GARDEN

1 Use a funnel of heavy paper or cardboard to pour the gravel, charcoal, and peat-moss-based potting mix into a narrow-necked bottle.

2 "Landscape" the soil to form a slight slope; then, with a teaspoon tied securely to a stake, scoop out a hole for the first plant in the place you have planned for it.

3 Holding the plant carefully between two bamboo stakes, maneuver it through the neck of the bottle and into the hole you have just made in the soil.

4 Firm the soil around the plant's roots by gently pressing it down with a spool tied to a stake. Repeat the process until all the plants are in their chosen positions.

Once the planting is complete and the plants have been watered, set the bottle close to a window where it will receive bright light but no direct sun.

PLANTING

First, wash out the container with water and detergent; then fill it with water that contains some bleach or disinfectant to kill off any fungus spores and rinse it thoroughly. Make sure that the inside of the container is completely dry before planting it.

Start by pouring in gravel until there is a layer about 1in/2.5cm deep in the bottom. (With a narrow-necked bottle, use heavy paper or cardboard rolled into a funnel to pour in the gravel.) Add a thin layer of charcoal pieces to keep the soil sweet, then add 2–3in/5–8cm of peat-moss-based potting mix. Landscape the mix to produce a slight slope.

You will find it much easier to plant the bottle if the opening is large enough for your hand to pass through. For planting narrow-necked bottles, you will either have to buy special tools or improvise by tying a fork, a teaspoon, and a spool to long stakes to use as planting and firming tools.

Plan the arrangement of the plants before you start to plant them. Take into account whether the garden will be viewed from one side only or all around. Remove the plants from their pots and tease out the roots; wash off some of the soil and trim the roots if necessary. Scoop a hole in the potting mix with the teaspoon, insert the plant by holding it between two stakes, and firm it gently into place with the spool.

AFTERCARE

When planting is finished, cover the surface of the potting mix with a thin layer of fine sand. Trickle some water down the sides of the bottle to wash any soil off the glass and moisten the potting mix; lightly mist the plants in a terrarium. Leave the container open for a few hours after planting, then replace the stopper; if there is no stopper, stretch some self-clinging plastic film or food wrap over the mouth of the container or close the door of a terrarium.

If the inside of the glass mists over and will not clear, ventilate the container for a short while. Changes in temperature will bring about temporary condensation, but once the garden has settled down, neither watering nor regular ventilation should be necessary. Keep the bottle garden or terrarium in a position where it receives good bright light but not direct sunlight.

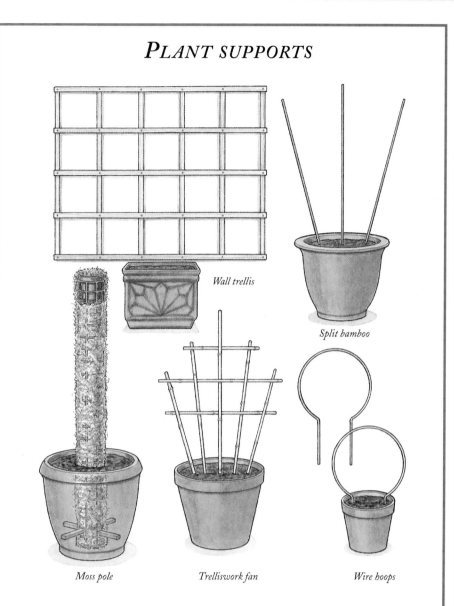

PLANT SUPPORTS

Wall trellis

Split bamboo

Moss pole

Trelliswork fan

Wire hoops

Many plants need supports to keep them shapely, to hold up flowering stems, or because they are climbers. Any type of support should be as unobtrusive as possible.

Climbers that produce aerial roots, such as *Monstera deliciosa*, the Swiss cheese plant, will grow well around a moss pole or a synthetic substitute. To encourage the roots to grow into the moss, the pole should be kept moist by frequent misting or by watering it through a tiny thumb pot set in the top of the moss. A deep container filled with soil-based potting mix is necessary to provide adequate stability for a tall pole.

Jasmine and other climbers look attractive trained around wire, plastic, or cane hoops. This keeps the plant neat and encourages flowering by bending the shoots down and slowing the flow of the sap. Two hoops set at right angles will form a plant ball.

Trelliswork, of wood, wire, or plastic, can take the form of a fan inserted into a pot or can be attached permanently to a wall to support scrambling plants. A free-standing trellis covered with a vigorous climber makes an attractive room divider.

Split bamboo stakes are useful as a temporary support or for training a wayward stem. Green stakes are the least conspicuous; cut them so they do not show above the plant. Use soft twine or plant ties to attach stems gently to their supports; a figure-eight loop prevents stem damage.

*T*HE PLANT DIRECTORY

THE PLANT DIRECTORY IS DIVIDED INTO TWO SECTIONS. The first part deals in depth with the most popular indoor plants, and the second part covers some of the less common subjects. All the plants in the main directory are illustrated with specially commissioned photographs. In order to include the maximum number of plants, the Secondary Plant List carries illustration only of some. However, the same type of information is given for the plants in both sections.

Two pages from the main directory are shown below. They contain most of the elements that appear in all the entries, and to help you make the best use of the information, these elements are clarified in the accompanying notes.

Botanical name Plants are listed alphabetically by their botanical name.

Family name Knowing what family a plant belongs to helps you understand its requirements and allows you to discover other indoor plants to which it may be related.

Common name This is the name by which the plant is most popularly known.

FACT FILE
Origin Tells you the geographical area in which the plant originated.
Height Gives the height most average specimens, kept in good growing conditions, are likely to reach in the home within two or three years. The ultimate height will, of course, be determined by the size of container, level of care, and any pruning carried out, so this is only a rough guide.
Potting mix Indicates whether the plant prefers a soil-based or peat-moss-based (soilless) medium. Where peat-moss-based medium is specified, the new peat-substitute mixtures may also be used.
Repotting Explains the best time of year to move the plant into a larger container, and gives an idea of how often this should be done. When you are advised to repot "as necessary," this means when the roots are showing through the base of the pot, or a plant is overcrowded in its container.
Propagation Tells the main methods of increasing the plant in the home. Methods that require special equipment, such as a heated propagator or that are difficult to do are noted.
Keeping plants A plant's preferences and special needs—for pruning and training, pinching off growing tips, deadheading, and the like—are listed, along with information about how to treat the plant in the different seasons of the year.

BELOPERONE GUTTATA (SYN. *JUSTICIA BRANDEGEANA*)
Acanthaceae

*S*HRIMP PLANT

The reddish brown bracts of this plant, resembling overlapping roof shingles, appear almost all year-round, and the white flowers that emerge at the end of the bracts are insignificant and short-lived. The leaves are 1–3in/2.5–8cm long, light green, oval, and pointed.

Disregard those who tell you to throw beloperone away after flowering: the plant is easy to care for and can survive for many years, reaching 3ft/90cm in height and spread. It is best to pinch out the stem tips regularly to make the plant bushier, and annual pruning will renew its vigor. If you do not prune, the plant will almost certainly be larger and will produce colorful bracts, but the relatively weak branches will probably require staking.

If bracts do not develop fully, prune the plant in midwinter, just as the show of bracts ends.

Whiteflies, mealybugs, scale insects, and aphids may attack the plant in hot weather; spray with a suitable insecticide.

Feed once a month during the winter, and from early spring give the plant plenty of direct sunlight.

Loss of leaves may indicate that the plant is rootbound; annual potting should alleviate this.

Overwatering can encourage the leaves to turn yellow. Do not water again until the soil has dried out completely.

FACT FILE
ORIGIN Mexico.
HEIGHT To 3ft/90cm.
POTTING MIX Soil-based.
REPOTTING Repot every spring and cut stems back by about half.
PROPAGATION Take 3-in/8-cm tip cuttings in spring; use the prunings but remove the bracts, which will rot if they are left.
KEEPING PLANTS The arching stems and drooping flower heads make this a good plant for a hanging basket.

PLANT CARE

A bright place, with direct sunlight for short periods during spring and summer will help to produce colorful bracts. ● Minimum winter temperature of 60°F/16°C; ideally 75°F/24°C at other times. ● Keep fairly dry during winter and moist, not wet, at other times. ● Feed every 2 weeks in summer with a weak solution of fertilizer.

BILLBERGIA NUTANS
Bromeliaceae

*Q*UEEN'S TEARS

One of the prettiest of bromeliads, this is also one of the easiest to grow. Its tough, straplike, tooth-edged, olive green leaves, which can be as much as 16in/40cm long and ½in/13mm wide, arch over in an attractively random fashion. The pendant flowers, which usually appear in late spring, are tinged with blue, yellow, pink, and green and are encased in pink bracts. Nectar formed within the small flowers sometimes drops out when the plant is touched or moved, giving it its common name; it is also called the friendship plant.

A much underrated, easy-care plant, this billbergia is seen to best effect when grown at eye-level, as in a hanging container, which will show off the pendulous bracts to full advantage. While most plants in elevated locations may suffer as a result of dry conditions, billbergias are much more tolerant, and small hanging pots can be plunged into water occasionally to give them a good soak.

FACT FILE
ORIGIN Argentina; Brazil; Uruguay.
HEIGHT To 16in/40cm in flower.
POTTING MIX Commercial bromeliad or orchid potting mixture, or soilless potting mix.
REPOTTING In spring, in a pot up to 5in/13cm in diameter.
PROPAGATION Detach offsets when they are half the size of the parent plant. Let the cut surface dry for a day or so before potting up.
KEEPING PLANTS Empty the water reservoir in the center of the rosette once a month and refill with fresh water.

PLANT CARE

Keep in good light but out of direct sunlight to maintain good leaf color and promote flowering. ● Normal room temperature, but will tolerate temperatures as low as 35°–40°F/2°–4°C for a short while. ● Water moderately all year-round, with rainwater or cool boiled water. ● Apply weak liquid fertilizer every 2 weeks both to the soil and as a foliar spray.

A month or two outdoors in a shady location during summer greatly improves the leaf color and usually encourages flowering.

The olive green leaves may become reddish the plant is placed direct sunligh

Illustration Photo shows typical plant of the size and form you are likely to find available for sale in garden centers and nurseries.

Plant description Introductory text describes the plant's main features and lists some of the varieties and allied species that may be available.

Second illustration On full-page entries, an interesting feature of the plant, or another variety or related species is pictured.

Annotation Tips on cultivation or information about pests and diseases that may affect the plant are given in annotations near the main illustration.

BOUGAINVILLEA GLABRA
Nyctaginaceae

*P*APER FLOWER

A true tropical exotic, in its natural environment this showy climber produces such dense and vivid color on 15-ft/4.5-m trailing stems that it outshines almost everything else in the vicinity. Its strong twining branches, which carry narrow, smooth, 3-in/8-cm-long leaves, have vicious barbs. This drawback is, however, more than compensated for when the colorful papery bracts, some 1½in/4cm long, appear at the beginning of summer.

Bougainvillea can be most frustrating to grow as a houseplant, for it is reluctant to flower in limited light. Fine indoor specimens can, however, be grown beside large windows and in greenhouses or sunrooms. Although a climber, this plant can be trained to keep it bushy indoors—wire hoops have become popular supports—and there are some dwarf types that do not require special training.

Bougainvillea glabra, with purple-pink bracts in summer and fall, is the species most easily obtained. This, and the less vigorous *B. x buttiana*, have given rise to dozens of hybrids with a range of highly colored bracts, many being smaller than the species.

FACT FILE

ORIGIN Brazil.

HEIGHT To 15ft/4.5m.

POTTING MIX Soil-based.

REPOTTING When new growth appears in spring, move the plant into a pot one size larger. When a pot size of 8in/20cm is reached, simply top-dress the plant.

PROPAGATION Not easy. In late spring or early summer put 3–4-in/8–10-cm stem cuttings in a heated propagator.

KEEPING PLANTS If the plant becomes straggly, prune it lightly in fall. But flowering is better if new growth is wound around established stems and tied in.

PLANT CARE

Bougainvillea needs 4 hours of direct sunlight daily. Place in a sunny window close to the glass, but do not allow it to bake in hot weather. Set outdoors in summer, if possible. ● Minimum winter temperature of 50°F/10°C. ● Water well during active growth, but the plant must not stand in water; do not water in winter until new growth appears. ● Apply a high-potash feed every 2 weeks in spring and summer.

ALSO RECOMMENDED

Bougainvillea glabra 'Alexandra' is rose pink and one of the most free-flowering. 'Variegata' has leaves bordered with cream. *B. x buttiana* hybrids 'Killie Campbell,' 'Orange King,' and 'Golden Glow' ('Hawaiian Gold') are shades of gold and orange; 'Jamaica Red' is crimson; 'Surprise' ('Mary Palmer') is rose purple or white or a combination of the two.

Bougainvillea x buttiana 'Amethyst', seen close up here, has bracts with a papery quality that enclose its insignificant yellow flowers.

This is a tough plant that does not suffer greatly from pests. But aphids, red spider mites, and mealybugs may attack it, so check often for signs of infestation.

Water left on the leaves or papery bracts may cause scorching when the plant is in full sun.

Yellowing of the leaves is caused by too much moisture at the roots. Make sure that the soil has good drainage.

PLANT CARE

The information is always given in the following order.

Light This tells you whether a plant needs bright, moderately bright, or shaded conditions. "Direct sun" or "Full sun" means a plant can be exposed to sunlight all day, all year-round: "Some direct sun" means it benefits from several hours of sun a day but does not require day-long exposure. "No direct sun" means that damage is likely to occur to leaves or flowers if sunlight is allowed to fall on the plant, particularly through glass. "Filtered" or "diffuse" light means sunlight should be filtered by a lightweight curtain.

Temperature Where plants are not very specific in their temperature requirements, "average" or "normal" room temperature is advised. This means ordinary, comfortable living conditions both winter and summer—usually around 65°–70°F/18°–21°C. Minimum recommended temperature is sometimes given; this is the lowest temperature possible for healthy growth and development, but plants will not necessarily be damaged by an occasional dip below this point.

Watering This gives advice as to watering the plant freely, moderately, or sparingly. (For step-by-step instructions on this topic, see pp. 196–97.) Keeping the potting mix moist means that it should be neither saturated nor allowed to dry out so that it shrinks away from the sides of the pot.

Feeding Explains the type of fertilizer to use and when and how often it should be applied. (For how-to instructions, see pp. 198–99.)

Other points Any other special needs such as increasing the level of humidity are noted here.

ALSO RECOMMENDED

This gives suggestions for other related plants you might consider growing.

***ABUTILON PICTUM* 'THOMPSONII'**
Malvaceae

$\mathscr{S}$POTTED FLOWERING MAPLE

Originating in tropical to warm temperate areas, particularly South America, where it grows in lightly wooded terrain, this is a tender plant related to the mallows. The genus is made up of about 150 shrubs, perennials, and annuals, which are grown for their bell-shaped, drooping flowers and maplelike leaves on long stalks.

This form has attractive green-and-yellow mottled leaves 3–5in/8–13cm long and with three to five lobes. Its red- and orange-veined flowers are 2–3in/5–8cm long and open from spring to fall. In the wild, the plant will grow into a large shrub, but as an indoor pot plant, it is best kept to 2–4ft/60cm–1.2m. Abutilons are long-lasting and therefore useful as semipermanent feature plants. And since they need plenty of direct sunlight, they do particularly well in front of a window.

All abutilons respond well to pruning, and you should not be afraid to use the shears when a plant grows beyond its allocated space. Cut back spindly growth in early spring; remove any thin shoots that crowd the center of the plant and reduce others by a third.

FACT FILE

ORIGIN Brazil.

HEIGHT To 7–10ft/2.1–3m.

POTTING MIX Soil-based.

REPOTTING Move plants into a pot one size larger each spring, until a 9-in/23-cm pot is reached. Top-dress large plants annually.

PROPAGATION Take 4-in/10-cm tip cuttings in spring and summer and root in equal parts of sand and peat at a temperature of 75°F/24°C.

KEEPING PLANTS Deadhead regularly during the summer. Pinch out growing tips occasionally to maintain bushy growth.

PLANT CARE

Direct sunlight, which will enhance the leaf variegation. ● Winter temperature of 45°–55°F/7°–13°C; the plant may lose some or all of its leaves during this dormant period. ● Little water in winter; water freely in summer. ● Apply a weak liquid fertilizer every 2 weeks from early spring to late summer. ● Large plants can be top-heavy, so make sure containers are large enough to prevent them from falling over.

ALSO RECOMMENDED

Abutilon x *hybridum* is the name given to a group of hybrids that are generally available from garden centers and stores. Look for *A.* x *h.* 'Savitzii,' with the palest of green leaves, 'Cannington Red,' with golden yellow foliage and striking rose red blooms. 'Pink Lady' has bright pink flowers with deeper pink veins, and 'Kentish Belle' bears vibrant orange flowers.

Abutilon x hybridum *'Red Belle' will grow into a large free-flowering shrub with deep red flowers up to 2in/5cm long that look like Chinese lanterns.*

Flowers appear between the leafstalk and the stem, so buy bushy plants with plenty of side shoots.

Check the leaves regularly for signs of infestation by aphids, whiteflies, red spider mites, and cyclamen mites.

Give the plant the greatest amount of direct sunlight possible, or leaf and flower color will be dull.

Mealybugs and root mealybugs both attack abutilons. Check the plant carefully for these pests.

ACALYPHA HISPIDA
Euphorbiaceae

ℛED-HOT CAT'S-TAIL

Guaranteed to be a conversation piece, this exotic plant is one of a few species in the genus to produce conspicuous taillike flowers. The tiny, bright red blooms, which emerge from the leaf axils, usually in late summer and fall, can reach 12–18in/30–46cm in length. They droop in tassels, without petals, and resemble lengths of chenille, hence the plant's other common name of chenille plant. The bright green, slightly hairy, pointed oval leaves are 5–8in/13–20cm long and 3in/8cm wide. *Acalypha hispida* 'Alba' is an attractive white-flowered form.

The plant will form a shrub 6ft/1.8m tall if allowed to grow unchecked; even if it is kept to just half this size, you should give it plenty of space. Acalyphas require a high level of humidity.

Dull green leaves with tiny brown spots are the first signs of red spider mites. Keep the atmosphere moist to discourage that pest.

Watch out for mealybug infestation. If you spot the cottonlike coating, pick off the bugs and spray the nest areas with insecticide.

Flowers may appear throughout the year, given the right conditions.

FACT FILE

ORIGIN Java; Papua New Guinea.

HEIGHT To 6ft/1.8m.

POTTING MIX Soil-based.

REPOTTING Cut back in early spring to 10in/25cm above a leaf and repot into a pot one size larger.

PROPAGATION Take 3–4-in/8–10-cm stem cuttings in spring and establish them in equal parts of sand and peat moss at 75°F/24°C.

KEEPING PLANTS Acalypha is naturally bushy, so there is no need to pinch out the growing tips. Prune it back annually or renew it each year from cuttings, which take readily, and discard the old plant. Plants are rarely worth keeping after 2 years.

PLANT CARE

Bright filtered sunlight. ● Temperature range of 65°–85°F/18°–29°C . ● Plenty of water in summer; less in winter. ● Stand the pot on a tray of damp pebbles and mist the foliage regularly except when the plant is in flower. ● Apply a weak liquid fertilizer every 2 weeks from early spring to late summer.

ACALYPHA WILKESIANA
Euphorbiaceae

𝒞OPPER LEAF

This plant is grown chiefly for its highly colored leaves, which vary enormously and come in tints of coppery green, mottled and streaked with purple, red, and copper, giving it its best-known common name. Other names include match-me-if-you-can, beefsteak plant, fire dragon plant, and Jacob's coat. Varieties include 'Can Can,' with mainly magenta, mauve, and cream leaves, and 'Marginata,' with heart-shaped olive green leaves tinged with bronze and edged with carmine.

Like *Acalypha hispida*, this plant can reach 6ft/1.8m. The leaves are about 5in/13cm long and 2in/5cm wide.

FACT FILE

ORIGIN Java; Papua New Guinea.

HEIGHT To 6ft/1.8m.

POTTING MIX Soil-based.

REPOTTING In late spring, or at any other time if growth has been rapid, move plants into pots one size larger when roots fill the pots.

PROPAGATION In early spring plant 3–4-in/8–10-cm tip or stem cuttings in equal parts of sand and peat moss. Keep at 75°F/24°C.

KEEPING PLANTS Do not pinch out the growing tips, since this plant is naturally bushy. Discard messy plants after 2 seasons.

PLANT CARE

Bright filtered light to retain leaf color. ● Minimum winter temperature of 60°F/16°C; up to 80°F/27°C in summer. ● Plenty of water at all times, particularly in summer when the soil dries out more quickly. ● High humidity: stand the plant on a tray of damp pebbles and mist the foliage regularly. ● Apply a standard liquid fertilizer every 2 weeks during the active growing period.

Reduce the plant's size by half each spring to encourage plenty of new stems and highly colored leaves.

Check for mealybugs and red spider mites, both of which attack acalyphas.

Keep the soil moist at all times, but plants will wilt if the soil becomes sodden.

ACHIMENES
Gesneriaceae

CUPID'S BOWER

There are more than 50 hybrid varieties of achimenes, which are more frequently grown than the species. They are among the most colorful and floriferous pot plants, producing abundant white, pink, purple, blue, or yellow flowers throughout the summer. These appear on short stalks from the leaf axils and comprise a narrow tube flaring out into five broad lobes. Each flower lasts only a few days, but the flowering period is extensive. Leaves are generally rich to dark green, slightly hairy, heart-shaped, and with toothed edges. Because achimenes have weak stems, they are ideal for a hanging basket where they can trail.

All achimenes grow from small, caterpillarlike rhizomes, which can be started into growth by dipping them in hot water before planting them, hence the unromantic common name of hot-water plant.

Direct sunlight over a long period may scorch the tender leaves, causing small brown spots to appear.

Aphids occasionally attack the fleshy growth at the growing tips.

Dormant tubers will survive the winter in any cool, dry place, but exposure to frost will kill them.

Do not water the plants during the dormant period. That would start them into growth at the wrong time.

FACT FILE

ORIGIN Guatemala; hybrids.

HEIGHT To 12in/30cm.

POTTING MIX Peat-moss- or soil-based.

REPOTTING In early spring, set 3–4 tubers horizontally, ½in/13mm below the surface of the potting mix in a 4-in/10-cm pot at a minimum of 50°F/10°C.

PROPAGATION Divide tubers when repotting or take 3-in/8-cm tip cuttings in early summer.

KEEPING PLANTS If allowed to dry out, even briefly, the plant will return to dormancy. But do not let flowering plants stand in water, or the root system will quickly start to rot.

PLANT CARE

Bright indirect sunlight. ● An average temperature of 65°F/18°C in the growing season; the plants will droop above 80°F/27°C. ● Water freely, particularly when the plant is in flower. ● Apply a high-potash liquid feed every 2 weeks in the flowering season.

ADIANTUM RADDIANUM
Adiantaceae

DELTA MAIDENHAIR FERN

Taken together, the four commonly grown species of adiantums are the most popular of all pot-grown ferns, with *Adiantum raddianum* the most widely grown. They are called maidenhair ferns because the leafstalks are shiny, thin, and black, much like human hair.

The plants grow from rhizomes, which spread horizontally and quickly just beneath the surface of the soil. The fronds are some 8–15in/20–38cm long and are divided into many small triangular leaflets, known more correctly as pinnae. Adiantums are very long-lasting and plants will reach a height of 12–15in/30–38cm and a width of 2ft/60cm or even larger.

FACT FILE

ORIGIN Tropical America.

HEIGHT To 15in/38cm.

POTTING MIX Open, peaty mixture.

REPOTTING Annually in spring. Pack the soil lightly; good drainage is essential.

PROPAGATION In spring, divide the clump, leaving a section of rhizome attached to each piece; pot up separately.

KEEPING PLANTS As needed to keep plants moist in summer and once a week in winter. Submerge the pot in water for 10 minutes, then drain.

PLANT CARE

No direct sunlight; adiantums do well in bathrooms and shaded parts of a sunroom. ● Winter temperature of 60°F/16°C, with a maximum in summer of 75°F/24°C. ● The roots must be kept moist at all times. ● To improve humidity, stand the pot on a tray of damp pebbles and mist the foliage twice a day. ● Apply a weak liquid fertilizer every 2 weeks from early spring to late summer.

If the fronds dry up, cut them off and spray the plant with water daily until new shoots appear.

Keep plants out of drafts and away from radiators.

Cut the plant right back if the leaflets drop off; maintain watering and humidity to encourage new growth.

Scale insects and mealybugs may attack this plant; check the fronds regularly for signs of infestation.

AECHMEA FASCIATA (SYN. *BILLBERGIA RHODOCYANEA*)
Bromeliaceae

URN PLANT

The natural home of this plant is near the floor of the rain forest, where water from the tree canopy drips onto the tough, leathery, strap-shaped leaves. These often grow to 12in/30cm in length, and they combine in the center of the plant to form a natural water-retaining vase shape, from which the common name of silver vase plant is derived.

In mature plants 3–4 years old, a central pointed pink flower stalk some 6in/15cm long emerges from the center of the leaves. The top of the stem opens into many bracts, and in summer the flowers themselves, which are small and blue, bloom on short stalks that rise between the bracts. They last for up to six weeks, after which the inflorescence gradually fades and shrivels, and then the rosette dies. At the same time, the plant produces two or three smaller spikes, or rosettes, which can be detached and potted as separate plants.

Aechmea cylindrata *produces a tall spike of flowers, enclosed in decorative bracts, that rises high above the rosette of leaves.*

FACT FILE

ORIGIN Brazil.

HEIGHT To 20in/50cm.

POTTING MIX Soilless mix with a little fresh sphagnum moss: free drainage is essential.

REPOTTING Every other year.

PROPAGATION Once the offsets at the base of the plant have grown to a viable size, after 4–6 months, remove them in spring and pot them into a rich, barely moist potting mix. Or cut out the old rosette, allowing the new offshoots to develop instead.

KEEPING PLANTS
Despite its exotic appearance, this plant is easy to care for. Simply make sure that neither the water well nor the soil dries out.

PLANT CARE

A tolerant plant, taking either direct or subdued sunlight. ● Minimum winter temperature of 55°F/13°C with, ideally, 80°F/27°C in the growing season. ● Water twice a week with rainwater if possible, keeping 1in/2.5cm depth of water in the well at all times. ● Do not feed this plant in the conventional way; instead, mist the leaves with weak liquid fertilizer occasionally in the spring and summer.

ALSO RECOMMENDED

Aechmea fasciata 'Purpurea' has striking maroon leaves and silver markings; the gray-green leaves of 'Variegata' are striped with cream-yellow along their length.

If flowers, or even the bract spikes, fail to appear, move the plant to a position receiving more light.

This plant may be attacked by aphids, scale insects, and mealybugs; check regularly for signs of infestation.

Overwatering or too low a temperature will cause the flower stem to rot; empty the rosette occasionally and allow the soil to dry out.

If the leaves develop brown tips and then shrivel, it is an indication that the plant is too hot and dry; increase watering.

AEONIUM ARBOREUM 'ATROPURPUREUM'
Crassulaceae

*P*URPLE TREE AEONIUM

This plant has dark bronze, spoon-shaped leaves 2–3in/5–8cm long; but the species plant has leaves of a fresh green color, and the variety 'Schwartzkopf' has almost black leaves. All form strong woody stems, which branch out freely and from which rosettes develop. The rosettes regularly shed some of the lower leaves, leaving the stems scarred at the points where the leaves were attached.

Panicles of small, bright yellow, star-shaped flowers form from the centers of the rosettes at the ends of the branches on mature four- to five-year-old plants. These blooms appear from winter through to spring, but once a rosette has flowered, it dies and must be cut out. Aeoniums need a lot of sunshine and fairly dry growing conditions.

FACT FILE

ORIGIN Spain; Portugal; Morocco; Sicily; Sardinia.

HEIGHT To 3ft/90cm.

POTTING MIX Two parts soil-based medium to one part coarse sand or perlite.

REPOTTING Move into a pot one size larger every spring. Newly potted plants should be firmly pressed into the potting mix.

PROPAGATION By seed, or by leaf or stem cuttings in spring or summer.

KEEPING PLANTS Use terra-cotta pots instead of plastic ones, since mature plants tend to become top-heavy and fall over; stake tall plants.

PLANT CARE

Full sunlight all year. ● Minimum winter temperature of 50°F/10°C; temperatures up to 75°F/24°C at other times. ● Keep the potting mix moist during the growing period, on the dry side at other times; leaves will shrivel if it gets too dry. ● Apply a weak liquid fertilizer every 2 weeks during the growing period. ● Let the plant rest in winter.

As the plant grows taller, it may need staking.

Overwatering encourages soft, untypical growth, which is likely to droop.

Too little light will result in sparse rosettes and elongated, prematurely falling leaves.

AESCHYNANTHUS LOBBIANUS
Gesneriaceae

*L*IPSTICK PLANT

This epiphytic plant is closely related to, and resembles, columneas. It is ideal for use in a hanging basket, since its habit is to sprawl, and a simple flowerpot cannot always confine it adequately.

The plant originates in tropical rain forests, where it thrives in the high humidity. In the wild its woody stems follow the line of the often moss-covered tree branches, while the roots grow down into any suitable material. The pale green, fleshy, elliptical leaves are up to 2in/5cm wide and 4in/10cm long. During the spring and summer, clusters of 6 to 20 flowers bloom on, or very near, the tips of the stems, which can extend to 2–3ft/60–90cm. The long, blood-red flowers, with yellowish throats, arise from deep purple "lipstick cases."

Aeschynanthus speciosus, the basket plant, has yellow-orange flowers, marked with red; *A. marmoratus* is grown not for its flowers, which are greenish yellow, but for its attractive foliage—mottled shiny and dark green on the upper surface, and flushed with red below.

Aphids may attack the plant; check it regularly for signs of infestation.

If the stems are pinned into the soil, they often branch and make side shoots. The more growing tips, the more flowers.

FACT FILE

ORIGIN Malaysia; Borneo; Java.

HEIGHT To 2ft/60cm.

POTTING MIX Coarse sphagnum moss, or a mixture of equal parts coarse peat, perlite, and leaf mold.

REPOTTING At any time; when the roots fill the pot, move the plant into a pot one size larger, or cut it back by one-third and repot it in the same pot.

PROPAGATION Take 4–6-in/10–15-cm tip cuttings in summer.

KEEPING PLANTS If kept in humid conditions, this plant does not have a rest period, so it will need watering and attention all year-round.

PLANT CARE

Bright light, with up to 2–3 hours of direct sunlight in winter; filtered light in summer. ● Normal room temperature. ● Plenty of water when the plant is in flower, less at other times. ● Raise the level of humidity by standing the pot on a tray of damp pebbles and misting the foliage daily. ● Apply a weak liquid fertilizer at every watering.

AGAVE AMERICANA
Agavaceae

ℰENTURY PLANT

A group of succulent plants grown for their "architectural" appeal, agaves are often referred to as century plants because of the mistaken belief that flowers appear only once every 100 years. In reality, plants will flower when they reach about 10 years of age; indoors, this is unlikely. This species grows so big that it can be used as a houseplant only when young—the leaves of a fully grown specimen may exceed 6ft/1.8m.

The plant forms a stemless open rosette of blue-gray leaves with needle-sharp points on the tips, so it must be kept out of the way of passersby and children, and gloves should be worn when inspecting it. In spite of these drawbacks, this agave is magnificent when grown as a specimen. Several variegated forms are available.

FACT FILE

ORIGIN Mexico.

HEIGHT Rosette to 6ft/1.8m and flower spike to 25ft/7.5m outdoors.

POTTING MIX Soil-based, with coarse sand or perlite added for drainage.

REPOTTING In spring, move into a pot one size larger; top-dress plants that have reached maximum convenient pot size.

PROPAGATION Detach offsets 3–4in/8–10cm long from the base of the plant. Leave them to dry for a day or two before potting them up.

KEEPING PLANTS In good conditions, plants will last for many years. If they flower, the rosette will die.

PLANT CARE

A sunny position at all times. ● Minimum winter temperature of 50°F/10°C; normal room temperature at other times. ● Allow the top two-thirds of the soil to dry out before watering. ● Apply a weak liquid fertilizer every 2 weeks from early spring to late summer.

Old leaves around the base eventually dry up and can be pulled off, often leaving scars on the woody stem.

During the summer, place agaves outdoors in a sunny place.

Mealybugs may leave their telltale signs—tufts of white, waxy wool—on the leaves; root mealybugs may also infest the plant's roots, which will hinder its growth.

AGLAONEMA 'SILVER QUEEN'
Araceae

𝒫AINTED DROP TONGUE

Also called Chinese evergreen, this is a hybrid whose parent plants came originally from the subtropical forests of Southeast Asia. An important quality of most aglaonemas is their ability to thrive in poor light. *Aglonema* 'Silver Queen' is a compact, low-growing plant, with leaves about 5–6in/12.5–15cm long, on short stems produced at soil level. It gains its name from the leaves, which are green only at the margins and along the main veins, with the rest of the leaf silvery white and cream. As the plant ages, it loses some of the lower leaves and develops a short, trunklike stem. Small, insignificant, petalless flowers appear in summer or autumn and are carried on a short stem at the top of which is a 2-in/5-cm-long arumlike spathe. Sometimes small orange poisonous berries are formed.

This plant likes warmth; a cold draft will soon damage the leaves.

Mealybugs and root mealybugs may attack aglaonemas.

Leaf spot disease may infect the plant, and botrytis fungus may appear if conditions are too cool.

FACT FILE

ORIGIN Southeast Asia.

HEIGHT To 3ft/90cm.

POTTING MIX Open, peaty mixture.

REPOTTING Repot in spring when necessary. Do not use a pot that is too large, since this plant grows best when its roots are confined.

PROPAGATION In spring, divide the root clump; take tip cuttings or use sections of the old plant's stem. Young plants need high humidity.

KEEPING PLANTS Do not grow this plant where there are children or pets; the sap and berries are poisonous.

PLANT CARE

Subdued light. ● Minimum winter temperature of 60°F/16°C with normal room temperature at other times. ● Water freely in summer; in winter keep the soil just moist. ● Apply a weak liquid fertilizer with every watering from early spring to late summer.

ALLAMANDA CATHARTICA
Apocynaceae

$\mathcal{G}$OLDEN TRUMPET

Although this plant is often referred to as the golden trumpet "vine"—it is after all a climber—its habit when grown in a pot is to sprawl or lean. Its demand for warmth, a humid atmosphere, and plenty of sun means that it is a plant for the sunroom or greenhouse, although it can be used as a short-term houseplant in other rooms. If grown in large containers, climbing allamandas can be trained on a trellis or wire support to cover a wall; and they are very attractive when encouraged to grow up into the ceiling space.

Allamandas are spectacular in flower, and if it were not for their rather weak constitution, they would undoubtedly be seen more often. The glossy, dark green, oval leaves are 4–6in/10–15cm long and are borne on long stems. The flaring, buttercup yellow trumpet blooms of *Allamanda cathartica* appear throughout summer and fall, and can be as much as 4in/10cm wide.

Leaves yellow and drop naturally. Prune any naked stems by half to encourage new leaf buds to break.

Check for mealybugs and scale insects, both of which attack this plant.

In damp conditions, collar rot fungus can attack the soft, fleshy stem. Scatter horticultural grit on the soil around the stem to help prevent it.

Honeydew, the sticky dark secretion from aphids, can be unsightly. If seen, wash the leaves with slightly soapy water.

FACT FILE

ORIGIN Guyana; Brazil.

HEIGHT To 8ft/2.4m and more with a similar spread.

POTTING MIX Soil-based.

REPOTTING Move into a pot one size larger each spring.

PROPAGATION Take 3–4-in/8–10-cm tip cuttings in early spring.

KEEPING PLANTS To keep the plant healthy, cut it back to roughly half its size just before growth resumes after the winter rest.

PLANT CARE

Bright light, with 3–4 hours of direct sunlight. ● Minimum of 60°F/16°C in winter. ● Water moderately in the growing season, sparingly in winter. ● Stand the plant on a tray of wet pebbles and mist it daily during summer. ● Apply a weak liquid fertilizer every 2 weeks from early spring to late summer. ● In smaller rooms, train this plant over a wire framework; although the stems are tough, they are flexible and easy to wind and unwind.

ALOCASIA SANDERIANA
Araceae

$\mathcal{E}$LEPHANT'S-EAR

Alocasias are not difficult to find, and they are worth looking for if you want a spectacular specimen plant. The erect, thick stems of *Alocasia sanderiana* carry arrow-shaped leaves 12–16in/30–40cm long and 6in/15cm wide. They are metallic silver-green, broken by yellowish gray veining, with scalloped edges and a thin white margin; the undersides have a purplish tinge. The rather insignificant petalless flowers are held on a spadix within a typical arumlike spathe.

This attention-grabbing plant is, unfortunately, not really happy in normal room conditions and should be returned to a greenhouse to recuperate after a few months. A rest period is essential in winter, during which the soil should be allowed to become almost dry between waterings, and feeding can cease completely.

FACT FILE

ORIGIN Philippines.

HEIGHT To 30in/76cm with a similar spread.

POTTING MIX Soil-based, with added peat moss or leaf mold.

REPOTTING Annually in spring.

PROPAGATION In spring, by division; by potting up the suckers; or by taking cuttings of the rhizomes.

KEEPING PLANTS Equally good as a solitary specimen plant or as part of a group of houseplants.

PLANT CARE

Bright light preferred; avoid direct sunlight in summer. ● Minimum of 65°F/18°C in winter; warm room temperature at other times, preferably above 70°F/21°C. ● Keep the soil moist during the active growth period; reduce watering in winter. ● Humidity is appreciated; so mist the leaves frequently, and stand the plant on moist pebbles. ● Feed every 2 weeks with a weak liquid fertilizer.

Check for mealybugs and red spider mites, both of which attack this plant.

Wiping dust from the metallic-looking surface can damage the leaves. It is a better idea to spray them with water to clean them.

ALOE BARBADENSIS (SYN. *A. VERA*)
Liliaceae

*M*EDICINE ALOE

Aloes are slow-growing succulents, and they display diverse size and habit. Many have leaves that are fiercely armed with hooked teeth and spines. *Aloe barbadensis,* today more frequently known as *A. vera,* is a rambling and rather messy-looking plant that has appreciably larger rosettes of growth than *A. variegata* (p. 38). It is a trouble-free houseplant and lives up to its common name in that the sap from a broken leaf has amazing curative and restorative qualities when rubbed on sores and bruises, and even when used on the hair. As its other common name, burn plant, indicates, it can also be used to alleviate the pain from burns. It has long been cultivated and has now become naturalized in many countries around the world and is used both in medicines and cosmetics.

The plant forms a stemless clump of dagger-shaped gray-green leaves, faintly spotted with white and edged with soft teeth in shades of pink and red. The leaves are 1–2ft/30–60cm long and 2–3in/5–8cm wide. A stalk up to 3ft/90cm long carries tubular 1-in/2.5-cm-long yellow flowers in spring.

FACT FILE

ORIGIN Northeast Africa; Arabian Peninsula.

HEIGHT To 2ft/60cm.

POTTING MIX Soil-based with added coarse sand.

REPOTTING Repot young plants into a pot one size larger in spring each year. When maximum convenient pot size has been reached, top-dress shoots, or offsets, when the leaves are just beginning to form rosettes. Sticky sap exudes from the shoot, so leave it for 2 days to dry before planting it in a just-damp mixture of soil and sand at normal room temperature.

PROPAGATION By removal of suckers, cuttings of young growth, and seeds, if available.

KEEPING PLANTS This aloe is reasonably hardy and trouble-free and should last for several years.

PLANT CARE

A bright location, with some direct sunlight in winter. ● Water by immersing the pot for 10 minutes; do not let water collect in the rosettes of leaves. Allow the soil to almost dry out before rewatering. In winter, water every 3–4 weeks. ● Feed monthly in spring and summer with high-potash fertilizer.

ALSO RECOMMENDED

Aloe jucunda is a pretty little plant, forming 3-in/8-cm-wide rosettes of spiny, rich green leaves with cream blotches. *A. humilis* has incurving, upright, 4–6-in/10–15-cm-long, spiny blue-green leaves. *A. h.* 'Globosa' is slightly smaller.

If the leaves turn brown and dry, the plant has not received enough water. Soak thoroughly for an hour and then drain.

Overwatering, particularly in winter, will induce black marks on the leaves and cause the plant to rot.

Check for scale insects, which attack this plant.

Mealybugs and root mealybugs both infest this plant. Check the leaves regularly for signs of the pest, and if the plant looks sickly scrape away the top ½in/13mm of potting mix and make sure there are no insects on the roots.

Aloe jucunda
produces a single spike of pale rose pink and white flowers from the center of each rosette.

ALOE VARIEGATA
Liliaceae

Partridge-Breast Aloe

All aloes grow well at normal room temperature and are particularly tolerant of dry air. The most popular dwarf species for indoor cultivation is *Aloe variegata*, which is especially easy to grow and usually does better in the home, even on a windowsill, than in a greenhouse.

The plant produces tight, spiraling rosettes of smooth-edged, V-shaped green leaves up to 6in/15cm long and 1½in/4cm wide. The leaves are marked with irregular paler bands of color, which give the plant its most frequently used common name. It is also known as the tiger aloe, pheasant's wings, and the kanniedood aloe, which translates as the aloe that cannot be killed—a tribute to its hardiness.

Coral pink flowers appear during late winter and early spring on stems up to 12in/30cm long, growing from the leaf axils. The flowers are at their best after the plant has been given a winter rest.

If the plant is grown in too shady a location, the foliage will become pale and soft.

Avoid wetting the leaves when watering; moisture lodging in the leaf axils can cause rotting.

This plant will rarely shed leaves, so it will eventually become top-heavy and prone to toppling over.

FACT FILE

ORIGIN South Africa (Cape Province, Orange Free State); Namibia.

HEIGHT To 12in/30cm.

POTTING MIX Soil-based with added coarse sand.

REPOTTING In spring, move into a pot one size larger or top-dress plants that are in pots of maximum desired size.

PROPAGATION From offsets taken from around the base of the plant. Use a mixture of soil and sand to start them off.

KEEPING PLANTS Shade from strong sunlight in summer.

PLANT CARE

A bright location, with filtered sunlight. ● Maximum temperature of 50°F/10°C during the winter rest period; otherwise, normal room temperature. ● Keep the soil moist during the spring and summer and on the dry side at other times. ● Feed occasionally with a high-potash fertilizer.

ANANAS BRACTEATUS VAR. *TRICOLOR*
Bromeliaceae

Red Pineapple

The common edible pineapple, *Ananas comosus*, is the best known and commercially the most important member of this genus. Its spiny-leafed relative *A. bracteatus* var. *tricolor* (which used to be known as var. *striatus*) is much more ornamental, however, and is sought as a pot plant for its dramatic foliage and occasional brown, edible fruits. It forms stiff, pointed rosettes of bronze green leaves with yellow margins. The swordlike leaves can be 2½in/6.5cm across and can grow to more than 3ft/90cm long, so the plant needs plenty of space. Always wear gloves when handling it, since the spines are sharp.

When the plant is five or six years old, a pink fruiting spike that contrasts attractively with the foliage may be produced. The fruit takes several months to form, usually maturing in spring.

FACT FILE

ORIGIN Southern Brazil; Paraguay.

HEIGHT To 3ft/90cm.

POTTING MIX Commercial bromeliad mix; or equal parts by volume of coarse sand and peat moss plus half a part of leaf mold.

REPOTTING Move into a pot one size larger every second spring. Once the plant has reached the desired size, top-dress it each spring.

PROPAGATION Use the top of the fruiting spike, which bears a small plant, or good-sized offsets from around the base of older plants and set them in a mixture of peat moss and coarse sand or perlite. Warm conditions in filtered sunlight or a propagator are needed to induce them to root.

KEEPING PLANTS Mature plants may become top-heavy. Repot them into heavier clay pots as they grow.

PLANT CARE

A bright location, with some direct sunlight. ● Minimum winter temperature of 64°F/18°C. ● Allow the top two-thirds of the soil to dry out before watering. ● Stand the plant on a tray of moist pebbles or plunge it into moist peat moss to keep humidity high. ● Apply a weak liquid fertilizer every 2 weeks from early spring to late summer.

If plants are kept in direct sunlight for short periods only, the variegated leaves will take on a rich pink color.

Leaf tips become brown, or the leaves shrivel, if the atmosphere is too dry and warm. Increase humidity and move the plant to a cooler location.

Ananas is prone to few diseases, but may be attacked by scale insects; check regularly for signs of infestation.

ANTHURIUM SCHERZERIANUM
Araceae

FLAMINGO FLOWER

The flamingo flower, also known as tailflower, is spectacularly colorful from spring right through to midfall. Each inflorescence, which can last for almost two months, comprises a large, waxy, scarlet, palette-shaped spathe from which a narrow, curly, orange spadix emerges. The pointed dark green leaves, up to 7in/18cm long, are equally handsome. When the plant is not in flower, the leaves harmonize with those of other tropical plants suitable for shady spots. Indeed, setting this plant in a group of other plants can help to support the flower stalks without the need for unsightly staking. In addition, tropical plants like high humidity and placing them together raises the humidity.

Anthurium scherzerianum does not grow quickly and may prove difficult for the beginner. It needs careful monitoring to make sure the conditions are right, and it must be free from drafts and variations in temperature.

FACT FILE

ORIGIN Guatemala; Costa Rica.

HEIGHT To 9in/23cm.

POTTING MIX Peat-moss-based, with added sphagnum moss. Good drainage is essential.

REPOTTING Move into a pot one size larger every spring until a pot size of 5–6in/13–15cm is reached, then top-dress annually.

PROPAGATION Divide crowded clumps in spring, making sure each piece has some roots attached and a growing point. Establish in humid conditions.

KEEPING PLANTS

When grown in ideal conditions, this plant should last for many years.

PLANT CARE

Strong, indirect sunlight in winter; some shade in summer.
● Minimum winter temperature of 60°F/16°C; an ideal top summer temperature of 70°F/21°C.
● Keep the potting mix moist during the active growth period; be more sparing with water in winter.
● Mist leaves daily during summer. ● Feed with a weak liquid fertilizer every 2 weeks while growth is evident.

Anthurium andreanum
has large waxy spathes, which shine as though they have been varnished. Its deep green, heart-shaped leaves, provide a brilliantly colorful focal point in a group of foliage plants.

ALSO RECOMMENDED

Although not easy to find, there are cultivars with darker red, pink, white, and spotted spathes. *Anthurium scherzerianum* 'Rothschildeanum' has a red spathe spotted with white and a yellow spadix, while *A.s.* 'Wardii' has a dark red spathe, with a long red spadix and unusual red stems as well.

Inflorescences may need staking; attach them to thin canes with soft twine or plastic-covered wire.

Mealybugs and red spider mites occasionally attack this plant. Aphids may also be present; check regularly for their telltale sticky secretions.

Remove dust from the leaves by spraying with clean water rather than wiping, which may damage their delicate surface.

Yellow leaves are a sign that conditions are too cold and wet or too dry.

The leaves can be prone to a leaf spot fungus. If dry brown spots appear on the leaves, spray with diluted fungicide and make sure the plants are well fed.

APHELANDRA SQUARROSA
Acanthaceae

ZEBRA PLANT

One of the most attractive indoor plants, this compact aphelandra is truly a dual-purpose specimen—its fabulous foliage catches the eye when the dramatic yellow bracts are absent. In the wild it thrives in the high humidity and regular downpours of the rain forest, and it has adapted well to indoor conditions but will not flourish unless humidity is high. The stem is stout and fleshy, and the 8–10-in/20–25-cm-long leaves are broadly elliptical, dark grayish green, and heavily striped in the vein areas with silvery white. Insignificant tubular yellow flowers peep through a much more impressive four-sided, cone-shaped spike of yellow bracts, tinged red—hence the plant's other common name, saffron spike. To add to the pleasure the plant gives, these bracts are long-lasting, often looking good for six or seven weeks.

Sciarid flies, or fungus gnats, can be a nuisance if the potting mixture becomes excessively wet and sour.

Watch out for scale insects and for aphids, which are drawn to the bracts and young foliage.

Falling leaves are a sign that the plant has been allowed to dry out.

FACT FILE

ORIGIN Brazil.

HEIGHT To 12in/30cm.

POTTING MIX Soil-based, with peat moss or leaf mold added.

REPOTTING Once a year, at any time other than the coldest winter months. Pot the plant firmly.

PROPAGATION Take tip cuttings and sideshoots in spring.

KEEPING PLANTS Plants that have flowered should be cut down to a pair of lower leaves in spring, or they will become too tall.

PLANT CARE

Bright to semishaded conditions; no direct sunlight. ● Minimum winter temperature of 62°F/17°C, normal room temperature at other times. ● Water plentifully during the period of active growth. Give less water for a few weeks after flowering to allow the plant to rest, but never allow the soil to dry out completely. ● Maintain a humid atmosphere by standing the plant on moist pebbles, or plunge it into moist peat moss. ● Apply full-strength liquid fertilizer every 2 weeks from early spring to late summer.

APOROCACTUS FLAGELLIFORMIS
Cactaceae

RAT'S-TAIL CACTUS

A popular plant that is easy to care for, the rat's-tail cactus produces long streamers of narrow, fleshy, bright green ribbed stems, covered with many rows of fine, prickly spines in radiating clusters. Striking cerise-pink trumpet-shaped flowers 3in/8cm long appear in spring, usually in good quantity. The flowering season extends for about two months, and individual blooms may last for a week. The plant is fast-growing.

Display *Aporocactus flagelliformis* in a hanging basket or on a shelf near a window that offers good light, locating it where no one will brush against it, since the spines are very difficult to remove from the skin and the lengthening stems can soon overbalance a freestanding pot. The rat's-tail cactus can also be displayed in an indoor cactus garden, with its long stems trailing through an arrangement of sand and rocks.

FACT FILE

ORIGIN Mexico.

HEIGHT To 2–4in/5–10cm; stems trail to 3ft/90cm or more.

POTTING MIX Two-thirds soil-based to one-third leaf mold mixed with sand.

REPOTTING Repot every year after flowering. When plants are in 6–9-in/15–23-cm pots, simply top-dress annually.

PROPAGATION By 6-in/15-cm tip cuttings in early summer. Allow them to dry for a day or two, then insert them in a peat moss and sand mixture. Seed can be sown in spring.

KEEPING PLANTS Set the plant outdoors in summer, in a sheltered sunny spot where it will receive occasional rain.

PLANT CARE

Bright sunlight. ● Winter rest temperature of 45°–50°F/7°–10°C; normal room temperature at other times. ● Allow to dry between thorough waterings, but water more sparingly in the rest period following flowering. ● Good drainage is essential; do not allow the plant to stand in water. ● Apply a high-potash fertilizer every 2 weeks from midwinter until flowering stops.

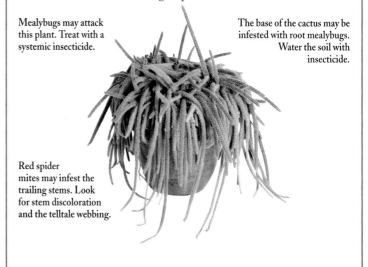

Mealybugs may attack this plant. Treat with a systemic insecticide.

The base of the cactus may be infested with root mealybugs. Water the soil with insecticide.

Red spider mites may infest the trailing stems. Look for stem discoloration and the telltale webbing.

ARALIA ELEGANTISSIMA see *DIZYGOTHECA ELEGANTISSIMA*

ARAUCARIA HETEROPHYLLA (SYN. *A. EXCELSA*)
Araucariaceae

Norfolk Island Pine

Discovered on Norfolk Island in the South Pacific by Sir Joseph Banks in 1793, this handsome conifer reaches a height of 200ft/60m in its natural habitat. As a houseplant, however, it will grow to a more suitable 3–6ft/90cm–1.8m. It is a slow grower and after reaching this height is past its best. The Norfolk Island pine is appealing because of its horizontally held branches covered with 1/2-in/13-mm-long needles, which are bright green in the spring, and turn dark green over time. The plant should last for many years and can be used as a Christmas tree.

Araucaria requires a bright, well-lit location and enjoys a spell outdoors on mild days. Frequent misting is important; this plant likes freely circulating air, but not dry heat, and in summer it needs an even more-humid atmosphere.

Aphids and mealybugs can attack this plant. Watch for signs of infestation and spray with a suitable insecticide.

Dry, yellowing needles indicate that conditions are too hot and dry. Move the plant to a cool, well-ventilated location, and water and mist it more frequently.

FACT FILE

ORIGIN Norfolk Island.

HEIGHT To 6ft/1.8m or more.

POTTING MIX Soil-based.

REPOTTING Move into a pot one size larger every 2–3 years, or when roots show on top of the soil. Top-dress plants more than 3ft/90cm tall in spring.

PROPAGATION By seed or stem cuttings by specialist growers.

KEEPING PLANTS Remove bare lower branches. General pruning is not advisable, but it will encourage bushier growth if the plant becomes straggly.

PLANT CARE

A bright location with some direct sunlight. ● Winter temperature of 50°F/10°C; otherwise normal room temperature. ● Keep the soil moist except in winter, when less water is needed. ● Mist-spray every 3 days. ● Apply a liquid fertilizer every 2 weeks in summer. ● Keep well away from radiators.

ARDISIA CRENATA
Myrsinaceae

Coral Berry

Few suppliers of houseplants stock this small erect shrub because it is so slow-growing. It is, however, an attractive plant and is easy to care for. In nature, it reaches 5–6ft/1.5–1.8m, almost twice the height it can attain as a houseplant. The leathery leaves are a glossy deep green, up to 4in/10cm long and 2in/5cm wide. And the tiny white or pale pink flowers are slightly fragrant. They grow from the leaf axils at the lower part of the foliage in summer and are followed by 1/4-in/6-mm round red berries—by far the most attractive feature of the plant. The berries, on almost horizontal stalks, usually appear at about Christmas-time in the Northern Hemisphere and remain until the onset of flowering the following season.

The coral berry, marlberry, or spiceberry will last for three or four years and even longer, though it easily loses its vigor. To retain a compact, bushy shape, prune the plant each spring before flowering.

FACT FILE

ORIGIN Southeast Asia.

HEIGHT To 3ft/90cm.

POTTING MIX Soil-based.

REPOTTING When the roots have filled the pot, move the plant to a container one size larger.

PROPAGATION By seed in spring, or by stem cuttings in spring or early summer. Ardisias can also be air-layered. None of these methods is easy.

KEEPING PLANTS If only a few berries are produced, use a small brush to pollinate the flowers the next time the plant is in bloom. Replace the plant when it begins to become spindly.

PLANT CARE

A bright location with some direct sunlight. ● Minimum winter temperature of 45°F/7°C; 45°–60°F/7°–16°C is best at other times. ● Never let the soil dry out. ● Maintain humidity by misting regularly, or stand the pot on a tray of damp pebbles. ● Apply a weak liquid fertilizer every 2 weeks from early spring to late summer; once a month at other times.

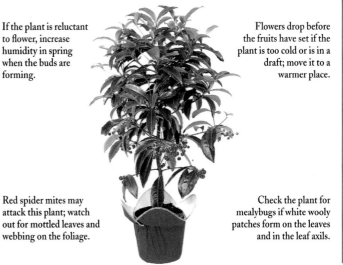

If the plant is reluctant to flower, increase humidity in spring when the buds are forming.

Flowers drop before the fruits have set if the plant is too cold or is in a draft; move it to a warmer place.

Red spider mites may attack this plant; watch out for mottled leaves and webbing on the foliage.

Check the plant for mealybugs if white wooly patches form on the leaves and in the leaf axils.

ASPARAGUS DENSIFLORUS 'SPRENGERI'
Liliaceae

ASPARAGUS FERN

Relatives of the lily, this plant and *Asparagus densiflorus* 'Myers' are frequently, but incorrectly, called ferns because of their finely divided foliage, which is actually modified stems or branches. In its natural habitat—temperate savanna and warm temperate forests—*Asparagus densiflorus* will scramble through and up stronger-stemmed plants, but the two cultivars most often grown indoors make excellent plants for hanging baskets. They produce fleshy roots, often with pronounced tubers on them, which store water and see the plants through brief periods of water shortage; the insignificant flowers are followed by reddish berries.

A.d. 'Sprengeri,' the emerald-feather fern, with its drooping stems clothed in 1-in/2.5-cm-long needlelike "leaves," makes an excellent trailing plant; a well-grown mature specimen can have a spread of 3ft/90cm. Arguably more attractive is *A.d.* 'Myers,' which has needle-like branchlets arranged around its stems like plumes, hence its common name of foxtail fern.

FACT FILE

ORIGIN South Africa.

HEIGHT Stems up to 3ft/90cm long.

POTTING MIX Soil-based.

REPOTTING Annually in spring. Leave the surface of the soil well below the rim of the pot; the thick, tuberous roots force the soil up as they grow.

PROPAGATION In spring, divide old overcrowded clumps that have lost their vigor with a sharp knife. Try to retain as many of the roots as possible.

KEEPING PLANTS Asparagus is a long-lived plant; cut out faded fronds to keep the plant looking decorative.

PLANT CARE

Bright filtered sunlight; avoid deep shade. ● Minimum winter temperature of 50°F/10°C; normal room temperature at other times. ● Water thoroughly, allowing the potting mix to dry out a little between waterings; water sparingly in winter. ● Feed every 2 weeks from spring to early fall with a standard liquid fertilizer.

If leaves drop off, the plant has either received too much direct sunlight or the soil has been allowed to dry out.

Erratic or too much watering may cause the roots to rot.

Scale insects or red spider mites will attack the plant if conditions are too dry.

ASPIDISTRA ELATIOR
Liliaceae

CAST-IRON PLANT

This is the only species of aspidistra in cultivation; although it is occasionally described as *Aspidistra lurida*, this is an entirely different plant. *A. elatior* is sometimes known as the parlor plant because it was popular with the Victorians, who also prized it for its ability to stand up to poor conditions—hence the name cast-iron plant.

Stemless, it sends up its 12–18-in/30–46-cm oval, dark green, arching leaves from a fleshy, creeping rootstock. It can flower in late winter or early spring, but this event is not frequent. The dull purple, star-shaped blooms are produced at soil level (in nature they are pollinated by snails) and often go unnoticed as a result.

Aspidistras are seen at their best as lone specimens, and a mature plant in an ornamental stand looks very dignified in a hallway or bay window (which should not receive direct sunlight). Although aspidistras are quite expensive to buy, they are virtually "everlasting."

Split and damaged leaves may be caused by overfeeding; if the leaves start to split, reduce the amount of fertilizer by half.

If the plant is too close to a heat source or receives direct sunlight, brown patches may form on the leaves.

Speckled leaves often indicate that the plant has been given either too much or too little water.

Aspidistras may be attacked by red spider mites, scale insects, and mealybugs. Check regularly for signs of these pests.

FACT FILE

ORIGIN China.

HEIGHT To 30in/76cm.

POTTING MIX Soil-based.

REPOTTING Repot only when essential until a 12-in/30-cm pot is required.

PROPAGATION Divide overcrowded clumps in spring. Single pieces or clusters of leaves with roots can be potted; the latter will produce a better plant more quickly.

KEEPING PLANTS Old plants are best left in their original pots; remove new shoots and some roots if necessary. Set outdoors in a sheltered spot in summer.

PLANT CARE

Moderate light, without direct sunlight. ● Minimum winter temperature of 50°F/10°C, with a maximum of 70°F/21°C. ● Water moderately, allowing the potting mix to almost dry out between waterings. ● Feed every 2 weeks during the growing season but do not overfeed. ● Wipe leaves free of dust periodically.

ASPLENIUM NIDUS
Aspleniaceae

*B*IRD'S-NEST FERN

The broad, fluted, straplike fronds of this fern are a shiny fresh green with a dark central vein. The foliage grows in the form of a rosette, from the center of which new fronds unfurl. In its natural habitat, the plant grows as an epiphyte in moist tropical rain forests, and in those conditions fronds can reach 4ft/1.2m in length. Asplenium makes an excellent houseplant; it grows relatively quickly.

An ideal place indoors is warm, humid, partly shaded, and well away from drafts. But aspleniums can tolerate heated houses if adequate humidity is provided. Even large fronds are relatively fragile and should be handled as little as possible.

Asplenium australasicum, commonly grown in Australia and New Zealand, is a very similar plant.

FACT FILE

ORIGIN Southeast Asia, Australia.

HEIGHT To 2ft/60cm or more in a pot indoors.

POTTING MIX Peat-moss-based, with some added loam and coarse sand.

REPOTTING In spring, when the roots fill the pot. The roots tend to cling to the side of the pot, so it may be necessary to break the pot to release the root ball.

PROPAGATION This fern can be raised only from spores.

KEEPING PLANTS Stand the plant outdoors in summer in mild climates. Clean the fronds by wiping them gently with a damp cloth. Alternatively, you can give the plant a shower. Do not use leaf shine.

PLANT CARE

Medium light, no direct sun; turn the pot regularly for even growth. ● Normal room temperature with a minimum winter temperature of 61°F/16°C. ● Keep the soil moist, especially in the growing period. ● Stand the pot on damp pebbles. ● Apply a weak liquid fertilizer every 2 weeks in spring and summer.

Damaged or dried fronds can be cut off at the base.

If scale insects (on both sides of the leaves) or aphids attack the plant, spray with soapy water, followed by clean water.

Brown spots on the fronds may indicate that the plant is in a position that is drafty or too cold. Move it to a warmer, more protected place.

BEAUCARNEA RECURVATA (SYN. *NOLINA RECURVATA*)
Liliaceae

*P*ONYTAIL PLANT

Originally from the desert of southern Mexico, this bizarre-looking succulent is most unusual and eye-catching. The bottle-shaped woody stem, which serves as a water reservoir, adds to the plant's odd appearance and gives rise to its common names of bottle palm and elephant foot. From this bulbous stem spring several slim, downward-curving "ponytails" of gray-green leaves up to 3ft/90cm long. Clusters of small white flowers are sometimes produced on older plants.

Beaucarnea recurvata grows slowly, but it is easy to keep and should live for several years. It is ideal in a modern room setting. Since it prefers dry air, it will thrive in heated houses. It likes a sunny position as well as fresh air, so should be sited near a window.

Check for scale insects and red spider mites, which may attack the plant.

If the leaf tips turn brown, trim back the damaged leaves, but do not decimate the plant.

Limp, pale leaves and soft stems indicate overwatering. Stand the pot on dry newspaper for a day or two, changing the paper when it gets wet. Do not water again until the top of the soil has dried out.

FACT FILE

ORIGIN Mexico.

HEIGHT To 10ft/3m or more.

POTTING MIX Soil-based, mixed with leaf mold or peat moss, and sand.

REPOTTING Every 2–3 years, always providing good drainage. Keep this plant in a pot relatively small for the plant's size.

PROPAGATION By seed or offsets in spring or summer, with an air temperature of 75°F/24°C, but propagation is not easy for the amateur.

KEEPING PLANTS Fading leaves can be gently peeled off. Put the plant in a sheltered spot outdoors in summer.

PLANT CARE

Bright light, preferably full sun, all year-round. ● Minimum winter temperature of 50°F/10°C. ● Keep the soil moist from early spring to late fall, but do not let the plant stand in water. ● Feed with a weak liquid fertilizer every 4 weeks during summer.

BEGONIACEAE

*B*EGONIAS

The begonia family contains more than 900 species and 10,000 hybrids and cultivars. Some are grown mainly for their flowers, others for their leaves, but most of the flowering types also have attractive foliage. Plants range in size from tiny ground creepers to climbers 10ft/3m high. In general, they do not need much direct sunlight, so most of them make suitable indoor plants.

Begonias bear male and female flowers, sometimes in clusters and sometimes separately. Male flowers last for only a few days, but usually compensate for this by being more striking, often having several layers of petals. Female flowers have four petals and are distinguished by a winged or strongly angled seed pod; they also remain on the plant for weeks or even months.

Since the genus is so large and diverse, it is best divided into three groups, distinguished by the root structure. The first group has fibrous-rooted plants, which grow from a tangle of fine roots that will fill a pot quickly. The second contains the rhizomatous begonias, most of which have a thick, fleshy rhizome that crawls over the surface of the potting mix, sending down roots as it goes. The final group contains the tuberous begonias, which are characterized by swollen underground stems, or tubers; they are deciduous and have an annual period of dormancy.

Begonia × *hiemalis* (tuberous), the winter-flowering begonia, has reddish stems up to 18in/46cm long. The most widely seen are the Elatior hybrids such as 'Heidi' (*right*).

Flowers are usually borne in groups of three—a large central male and two smaller female flowers.

Fleshy erect stems up to 1in/2.5cm thick.

Soft, dark green leaves 6–8in/15–20cm long, with paler green veining.

Tuber (swollen underground stem) just on the surface of the soil.

ALSO RECOMMENDED

Begonia 'Corallina de Lucerna' (fibrous) is a vigorous plant up to 6ft/1.8m high. The big lance-shaped glossy leaves are spotted with white and deep red below; flowers in large clusters are deep pink to bright red.

Begonia × *tuberhybrida* is the most popular tuberous begonia. The 12-in/30-cm-tall fleshy-stemmed plants carry large and showy single, semidouble, and double blooms in a wide range of colors.

Begonia sutherlandii (tuberous) is 6–8in/ 15–20cm high, with pendulous deep pink stems and red-edged bright green leaves. It bears dainty salmon-pink flowers for 8 months of the year from early spring.

Young shoots distorted by tarsonemid mites chewing them.

The leaves and stems of deciduous begonias start to fall off as the growing seasons nears its end. Do not pull these away from the tuber, since this could damage it; wait for the stems to fall away naturally.

Botrytis fungus will attack plants in cool, damp conditions. Remove and destroy infected leaves and move the plant to a warmer spot; treat with a fungicide if severely affected.

Overwatering, coupled with low temperatures, causes leaves to wilt and turn brown.

Most begonias are prone to powdery mildew on leaves, leafstalks, and stems. Spray regularly with a suitable fungicide.

When potting or repotting, sprinkle soil around the roots, rhizome or tuber and tap the pot to settle the mixture; do not compact it with your fingers.

FACT FILE

ORIGIN Tropical America; Africa; Asia; hybrids.

HEIGHT To 18in/46cm and more.

POTTING MIX Peat-moss-based, or peat-moss- and soil-based in equal parts by volume.

REPOTTING Fibrous: Move plants into pots one size larger every spring until 6–8-in/15–20-cm pots are reached, then top-dress annually instead. **Rhizomatous:** Shallow-rooted and best grown in shallow pots. Move into a pot one size larger only when the rhizome has covered much of the surface of the soil. **Tuberous:** Move semituberous types into pots one size larger each spring.

PROPAGATION Fibrous: Take 3–4-in/8–10-cm stem cuttings of nonflowering shoots in spring or summer. **Rhizomatous and tuberous:** By seed, division, leaf, or stem cuttings in spring or summer.

KEEPING PLANTS All begonias suffer in dry air, so increase humidity by standing pots on moist pebbles, particularly if the temperature rises above 65°F/ 18°C.

PLANT CARE

Fibrous: Foliage plants require bright light, not direct sun; flowering plants need up to 4 hours' direct sunlight. ● Minimum winter temperature of 55°F/13°C; normal room temperature at other times. ● Allow the top 1in/2.5cm of the potting mix to dry out between waterings; water less frequently in winter. ● Apply a weak liquid fertilizer every 2 weeks during the period of active growth. **Rhizomatous and tuberous:** Bright, filtered light; plants that lose their top growth do not require light during dormant periods. ● Minimum winter temperature of 55°F/13°C. ● Let the top 1in/2.5cm of soil dry out between waterings; do not water dormant plants. ● Apply a high-potash liquid feed every 2 weeks in the period of active growth.

PESTS & DISEASES

Begonias are affected by root knot eelworm, tarsonemid mites, weevils, powdery mildew, and botrytis.

Begonia masoniana (rhizomatous), the iron cross begonia, has deeply puckered leaves. They are bright green, with a mahogany-red cross resembling the German iron cross in the center.

Begonia rex (rhizomatous) has decorative heart-shaped foliage with zones of silver, pink, purple, cream, and near black on the corrugated leaf surfaces. Many named forms are available.

BELOPERONE GUTTATA (SYN. *JUSTICIA BRANDEGEANA*)
Acanthaceae

Shrimp Plant

The reddish brown bracts of this plant, resembling overlapping roof shingles, appear almost all year-round, and the white flowers that emerge at the end of the bracts are insignificant and short-lived. The leaves are 1–3in/2.5–8cm long, light green, oval, and pointed.

Disregard those who tell you to throw beloperone away after flowering: the plant is easy to care for and can survive for many years, reaching 3ft/90cm in height and spread. It is best to pinch out the stem tips regularly to make the plant bushier, and annual pruning will renew its vigor. If you do not prune, the plant will almost certainly be larger and will produce colorful bracts, but the relatively weak branches will probably require staking.

If bracts do not develop fully, prune the plant in midwinter, just as the show of bracts ends.

Whiteflies, mealybugs, scale insects, and aphids may attack the plant in hot weather; spray with a suitable insecticide.

Feed once a month during the winter, and from early spring give the plant plenty of direct sunlight.

Overwatering can encourage the leaves to turn yellow. Do not water again until the soil has dried out completely.

Loss of leaves may indicate that the plant is rootbound; annual potting should alleviate this.

FACT FILE

ORIGIN Mexico.

HEIGHT To 3ft/90cm.

POTTING MIX Soil-based.

REPOTTING Repot every spring and cut stems back by about half.

PROPAGATION Take 3-in/8-cm tip cuttings in spring; use the prunings but remove the bracts, which will rot if they are left.

KEEPING PLANTS The arching stems and drooping flower heads make this a good plant for a hanging basket.

PLANT CARE

A bright place, with direct sunlight for short periods during spring and summer will help to produce colorful bracts. ● Minimum winter temperature of 60°F/16°C; ideally 75°F/24°C at other times. ● Keep fairly dry during winter and moist, not wet, at other times. ● Feed every 2 weeks in summer with a weak solution of fertilizer.

BILLBERGIA NUTANS
Bromeliaceae

Queen's Tears

One of the prettiest of bromeliads, this is also one of the easiest to grow. Its tough, straplike, tooth-edged, olive green leaves, which can be as much as 16in/40cm long and ½in/13mm wide, arch over in an attractively random fashion. The pendant flowers, which usually appear in late spring, are tinged with blue, yellow, pink, and green and are encased in pink bracts. Nectar formed within the small flowers sometimes drops out when the plant is touched or moved, giving it its common name; it is also called the friendship plant.

A much underrated, easy-care plant, this billbergia is seen to best effect when grown at eye-level, as in a hanging container, which will show off the pendulous bracts to full advantage. While most plants in elevated locations may suffer as a result of dry conditions, billbergias are much more tolerant, and small hanging pots can be plunged into water occasionally to give them a good soak.

FACT FILE

ORIGIN Argentina; Brazil; Uruguay.

HEIGHT To 16in/40cm in flower.

POTTING MIX Commercial bromeliad or orchid potting mixture, or soilless potting mix.

REPOTTING In spring, in a pot up to 5in/13cm in diameter.

PROPAGATION Detach offsets when they are half the size of the parent plant. Let the cut surface dry for a day or so before potting up.

KEEPING PLANTS Empty the water reservoir in the center of the rosette once a month and refill with fresh water.

PLANT CARE

Keep in good light but out of direct sunlight to maintain good leaf color and promote flowering. ● Normal room temperature, but will tolerate temperatures as low as 35°–40°F/2°–4°C for a short while. ● Water moderately all year-round, with rainwater or cool boiled water. ● Apply weak liquid fertilizer every 2 weeks both to the soil and as a foliar spray.

A month or two outdoors in a shady location during summer greatly improves the leaf color and usually encourages flowering.

The olive green leaves may become reddish if the plant is placed in direct sunlight.

BOUGAINVILLEA GLABRA
Nyctaginaceae

Paper Flower

A true tropical exotic, in its natural environment this showy climber produces such dense and vivid color on 15-ft/4.5-m trailing stems that it outshines almost everything else in the vicinity. Its strong twining branches, which carry narrow, smooth, 3-in/8-cm-long leaves, have vicious barbs. This drawback is, however, more than compensated for when the colorful papery bracts, some 1½in/4cm long, appear at the beginning of summer.

Bougainvillea can be most frustrating to grow as a houseplant, for it is reluctant to flower in limited light. Fine indoor specimens can, however, be grown beside large windows and in greenhouses or sunrooms. Although a climber, this plant can be trained to keep it bushy indoors—wire hoops have become popular supports—and there are some dwarf types that do not require special training.

Bougainvillea glabra, with purple-pink bracts in summer and fall, is the species most easily obtained. This, and the less vigorous *B.* x *buttiana*, have given rise to dozens of hybrids with a range of highly colored bracts, many being smaller than the species.

Bougainvillea x buttiana *'Amethyst,' seen close up here, has bracts with a papery quality that enclose its insignificant yellow flowers.*

FACT FILE

ORIGIN Brazil.

HEIGHT To 15ft/4.5m.

POTTING MIX Soil-based.

REPOTTING When new growth appears in spring, move the plant into a pot one size larger. When a pot size of 8in/20cm is reached, simply top-dress the plant.

PROPAGATION Not easy. In late spring or early summer put 3–4-in/8–10-cm stem cuttings in a heated propagator.

KEEPING PLANTS If the plant becomes straggly, prune it lightly in fall. But flowering is better if new growth is wound around established stems and tied in.

PLANT CARE

Bougainvillea needs 4 hours of direct sunlight daily. Place in a sunny window close to the glass, but do not allow it to bake in hot weather. Set outdoors in summer, if possible.
● Minimum winter temperature of 50°F/10°C. ● Water well during active growth, but the plant must not stand in water; do not water in winter until new growth appears. ● Apply a high-potash feed every 2 weeks in spring and summer.

ALSO RECOMMENDED

Bougainvillea glabra 'Alexandra' is rose pink and one of the most free-flowering. 'Variegata' has leaves bordered with cream. *B.* x *buttiana* hybrids 'Killie Campbell,' 'Orange King,' and 'Golden Glow' ('Hawaiian Gold') are shades of gold and orange; 'Jamaica Red' is crimson; 'Surprise' ('Mary Palmer') is rose purple or white or a combination of the two.

This is a tough plant that does not suffer greatly from pests. But aphids, red spider mites, and mealybugs may attack it, so check often for signs of infestation.

Water left on the leaves or papery bracts may cause scorching when the plant is in full sun.

Yellowing of the leaves is caused by too much moisture at the roots. Make sure that the soil has good drainage.

BROMELIACEAE

BROMELIADS

Guzmania lingulata, scarlet star, is a commonly found terrestrial bromeliad. It has smooth, glossy strap-shaped leaves up to 18in/46cm long, which overlap at the base to form a central well, or urn, that holds water. At almost any time of the year it may bear white flowers, which are almost hidden by the scarlet star-shaped bracts that give this plant its common name.

This group of some 2,000 species in more than 50 genera, ranging from pineapples to Spanish moss, provides us with some exciting and colorful indoor plants. Typically, they produce wide rosettes of more or less leathery, strap-shaped leaves, often striped or patterned, and with a central zone that becomes brightly colored at flowering time. Flower heads on stout stems, with numerous small flowers, are borne between long-lasting colorful bracts.

There are two types of bromeliad, epiphytic and terrestrial. In the wild, epiphytic plants grow on trees or rocks. They have small, weak root systems, and they obtain much of their nourishment from the air and from the detritus that collects within their leaves. Some of the most beautiful of the epiphytic bromeliads, such as *Aechmea fasciata*, the urn plant, are easy to grow. It is typical of most bromeliads in having a water-holding vessel formed by the bases of the leaves. Air plants, *Tillandsia* spp., are epiphytic bromeliads that live by absorbing water from the atmosphere and trapping dust particles between the tiny scales on their foliage. Among the terrestrial types—those that live in the ground—are *Cryptanthus, Dyckia, Nidularium, Neoregelia,* and one of the most widely seen genera, *Ananas,* the pineapple, several species of which make good houseplants.

The scarlet star-shaped bracts conceal small white flowers.

Long strap-shaped leaves overlap at their bases to form an urn that holds water.

ALSO RECOMMENDED

Cryptanthus bivittatus is a small species that grows in the ground and thrives in terrariums. It forms a rosette of 2–3in/5–8cm-long leaves, with spiny edges, which are striped dark green and in strong light become tinged with pink.

Nidularium billbergioides, another terrestrial bromeliad, forms an upright rosette of glossy light green leaves about 12in/30cm high. The flower spike has white flowers, up to 2in/5cm wide, enclosed in bright yellow bracts.

If flowers, or even the bract spikes, fail to appear, move the plant to a location that receives more light.

If the thick leaves develop brown tips and then shrivel, that is an indication that the plant is too hot and dry; increase watering accordingly.

Bromeliads may be attacked by aphids, scale insects, and mealybugs; check regularly for signs of infestation.

Overwatering or too low a temperature will cause flower stems to rot; empty the well in the center of the rosette and allow the soil to dry out before rewatering.

FACT FILE

ORIGIN Southern US to Tropical America; Africa.

HEIGHT 4in–6ft/10cm–1.8m.

POTTING MIX Equal parts of peat moss and peat-moss-based mix, with some fresh sphagnum moss. Good drainage is essential.

REPOTTING Every 2 years. Since rooting systems are not extensive, fairly small pots are suitable.

PROPAGATION Remove good-sized offsets from the base of the plant in spring and pot them in rich, just-moist potting mix.

KEEPING PLANTS Make sure that neither the plant's urn nor the soil is allowed to dry out. Put plants outside in summer, particularly in mild climates, since they love the rain.

PLANT CARE

These are tolerant plants, which can take either direct or subdued sunlight. ● Average room temperature is suitable for growth, with a minimum winter temperature of 55°F/13°C. A temperature of about 75°F/24°C is needed for flowering. ● Water twice a week with tepid rainwater or soft water. Do not overwater bromeliads, although the vessel, or urn, which is the plant's growing point, must be kept full of water at all times. ● Mist the leaves with weak liquid fertilizer occasionally in spring and summer.

AIR PLANTS

Most of these types of epiphytic bromeliads should not be planted in soil, since this would rot the small roots, which are used more for support than for feeding the plant. Instead, wrap the bottom of the plant and any roots in sphagnum moss and wire the plant to a piece of wood or cork. Hang the plant up and spray the moss and leaves twice a day year-round to keep them moist. *Tillandsia* spp. and *Neoregelia tristis* do well grown this way.

PESTS & DISEASES

Bromeliads may be attacked by aphids, scale insects, and red spider mites. Check regularly for these pests and spray with insecticide; remove scale insects by hand.

Neoregelia '**Meyendorffii**' is a cultivar typical of most neoregelias, with the leaves arranged in a rather flat rosette. During the flowering period the leaves change color to a striking scarlet.

Tillandsia cyanea, pink quill, can be planted in potting mix. Its grasslike leaves form a rosette up to 12in/30cm wide, and in early summer it bears a spectacular flower head with blue flowers held between bright pink bracts.

BROWALLIA SPECIOSA 'MAJOR'
Solanaceae

Sapphire Flower

The violet-blue blooms of this plant, sometimes known as the bush violet, are carried in the leaf axils of slender semitrailing stems. They are trumpet-shaped, opening out to a flat-faced bloom about 2in/5cm wide, and have an attractive white throat. Plants, which are also grown as summer annuals, may be bought in flower from midsummer right through the fall and winter; winter-flowering plants are popular. The rather drooping foliage is ovate and mid green. Stems can be supported by thin stakes to give a bushy plant, or they can be allowed to trail gracefully. The tips of the stems should be pinched off regularly to keep the plant reasonably compact. Browallias are difficult to keep in good condition for a further flowering season and are usually discarded once flowering has finished.

Browallia speciosa 'Blue Troll,' with a compact habit, and *B.s.* 'White Troll,' its counterpart with white flowers, are the most popular varieties.

FACT FILE

ORIGIN Colombia.

HEIGHT To 2ft/60cm.

POTTING MIX Soil-based.

REPOTTING Not usually done.

PROPAGATION Easily grown from seed sown in spring or summer.

KEEPING PLANTS Discard after flowering.

PLANT CARE

Bright light with some direct sun. ● Prefers cool conditions of 50°–60°F/10°–16°C. ● Keep the soil just moist and mist the foliage occasionally. ● Apply a standard liquid fertilizer every 2 weeks throughout the flowering period. ● Remove flowers as they fade.

To extend the flowering period, pick off the flowers as they fade.

Keeping the plant in a cool room will help the flowers to last as long as possible.

The slender stems often need staking to produce a bushy, upright plant.

BRUNFELSIA PAUCIFLORA (SYN. *B. CALYCINA*)
Solanaceae

Yesterday-Today-and-Tomorrow

This plant's strange common name arises from the rapidly changing appearance of the flowers: they open deep purple and fade to lavender the next day, then to white. The flowers are fragrant, about 2in/5cm across with a central white eye; and even though they are short-lived individually, there are always plenty more blooms to follow. Given the right conditions, brunfelsias can flower at any time of year.

Leaves are long and lance-shaped, glossy mid to deep green, and leathery. Stems should be pruned back in early spring to produce well-shaped plants, and growing tips pinched off throughout the season to keep the plant bushy. Brunfelsias will flower better if they are put in a sheltered place outdoors during warm summer weather, a practice that helps to ripen the wood.

Flowers appear in clusters at the tips of the stems, opening one by one and changing color day by day.

The leathery leaves are sometimes attacked by scale insects; check the undersides regularly.

Mist foliage regularly in the growing season.

Allow the surface of the soil to dry out between waterings in winter.

FACT FILE

ORIGIN Tropical America; West Indies.

HEIGHT To 2ft/60cm.

POTTING MIX Soil-based.

REPOTTING Every spring, in a pot up to 8in/20cm maximum. Do not use an overlarge pot as the plant flowers better when the roots are confined.

PROPAGATION By soft stem cuttings in spring and early summer.

KEEPING PLANTS Prune in early spring and pinch off growing tips during the flowering season to keep the plant bushy.

PLANT CARE

Bright light with some direct sunlight. ● Give moderate warmth, with a minimum of 50°F/10°C in winter. ● Keep the soil moist in the growing season, but water more sparingly in winter. ● Apply standard liquid fertilizer every 2 weeks while the plant is actively growing.

CALADIUM × *HORTULANUM*
Araceae

Angel Wings

An exception to the rule that foliage houseplants are decorative all year-round, this hybrid tuberous-rooted plant dies down in autumn and remains dormant over the winter. That characteristic, together with the fact that the plants are not easy to grow—they require high temperature and high humidity—leads to many of them being discarded after their first season.

The large, 12–16-in/30–40-cm heart-shaped leaves, which are carried on long, arching stalks, are paper thin and spectacularly marked. The range of varieties is wide, and leaf colors vary from white with green edges and crimson veins, as in 'White Queen' shown here, through rose pink with green margins, to spotted and marbled red, pink, white, orange, and green. Arumlike flowers may be produced, but they are insignificant compared with the foliage. The plant is also known as elephant's-ear.

FACT FILE

ORIGIN Tropical; South America; West Indies.

HEIGHT To 2ft/60cm.

POTTING MIX Peat-moss based.

REPOTTING In spring, add plenty of pot shards to guarantee good drainage.

PROPAGATION When repotting, you can break off small tubers from the parent and pot them separately, at the same depth as they are thick, to produce new plants.

KEEPING PLANTS Allow the potting mix to dry out completely when the foliage dies down. Keep it dry until spring, when repotting takes place.

PLANT CARE

Bright light but no direct sunlight.
● Warm conditions: at least 70°F/21°C, but 80°F/27°C is better. ● Keep the soil moist throughout the growing season and mist the foliage daily. ● Set the plant on a tray of moist pebbles to raise the humidity. ● Apply half-strength liquid fertilizer every 2 weeks during the period of active growth.

ALSO RECOMMENDED

Caladium × *hortulanum* 'Pink Beauty' has green leaves with red ribs and pink marbling in the center. The leaves of 'Carolyn Morton' are bright pink with red ribs and broad dark green edges. The bushy 'Frieda Hempel' has bright red leaves, red ribs, and dark green margins.

Caladium leaves have a magnificent coloration which differs from variety to variety and within the leaves on a single plant. And the paradoxically fragile translucency of the leaves increases their attractiveness. In addition, their shape and huge size are reminiscent of an elephant's ears.

Paper-thin leaves are available in a spectacular choice of colors, and need to be protected from cold and drafts at all times.

Keep the tuber virtually dry during the winter and restart it into growth in warm conditions (about 75°F/24°C) in spring.

Keep the humidity high by misting the foliage and standing the pot on a tray of damp pebbles.

Direct sunlight will scorch the delicate foliage.

CALATHEA MAKOYANA
Marantaceae

PEACOCK PLANT

The "eyes" and the very fine lines of this plant's decorative foliage create the appearance of a peacock's tail and give the plant its most widely used common name, peacock plant. It is also, but less commonly, called cathedral windows. Calatheas are closely related to marantas (see p. 107) but are rather more delicate.

Leaves are thin, oval in shape, and about 12in/30cm long. They are light green, feathered with fine, dark green lines running from the midrib to the edge of the leaf, and have elongated, irregularly shaped blotches occurring at intervals. The underside of the leaves is also marked and tends to be pinkish maroon rather than green. The foliage is held upright on long slender stems.

Yellowing and browning of the leaves is often caused by dry air. Mist regularly and set the plant on a tray of moist gravel to raise humidity.

Never allow the soil to dry out during the growing season.

The undersides of calathea leaves are an attractive maroon color.

FACT FILE

ORIGIN Brazil.

HEIGHT To 2ft/60cm.

POTTING MIX Peat-moss-based or soil-based with one-third peat moss or leaf mold added.

REPOTTING Every year, or every other year, move the plant into a pot one size larger in spring.

PROPAGATION Divide and repot established plants in spring.

KEEPING PLANTS Calatheas are fairly long-lived, given the right growing conditions.

PLANT CARE

Light shade; no direct sun. ● Keep in evenly warm conditions with a minimum temperature of 60°F/16°C. ● Water freely with warm, preferably lime-free, water during the growing season, more sparingly in winter. ● Mist the foliage regularly. ● Give plants plenty of standard liquid fertilizer every 2 weeks in the growing period.

CALCEOLARIA × HERBEOHYBRIDA
Scrophulariaceae

SLIPPER FLOWER

Calceolaria's curious pouch-shaped flowers have given rise to several common names for these hybrid plants, among them pocketbook plant and slipperwort. The brightly colored flowers are often yellow spotted with red or brown, but orange and red varieties with darker blotches are also available. Flowers are normally borne in spring, in clusters on tall stems that rise above the roughly heart-shaped, light green, downy foliage. The soil needs to be kept moist at all times, since these plants are difficult to revive if they are ever allowed to dry out. The flowering season will be extended if they are kept in moderately cool conditions.

Calceolaria × *herbeohybrida* 'Anytime Mixed' is an early-flowering strain that if sown in summer will produce flowering plants in early winter. However, as its name implies, it can be sown virtually all year-round and will flower four to five months later.

FACT FILE

ORIGIN Hybrid.

HEIGHT To 18in/46cm.

POTTING MIX Soil-based with added coarse sand.

REPOTTING None.

PROPAGATION Can be raised from seed sown in summer and fall for flowering the following spring; best left to professional growers.

KEEPING PLANTS Once flowering has finished, discard the plant.

PLANT CARE

Bright light but no direct sunlight. ● Keep in a fairly cool room at about 45°F/7°C at night, 50°F/10°C during the day. ● Water plentifully and regularly. ● Provide humid conditions by standing the plant on a tray of wet pebbles or peat moss.

Always choose a plant with plenty of unopened buds. The flowering season should extend for about a month under the right conditions.

Check the undersides of the leaves regularly for aphids and spray with a contact insecticide if they are present.

Keep in a cool location that is free from drafts.

CALLISIA REPENS
Commelinaceae

CALLISIA

This easily grown callisia is related to tradescantia and is similar in appearance. It produces trailing stems up to 2ft/60cm long, which start erect but droop as they mature. The stems are densely clothed in small, rounded, rather fleshy bright green leaves.

Callisia elegans (syn. *Setcreasea striata*), the striped inch plant or wandering Jew, has leaves striped with white down their length. The undersides of the leaves, which are visible because of the plant's trailing habit, are purple.

Like many plants that are easy to grow and to propagate, these plants are often treated with disdain, but a well-grown specimen makes an attractive subject for a hanging basket. Set three or four plants around the edge of a pot to make a well-filled basket. After two or three years, plants begin to look jaded and straggly and are best replaced; new plants are easily raised from cuttings.

FACT FILE

ORIGIN South and Central America; USA (Texas).

HEIGHT To about 4in/10cm; stems trail to 2ft/60cm.

POTTING MIX Either peat-moss-based or soil-based.

REPOTTING Generally unnecessary.

PROPAGATION Take 2-in/5-cm stem cuttings in spring and summer.

KEEPING PLANTS Pinch off stem tips regularly to keep the plant compact. Replace the plant with a rooted cutting when it becomes leggy—usually after about 2 years.

PLANT CARE

Bright indirect light with several hours of direct sun daily.
● Moderately warm rooms, with a minimum winter temperature of 60°F/16°C. ● Keep the soil moist during the growing season, but allow the surface to dry out between waterings in the winter rest period.
● Mist the foliage occasionally. ● Liquid fertilizer every 10 to 14 days in summer helps to keep the foliage dense and the growth compact.

Excessively dry conditions may cause brown marks on the foliage. Mist the plants to increase humidity.

Red spider mites are sometimes attracted to the tips of the stems, where their fine webbing can be seen. Increase humidity to combat this pest.

Bright light with direct sun helps to prevent plants from becoming straggly.

CALLISTEMON CITRINUS
Myrtaceae

CRIMSON BOTTLE BRUSH

Although this attractive and unusual houseplant will grow well in normal room conditions, it is ideal for a greenhouse or sunroom, where it can be allowed to develop into a moderately large shrub. The flower spikes have no petals but consist of tightly packed, bright red stamens with yellow tips. These 4-in/10-cm spikes have the appearance of a particularly colorful bottle brush. Leaves are long, narrow, and pointed, giving the plant a rather spiky appearance.

Flowering occurs in summer; once it is over, move the plant outdoors into a sunny, sheltered location to help ripen the wood for good flowering the following season. Bring it back indoors when the nights start to become cold. Callistemons need a winter rest period, during which they should be kept cool and watered moderately.

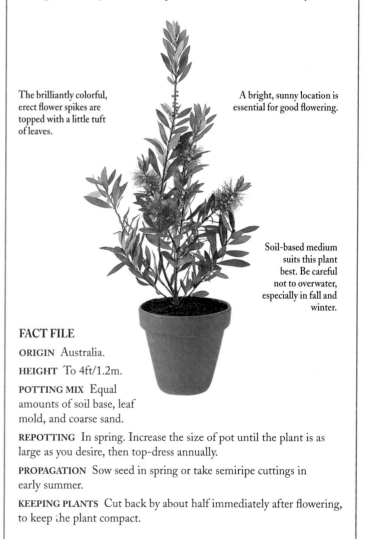

The brilliantly colorful, erect flower spikes are topped with a little tuft of leaves.

A bright, sunny location is essential for good flowering.

Soil-based medium suits this plant best. Be careful not to overwater, especially in fall and winter.

FACT FILE

ORIGIN Australia.

HEIGHT To 4ft/1.2m.

POTTING MIX Equal amounts of soil base, leaf mold, and coarse sand.

REPOTTING In spring. Increase the size of pot until the plant is as large as you desire, then top-dress annually.

PROPAGATION Sow seed in spring or take semiripe cuttings in early summer.

KEEPING PLANTS Cut back by about half immediately after flowering, to keep the plant compact.

PLANT CARE

Strong, bright light with several hours of direct sun. ● Normal room temperature; keep cool during the winter rest period, with a minimum temperature of 45°F/7°C. ● Keep the soil thoroughly moist in spring and summer; water moderately in winter. ● The plant prefers low humidity and good ventilation.

CAMELLIA JAPONICA
Theaceae

CAMELLIA

In the home, the beautiful waxy blooms of this winter- and early spring-flowering shrub can be appreciated at close quarters, and they are secure from damaging frosts. The flowers may be single, double, or semidouble, carried in clusters or singly, depending on variety. They may be white, pink, or red, or a combination of either pink or red and white, and may be about 5in/13cm wide. The glossy, dark green leathery leaves are carried on woody branches and tend to curl under slightly from the tips and sides.

Camellias are ideal plants for a cool, airy room. And they do not like the hot, dry conditions of centrally heated houses. They need regular misting and should be set on a tray of gravel to raise the humidity, especially when the buds are forming. Do not move flowering plants; the buds are likely to drop off if you do.

FACT FILE

ORIGIN China; Japan; India; Indonesia.

HEIGHT To 10ft/3m or more.

POTTING MIX Equal parts of lime-free soil-based potting mix, peat moss, and coarse leaf mold.

REPOTTING When necessary, move the plant into a pot one size larger after flowering until maximum practical size is reached; thereafter, top-dress at the end of the rest period.

PROPAGATION By semiripe cuttings in early summer; difficult for the amateur.

KEEPING PLANTS Leave outdoors in a sheltered place in summer; bring under cover in late fall.

PLANT CARE

Bright light but no direct sun. ● Must have cool conditions of 45°–60°F/7°–16°C. ● Keep the soil evenly moist when the buds are forming. After flowering, allow the surface of the soil to dry out between waterings. ● Mist-spray daily. ● Give a liquid feed every 10 to 14 days during the growing season.

Stand the plant outside in summer to encourage buds to form.

Check the undersides of the leaves for scale insects and push off any scales with a fingernail.

Buds will drop if soil dries out in the flowering season.

CAMPANULA ISOPHYLLA
Campanulaceae

STAR OF BETHLEHEM

This trailing plant is ideal for a hanging basket or any location where its long stems, studded with blue bell-like flowers, can be allowed to trail. The soft, pale green leaves are heart-shaped, and under good conditions are almost hidden by the clusters of star-shaped blooms. Stems reach up to 12in/30cm in length.

Flowers are generally light blue, although a white variety is available: *Campanula isophylla* 'Stella Blue,' 'Stella White,' 'Alba,' and 'May' are popular varieties. Also known as falling stars and bellflower, this campanula is easy to grow, demanding only a fairly cool room and regular watering thoughout the growing season.

Check the young leaves for the presence of aphids; treat with a contact insecticide.

If humidity is too high, gray mold may occur; treat with a fungicide.

Display plants in a hanging basket or on a tall pot stand; allow stems to trail gracefully.

Reduce watering and keep the plant cool during the winter.

FACT FILE

ORIGIN Northern Italy.

HEIGHT To 6in/15cm, trailing stems to 12in/30cm long.

POTTING MIX Soil-based.

REPOTTING When roots appear on the surface of the soil, move plants to pots one size larger up to a maximum of about 5in/13cm.

PROPAGATION By soft tip cuttings in spring and summer or by seed.

KEEPING PLANTS Campanulas do not like too much humidity. Cut back stems after flowering and reduce watering in the winter.

PLANT CARE

Bright light but no direct sun. ● Cool conditions up to 60°F/16°C. ● Water regularly during the growing season. ● Apply a standard liquid fertilizer every 2 weeks while the plant is in flower. ● Remove faded blooms to encourage a long flowering season.

CAPSICUM ANNUUM
Solanaceae

ORNAMENTAL PEPPER

Grown for its brightly colored fruits rather than its foliage or flowers, this plant is a variety of the chili pepper and is also often called the ornamental chili pepper. The medium green leaves are oval and pointed, and white, star-shaped flowers appear in summer and early fall. Stand the plant out doors in summer to make sure of good pollination. The usually cone-shaped peppers, which are held erect, change color from green through yellow and orange to red. And there are purple varieties and also some that have round, ball-shaped fruits similar to the false Jerusalem cherry, *Solanum capsicastrum* (see p. 137). The peppers ripen in fall and winter, which accounts for their most usual common name in the Northern Hemisphere: Christmas pepper.

Keep plants out of the reach of children, who may be tempted to sample the peppers; the fruits of all species are intensely fiery and are not suitable for eating. Juice from the fruits can cause painful burning and stinging of the delicate skin near the eyes and mouth, so be very sure to keep your hands away from your face after handling the peppers.

Capsicum annuum produces either cone-shaped or round fruits, according to the variety. The fruits change color as they mature.

FACT FILE

ORIGIN South America.

HEIGHT To 12in/30cm.

POTTING MIX As provided.

REPOTTING Usually none.

PROPAGATION By seed sown in early to mid spring.

KEEPING PLANTS Usually discarded after fruiting.

PLANT CARE

A brightly lit, sunny location is required.
● Fairly cool conditions, about 55°F/13°C.
● Keep the soil moist at all times, particularly during the flowering period.
● Mist the foliage regularly.
● Stand the plants in an open sheltered location outdoors in summer to aid pollination and fruiting.

ALSO RECOMMENDED

Capsicum annum 'Holiday Cheer' has round berries that change from cream through yellow and purple to holly red; fruits at various stages on the same plant give an attractive multicolored effect. *C.a.* 'Red Missile' has large, tapered fruits that are brilliant red when ripe; *C.a.* 'Fireball' has round fruits, maturing from cream through orange to scarlet on compact plants.

Juice from the berries is a powerful irritant, so take care when handling them.

If leaves look papery and fine webbing can sometimes be seen, check for red spider mites. Stand the plants on moist gravel to increase humidity, which helps to combat this pest.

Hot, dry air leads to foliage shriveling and falling and encourages attack by red spider mites. Mist the foliage regularly.

CAREX MORROWII 'VARIEGATA'
Cyperaceae

JAPANESE SEDGE GRASS

The sedges are usually found growing outdoors in boggy soil at the sides of rivers and ponds, but one variety, *Carex morrowii* 'Variegata,' makes a useful houseplant. The narrow, grassy leaves, striped pale green and white, arise from a rhizomatous root to make a gracefully arching fountain of foliage up to 18in/46cm long.

Plants are easy to grow and are not fussy about conditions, although they prefer a cool, humid atmosphere. They are useful plants for groups, where their slender, upright, grassy foliage contrasts well with broad-leaved plants that have more rounded shapes.

FACT FILE

ORIGIN Japan.

HEIGHT To 12in/30cm.

POTTING MIX Soil-based preferably.

REPOTTING In spring, when the roots can be seen growing through the base of the pot.

PROPAGATION Divide plants into two or three clumps at any time during the growing season; very small clumps will not grow well.

KEEPING PLANTS This plant is long-lived and if given minimum attention will thrive for years.

PLANT CARE

Bright filtered light helps to guarantee well-colored foliage. ● Cool to moderately warm conditions; winter temperature of 40°–45°F/4°–7°C. ● Keep the soil moist but not waterlogged. ● Mist the foliage frequently at temperatures of 65°–70°F/18°–21°C. ● Apply standard liquid fertilizer every 4 weeks in spring and summer.

The grassy foliage makes a graceful arching shape.

The variegation of the leaves is more marked when plants are grown in bright light with some direct sun.

Keep the soil just moist, never saturated.

CATHARANTHUS ROSEUS
Apocynaceae

MADAGASCAR PERIWINKLE

This plant is related to the blue-flowered periwinkles, *Vinca* spp., but produces white, pale violet, or pink star-shaped flowers with a deeper-colored throat. The oval leaves are bright green and shiny, and flowers are produced in profusion at the tips of the stems. This periwinkle forms a rounded, shrubby plant with a flowering season that lasts for the whole of the summer into fall.

Catharanthus roseus aroused much interest some years ago when its wild form was found to produce a drug useful in the treatment of leukemia. It is not demanding and is available at garden centers in spring. It fairly easy to raise from seed and can be a good outdoor annual.

Shiny, healthy-looking oval leaves have a light-colored midrib.

Star-shaped flowers, with slightly reflexing petals, are about 1in/2.5cm across and are often carried in large numbers.

Seedlings produce the healthiest, most free-flowering plants.

A well-grown plant can quickly fill a 5-in/13-cm pot. Repot as necessary to keep the plant growing strongly.

FACT FILE

ORIGIN Madagascar.

HEIGHT About 10in/25cm.

POTTING MIX Soil or soil-based medium.

PROPAGATION Sow seed in a warm sheltered spot in late winter or early spring, or in a warm greenhouse in winter. Soft-tip cuttings can be taken in spring and early summer.

REPOTTING Move vigorous plants into pots one size larger as necessary.

KEEPING PLANTS Not easy to bring into flower again, so plants are often discarded after flowering.

PLANT CARE

Bright light with some direct sun will encourage good flowering. ● Moderate warmth with a minimum temperature of about 60°F/16°C. ● Keep the soil moist throughout the flowering period and mist the leaves occasionally. ● Apply a standard liquid fertilizer every 10 to 14 days.

CATTLEYA SPP.
Orchidaceae

*C*ATTLEYA

Many species of orchids are becoming increasingly popular as plants to grow in the home, cattleyas among them. They are not as difficult to grow as many people believe, and the exotic, waxy, long-lasting flowers are very rewarding. There are several species and varieties of cattleya suitable as houseplants. All are epiphytic—in the wild they do not grow in soil but on the stems of other plants, receiving moisture and nutrients from the atmosphere and from rain. Under cultivation, they are grown in a special orchid potting mix, often consisting of a mixture of bark, sphagnum peat moss, and osmunda fiber.

Cattleyas produce swollen pseudobulbs with long, strap-shaped leaves. Flowers in shades of pink and red, often splashed with yellow and with a ruffled lip, arise in clusters or singly on long stems. The flowers can be 5in/13cm wide and may last for more than a month; after flowering, plants rest for about six weeks.

Among the species available are *Cattleya intermedia*, with clusters of rose pink and deep purple blooms in late spring or early summer; and *C. labiata*, which produces groups of large flowers in shades of pink and red marked with yellow in early winter.

FACT FILE

ORIGIN Tropical South America; Mexico; West Indies.

HEIGHT To 2ft/60cm.

POTTING MIX Special orchid mix available from specialist growers.

REPOTTING Move into a pot 2in/5cm larger when the pseudobulbs appear crowded.

PROPAGATION After the rest period, divide overcrowded plants into two, using a sharp knife to cut between the pseudobulbs.

KEEPING PLANTS Place repotted plants in medium light for about a month, until new roots have formed.

PLANT CARE

Bright light but no direct sunlight. ● Warm conditions, with a minimum temperature of 60°F/16°C. ● Water frequently during the growing period, sparingly during the rest period. ● Mist the plant regularly, especially in temperatures over 70°F/21°C, and stand the pot on a tray of moist pebbles—humidity must be high. ● Give a foliar feed every 3 or 4 waterings during the period of active growth.

ALSO RECOMMENDED

Many hybrids and named varieties have larger flowers than the species. Among them are *Cattleya* Bob Betts 'White Wings,' a large-flowered, spring-blooming plant, and *C.* Nigritian 'King of Kings,' which produces many-flowered clusters of splendid lavender-colored blooms. *C.* 'Guatemalensis,' with small salmon pink flowers in spring, is a natural hybrid.

Pseudobulbs are swollen stem bases from which the leaves and flower stems arise. Wait until the pot is crowded with pseudobulbs before repotting; otherwise, flowering will be adversely affected.

Allow the potting mix to dry out between waterings, and give a rest period with very little water for about 6 weeks after flowering. Use lime-free water if possible.

Old, shriveled pseudobulbs may remain on the plant for several years. They do not need to be removed.

Flowers consist of three sepals and three petals, the lower one of which is tubular and frilled to form a lip. Remove flowers as they fade.

The hybrid 'Violacea' is a charming small-flowered cattleya. Its pale-colored flowers are borne in abundance and it produces 3 or 4 blooms to a stem.

CHAMAEDOREA ELEGANS
Palmae

PARLOR PALM

One of the most popular palms for the home, *Chamaedorea elegans* (also known as *Neanthe elegans*) has long, arching leaves divided into pairs of leaflets on each side of the central midrib. It eventually develops a short trunk and after three or four years may produce sprays of tiny yellow flowers. It remains a small, compact plant and is easy to look after. Young plants are particularly suitable for terrariums. Because of their slow growth rate, older, larger plants can be very expensive; small young plants are a better buy. The parlor palm is also known as the good luck or dwarf mountain palm.

FACT FILE

ORIGIN Mexico; Guatemala.

HEIGHT To 6ft/1.8m after several years.

POTTING MIX Soil-based mixed with added peat moss.

REPOTTING Necessary only when the roots have completely filled the pot; firm soil gently but thoroughly around the roots.

PROPAGATION From seed. Practicable only by specialists.

KEEPING PLANTS Plants will survive for many years if good growing conditions are provided.

PLANT CARE

Moderately bright light or light shade. ● Minimum winter temperatures of 50°–55°F/10°–13°C. ● Keep the soil moist during the growing season; allow the top third to dry out between waterings in winter. ● Mist the foliage regularly and stand the plants on a tray of moist pebbles to increase humidity. ● Apply half-strength liquid fertilizer monthly during the growing period only.

Brown tips to the leaves are usually caused by an excessively dry atmosphere. Increase the humidity.

Sprays of tiny yellow flowers may appear on a 3- to 4-year-old plant if it is grown in good light.

Dry-looking leaves with a silvery or mottled appearance may indicate attack by red spider mites. Maintain a humid atmosphere to combat this pest.

CHAMAEROPS HUMILIS
Palmae

EUROPEAN FAN PALM

There are several other fan palms, but this is the only one that is native to Europe. The large, deeply divided, fan-shaped fronds give this plant its other frequently used common names: dwarf fan palm and hair palm. Each dark green leaf measures about 2ft/60cm across and consists of a number of stiff, spiky segments radiating from the base. The leaf stalk, which is usually 1–2ft/30–60cm long, is sharply toothed.

The plant makes a bushy, architectural shrub, which is generally not difficult to grow in room conditions. Where winter temperatures fall below 55°–60°F/13°–16°C, water this palm sparingly and allow the top half of the soil to dry out between waterings.

Even well-established plants do not produce flowers or fruit when grown indoors.

Take care when handling the palm: the leaf stems are covered with sharp teeth.

The long, stiff leaf segments often become shaggy and split at their tips.

FACT FILE

ORIGIN Western Mediterranean countries.

HEIGHT To 4ft/1.2 m.

POTTING MIX Soil-based.

REPOTTING Move into a pot one size larger every 2 years in spring until maximum convenient size has been reached; thereafter top-dress.

PROPAGATION Sow fresh seed in a propagator, or carefully separate 8–10-in/20–25-cm suckers, with roots, from the parent plant and pot up individually.

KEEPING PLANTS This palm can survive for several years, given good growing conditions.

PLANT CARE

Bright light with some direct sun, although the plant will tolerate light shade. ● Minimum temperature 50°F/10°C. ● Keep the soil moist at all times in the growing period, but do not allow the pot to stand in water. ● Liquid-feed every 10 to 14 days in summer.

CHLOROPHYTUM COMOSUM '*VITTATUM*'
Liliaceae

*S*PIDER PLANT

Probably because it is so easy to grow and propagate, the spider, or ribbon, plant is one of the most popular of all plants both in homes and offices. The grassy, ribbonlike leaves, which form an arching clump, are 6–12in/15–30cm long and are green, with central bands of creamy white.

In spring and summer, sprays of small white flowers are produced on long, yellow, wiry stems that cascade gracefully down from the parent plant. Spider plants are especially attractive in hanging baskets or wall-mounted pot-holders. The flowers are followed by clusters of baby plants, each producing a miniature clump of variegated leaves. Roots soon develop on these plantlets, which can be removed from the parent and potted individually.

FACT FILE

ORIGIN South Africa.

HEIGHT To 10in/25cm.

POTTING MIX Soilless or all-purpose mix.

REPOTTING Move into a container one size larger when roots start to appear through the base of the pot.

PROPAGATION Pot baby plantlets when they start to develop roots, or divide the rosettes in spring.

KEEPING PLANTS These are hardy plants and will go on for years, provided they are given good growing conditions and are repotted when necessary.

PLANT CARE

Bright light is essential for well-colored leaves; too much direct sunlight will scorch the foliage. ● Minimum temperature 45°F/7°C. ● Keep the soil moist at all times in spring and summer; water more sparingly in winter. ● Feed with a standard liquid fertilizer every 10 to 14 days from early spring to late fall.

Brown tips to the leaves develop if the plant is allowed to dry out or if the air is excessively hot and dry. Mist the foliage occasionally.

The plant needs good light to ensure the best color contrast on the variegated leaves.

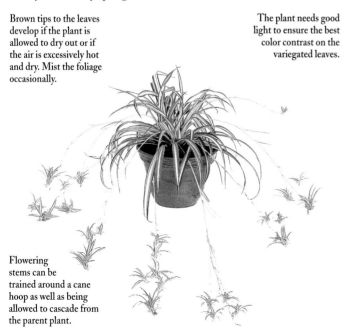

Flowering stems can be trained around a cane hoop as well as being allowed to cascade from the parent plant.

CHRYSALIDOCARPUS LUTESCENS
Palmae

*B*UTTERFLY PALM

This upright palm produces tall, bamboolike stems topped with arching fronds, which are divided into leaflets in more or less opposite pairs. The fronds are pale yellow-green and up to 4ft/1.2m long. Previously called *Areca lutescens*, this plant is sometimes also known as the areca palm, golden feather palm, or yellow palm.

With its bold, striking outline, chrysalidocarpus makes a good specimen plant. It is fairly slow-growing, so large specimens tend to be expensive to buy.

The canelike stems of mature plants are marked with notches, indicating the position of previous leaf stalks.

Old fronds at the base of the plant turn brown and shrivel, and should be removed. Their removal leads to the development of the typical reedlike stems.

Mottled, grayish, dry-looking leaves may indicate attack by red spider mites. Keep the pest at bay by providing a humid atmosphere.

FACT FILE

ORIGIN Madagascar.

HEIGHT To 5ft/1.5m or more after several years.

POTTING MIX Soil-based.

REPOTTING Move into a pot one size larger every other year in spring. Top-dress annually once the pot is as large as is practical.

PROPAGATION When repotting, detach suckers (ideally, those about 12in/30cm high with good root growth) complete with roots from the base of established plants and pot them individually.

KEEPING PLANTS These palms are hardy and will last for many years.

PLANT CARE

Bright filtered light. ● Minimum temperature of 55°F/13°C. ● Keep the soil moist at all times during the growing season. In winter reduce watering in lower temperatures. ● Mist the foliage daily to maintain a humid atmosphere. ● Apply liquid fertilizer every 2 weeks in the growing season.

CHRYSANTHEMUM* x *MORIFOLIUM
Compositae

*F*LORISTS' *CHRYSANTHEMUM*

A popular short-term flowering plant, the florists' chrysanthemum (*Dendranthema* x *grandiflorum* as it is currently known) requires production techniques beyond the capability of the amateur. Deep green, aromatic, lobed leaves are set on short stems topped with double, semidouble, or single flowers in a wide range of colors: white, cream, red, orange, yellow, and pink. Anemone-centered flowers are also available, as are fine-petaled "spiders," and "spoons" with rolled petals opening out at the ends. Most florists' chrysanthemums consist of several cuttings inserted around the edge of a pot, and because the soil is filled with roots, plants tend to dry out quickly.

In nature, the flowering time of chrysanthemums is controlled by day length: they are "short-day" plants that flower naturally in late summer and fall. Commercial growers manipulate artificial lighting to bring plants into flower throughout the year, but they are probably most popular as fall and winter plants. (Buy only plants that are showing color in the buds; others may not open.)

Plants are also treated with dwarfing chemicals to keep them compact; without these chemicals, most varieties would flower at 3–4ft/90cm–1.2m high. These are only temporary houseplants, and they can sometimes be successfully planted outdoors in mild climates, where they will revert to their full height and natural flowering season the following year.

FACT FILE

ORIGIN Northern temperate zones; hybrid.

HEIGHT To 12in/30cm.

POTTING MIX Not applicable.

REPOTTING None.

PROPAGATION Take soft stem cuttings to produce garden plants; it is not possible for the home gardener to produce successful houseplants.

KEEPING PLANTS Discard after flowering, or plant outdoors.

PLANT CARE

Moderately bright light without direct sun. ● Flowers last best in reasonably cool conditions of 55°–60°F/13°–16°C. ● Keep the soil moist at all times.

ALSO RECOMMENDED

Chrysanthemum frutescens (syn. *Argyranthemum frutescens*), the white marguerite, has masses of daisylike flowers with a bright yellow central disc. It can grow to 3ft/90cm, but on pot plants—best bought from a grower in early spring—the growing shoots are usually pinched off, and the plants are about 18in/46cm high. *C.f.* 'Etoile d'Or' has lemon yellow petals, and 'Mary Wootton' rose pink petals.

A wide variety of flower types and shapes is available, though the doubles are probably the most popular.

Compact, low-growing plants are produced by the use of dwarfing compounds. Surviving plants will eventually return to their natural height.

Chrysanthemum frutescens, *the white marguerite, is one of the most floriferous and rewarding of summer-flowering plants.*

The colorful flowers should last for several weeks in reasonably cool, bright conditions.

Water frequently to keep the soil thoroughly moist.

CISSUS ANTARCTICA
Vitadacae

*K*ANGAROO VINE

A fast-growing, scrambling plant, this cissus can cover large areas of trellis with its bright green, healthy-looking leaves and is useful as a screen or room divider. The pointed, oval leaves are shiny, with toothed edges, and are carried on tough stems that climb upward and outward rapidly, clinging to any support by means of curling tendrils. *Cissus antarctica* can also be grown in hanging baskets and allowed to trail. *C.a.* 'Minima' is probably best for this, since it has a more spreading growth habit. These plants are suitable for a wide range of conditions and are popular because of their adaptability.

Cissus rhombifolia 'Ellen Danica,' a quick-growing grape ivy, has handsome, glossy three-lobed leaves and is an excellent plant for a hanging basket or for growing up a trellis to form a room divider.

FACT FILE

ORIGIN Australia.

HEIGHT To 10ft/3m.

POTTING MIX Soil- or peat-moss-based.

PROPAGATION Take young tip cuttings in spring and early summer; strip off the lower leaves, dip in hormone rooting powder, insert into a mixture of peat and sand, and enclose the pot in a plastic bag. Roots should form within 6–8 weeks.

REPOTTING In spring, when roots have filled the pot.

KEEPING PLANTS Pinch shoot tips back to keep plants within bounds; if they become bare at the base, cut them well back in spring.

PLANT CARE

Ideally, bright light but no direct sun, but the plant will adapt to a wide range of light conditions. ● Cool conditions, with a minimum of 45°–50°F/7°–10°C in winter. ● Keep the soil moist throughout the growing season; allow the surface to dry out between waterings in winter. ● Liquid-feed every 10–14 days in spring and summer. ● Provide a suitable support before stems become tangled or misshapen.

ALSO RECOMMENDED

Cissus rhombifolia (often sold as *Rhoicissus rhomboidea*), the grape ivy, has leaves that are a deep green, although young shoots are covered in fine hairs, which gives them a silvery appearance. Tendrils are forked at the tips. The variety 'Ellen Danica' has attractively lobed leaflets.

Cissus discolor is much more unusual, and more difficult to grow. The velvety, spear-shaped leaves are marked with silver and pink in a similar fashion to those of *Begonia rex*. This plant needs warm conditions and high humidity to do well.

Train the plant up a trellis, netting, or pole covered with moss. Make sure supports are firmly anchored, since the weight of the foliage on well-grown plants can easily cause them to topple over.

Cissus needs good light, but should be protected from direct sun, which causes scorch marks on the leaves. The plant will tolerate light shade.

Aphids often attack young shoots. Inspect them regularly during spring and early summer and treat with a contact insecticide if the pests are present.

Mist the foliage regularly to keep it healthy. Brown leaf tips indicate that the atmosphere is too dry.

x *CITROFORTUNELLA MICROCARPUS*
Rutaceae

Calamondin

Citrus plants make attractive shrubs particularly suitable for a sunroom. This cross between a tangerine and a kumquat—also known under the name of x *Citrofortunella mitis*—is one of the best to grow indoors, since it makes a compact tree that bears flowers and fruits while still young. The glossy, dark green, oval leaves are aromatic when crushed and are carried on woody branches that, unlike those of many other species of citrus, are spineless. White, star-shaped, fragrant flowers are borne mainly in summer but may appear sporadically at any time of year. They are followed by small round fruits, carried in clusters of two or three at the tips of the branches, which tend to bend the stems down as they develop. The fruits ripen slowly, changing from deep green to orange, and measure about 1½in/4cm in diameter; they are decorative and, although very bitter, are sometimes used in jams. Flowers and fruits are often seen on the tree at the same time, adding to its interest.

To ensure fruiting, if the plant is indoors, pollinate the flowers with a soft brush. Pollination is improved by standing the plant outdoors in summer.

Yellowing or mottled leaves may indicate nutrient deficiency. Apply a foliar feed containing trace elements.

Scale insects can be a problem. Check the undersides of the leaves, pushing off any scales with a fingernail.

Attack by red spider mites can be combated by misting to increase humidity and by standing the pot on moist gravel.

FACT FILE

ORIGIN Hybrid.

HEIGHT To 4ft/1.2m.

POTTING MIX Soil-based.

REPOTTING Move the plant into a pot one size larger every spring until the maximum convenient size is reached; thereafter top-dress annually.

PROPAGATION Difficult; by semiripe cuttings in early summer.

KEEPING PLANTS Stand outdoors in a sheltered place in summer; bring under cover in late fall.

PLANT CARE

Bright light with several hours of direct sun daily. ● Minimum winter temperature of 50°F/10°C. ● Allow the surface of the soil to dry out between waterings. ● Mist the foliage frequently and stand the pot on a tray of moist gravel to increase humidity. ● Give a high-potash liquid feed every 10–14 days in the growing season.

CLERODENDRUM THOMSONIAE
Verbenaceae

Bleeding-Heart Vine

This climbing plant can be trained up a trellis or around a hoop, or allowed to trail from a hanging basket or raised pot. It can also be kept bushy by regularly pinching off the tips of shoots. The deep green ovate leaves are attractively veined, but the plant's chief glory is the striking red-and-white flowers, which consist of a white lantern-shaped calyx from which the bright scarlet blooms with prominent stamens emerge. The flowers are produced from spring to fall in clusters at the ends of the stems. *Clerodendrum thomsoniae* 'Variegatum,' with marbled green leaves, is sometimes available.

FACT FILE

ORIGIN Tropical West Africa.

HEIGHT To 8ft/2.4m.

POTTING MIX Soil-based.

REPOTTING When the potting mix is filled with roots, move to a pot one size larger in spring; top-dress when maximum convenient pot size is reached.

PROPAGATION Take stem cuttings in late spring, pot in a mixture of equal parts of coarse sand and peat moss; move to a soil-based mix after 3–4 months.

KEEPING PLANTS Prune in spring, just as the plant is starting into growth. Cut back the stems by about half to keep it at a manageable size indoors.

PLANT CARE

Bright light is required for good flowering, but protect from direct sunlight. ● Moderate warmth during the growing season, but keep warm (62°–85°F/17°–29°C) in winter. ● Keep the soil moist throughout the flowering season; water sparingly in the winter rest period. ● Mist frequently with tepid water from springtime onward. ● Apply standard liquid fertilizer every 2 weeks in the growing season.

The striking red-and-white flowers are produced most freely in warm, humid conditions.

The plant flowers best when slightly pot-bound.

Pinch off the shoot tips occasionally to keep the plant neat.

The twining stems can be trained up supports or left to trail from a hanging basket.

CLIVIA MINIATA
Amaryllidaceae

CLIVIA

Although this is a long-established favorite, it often fails to flower indoors, usually because it has not been given a winter rest. The long, strap-shaped, deep green leaves overlap at the base, rather like those of a leek, then fan out at the top. In late winter or early spring, a tall flower stem, carrying a head of about 10–15 trumpet-shaped flowers, pushes out from between the leaves. The flowers are usually orange with yellow throats, but deeper reddish shades and yellow or cream varieties are sometimes available.

The roots of clivias are thick, fleshy, and rather brittle, and plants flower best when slightly potbound. Offsets are produced on established plants, and while they can be used for propagation, they will produce an impressive specimen with a number of flower heads if they are allowed to remain.

FACT FILE

ORIGIN South Africa.

HEIGHT To 18in/46cm.

POTTING MIX Soil-based or peat-moss-based.

REPOTTING The fleshy roots soon appear to crowd the pot, but plants should be repotted only every 3–4 years. Instead, top-dress in late winter.

PROPAGATION Carefully detach offsets complete with roots from the parent and pot individually.

KEEPING PLANTS Cut out embryo fruits that form after the flowers drop; pull withering flower stalks off the plant.

PLANT CARE

Bright light with some direct sun in spring. ● A winter rest period is essential, with a temperature of about 50°F/10°C for 6–8 weeks from late fall. ● Keep the soil moist during the growing season, and water very sparingly during the rest period. ● Give a liquid feed every 12–14 days during the growing season.

ALSO RECOMMENDED

Clivia miniata 'Striata' has variegated leaves but is difficult to find.

Wipe the glossy, deep green leaves with a damp cloth occasionally to keep them looking fresh.

Snap off the flower head once all the blooms have faded, but wait until the flower stem begins to shrivel before pulling it gently from the plant.

Fluffy white mealybugs can sometimes be found between the leaf bases. Use a systemic insecticide to deal with any infestation.

The thick, fleshy roots often appear on the surface of the soil, but do not repot the plant until it is essential. It will flower best when the roots are restricted.

If the plant is not given a cool winter rest period, the flower stalk may not develop properly or flowers may fail to form.

The flower stem of **Clivia miniata** *bears an umbel of fragrant trumpet-shaped flowers in a bright, soft orange.*

CODIAEUM VARIEGATUM PICTUM
Euphorbiaceae

*C*ROTON

Another name for this popular plant is Joseph's coat, and a look at the variety of forms available will soon explain why. The tough, leathery leaves are indeed of many colors, largely yellows and greens mottled or veined with rosy pink, red, or orange. Their shapes, too, vary enormously, from long and pointed to short and broad; from slender, wavy-edged ribbons to deeply lobed and fiddle-shaped. The plant forms a small, sturdy shrub, often with a bare lower stem.

In some forms the colors remain the same; in others they darken with age. Mature plants may produce insignificant, fluffy, cream-colored flowers.

Codiaeum *'Golden Bell,' a recently developed variety, has long, square-ended multicolored leaves, some with smaller leaflets growing from them.*

FACT FILE

ORIGIN Malaysia; Pacific islands; Northern Australia.

HEIGHT To 3ft/90cm and more.

POTTING MIX Soil-based.

REPOTTING Move into a pot one size larger in spring; when maximum desired size is reached, top-dress instead.

PROPAGATION By tip cuttings in spring.

KEEPING PLANTS Plants are naturally bushy, so should not need pruning. But if they become too large, cut them well back in early spring, and use the prunings for propagation.

PLANT CARE

Bright light with some direct sun.
● Warm conditions with a minimum of 60°F/16°C in winter. ● Keep the soil evenly moist during the growing period. Reduce watering in winter, but do not allow the soil to dry out completely. ● Mist often and stand the plant on a tray of moist pebbles. ● Liquid-feed every 2 weeks during the growing season.

ALSO RECOMMENDED

Many varieties are available which are often sold unnamed. *Codiaeum variegatum pictum* 'Aucubifolium' has green, laurel-like leaves spotted with yellow; 'Craigii' has deeply lobed leaves with yellow veins; 'Reidii,' deep red veins and leaves suffused with red, yellow, and pink; and 'Bravo,' lightly lobed leaves splashed with yellow.

Keep the plants in bright light to ensure the best foliage color and to avoid a bare lower stem where leaves have fallen prematurely.

Check the undersides of the leaves, especially along the midrib, for scale insects. If you find any, scrape them off with a fingernail.

Colors fade if the light is poor, especially in winter; move the plant to a brighter location.

Mealybugs and red spider mites both attack this plant; high humidity will help to keep the latter pest at bay.

The choice of different shapes and color combinations of codiaeum leaves is vast.

COELOGYNE CRISTATA
Orchidaceae

*C*OELOGYNE

This orchid produces two strap-shaped, slightly arching leaves from each of the rounded or egg-shaped pseudobulbs, which are tightly clustered. Flower stalks some 12in/30cm long arise from the pseudobulbs in winter or early spring and carry 6–8 scented white flowers with golden yellow markings on the lip, and undulating petals.

Coelogynes are not the easiest orchids to grow in the home. They require high humidity during the growing season and a short winter rest period in order to produce their flowers. The pure white-and-gold flowers are, however, carried in quite large numbers on established plants, making coelogyne's cultivation a tempting prospect. It grows well mounted on a log or bark or in a hanging wooden basket, where its long, drooping flower stems will show to best advantage.

FACT FILE

ORIGIN Himalayas.

HEIGHT To 12in/30cm.

POTTING MIX Use only special orchid mix, which may consist of shredded bark, tree-fern fiber, and sphagnum moss.

REPOTTING In spring every 3–4 years. The plant resents disturbance.

PROPAGATION Cut off part of the rhizome together with a small number of pseudobulbs and pot up in special orchid mix.

KEEPING PLANTS With proper care, this orchid will last for many years.

PLANT CARE

Bright filtered light at all times. ● Minimum winter temperature of 55°F/13°C during the day, 45°F/7°C at night. In summer, keep temperatures below 75°F/24°C. ● To water, stand plants in water for 10 minutes. Always keep the soil moist in the growing period. During the rest period, water just enough to prevent the soil from drying out completely. ● Mist the foliage regularly to ensure high humidity. ● Apply a foliar feed every 2 to 3 waterings.

A 6-week winter rest period is essential to ensure good flowering.

Pseudobulbs become wrinkled and yellow after flowering, but the new ones are shiny and light green. Take care not to splash the pseudobulbs when watering.

COLEUS BLUMEI
Labiatae

*F*LAME NETTLE

Known today as *Solenostemon scutellarioides*, but usually offered in the trade as *Coleus blumei*, this plant is cheap and easy to grow. These qualities, along with its brilliantly colored foliage, have made it a popular, if fairly short-lived, houseplant. The toothed leaves are usually ovate or heart-shaped, although some varieties have lance-shaped, or interestingly lobed or contorted foliage. The square, fleshy stems are typical of the mint family. Spikes of small blue flowers are often produced, but these are rather insignificant and detract from the foliage, so they are usually removed.

Foliage colors vary from green with yellow markings to intense reds, brilliant yellows and oranges, deep maroon, and brown. Leaves may be edged or veined with contrasting colors or simply splashed with several different colors; some varieties have no green on the leaves at all. No wonder the plant is also called the painted nettle.

If winter temperatures drop much below 55°F/13°C, leaves may wilt and fall.

Pinch off the stem tips occasionally to keep plants bushy, and remove flower spikes as soon as they appear.

If aphids attack the soft young foliage, spray with insecticide or soapy water, or pinch off and destroy the affected shoot tips.

Lower leaves fall in poor light, or if the plant is short of water.

FACT FILE

ORIGIN Tropical Africa; Asia.

HEIGHT To 2ft/60cm.

POTTING MIX Soil-based.

REPOTTING Move the plant into a larger pot as necessary during the growing season.

PROPAGATION In spring by seed or stem cuttings. In late summer by cuttings.

KEEPING PLANTS Discard the plant when it becomes leggy.

PLANT CARE

Bright light with some direct sun is essential for good leaf color; intense summer sun will scorch the foliage. ● Moderately warm rooms, with a minimum of 60°F/16°C. ● Keep the soil evenly moist at all times, using lime-free water if possible. ● Mist the foliage regularly. ● Liquid-feed every 2 weeks during the growing season.

COLUMNEA × BANKSII
Gesneriaceae

GOLDFISH PLANT

Several species of columnea are available, but not all are easy to grow as houseplants. *Columnea × banksii* is one of the most tolerant. Its dark green leaves are smooth and almost succulent. They are carried in opposite pairs along trailing stems that can reach 3ft/90cm or more, making this columnea an ideal plant for a hanging basket.

The bright red tubular flowers, about 2½–3in/6.5–8cm long, have yellow throats, with the upper petals forming a hood. They are borne in profusion in winter and early spring and occasionally at other times.

FACT FILE

ORIGIN Tropical America; hybrids.

HEIGHT Stems trail to 3ft/90cm or more.

POTTING MIX Peat-moss-based.

REPOTTING In spring, when the roots fill the pot.

PROPAGATION In spring or summer take cuttings from stems that are not flowering. Root them with bottom heat or sow seed in spring.

KEEPING PLANTS In good conditions, plants will last for several years.

PLANT CARE

Columneas need bright light but not direct sun. ● Warm conditions, with a minimum of about 60°F/16°C in winter. ● Keep the soil just moist, allowing the top third to dry out between waterings. Reduce watering in lower winter temperatures. ● A humid atmosphere must be maintained at all times. Mist the foliage with tepid water daily. ● Liquid-feed with a high-potash fertilizer every 10–14 days during the growing season.

ALSO RECOMMENDED

Columnea gloriosa has leaves that are densely covered with fine brownish hairs and produces large, striking orange-red hooded flowers with yellow throats. The leaves of *C.g.* 'Purpurea' are covered with purple hairs.

Among the many hybrids are 'Alpha,' with bright yellow flowers freely produced sporadically throughout the year, and 'Chanticleer,' one of the easiest and most popular varieties, with a compact, branching habit and orange flowers produced all year. 'Mary Ann' produces unusual deep pink blooms at intervals during the year, and 'Stavanger' has smooth, glossy leaves and large, orange-red flowers.

Columnea gloriosa *has slender stems that trail to about 3ft/90cm before they branch. It bears brilliant orange-red single flowers, which can be 3in/8cm long. These are followed by large white berries.*

The bright orange-red hooded flowers give columneas their common name of goldfish plant.

All columneas need the high humidity provided by frequent misting.

Smooth-leafed varieties are easier to grow than the hairy-leafed types.

Small brown spots on the leaves can be caused by misting with cold water; use tepid water instead.

CORDYLINE AUSTRALIS
Agavaceae

*C*ABBAGE TREE

Cordylines are sometimes confused with dracaenas, to which they are related, and *Cordyline australis* may be offered as *Dracaena indivisa*. It makes a fountain-shaped plant, with long, narrow, arching leaves on top of a short, stout stem. It has something of the appearance of a palm tree, and plants in this group are often known as "false palms." Also known as palm lily, grass palm, New Zealand cabbage palm, and fountain dracaena, *C. australis* is an architectural plant, popular in modern settings.

Leaves are sword-shaped and leathery, mid to dark green, and up to 3ft/90cm long. The variety *C.a.* 'Purpurea' has deep, rich purple-bronze leaves, and *C.a.* 'Atropurpurea' has a purple flush at the base and up the center of the leaf. Small white flowers in long panicles appear on mature plants, but are rarely produced in the home. It is a long-lived, fairly tolerant plant and can withstand lower temperatures than other cordylines.

FACT FILE

ORIGIN New Zealand.

HEIGHT 6–10ft/1.8–3m or more.

POTTING MIX Soil- or peat-moss-based.

REPOTTING Move into a pot one size larger every spring. Once the maximum desired pot size is reached, top-dress annually with fresh soil.

PROPAGATION In spring, sow seed, or take shoot tip cuttings from basal or stem shoots. Cut back overgrown plants and use 2-in/5-cm sections of the old stems with growth buds as cuttings.

KEEPING PLANTS The plant will benefit from a spell in the shade outdoors in summer.

PLANT CARE

Bright indirect sunlight; the plant will stand some shade. ● Minimum winter temperature of 50°F/10°C. ● Keep the soil moist during the growing season but allow it to dry out slightly between waterings in winter. ● Apply a balanced liquid fertilizer every 2 weeks in spring and summer.

Brown tips to the foliage indicate that the air is too dry. Mist the foliage regularly to increase humidity, and stand the pot on a tray of moist gravel.

The arching foliage makes an attractive, fountain-shaped plant that requires plenty of space. Constantly brushing past the leaves will damage them.

Lower leaves naturally yellow and die off. Overwatering, particularly in winter, can cause leaves to yellow.

CORDYLINE TERMINALIS
Agavaceae

*G*OOD LUCK PLANT

Also known as ti tree or plant and red dracaena, *Cordyline terminalis* is sometimes incorrectly sold as *Dracaena terminalis*. It has more or less lance-shaped leaves up to 2ft/60cm long and 4in/10cm or so wide. Young foliage is pinkish red, gradually becoming deep coppery green. Several attractively colored varieties are available, including *C.t.* 'Rededge,' probably the most popular, with leaves streaked and outlined in red and a relatively compact habit. 'Baptistii' is flushed with red and yellow, and 'Kiwi' has leaves of mid green, light green, and cream, edged and flushed with pink. As the plant grows, the lower leaves fall to produce a plant with a rosette of foliage at the top of a long stem. It will last for several years.

The broad leaves have long leaf stalks and spread out like a fan from the central stem.

Dry air causes brown edges on the foliage. Regular frequent misting is required.

Bright, filtered light is needed for the most intense leaf color.

Watch out for aphids on the young leaves, particularly on the undersides. Treat with a contact insecticide.

FACT FILE

ORIGIN Polynesia.

HEIGHT 3–5ft/90cm–1.5m in a container indoors.

POTTING MIX Soil- or peat-moss-based.

REPOTTING In spring move into a pot one size larger until maximum required pot size is reached; thereafter top-dress annually.

PROPAGATION In spring separate suckers from the base of the plant and keep them in warm, humid conditions until established. In early summer, cut the stems from old plants into 2-in/5-cm sections, each with a bud, and insert into seed mix with added sharp sand.

KEEPING PLANTS This is a long-lived plant under favorable conditions.

PLANT CARE

Bright conditions with filtered sun. ● Minimum winter temperature of 60°F/16°C. ● Keep the soil evenly moist during the growing season. Allow the surface to dry out between waterings in winter. ● Mist the foliage regularly. ● Feed with a balanced liquid fertilizer every 2 weeks in spring and summer. ● Protect from drafts.

CRASSULA ARBORESCENS (SYN. *C. COTYLEDON*)
Crassulaceae

CHINESE JADE PLANT

Most crassulas are low-growing, but some make small bushy shrubs. In their native habitat – the drier areas of South Africa – day temperatures can be high with a huge drop at night, causing heavy dew. The flowers of most crassulas are tiny, but they may appear in very large numbers.

The Chinese, or silver, jade plant can grow to 4ft/1.2m high and, with its thick, trunklike stem and many branches, which are symmetrical in mature specimens, it makes a perfect miniature "tree." No training or pruning is required. The 1–2-in/2.5–5-cm-wide fleshy leaves are almost round and gray-green, rimmed with red. Flowers rarely appear indoors, but if you are lucky you will see them—tiny stars in white through to pink, carried in clusters during spring.

C.a. 'Variegata' is an attractive, slower-growing variegated form, with yellowish leaf markings.

Gray mold may develop if the plant is overwatered or drainage is inadequate.

Mealybugs may attack this plant; check for signs of the white waxy wool on leaves and stems.

If the plant is limp, wilting or discolored, knock it out of its pot and check for root mealybugs or weevil grubs. Waterlogging could also cause these symptoms.

Brown, shriveled or shrunken patches on leaves are caused by underwatering or the roots being dry for too long.

FACT FILE

ORIGIN South Africa (Cape Province, Natal).

HEIGHT To 4ft/1.2m.

POTTING MIX Soil-based, with some added peat.

REPOTTING Move into pots one size larger each spring. Once plants are in 8-in/20-cm pots, top-dress annually instead.

PROPAGATION Take tip cuttings in spring or summer.

KEEPING PLANTS Stand the plant in a sunny window and set it outdoors in summer to toughen up the stems and improve leaf color.

PLANT CARE

Bright light, with some direct sunlight. ● Minimum winter temperature of 45°F/7°C, with normal room temperature at other times. ● Water liberally during spring and summer, but allow the soil to dry out between waterings. ● Apply a weak liquid fertilizer every 2 weeks from spring to fall.

CRASSULA OVATA (SYN. *C. PORTULACEA*)
Crassulaceae

JADE TREE

Similar in many respects to its close relative *Crassula arborescens*, this succulent has glossy, dark green, spoon-shaped fleshy leaves which grow from a treelike trunk. It may produce pretty, but short-lived, pink or white flowers in spring.

C. ovata likes the warm, dry atmosphere of a heated home and does not require much attention. If it is necessary to prune the plant, dust the wounds with sulfur or cigarette ash to stem the flow of sap. Mist the leaves occasionally to clean them. The jade tree, or money tree as it is sometimes called, is a slow grower and should last for many years.

FACT FILE

ORIGIN South Africa (Namaqualand to Transvaal).

HEIGHT To 3ft/90cm.

POTTING MIX Soil-based and perlite or sand in a ratio of 3:1.

REPOTTING Move only when necessary, probably every other year. Once plants are in 8-in/20-cm pots, top-dress annually instead.

PROPAGATION Sow seed in a propagator or root individual leaves or stem cuttings in a peat/sand mixture at room temperature. Allow cuttings to dry out for a few days before planting.

KEEPING PLANTS Stand the plant outside in summer in a sunny, protected spot.

PLANT CARE

Bright light with some direct sunlight. ● Minimum winter temperature of 45°F/7°C; this plant can withstand high temperatures. ● Water 2 or 3 times a week in spring and summer, once a month in winter. ● Apply a high-potash fertilizer every 2 weeks from spring to fall only.

Leaves drop in winter if the room is too warm; move the plant to a cooler location.

If the plant becomes spindly, move it to a brighter location.

Check stems and roots regularly for mealybugs; check roots for signs of weevil grubs.

CROCUS HYBRIDS
Iridaceae

DUTCH CROCUS

The crocuses most commonly seen in the home are Dutch hybrids, which have larger and more striking flowers than the species. The leaves are striped green and white, and the cup-shaped flowers, which appear in winter and early spring, may be white, yellow, bronze, purple, or multicolored.

Dry corms are offered for sale in late summer, and ready-planted pots are available from late fall onward. Among the best for growing indoors are 'Pickwick,' shown here, which is pale silver-lilac with deep lilac stripes and a bright orange stigma, and the silvery, amethyst blue 'Little Dorrit,' one of the largest of all crocuses. 'Snowstorm,' with pure white globular flowers, is free-flowering and long-lasting.

FACT FILE

ORIGIN Hybrids.

HEIGHT To 4in/10cm.

POTTING MIX Soil-based.

PROPAGATION Remove small corms that may form around the parent bulb, or sow seed. The seedlings will take 3–4 years to bloom.

REPOTTING Plant several corms together in early fall; set them just below the surface of the potting mixture. Corms must be 'wintered' for about 10 weeks and brought into a warm room only when the flower buds are visible.

KEEPING PLANTS After flowering, either let the corms dry out in the pot and keep them until the next fall, or plant them out in the garden. They will not bloom again indoors.

PLANT CARE

Filtered sunlight. ● Cool conditions, with a maximum temperature of 60°F/16°C. ● Keep the soil moist at all times. ● Apply weak liquid fertilizer every 4 weeks from planting to the start of flowering.

It is better to mass crocuses of one variety in a shallow bowl rather than to mix them, because they tend to bloom at different times.

CROSSANDRA INFUNDIBULIFORMIS
Acanthaceae

FIRECRACKER FLOWER

This striking plant, also known as *Crossandra undulifolia*, is a small shrub from the rain forests of southern India and Sri Lanka. Its shiny, dark green leaves with wavy edges are held in opposite pairs and are 2½–5in/6.5–13cm long. From spring to late fall, the flowers—in shades of yellow, orange, and red—rise in twos and threes from upright tufts of green bracts. Each has a tube-shaped base, but flares out into a lobed disc up to 1½in/4cm wide. Even young specimens will flower readily, but after about two years they tend to lose their vigor and should be replaced. The form 'Mona Walhead' has salmon pink blooms; those of *Crossandra pungens* are yellow.

Crossandras are good for groups, since they flourish best when surrounded by other plants and enjoy humid conditions.

Check for red spider mites; regular misting will help to discourage this pest.

A reluctance to flower may mean that the plant is in too much shade. Move to a brighter place and pinch off some leaf growth to stimulate flower buds.

Falling leaves and a drooping appearance may indicate that the plant is standing in a cold draft; move it to a warmer place.

FACT FILE

ORIGIN India; Sri Lanka.

HEIGHT To 15in/38cm.

POTTING MIX Soil-based, with added peat moss.

REPOTTING Repot each spring, in a pot one size larger. Ensure good drainage as waterlogging can be fatal to the plant.

PROPAGATION Take 2–3-in/5–7.5-cm-long tip cuttings in spring and root them in a heated propagator.

KEEPING PLANTS Stand the plant outdoors in the sun in summer.

PLANT CARE

Bright filtered light; avoid direct sunlight. ● Stable year-round temperatures no lower than 65°F/18°C. ● From spring to fall water thoroughly, allowing the soil to almost dry out before adding more; water sparingly in winter. Water should be tepid. ● Stand the plant on a tray of moist pebbles for extra humidity, and mist regularly. ● In spring and summer, feed every 2 weeks with a high-potash liquid fertilizer.

CRYPTANTHUS ACAULIS
Bromeliaceae

Green Earth Star

All cryptanthus species make good houseplants. They thrive in the sunniest places and if treated well are almost trouble-free. In the wild, these ground-hugging star-shaped bromeliads (see pp. 48–49) are found growing mainly on rocks, on the moss-covered roots of trees, or in the debris on the floor of the rain forest. *Cryptanthus acaulis*, also called the starfish plant, spreads to 9in/23cm across and has medium green, tough leaves covered with gray scales, or "scurf." The leaves are not easily spoiled by handling. The scales absorb water and nutrients from the air or from tropical downpours.

The root system is shallow. Special care must be taken to ensure that it does not dry out completely, especially in winter, since that may encourage infestation by root mealybugs. *C.a.* 'Ruber' has leaves with the margin and center purple-bronze and deep buff-yellow scales; the leaves of *C.a.* 'Roseo-pictus' and *C.a.* 'Roseus' have a reddish tinge.

FACT FILE

ORIGIN Brazil.

HEIGHT To 5in/13cm.

POTTING MIX Peat-moss-based or equal parts of peat moss and leaf mold, with a little fresh sphagnum moss to ensure good drainage.

REPOTTING When the rosettes need separating, probably only every 2 years or so.

PROPAGATION In spring, remove offsets at the base of the plant and pot in a barely moist mix of peat moss and sand.

KEEPING PLANTS In the right conditions, these are long-lived plants.

PLANT CARE

Direct or subdued sunlight. ● About 75°F/24°C for flowering; a minimum winter temperature of 60°F/16°C. ● Water sparingly; allow the top half of the soil to dry out between waterings. ● Mist the leaves with weak liquid fertilizer occasionally during the spring and summer.

If the atmosphere is too dry, leaves will shrivel or turn brown; trim off damaged leaves.

Lack of light will make the leaves appear dull; move the plant to a brighter position.

Free drainage is essential; the plant will rot at the base if the soil is too wet.

CTENANTHE OPPENHEIMIANA '**TRICOLOR**'
Marantaceae

Never-Never Plant

Ctenanthes are closely related to calatheas and marantas, and this attractive plant is prized for the unusual coloring of its leaves. Silvery markings along the veins are overlaid with creamy green, and the undersides of the leaves are wine red. The red tinges the paler areas on the upper sides, making this truly a three-colored plant. The long, almost vertical, leafstalks produce large pointed elliptical leaves up to 12in/30cm in length.

Ctenanthe's native habitat is beneath the tree canopy of hot, humid rain forests, but it has adapted well as a houseplant. It enjoys average room temperatures, and as long as it is not overwatered and has high humidity, it should do well. The plant has a dormant period in winter when it needs simply to be kept warm and the soil prevented from drying out.

Red spider mites, scale insects, and mealybugs all attack this plant; check regularly for signs of these pests.

Leaves will curl in hot, dry conditions or in very bright light or full sun. Increase humidity by spraying, and ensure adequate watering.

If the plant shows signs of root rot in winter, conditions are too cold. Move the plant to a warmer spot and allow it to dry out.

FACT FILE

ORIGIN Brazil.

HEIGHT To 3ft/90cm with a similar spread.

POTTING MIX Soil-based, with added peat moss or leaf mold.

REPOTTING Move into larger pots in spring as necessary.

PROPAGATION In spring, take stem cuttings with several leaves, or separate basal offsets and grow them on as mature plants.

KEEPING PLANTS The plant should last for 5–6 years or more.

PLANT CARE

Semishade in summer, bright filtered light in winter. ● Minimum winter temperature of 62°F/17°C; otherwise, normal or high room temperature. ● Keep soil moist in spring and summer; in winter water just enough to prevent it from drying out completely. ● Stand the pot on a tray of damp pebbles to maintain humidity. ● Feed every 2 weeks in spring and summer with weak liquid fertilizer.

CUPHEA IGNEA (SYN. C. PLATYCENTRA)
Lythraceae

CIGAR FLOWER

A quick-growing plant, the cigar, or cigarette, flower can reach its mature height in a single year, forming a bushy small shrub. From early summer to late fall, the flowers are borne in profusion among narrow, smooth, 2-in/5-cm-long leaves, which are up to ½in/13mm wide. The flowers grow singly in the axils of the leaves, and each flower, which lacks petals, consists of a red tubular calyx 1in/2.5cm long, with a white and purple mouth. It takes only a little imagination to see the resemblance to a cigar or cigarette with ash at the tip.

Another good species for growing indoors is *Cuphea hyssopifolia*—elfin herb, or false heather. This slightly larger, shrubby plant has small trumpet-shaped flowers, with a green tube and petals of pink, white, or most commonly, pale lilac with deeper mauve veining.

Lack of light will make the leaves appear dull. Move the plant to a brighter position, where leaf edges will redden.

Good drainage is essential; the plant will rot at the base if the soil is too wet. Allow it to dry out before watering again.

Red spider mites and aphids may attack this plant; check regularly for signs of infestation.

Leaves will become dry and fall if the plant is kept in a cool, drafty place.

FACT FILE

ORIGIN Mexico, Jamaica.

HEIGHT To 2ft/60cm.

POTTING MIX Soil-based

REPOTTING In spring and again in summer if necessary, up to a maximum pot size of 10in/25cm.

PROPAGATION Take 2–3-in/5–8-cm-long stem cuttings in summer or early fall. Sow seeds in early spring.

KEEPING PLANTS Cut back stems by two-thirds in late winter to encourage new, flower-bearing growth. The plant is not long-lasting; it becomes straggly as it ages. Discard it after about 2 years and replace it with a new plant raised from a cutting or seed.

PLANT CARE

Bright light with some direct sunlight. ● Minimum winter temperature of 50°F/10°C, with normal room temperature at other times. ● Do not let the soil become dry in summer; water more sparingly in winter. ● Apply a high-potash liquid fertilizer every 2 weeks between spring and fall.

CYCAS REVOLUTA
Cycadaceae

JAPANESE SAGO PALM

Despite its common name, this exotic plant is not a true palm but a cycad, one of the most primitive of plants. It is extremely slow-growing and therefore usually quite expensive to buy. Originally from Japan, where it grows under the tree canopy, it has a brownish pineapple-shaped stem from which projects a loose rosette of feathery fronds up to 3ft/90cm long. Each evergreen frond has a stiff central rib, from which emerge many closely packed 3–6-in/8–15-cm-long needlelike leaflets, arranged in a chevron pattern. Some of the inner fronds are almost vertical, but most arch gracefully; the plant produces only one new set of leaves a year. Both male and female specimens are needed for cycas to produce its large red seeds, but they are not very likely to flower in pots, and if they do, must be hand-pollinated.

FACT FILE

ORIGIN Japan.

HEIGHT To 6ft/1.8m or more.

POTTING MIX Equal parts of soil-based medium, peat moss, and coarse sand or perlite.

REPOTTING Repot every 2–3 years, in spring or fall.

PROPAGATION In spring, by potting the basal suckers, if any, or by sowing seed. Both methods are difficult for the amateur.

KEEPING PLANTS Put the plant outdoors in summer if it is warm. Plants live for many years; 60-year-old specimens are not unusual.

PLANT CARE

Strong indirect light or sunlight all year. ● Minimum winter temperature of 40°F/4°C, with temperatures up to 65°F/18°C at other times. ● Allow to dry between thorough waterings; water less in winter, especially if temperature is at the minimum. ● Feed once a month from spring to fall with weak liquid fertilizer.

New leaves unfurl like those of ferns. Take care: these tender young leaves are delicate and easily damaged.

Scale insects, mealybugs, and red spider mites may attack this plant; check regularly for these pests.

Overwatering causes the leaves to develop brown spots or patches; underwatering turns them yellow.

PRIMULACEAE

CYCLAMENS

At one time it took an expert to grow first-class cyclamens, but that has changed with the recent introduction of modern F1 hybrid varieties, which are available mainly as pot plants and as seed from the larger seed houses. *Cyclamen persicum* hybrids, florists' cyclamen, are dramatic, vigorous, and free-flowering; they are no longer seasonal flowers that appear only in the fall. Hybridists have made it possible for cyclamens to bloom year-round, but these plants tend to be most popular during the winter months.

There are large types, typically reaching 12in/30cm in height and spread, and intermediates, growing to 9in/23cm; both will often have more than 30 flowers on the plant at a time. Many varieties are available, and the color of their swept-back petals ranges from white to pink, salmon, red, and purple; bicolored flowers are also found. Some cyclamens have frilly petals, and a few varieties have fragrant flowers. More recently, miniature strains have been developed with small leaves and charming little long-stemmed flowers in white, many shades of pink, red, mauve, and bicolors. In some varieties of both larger and miniature cyclamens, the leaves are marbled with silver or a different shade of green or have a silver margin.

Although usually treated as annuals, cyclamens can last for several years if the tubers are dried off in the late spring and rested during the summer months.

Cyclamen persicum hybrids are so numerous and so varied—many are not even named—that it is difficult to recommend one over another. More important when buying a plant is its condition.

Fresh-looking and upright stems, leaves, and flowers.

Plenty of well-formed flower buds visible among the leaves.

Leaves are well-formed and attractively marked.

Cyclamens do not mix well with other plants, but they are excellent long-lasting specimen plants for a cool room.

ALSO RECOMMENDED

The foliage of cyclamens may be heavily marbled or bordered with silver and pale green. Still other plants have plain deep green leaves.

Cyclamen flowers may be striped. Above, cerise petals of a large cyclamen have a paler pink stripe. Most plants have flowers that spread sideways, almost like wings.

Frilled petal edges provide a striking variation to the brilliant orange-pink flowers of this intermediate-size cyclamen, which has stems 7–8in/18–20cm long.

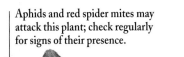

Aphids and red spider mites may attack this plant; check regularly for signs of their presence.

Yellowing leaves with brown patches are a sign of botrytis. Gray mold may soon appear and can quickly kill the plant. Cut away affected leaves or stems, and move the plant to a better ventilated place.

If leaves become stunted and hard, the plant may be infested with cyclamen mites, which look like dust on the underside of the leaves. There is no effective control, and the plant should be destroyed.

Yellowing, falling leaves are an indication that the plant is in a location that is too warm.

FACT FILE

ORIGIN Mediterranean regions; Iran; Europe; hybrids.

HEIGHT 5–12in/13–30cm, with a similar spread.

POTTING MIX Soil-based.

REPOTTING In midsummer, when growth has started, repot rested plants with the tuber only half-buried. Use the same size pot each year; cyclamens flower best if they are slightly pot-bound.

PROPAGATION Divide the tuber into sections at potting time. Alternatively, sow seed from late summer to early winter. The earlier this is done, the stronger the plant will be for the first season of flowering. Most varieties take up to 18 months to flower; miniatures may take only half this time. The temperature must be about 70°F/21°C for germination—the highest this plant will ever require.

KEEPING PLANTS After the leaves die down, dry the plant out slightly and rest it in a cool, frost-free place until new growth starts.

PLANT CARE

Bright, filtered light away from direct sunlight. ● A cool temperature of 55°–65°F/13°–18°C all year. ● Do not pour water onto the tuber, since this will cause it to rot. Water from below, but do not leave the plant standing in water for longer than 10 minutes or so; it does no harm to allow the leaves to droop slightly before applying water. ● Feed with standard liquid fertilizer every 2 weeks while the plant is in bud and flower. ● As flowers fade, remove the entire stalk by twisting it off at the base. Remove any yellowing or damaged leaves in the same way. Do not cut the stems.

PESTS & DISEASES

Cyclamens are prone to infestation by aphids, red spider mites, and cyclamen mites. If the soil is too wet and ventilation is poor, they may suffer from fungal diseases, particularly botrytis.

The sweet-scented deep pink flowers with fringed borders make this miniature cyclamen extremely attractive. These tiny plants are among the most charming.

Miniature cyclamens, which are 3–5in/ 8–13cm high, have dainty flowers and petite foliage. They will bloom well some 7–9 months from sowing.

CYMBIDIUM **HYBRIDS**
Orchidaceae

CYMBIDIUMS

Of all the orchids suitable for growing in homes, cymbidiums are the most easy-going and adaptable. A handful of species are in cultivation as houseplants, but these have largely been replaced by the thousands of hybrids, which are available with flowers in widely differing sizes. The smaller hybrids are best for heated rooms and produce flowers some 1½–3in/4–7.5cm across. Flower colors, too, are varied, from white, green, and yellow to pink, red, and maroon; those of *Cymbidium* 'Mem Rosl Greer,' shown here, are a creamy pink with a deeper spotted center. The waxy blooms generally have elliptical petals radiating from a prominent, differently colored, three-lobed center.

Cymbidiums produce clumps of pseudobulbs, which are surrounded by leathery straplike leaves. Flower spikes appear from around the bases of the pseudobulbs, mature gradually, and bear one or many flowers along the length of the spike. A mature plant may bear as many as 100 blooms in a season. To encourage flowering, cymbidiums need cool temperatures and a rest period of four to six weeks in late fall. After that, they can be returned to their normal location.

FACT FILE

ORIGIN Tropical Asia; Australia; hybrids.

HEIGHT 30in–5ft/76cm–1.5m.

POTTING MIX Special orchid medium: a mix of fibrous peat moss or osmunda fiber, perlite and/or grit, and small pieces of charcoal to aid drainage.

REPOTTING Every 3 or 4 years.

PROPAGATION From seed or by division of mature plants after flowering. Divide the pseudobulbs with a sharp knife; select bulbs with shoots and pot up 3–4 to a pot, discarding any dead growth.

KEEPING PLANTS Set plants outdoors to rest in summer. The sun will ripen the plants and encourage them to flower later in the year.

PLANT CARE

Filtered light in summer; direct sunlight in winter. ● Minimum winter temperature of 45°F/7°C; slightly cooler than normal room temperature at other times. ● Water every day in summer, preferably in the morning, using tepid rainwater if possible. Water once or twice a week in spring and fall, and once every 2 weeks in winter. ● Stand the pot on a tray of moist pebbles to increase humidity. ● Apply a weak liquid fertilizer every 2 weeks in summer; do not feed while the plant is resting.

ALSO RECOMMENDED

Cymbidium 'Minuet' has flower stems about 15in/38cm long, each bearing up to 20 brown, green, or yellow flowers, which are 1–1½in/2.5–4cm wide. *C.* 'Peter Pan' bears fewer flowers, but they are exotically colored greenish yellow, with a lip spotted with a deep maroon brown.

Aphids may attack flower spikes and buds, particularly during winter.

Look for signs of red spider mites; while not common on cymbidiums, these pests will infest plants that are kept in dry conditions.

Mosaic virus will occasionally get a hold on this plant, causing the leaves to become mottled and yellow. There is no cure, so the plant should be destroyed. Failure to take immediate and swift action will allow aphids to spread the virus to other plants.

Cymbidium *'Western Rose'* is one of the most beautiful cultivars of this orchid. It has sprays of large dusky pink flowers, each with a spotted creamy lip.

CYPERUS ALTERNIFOLIUS
Cyperaceae

UMBRELLA PLANT

The name cyperus derives from the Greek for sedge, a plant that grows in wet places. The umbrella plant is one of the few aquatic plants suitable for growing indoors, where with reasonable care it will do well. It will, with time, adapt itself to almost any location. The plant forms clumps of rather thin, pale green, grassy leaves, which radiate from the tops of the stems and are not in themselves particularly attractive. But the petalless flowers, enclosed in tiny bracts and arranged in umbrellalike flower heads, add much to the plant's appearance. *Cyperus alternifolius* is usually available during the summer months. It has an almost Oriental quality and suits uncluttered, modern interiors. *C.a.* 'Variegatus' is an attractive variety with leaves striped with white or, often, completely white.

FACT FILE

ORIGIN Madagascar; Mauritius.

HEIGHT 2ft–4ft/60cm–1.2m, with a spread of up to 3ft/90cm.

POTTING MIX Soil-based, with charcoal added to keep the soil fresh and to lessen odors caused by sour soil.

REPOTTING Move into a pot one size larger each spring.

PROPAGATION When the plant fills the pot, remove it from the pot. Make an initial knife cut across the clump, then tear it apart by hand. Pot sections individually.

KEEPING PLANTS As stems die, cut them off to allow for new growth.

PLANT CARE

Full, bright sunlight or light shade. ● Minimum winter temperature of 50°F/10°C, with constant room temperature at other times. ● The pot should stand in a pan of water at all times; it can be immersed in water to the top of the pot. ● Apply weak liquid fertilizer once a month from spring to fall, or push fertilizer tablets into the soil around the roots.

Pale leaf coloring, unsightly blotches on the leaves, or the plant's failure to produce many stems may indicate that its location is too shady.

Mealybugs may infest the green flowers at the top of the plant.

Aphids and whiteflies may attack young leaves; check regularly for signs of these pests.

If leaves develop brown patches or edges, make sure the plant is receiving enough water.

DAVALLIA FEJEENSIS
Davalliaceae

RABBIT'S-FOOT FERN

Practically all other ferns require a good deal of humidity, but this elegant and vigorous example does not and so thrives indoors. The unusual creeping rhizome, rather like a rabbit's or hare's foot, which grows over the edge of the pot, is the main feature of the plant. These brown rhizomes, which are covered with white-tipped hairs, can extend to 3ft/90cm, and if several of them are placed in a hanging basket or in a pot on a high window ledge, they will in time take on an almost spiderlike appearance. Dark wiry stalks emerge from the rhizomes, and these produce light green, triangular, leathery fronds as much as 12in/30cm long. Plants lose and then replace their leaves once a year.

If the fronds turn brown or become sparse, the conditions are too hot or dry. Raise the humidity level around the plant and water it more regularly.

Aphids and scale insects tend to attack this plant; check frequently for signs of infestation.

FACT FILE

ORIGIN Fiji.

HEIGHT To 18in/46cm.

POTTING MIX Peat-moss- or soil-based.

REPOTTING In spring move the plant into a pot one size larger; top-dress a mature plant. The root system is shallow, so use a half-pot.

PROPAGATION In spring by sections of rhizome, each with some roots and frond growth. Plant the sections in a mixture of peat and sand, then water and place in a propagator. Keep out of direct sunlight.

KEEPING PLANTS Plants will last for 5 or 6 years if well cared for.

PLANT CARE

Bright light at all times but not direct sunlight. ● Minimum winter temperature of 55°F/13°C, with normal room temperature at other times. ● Water thoroughly during the growing period but do not allow the plant to become waterlogged. In winter, allow the top of the soil to dry out between waterings. ● Stand the pot on a tray of moist pebbles to increase humidity, and mist the plant regularly. ● Apply weak liquid fertilizer every 2 weeks throughout the year.

DIEFFENBACHIA MACULATA (SYN. *D. PICTA*)
Araceae

*D*UMB CANE

This plant is grown almost entirely for its attractive shape and striking foliage, although it does produce insignificant spathe flowers. Some of the more robust forms can reach a height of about 6ft/1.8m in six years or so, but dieffenbachias are grown principally as compact plants that seldom get out of hand if confined to pots of reasonable size. Dieffenbachia leaves, which can be up to 10in/25cm long, are usually green, and the more commonly seen forms have patches, blotches, or variegations in shades of white, cream, yellow, or pale green giving rise to the frequently used common names of leopard lily or spotted dumb cane.

All parts of this plant are poisonous; the sap has a most unpleasant effect on the mouth and throat, causing swelling, pain, and temporary loss of speech, a fact reflected in the name dumb cane. Wear gloves when handling dieffenbachias and wash your hands well afterward.

Dieffenbachia maculata *'Camilla,'* which grows to only about 15in/38cm high, is a smaller plant than the species. It has cream leaves edged in rich green.

FACT FILE

ORIGIN Brazil; hybrids.

HEIGHT 18in–6ft/46cm–1.8m.

POTTING MIX Soil- and peat-moss-based in equal quantities.

REPOTTING In summer, when the plant has become too big for its pot.

PROPAGATION Take 3–5-in/8–13-cm-long stem cuttings in spring or summer (cuttings must have a node with an eye); lay them horizontally, half submerged, in a peat moss and sand mixture. Keep at a temperature of 70°–75°F/21°–24°C.

KEEPING PLANTS Cut back plants that are too tall; new growth will sprout from the cuts.

PLANT CARE

Fairly light, but shaded from direct sun.
● Minimum winter temperature of 60°F/16°C, with normal to high room temperature at other times. Keep away from heat sources and out of cold drafts.
● In spring and summer water generously; in winter water less and use tepid water. ● Stand the plant on a tray of damp pebbles and mist the foliage when temperature is high. ● In spring and summer apply weak liquid fertilizer with each watering; feed only every second watering at other times.

ALSO RECOMMENDED

Dieffenbachia maculata 'Exotica' has deep green leaves, regularly blotched with cream and pale green. 'Rudolph Roehrs' has creamy white leaves when young, but develops pale green spots, with a green midrib and margins. In the variety 'Tropic Snow,' the leaves are splashed with creamy white along the main veins. *D. seguine* is similar in many respects to *D. maculata*, but is more vigorous, with longer, narrower dark green leaves.

D. × *bausei* is a fairly robust hybrid, growing to 3ft/90cm in height. Leaves are 12in/30cm long, and are yellow-green with dark green blotches and margin and numerous small white spots.

The color in variegated leaves will suffer if the plant does not receive adequate light, and growth will be weak.

Falling leaves may mean that the atmosphere is too cool or too damp.

Leaf scorch can occur if the plant has been placed too near a heat source or has been left in strong, direct sunlight. Remove scorched leaves, since they will not recover.

Aphids may infest both the plant and the soil; check regularly for signs of these pests.

If the plant is overwatered, the stems may rot.

DIMORPHOTHECA SINUATA (SYN. *D. AURANTIACA*)
Compositae

*S*TAR OF THE VELDT

In the wild this plant is a shrubby perennial, but as an indoor plant it is best treated as an annual. It makes a colorful summer-flowering potted plant for the greenhouse or sunroom.

Dimorphothecas, or African daisies, are spreading plants, and this species will form a mound up to 12in/30cm high. The coarsely toothed oblong leaves, some 3in/8cm long, are aromatic, and the daisylike flowers, which open from early summer to fall, can be as much as 2in/5cm wide. They are generally bright orange-yellow, sometimes with a purplish tinge at the base of the petals.

Recent hybrids have been bred in many different colors. Among the best are the compact 'Salmon Queen' with salmon pink flowers, the aptly named 'Glistening White' with 7-in/18-cm stems, and 'Giant Orange' (sometimes called 'Goliath') with larger than normal bright orange-yellow flowers.

FACT FILE

ORIGIN South Africa.

HEIGHT To 12in/30cm.

POTTING MIX Soil-based, with the addition of coarse sand for good drainage.

REPOTTING Not required.

PROPAGATION Sow seed in winter or spring, or take stem cuttings in midsummer for overwintering.

KEEPING PLANTS Usually treated as an annual.

PLANT CARE

Bright light with full sun. ● Warm room temperature with good ventilation, in summer; a minimum winter temperature of 50°–55°F/ 10°–13°C for overwintering plants. ● Water sparingly at all times; overwatering may cause the stems to rot. ● Feed every 2 weeks from spring to fall with a half-strength solution of liquid fertilizer.

Good ventilation is essential for this plant. In damp conditions, botrytis (gray mold) may develop.

Dimorphothecas require full sunlight to guarantee blooming. Under good conditions, the plant will be covered with flowers from late spring through to fall.

DIONAEA MUSCIPULA
Droseraceae

*V*ENUS'S-FLYTRAP

Carnivorous plants generally come from areas where their roots are unable to obtain enough nutrients from the soil, so they have developed a way of absorbing nutrients from animals, live or dead. Plants such as dionaea feed on small insects by trapping them and then digesting the contents of their bodies.

Venus's-flytrap—the only species in this genus—is arguably the most interesting insect-eater, not for its appearance, but more for its action. It is a perennial with rosettes of heart-shaped leaves 3–6in/ 8–15cm long that are hinged in the middle and armed with sharp teeth. Inside the leaf are many bristles and, more important, three particular hairs that when touched trigger the leaf to close up, trapping any insect attracted by the plant's secretions. The action is immediate, and the leaves may stay shut for as long as two weeks, after which they open again and reset themselves for the next victim. In summer, clusters of white flowers, some ³⁄₄in/2cm wide, appear on short stems.

If the leaves and stems become limp, it may mean that the plant is being kept too dry. Water it well; even then the plant may not recover.

The plant can also make food by photosynthesis, so bugs are not critical to its survival.

FACT FILE

ORIGIN North and South Carolina.

HEIGHT 3–8in/8–20cm.

POTTING MIX Half peat moss, half sphagnum moss, or all sphagnum moss.

REPOTTING Not necessary.

PROPAGATION In spring, divide the rhizome, planting each piece separately; or sow seeds in fall, in peat moss mixed with spaghnum moss. In both instances, cover with plastic until the new plants are established.

KEEPING PLANTS Dry rooms can be fatal, so cover the plant with a plastic dome that will retain humidity.

PLANT CARE

Bright light with some direct sunlight. ● Minimum winter temperature of 50°F/10°C; normal room temperature at other times. ● Stand the pot in a shallow container of rainwater and keep the soil moist at all times. In winter cover the pot with a plastic dome and keep the soil just moist. ● From spring to fall, if there are no flies about, feed occasionally with newly swatted insects or small pieces of meat.

DIPLADENIA x *AMABILIS* see *MANDEVILLA* x *AMOENA*

DIZYGOTHECA ELEGANTISSIMA
Araliaceae

FALSE ARALIA

Sometimes sold as *Schefflera elegantissima* or *Aralia elegantissima*, this is a graceful shrub with a slim, mottled stem from which grow palmlike, leathery serrated leaves about 3in/8cm long and ½in/13mm wide. An interesting feature of the plant is the manner in which the character of the leaves alters as they mature. The young delicate filigree copper brown foliage changes to coarser dark green, almost black leaves, which are much more typical of the Araliaceae family to which the plant belongs.

False, or finger, aralias are beautiful enough to stand alone, but in the tropical islands of their native habitat, they grow with cordylines, crotons, cycas, and epipremnums, and indoors they can be used in a similar collection of tropical plants to add height and grace. For the best effect, plant two or three to a pot. Flowers are not produced on pot specimens.

FACT FILE

ORIGIN New Caledonia; Polynesia.

HEIGHT To 6ft/1.8m.

POTTING MIX Soil-based.

REPOTTING Move into a pot one size larger in spring, only when the roots have filled the pot.

PROPAGATION New plants can be raised from fresh seeds or stem cuttings in spring, but both operations are difficult for amateurs.

KEEPING PLANTS Dizygothecas do best in a warm sunroom and can last for 5 years or so. Prune in spring to improve the shape or promote bushiness.

PLANT CARE

Bright light, but avoid direct sunlight. ● Year-round warmth, with a minimum winter temperature of 60°F/16°C. ● Thoroughly soak the potting mix with each watering, but allow it to almost dry out before rewatering. ● Improve humidity by standing the pot on damp pebbles and misting the plant each day. ● Apply a weak liquid fertilizer every 2 weeks between spring and autumn.

Drooping leaves are a sign of overwatering.

Aphids and mealybugs may attack this plant; check for signs regularly.

Falling leaves may mean that the plant is too dry at the roots. Water well and improve the humidity level.

DRACAENA FRAGRANS 'MASSANGEANA'
Agavaceae

CORN PLANT

A popular and hardy houseplant, *Dracaena fragrans* is one of the more tolerant of the dracaena group; it originates in tropical Africa but is sufficiently hardy to grow farther east in the higher elevations of Ethiopia. As a houseplant, it will withstand a variety of temperatures and conditions as long as it has adequate humidity.

The straight *D. fragrans* produces rosettes of strong plain green curving leaves 2ft/60cm long, and 4in/10cm wide. As it grows, the plant sheds its lower leaves, so after a few years it will probably consist of a cluster of attractive leaves on top of a stout bare stem, occasionally with a leafy side branch or two. Occasionally scented yellow flowers are produced; these are followed by orange-red berries.

The variegated form 'Massangeana' is much more widely grown, mainly for its attractive leaves, each of which carries a central corn-yellow band and is bordered by narrower yellow stripes.

If the plant is too cold or damp, botrytis may get a hold; look for brownish spots on the leaves.

The plant sheds older, lower leaves from time to time. If younger leaves turn yellow and droop, the plant is being kept too dry and hot. Water well and increase the frequency of misting.

Rotting stems and leaves are an indication of overwatering.

Red spider mites and scale insects may attack the plant; check for signs regularly.

FACT FILE

ORIGIN Upper Guinea; Ethiopia; tropical Africa.

HEIGHT To 5ft/1.5m.

POTTING MIX Soil- or peat-based.

REPOTTING Every 2 or 3 years, in spring.

PROPAGATION By 3-in/8-cm tip or stem cuttings in spring or late summer, or by air layering.

KEEPING PLANTS This plant does not like drafts, so stand it in a protected spot. It grows slowly and should last for several years.

PLANT CARE

Bright light, but not long periods of direct summer sun. ● This plant can stand fluctuating temperatures, with a minimum of 55°F/13°C. ● Keep the soil moist; water once or twice a week in the active growing period; less in winter. ● Stand the pot on a tray of damp pebbles and mist the plant often, but not while it is in the sun. ● Apply a weak liquid fertilizer every 2 weeks from spring to fall.

DRACAENA MARGINATA
Agavaceae

*M*ADAGASCAR DRAGON TREE

This exotic-looking plant produces leaves from its base. Over the years, the lower leaves fall. So as the plant grows, it develops a slender ringed trunk. On top of these stems are dense tufts of spiky 12–16-in/ 30–40-cm-long deep green leaves with fine red or purple edgings. In its native habitat it can be quite a substantial plant, growing to a height of 9ft/2.7m or more; indoors it will reach a more suitable 6ft/1.8m after several years. This is perhaps the easiest dracaena to grow indoors, since it is slow-growing and tolerant of varying room conditions and different degrees of humidity.

Dracaena marginata 'Tricolor,' called by some the rainbow plant, has cream-striped leaves with a red edging. The variety 'Colorama' has a lighter leaf, with a narrow edge of red, an inner band of cream, and a light and dark green central stripe.

The plant's growth rate will slow down and more leaves than normal will fall off if the temperature is too low.

The lower leaves will droop if conditions are too dry; water and spray more frequently.

Mealybugs may lodge in the leaf axils; check for signs regularly.

FACT FILE

ORIGIN Madagascar.

HEIGHT To 6ft/1.8m.

POTTING MIX Soil-based with added peat.

REPOTTING Every 2 or 3 years, in spring.

PROPAGATION Take 3–4in/8–10cm stem cuttings in spring; leave for 24 hours before planting them in a sandy rooting mixture.

KEEPING PLANTS In warmer areas this plant will appreciate a spell outdoors in summer, but place it in a sheltered position.

PLANT CARE

Bright light to bring out the leaf color, but avoid direct sunlight in summer. ● Minimum winter temperature of 55°F/13°C, up to 70°F/21°C at other times. ● Water once or twice a week from spring to fall; less in winter. ● Humidity is not as crucial with this plant as it is with *Dracaena fragrans*, but it will benefit from a twice-weekly misting between spring and fall. ● Feed every 2 weeks during the active growing period with a weak liquid fertilizer.

DRACAENA SANDERIANA
Agavaceae

*B*ELGIAN EVERGREEN

The daintiest of the dracaenas, *Dracaena sanderiana* is a slow-growing, slender, upright shrub from the tropical rain forests of Cameroon. It is sometimes called ribbon plant, on account of its narrow, slightly twisted leaves of deep gray-green with broad creamy white margins that grow to 9in/23cm long and 1in/2.5cm wide, and is perfect where space is limited. The plant rarely branches from the base, so three or four specimens should be planted together in a large planter to create an interesting mass of spiky foliage. Provided it is not scaldingly hot, this plant can tolerate standing close to a radiator, but cold drafts can be detrimental.

FACT FILE

ORIGIN West Africa.

HEIGHT To 3ft/90cm.

POTTING MIX Soil-based.

REPOTTING Only when necessary. Once plants are in 5-in/13-cm pots, top-dress with fresh soil annually.

PROPAGATION Take stem, tip, and basal cuttings in spring. Stem cuttings, 3–4in/8–10cm long, will root readily if set upright in a peat and sand mixture and kept warm. Root tip cuttings in a propagator; basal shoots with some roots will grow if enclosed in a plastic bag.

KEEPING PLANTS Keep the plant in a protected spot.

PLANT CARE

Bright, filtered light enhances the leaf color. ● Minimum winter temperature of 50°F/10°C; normal room temperature in summer. ● Water plentifully when in active growth, more sparingly in winter. ● Feed every 2 weeks from spring to early fall with weak liquid fertilizer.

Mealybugs may inhabit the leaf axils, and scale insects may attach themselves to the leaves and stems; check regularly for signs of these pests.

Rotting stems and leaves are an indication of overwatering.

ECHINOCEREUS PECTINATUS
Cactaceae

ℋEDGEHOG CACTUS

One of the so-called desert cacti, the hedgehog cactus has a columnar stem that can eventually reach 10in/25cm in height and 3in/8cm across, although it usually remains smaller than this when it is grown indoors. Being a slow grower, it may take as long as five years to reach a height of 3in/8cm, and it will begin to branch from the base only when it is about 5in/13cm high. The broad, medium green ribs are covered with areoles, each of which bears about 25 short radial white spines in an unusual formation that resembles the teeth of a comb. They are so closely packed as to give the plant a white appearance.

All species of echinocereus, about 15 of which are in general cultivation as houseplants, bloom only when they are a few years old. The freely produced cup-shaped flowers of the hedgehog cactus are deep pink, covered with soft spines on the outside, and up to 3in/8cm across.

Scale insects and mealybugs attack this plant; check often for signs of infestation.

Thin, elongated stems may result from too little light during the growing period, or too much warmth in winter. These stems may not flower freely.

Corky patches on the stems may be caused by insect damage, sudden chilling, physical injury, or underwatering during the growing period.

If the plant rots from the base, it has been kept too wet, usually in winter when it is resting.

FACT FILE

ORIGIN Northern Mexico; southwestern USA.

HEIGHT To 10in/25cm.

POTTING MIX Soil- or peat-moss-based, both with added perlite or sand.

REPOTTING In spring. If the roots fill the pot, move the plant to a pot one size larger or replant it in the same pot, using fresh soil.

PROPAGATION In spring or summer remove a branch from a mature plant. Allow the cutting to dry for 3 days, then insert the base into sand or rooting mix and keep it out of direct sunlight for a month.

KEEPING PLANTS Stand the plant outdoors in the sun in summer.

PLANT CARE

Full sunlight all year-round to stimulate flowering. ● Temperatures of 35°–40°F/2°–4°C during the winter rest. Light frost can be endured as long as the soil is completely dry. ● Barely moisten the soil, and allow the top two-thirds to dry out before rewatering in the growing period; do not water in winter if plants are kept below 40°F/4°C. ● Apply a high-potash liquid feed every 2 weeks to a plant in peat-moss-based soil, every 4 weeks to one in a soil-based medium.

EPIPHYLLUM ACKERMANNII
Cactaceae

𝒪RCHID CACTUS

The epiphyllums grown as houseplants are almost all hybrids; their wild-plant parents are found as epiphytes in the tropical rain forests. The true orchid cactus, now renamed *Nopalxochia ackermannii* but still generally known as *Epiphyllum*, produces cup-shaped crimson blooms, 4–6in/10–15cm wide, all year-round. It is, however, rarely seen today , having been surpassed in flower color by the many hybrids that have been created. The species and the hybrids have leafless stems, up to 2ft/60cm long and 2in/5cm wide, which are notched at the edges and segmented. The newer hybrids bloom prolifically, mainly in spring. The flowers may be white, cream, yellow, and orange, all shades of pink and red, or even bicolored, and can be large (up to 6in/15cm wide) or small. Those with smaller flowers look good in hanging baskets with their stems trailing.

FACT FILE

ORIGIN Southern Mexico; hybrids.

HEIGHT To 2ft/60cm.

POTTING MIX Half peat moss, half soil-based, with added perlite or sand.

REPOTTING This plant flowers best if slightly pot-bound. In spring, move into a pot one size larger until a 6-in/15-cm pot is reached; thereafter top-dress instead.

PROPAGATION Detach 4–6-in/10–15-cm sections of stem in spring or early summer. Allow to dry for 2 days, then plant in soil as above.

KEEPING PLANTS Cut back old stems when they become too long. Put the plant outdoors in a sheltered spot from late spring to early fall.

PLANT CARE

Bright, filtered light; no direct sunlight. ● Minimum winter temperature of 40°F/4°C; normal room temperature at other times. ● Water generously while plant is growing; moderately at other times. ● Stand the pot on a tray of damp pebbles to increase humidity; mist daily in warm room conditions. ● From early spring until flower buds are well developed, feed every 2 weeks with a high-potash liquid fertilizer. Stop feeding for 4 weeks, then resume until early fall.

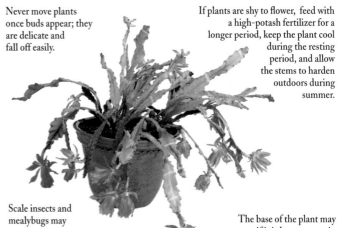

Never move plants once buds appear; they are delicate and fall off easily.

If plants are shy to flower, feed with a high-potash fertilizer for a longer period, keep the plant cool during the resting period, and allow the stems to harden outdoors during summer.

Scale insects and mealybugs may attack orchid cacti; check for signs of these pests.

The base of the plant may rot if it is kept too wet in the winter rest period.

EPIPREMNUM AUREUM
Araceae

*D*EVIL'S IVY

The golden pothos, taro vine, or devil's ivy, as it is commonly known, is one of the most remarkable of all foliage plants. Epipremnums come in many shapes and sizes, and may be displayed as climbers or as trailing plants. There are about 10 species in this genus with aerial roots, each with a characteristic tendency to wrap itself around the nearest object.

Epipremnum aureum (syn. *Pothos aureus, Scindapsus aureus*) is highly decorative, with mustard and green variegation on the 6-in/15-cm-long heart-shaped leaves. It is tolerant of a wide range of conditions, though when placed far from the light source, the leaves lose their variegation. Indoors it should not be allowed to exceed 6–8ft/1.8–2.4m in extent, but it can grow five times as high in the wild, where plants produce flowers rather like those of the arum; pot plants do not flower.

FACT FILE

ORIGIN Solomon Islands.

HEIGHT To 6–8ft/1.8–2.4m.

POTTING MIX Soil-based.

REPOTTING Move the plant to a pot one size larger each spring, but do not overpot.

PROPAGATION Take 4–5-in/10–13-cm stem cuttings with two good leaves attached at any time of year, or tip cuttings when pruning in spring. The plant can also be layered.

KEEPING PLANTS Although slow to start, this plant is an excellent climber and will last for many years. Pinch off the growing tips regularly to promote bushy growth, and prune the plant in early spring to reduce its size.

PLANT CARE

Bright, indirect light. ● Minimum winter temperature of 60°F/16°C; normal room temperature at other times. ● Allow the top two-thirds of the potting mixture to dry out between waterings. ● During the growing period, apply weak liquid fertilizer every 2 weeks.

ALSO RECOMMENDED

Epipremnum aureum 'Marble Queen' is similar to the type and is an attractive alternative but it can be difficult to care for.

E.a. 'Tricolor,' as the name suggests, has leaves marbled with three colors: pale green, yellow, and cream.

Epipremnum aureum
'Marble Queen' has beautiful leaves that are boldly streaked and marbled with soft green and white.

Wet brown patches on leaves indicate infection by botrytis; destroy any such leaves.

Aphids may attack young plants, and mealybugs may infest both young and old plants. Check regularly for signs of the pest.

Stems will rot at the base if the plant is constantly overwatered.

EPISCIA CUPREATA
Gesneriaceae

FLAME VIOLET

The creeping or trailing stems of *Episcia cupreata*, from which emerge nodeless red or green stolons bearing new plants at their tips, will rapidly cover the surface of a shallow pan or trail from a hanging basket. The oval, hairy leaves, 2–3in/5–8cm long and 1–2in/2.5–5cm wide, have toothed edges and are arranged in a rosette; their coloring ranges from deep bronze green to bright green, usually with silvery markings around the veins.

The 1-in/2.5-cm-long flowers, which appear in spring and continue until fall, are bright red and tubular. They flare out at the tip into lobes that may be fringed at the edges. Deep in the center of the tube, which is lined with soft hairs, lies a yellow "eye." Although in the wild the plants are shielded from the fierce sun by the leaf canopy, they need bright light to flower well in the home.

Watch out for aphids, which may infest young leaves.

Humidity must be high, or leaves will develop brown edges and flower buds will shrivel.

FACT FILE

ORIGIN Colombia; Venezuela.

HEIGHT To 6in/15cm.

POTTING MIX Cornell mix, or equal parts of sphagnum peat moss, leaf mold, and perlite to provide good drainage.

REPOTTING Move into a pot a size larger only when roots fill the current pot.

PROPAGATION Detach plants that develop at the ends of the stolons and pot up individually. Single leaves with short stalks will also root.

KEEPING PLANTS These shallow-rooting plants do best in wide-topped pans and hanging baskets in which the offsets can hang down.

PLANT CARE

Bright light; no direct sunlight. ● Warm conditions; minimum winter temperature of 60°F/16°C. ● Water generously during the growing season, more sparingly in winter. Do not wet leaves at night. ● Stand the pot on a tray of moist pebbles to provide added humidity. ● Every 2 weeks apply a weak liquid fertilizer to actively growing plants.

EUPHORBIA MILII VAR. *SPLENDENS*
Euphorbiaceae

CROWN OF THORNS

There are about 2,000 known species in the spurge family, and this is one of the easiest to grow indoors. For a succulent shrub, it is not fussy. It readily produces bright green leaves and, from late winter until early fall, clusters of tiny flowers surrounded by two cheery red bracts. In the form *lutea* the bracts are yellow. Flowering can be almost continuous if plenty of good, bright light is provided.

In its native habitat the plant grows happily in granite crevices, reaching up to 6ft/1.8m, but as a houseplant it rarely achieves this height. The woody stems are about as thick as a little finger and carry sharp spines, most of which are around ³⁄₄in/2cm long; wear gloves when handling the plant. The relatively few leaves are bright green, elliptical, and up to 2¹⁄₂in/6.5cm wide.

FACT FILE

ORIGIN Madagascar.

HEIGHT To 2ft/60cm.

POTTING MIX Soil-based, with sand or perlite added to improve drainage.

REPOTTING Every 2 years; once 5 or 6 years old, top-dress it.

PROPAGATION In spring or summer take 3-in/8-cm stem cuttings. Dip the cut ends into tepid water to halt the flow of sap, then leave them for 24 hours to dry before inserting them into a rooting medium.

KEEPING PLANTS Prune if necessary before new growth appears in spring, but beware: when cut, the plant exudes a poisonous white latex. Do not allow it to come into contact with the eyes or mouth.

PLANT CARE

Full sunlight, but shade it from very strong summer sun. ● Minimum winter temperature of 55°F/13°C; normal room temperature at other times. The plant likes warm, dry conditions. ● Allow the surface of the soil to dry out between waterings; water sparingly in winter. ● Apply a weak liquid fertilizer every 2 weeks while in bloom.

Leaves appear only on new growth and are not replaced if they fall.

Move plants that are shy to flower to a brighter location.

If leaves drop at any time other than winter, the plant may be waterlogged or too cool.

EUPHORBIA PULCHERRIMA
Euphorbiaceae

Poinsettia

Most people treat the poinsettia (also called Christmas star, Mexican flame leaf, or lobster plant) as an annual, purchasing a new plant at the beginning of the traditional winter flowering period and discarding it at the end. But in suitable climates, it can be planted in the garden after its use indoors. The plant's leaves are pale green and the small greenish yellow flowers uninteresting, but the vibrantly colored bracts can be magnificent. These are, in fact, colored leaves that develop at the top of the stems in fall, and they can be as long as 10in/25cm. Initially only the striking, brilliant red version was common, but there are now varieties with pink, creamy white, and bicolored bracts.

FACT FILE

ORIGIN Mexico.

HEIGHT 15in–3ft/38–90cm.

POTTING MIX Peat-moss-based.

REPOTTING Every year in midsummer; but do not overpot.

PROPAGATION Take 4–6-in/10–15-cm stem cuttings from the top of the plant in midsummer. Seal the ends in hot water, let them dry out for 24 hours, then insert them into sandy potting mix.

KEEPING PLANTS See box above right.

PLANT CARE

Keep young plants in bright filtered light; direct winter sun will not harm mature plants. ● Winter temperature of 60°–70°F/116°–21°C; cooler when the plant is not in color. ● Keep the soil moist in winter and spring; reduce watering after flowering. ● Apply weak liquid fertilizer every 2 weeks from midfall to late spring.

ALSO RECOMMENDED

Euphorbia pulcherrima 'Diva' has brick red bracts. On 'Rosea' the bracts are pale pink, darkly veined. They are salmon pink on 'Pink Peppermint,' strong lemon yellow on 'Lemon Drop.'

Euphorbia pulcherrima *'Ecke's White' has cream bracts. Other Ecke cultivars are 'Top White' and 'Hot Pink.'*

KEEPING PLANTS

In spring, when the plant has finished flowering, cut it back to 4–6in/10–15cm. Store it in a warm place, and keep the soil almost dry until new growth appears, usually after about 2 months. Then, in early summer, water the plant well, and when growth restarts, repot it in fresh soil in the same-size pot.

Beginning in midfall it is essential to keep a poinsettia in total darkness for 14 hours each day if the colored bracts are to appear. For 2 months, cover the plant with a black plastic bag in the early evening and remove it the following morning, while increasing watering and feeding. When the bracts begin to show color, leave the plant uncovered.

Nurserymen use a growth retardant to limit the size and bushiness of the plants sold in stores, but this is not possible for the home grower, and plants kept for a second or third year will inevitably be larger.

Red spider mites and mealybugs may attack this plant; check for signs regularly. Increase humidity and watering to help deter the mites.

A milky sap leaks from wounds to the stem and leafstalks. It may stain clothing. Keep it from contact with the eyes or mouth.

If leaves fall without wilting, the light is inadequate or the temperature is too low.

When leaves wilt and then fall, the plant is being overwatered; allow the soil to dry out before watering again.

EXACUM AFFINE
Gentianaceae

GERMAN VIOLET

A member of the gentian family, this plant also goes under the names of Arabian and Persian violet. It is a small plant, with a height and spread of 6–8in/15–20cm, and has 1-in/2.5-cm-long, glossy olive green leaves. In late spring countless mauve-purple or white scented flowers, each with a yellow eye, appear and continue to bloom until late fall. *Exacum affine* 'Rococo' has double lavender-blue flowers. Although it is generally treated as an annual, exacum is a biennial. It is raised commercially from seed sown in early fall or early spring and is sold as an indoor plant. For an eye-catching effect, you can mass several plants that are just coming into flower in a large bowl.

FACT FILE

ORIGIN Socotra (Gulf of Aden).

HEIGHT To 8in/20cm.

POTTING MIX Peat-moss-based.

REPOTTING In spring move overwintered plants into pots one size larger.

PROPAGATION In winter or spring sow seed on the surface of an open peat-moss or sphagnum-rich medium in a shallow 4-in/10-cm pot.

KEEPING PLANTS Pinch off blooms as they fade to prolong flowering. If the plant withers after flowering, discard it, but if you want to overwinter it, prune it back hard to maintain its bushiness.

PLANT CARE

Bright, filtered light but not strong direct sunlight. ● Normal room temperature; a minimum of 60°F/16°C if plants are overwintered. ● Keep the soil moist, never sodden. ● Place the pot on a tray of damp pebbles to increase humidity. ● Feed every 2 weeks throughout the year with weak liquid fertilizer.

If flowers fail to appear, move the plant to a warmer location and increase the humidity.

The flowers will fade and quickly die if the rootball ever becomes dry.

Wilting plants may mean that they are in a drafty position.

x *FATSHEDERA LIZEI*
Araliaceae

TREE IVY

This cross between two plants of different genera but the same family (known as a bigeneric hybrid) was raised by a French nursery just before World War I. *Fatsia japonica* 'Moseri,' the Japanese fatsia or aralia, was one parent and *Hedera helix* var. *hibernica*, Irish ivy, the other. The habit and shape of x *Fatshedera lizei* show the characteristics of both parents. The broad spread of the fatsia has been enlarged, and the stem of the ivy has been strengthened. The leaves are shiny, with a tough leathery texture, and the ivy shape has been enlarged: leaves may be up to 5in/13cm wide. From the ivy the plant has also inherited a partially climbing habit and so needs some form of support, such as a pole covered in spaghnum moss. For the best effect, set three or four plants around the edge of a single pot. Indoor plants do not often flower.

Aphids may infest the soft growing tips.

Leaf loss is natural on older plants; if the plant becomes unattractive and leggy, take cuttings and start new plants.

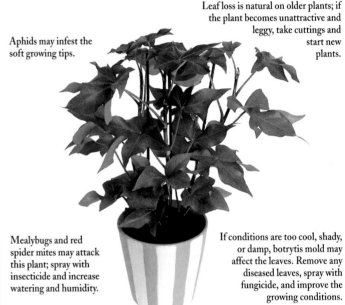

Mealybugs and red spider mites may attack this plant; spray with insecticide and increase watering and humidity.

If conditions are too cool, shady, or damp, botrytis mold may affect the leaves. Remove any diseased leaves, spray with fungicide, and improve the growing conditions.

FACT FILE

ORIGIN Hybrid.

HEIGHT To 8ft/2.4m.

POTTING MIX Soil-based.

REPOTTING Each spring, move into a pot one size larger. Once the plant has reached maximum desired size, top-dress annually instead.

PROPAGATION Take 3–4-in/8–10-cm tip cuttings in spring or early summer.

KEEPING PLANTS Pinch off growing tips to encourage bushiness; prune in spring if necessary to restrict the plant's size. In summer put the plant outdoors in a sheltered spot, out of direct sunlight.

PLANT CARE

Medium shade to bright filtered light; avoid extremes. ● Minimum winter temperature of 45°F/7°C, not above 60°F/16°C at other times. ● Keep the soil moist in the growing season, water less often in winter. ● Spray the leaves with water every other day. ● Feed with weak liquid fertilizer every 2 weeks in the period of active growth.

FATSIA JAPONICA
Araliaceae

JAPANESE FATSIA

Also known as Japanese aralia and false castor-oil plant, this has been a popular garden and houseplant since Victorian times. When it is grown outdoors, it makes a large shrub 6–8ft/1.8–2.4m high and with a spread of some 4ft/1.2m. Indoors it can be kept much smaller—it can withstand quite drastic pruning. It does best in cool rooms and enclosed porches, since in high temperatures the stems and the glossy lobed and pointed leaves become soft and sappy, easily damaged and prone to attack by pests. More-typical plants, with leathery light green, hand-shaped leaves, often as much as 16in/40cm wide, develop under cooler conditions. Creamy white flowers, followed by shiny black berries, may appear in fall.

Mealybugs, red spider mites, and aphids may attack this plant; check regularly for signs of these pests .

Loss of the oldest, lower leaves is normal on mature plants.

Botrytis mold may affect the leaves if the plant's location is too cool, shady, or damp. Remove damaged leaves, spray with fungicide, and move the plant to a better location.

FACT FILE

ORIGIN Japan; Korea.

HEIGHT To 6ft/1.8m.

POTTING MIX Soil-based.

REPOTTING In spring move the plant into a pot one or two sizes larger. Once it has reached its maximum size, top-dress annually.

PROPAGATION In spring take basal or side shoots as cuttings; keep them warm and humid inside a plastic bag or propagator.

KEEPING PLANTS Cut back by half in spring if necessary; pinch off growing tips to encourage dense growth. Stand the plant outdoors in a sheltered, shady position in summer. It should last for many years.

PLANT CARE

Bright light with some shade; no strong summer sun. ● Minimum winter temperature of 45°F/7°C; not above 60°F/16°C at other times. ● Keep the soil moist at all times. ● Spray with water every 2 days; in warm weather stand the pot on a tray of moist pebbles. ● Apply standard liquid fertilizer every 2 weeks in spring and summer. ● Clean the leaves with a damp sponge; do not use leaf shine.

FAUCARIA TIGRINA
Aizoaceae

TIGER JAWS

The fleshy grayish green leaves of *Faucaria tigrina* are 2in/5cm long, spotted with many tiny white dots, and are distinctly jawlike, complete with spines that resemble teeth. It is a small succulent plant from a dry area of South Africa, where it grows in rock crevices. In its natural habitat faucaria gains moisture from dews caused by rapid changes in night temperature and from humid winds off the sea.

This plant makes a low-growing, star-shaped rosette. In summer and fall golden yellow stalkless flowers reminiscent of daisies emerge from the rosette. They are up to 2½in/6.5cm wide and tend to open most fully in the afternoon.

FACT FILE

ORIGIN South Africa (Cape Province).

HEIGHT 2–4in/5–10cm.

POTTING MIX Soil-based and perlite or grit, to aid drainage, in a ratio of 2:1.

REPOTTING In spring every 2 or 3 years, when the plant has completely covered the surface of the soil.

PROPAGATION Divide overcrowded clumps in late spring or early summer; if a rosette has no root attached, allow it to dry for 24 hours before inserting it in a sand-loam mix.

KEEPING PLANTS The plant has relatively little root, so it is best planted in a shallow pan or half-pot.

PLANT CARE

Bright light; requires 3–4 hours of sunlight daily to ensure flowering. ● Minimum winter temperature of 50°F/10°C; normal room temperature at other times. ● Water copiously from spring to early fall; keep plants almost dry in winter. ● Apply a weak liquid fertilizer every 4 weeks to actively growing plants.

Mealybugs may infest the leaves; look for the tufts of waxy wool and scrape them off with a fingernail.

Root mealybugs leave wool tufts on the roots of the plant. Every few weeks, gently knock it out of its pot and check for this pest.

Overwatering during the winter rest period will cause rotting at the base of the plant and limp growth.

MORACEAE

FICUS

This is a large and diverse genus of plants that are generally natives of the warmer parts of the world. Most ficuses have evergreen foliage, although there are some variegated forms. Many make excellent indoor plants, and a suitable ficus can be found for any indoor situation. *Ficus* is the Latin word for the edible fig, and that plant is one of this group, which includes trees, shrubs, and climbers. Most of these plants are tolerant of a wide range of temperatures, and they adapt well to different conditions in the home, although they seldom flower or fruit in containers.

One of the most common indoor plants is the rubber plant, *Ficus elastica*, and its many improved hybrids such as 'Decora,' which has oval, glossy dark green leathery leaves up to 12in/30cm long. The leaves emerge from a rust-red protective sheath, and the vein on the underside of the leaf is also red. The sturdy *F.e.* 'Robusta' is shown here.

Among other species commonly found in the home are *F. benjamina*, the weeping fig; and *F. pumila* (*F. repens*), the creeping fig, which is ideal for a hanging basket or as ground cover. Several less well known species are also available, such as *F. rubiginosa*, the Port Jackson fig, or rusty fig; and *F. microcarpa* (*F. retusa*), Indian laurel. *F.m.* 'Hawaii,' with variegated leaves, is often sold as *F. benjamina*. *F. benghalensis*, the banyan tree, has leaves and stems covered with fine reddish hairs.

Ficus elastica 'Robusta' is a sturdy plant with leaves that are larger and rounder than those of 'Decora.' The shiny, leathery leaves are up to 12in/30cm long and have a pronounced mid-rib. When well cared for, this ficus can reach 10ft/3m in a pot. It does not fruit until it is about 30 years old.

When cleaning or handling young leaves, be very careful; they are easily damaged, and the scars will remain for the plant's entire life.

The central stem tends to grow straight, without branching, although branching will occur if the growing tip is removed.

ALSO RECOMMENDED

Ficus deltoidea var. *diversifolia* is the only species commonly grown indoors that regularly produces fruit (albeit inedible). It forms a much-branched small tree up to 3ft/90cm tall with thick dark green leaves.

Ficus pumila, the creeping or climbing fig, grows to about 4in/10cm high, but will trail to over 2ft/60cm. It thrives in damp shade and has thin, heart-shaped leaves, which are usually pale green and puckered.

Ficus lyrata, fiddle leaf fig, has 12-in/30-cm-long, glossy dark green leaves. In the wild, it starts as an epiphyte and becomes a tree up to 40ft/12m high, but in a pot it can easily be kept to a modest 3ft/90cm.

Mealybugs may attack older plants; check regularly for signs of infestation.

When the stem is cut or leaves break off, latexlike sap will bleed from the plant. This can be stopped by applying powdered charcoal or cigarette ash to the wound.

Drooping, lifeless-looking leaves that gradually turn yellow and fall indicate that the plant is being overwatered.

Scale insects can become a problem if left unchecked; inspect stems and leaves regularly—especially the undersides—of all ficus types.

Sooty mold will readily grow on leaves, establishing itself in the excreta of scale insects. Wipe the leaves with soapy water to remove it.

Leaf spot, a fungal disease, causes black spots on the leaves. Spray the plant with a suitable insecticide.

Older leaves turn yellow, then brown naturally and fall.

Prolonged overwatering will cause the roots to rot.

FACT FILE

ORIGIN Tropical and subtropical regions, particularly India and Malaysia.

HEIGHT 4in–10ft/10cm–3m.

POTTING MIX Soil-based for large-leafed ficuses; peat-moss-based for smaller types.

REPOTTING In spring, move all types into a pot one size larger only when roots fill the pot. Ficuses grow best if slightly pot-bound.

PROPAGATION It is difficult for the amateur to propagate large-leafed types. Plants are slow to root from cuttings because of high water loss from the large leaves, and are better air-layered instead. But this is a slow and difficult process. Small-leafed types, such as *Ficus pumila*, root easily from tip cuttings taken in spring.

KEEPING PLANTS These are not overly demanding plants, and all ficus species are long-lasting, some exceptionally so, provided the growing conditions are right.

PLANT CARE

Medium to bright light; some direct sunlight will not harm the plants. *Ficus pumila* prefers semishade.
● Minimum winter temperature of 50°–55°F/10°–13°C; normal warm room temperature at other times.
● Allow the top two-thirds of the soil to dry out before rewatering. Do not overwater. ● Apply a weak liquid fertilizer every 2 weeks in spring and summer. ● Spray smaller plants or plants with hairy leaves to clean the foliage. Sponge glossy leaves regularly to clean off any dust. To avoid damage, support the leaf with one hand while sponging it off.

PESTS & DISEASES

Scale insects and mealybugs infest these plants; check regularly for signs of these pests. Plants are also prone to attack by sooty mold.

Ficus benjamina, the weeping fig, has glossy 2–4in/5–10cm tapering leaves. In the wild it is a large tree, but can be kept to 6ft/1.8m in a pot. Stems are often plaited together for decorative effect.

Ficus benjamina '**Starlight**' is a variegated form whose leaves are a fresh apple green and white. Like other weeping figs, it has a pronounced graceful drooping habit and is highly ornamental.

FITTONIA VERSCHAFFELTII ARGYRONEURA
Acanthaceae

₷ILVER NET LEAF

Originally from the tropical rain forests of South America, this attractive plant has delicate oval olive green leaves with an overall pattern of distinct white veining; hence its other common name of the nerve plant. In summer insignificant yellow-green flowers that may appear should be removed or they will hinder the plant's growth.

In its natural habitat the plant grows as a low ground-cover creeper, flourishing in the shady environment. It is quite difficult to grow successfully indoors because it needs a humid atmosphere, with a temperature always above 64°F/18°C. Avoid the three D's: direct sunlight, drafts, and dry air. The plant is, however, ideal for terrariums and in mixed bowls, where it will spread to about 12in/30cm.

FACT FILE

ORIGIN Peru.

HEIGHT To 6in/15cm.

POTTING MIX Peat-moss-based or soil-based.

REPOTTING Each spring in the same pot. The plant is shallow-rooting, so shallow bowls or half-pots are best.

PROPAGATION In spring, by rooting 2-in/5-cm stem tip cuttings in warm humid conditions, or by layering.

KEEPING PLANTS Pinch off growing points regularly to encourage dense growth.

PLANT CARE

Bright location or light shade; avoid direct sunlight. ● Minimum winter temperature of 60°F/16°C; warmer room temperature at other times. ● Use tepid water to keep the potting mix damp but never sodden. ● Mist the plant regularly and stand the pot on a tray of moist pebbles to increase humidity. ● Apply a weak liquid fertilizer once a month in summer.

Shriveling leaves indicate that the air is too dry or the plant is in direct sunlight. Increase humidity and move to a semishady location.

If leaves turn yellow, the plant is being overwatered. Remove the damaged leaves and allow the soil to become almost dry before rewatering.

Leaves will drop if the plant is placed in a cool or drafty location.

Aphids may attack this plant; check regularly for their presence.

FREESIA
Iridaceae

₣REESIA

Hybrid freesias are attractive, sweet-smelling plants that will flower well in the house. The 2-in/5-cm funnel-shaped flowers grow on one side of wiry stems, 12–18in/30–46cm long, which emerge between narrow, straplike leaves. Freesias are available in white, yellow, mauve, pink, red, and orange. 'Super Giant' hybrids are a high-yielding and early-flowering strain in all colors.

Freesias grow from corms, which should be planted up in batches from late summer to early winter for flowering in succession through to the middle of spring. Set the corms 2–3in/5–8cm apart, just covering the tops with potting mix, followed by a layer of peat 1in/2.5cm deep; for maximum impact, plant six corms in a 5-in/13-cm pot. Keep the pots in a greenhouse or sunroom and give the plants small amounts of water until growth is visible.

Aphids infest the stems and leaves and can transmit plant viruses.

Red spider mites may attack plants in a greenhouse. Mist plants regularly and increase watering to combat that pest.

Corms may suffer from gladiolus dry rot, which causes them to become rotten and corky. When they are lifted, burn all diseased corms or seal them in a plastic bag and dispose of them.

FACT FILE

ORIGIN South Africa; hybrids.

HEIGHT To 18in/46cm.

POTTING MIX Soil-based with added sharp sand.

REPOTTING Pot up dry corms from late summer to early winter.

PROPAGATION By seed sown in mid-spring, avoiding excessively high temperatures, or by corms planted from late summer to early winter.

KEEPING PLANTS Support plants by pushing light stakes into the compost and stretching string between them. After flowering, allow plants to dry out; in midsummer lift, dry, and store the corms.

PLANT CARE

Bright light, with some direct sunlight. ● Minimum temperature of 40°F/4°C from mid fall to early spring; cooler room temperature at other times. ● Water actively growing plants well; ease off once the flowers fade. ● Apply weak liquid fertilizer every 2 weeks from the time flower buds show until the end of flowering.

FUCHSIA
Onagraceae

Fuchsia

Some modern hybrids can grow as tall as 6ft/1.8m outdoors, but under cool indoor conditions, the most suitable are dwarf or hanging varieties. Plants flower from early spring to late fall and produce distinctive, ornamental, pendulous blooms, which consist of a bell-shaped flower surrounded by four sepals, long stamens, and an extremely long style. Flowers may be single, semidouble, or double in almost every color except yellow. Some of the most attractive fuchsias have sepals of one color and petals of another. Buy small plants in spring and stand the pots on trays filled with wet gravel to increase humidity. In summer, plants that are kept indoors will thrive if given short spells outside in bright light, but not direct sun. In winter, the leaves drop, but the plants remain alive and dormant if kept in a cool, frost-free place. They are often discarded at the end of the season.

FACT FILE

ORIGIN Central and South America; New Zealand; hybrid.

HEIGHT To 2ft/60cm (dwarf varieties).

POTTING MIX Soil-based, peat moss and sand in equal quantities.

REPOTTING Each spring, in the same pot or one a size larger. In too big a pot the plant will not flower so well.

PROPAGATION Take 3–4-in/8–10-cm-long tip cuttings in spring or fall and root them in warm conditions.

KEEPING PLANTS Pinch off growing tips in spring and early summer to encourage bushy growth. Cut back stems by two-thirds when the plant stops flowering and overwinter in cool conditions.

PLANT CARE

Bright position but not full sun. ● Minimum winter temperature of 46°F/8°C; warm room temperature at other times. ● Water actively growing plants well; in winter allow dormant plants to dry out between waterings. ● Stand the plant on a tray of damp pebbles to increase humidity. ● Feed with a weak liquid fertilizer once a week between spring and fall.

ALSO RECOMMENDED

'Cascade' has white sepals streaked with pink, and crimson petals; 'Checkerboard,' white and red sepals, with deep red petals. The sepals of 'Display' are rose pink and the petals cerise, while 'Swingtime' has red sepals and white double petals faintly streaked with pink; both are particularly good for hanging baskets. 'Dollar Princess' has cerise sepals and purple petals, and 'Falling Stars,' red sepals with deep red petals. The flowers of 'Golden Marinka' are all red, but the foliage is variegated green, white, and cream.

If spider mites attack the plant, spray it with insecticide and increase the humidity around it.

Leaves that drop prematurely may mean that the atmosphere is too hot and dry. Increase the humidity and move the plant to a cooler place.

Fuchsia 'Little Charmer,' a hybrid miniature, is ideal for an indoor hanging basket.

Aphids and whiteflies may attack fuchsias; check frequently for signs of these pests and spray with a suitable insecticide if they are present.

Brown spotting with yellow margins on the leaves may mean that the plant is being overwatered; allow it to dry out before rewatering and improve the drainage.

When a new plant is purchased, or a greenhouse-grown specimen is brought into a dry room, flowers may shed rapidly. To counteract this difficulty, choose plants in bud, not in flower, and put them in a bright, cool location near a window.

GARDENIA AUGUSTA
Rubiaceae

Gardenia

There are several species of gardenia—also called Cape jasmine—but *Gardenia augusta*, (syn. *G. jasminoides*, *G. grandiflora*) is the one most commonly seen. This old-fashioned, attractive flowering shrub is not difficult to grow, but it does need particular attention if it is to fill a room with its powerful perfume. It is best regarded as a greenhouse or patio plant that is brought indoors when in flower. The delicate buds can suffer during transit, so take care when moving the plant and make sure that it is well protected within a draft-free carrier.

The glossy, dark, evergreen leaves resemble the foliage of camellia, but gardenia leaves, which can be 4in/10cm long, are softer and less rounded. The flowers, 2–4in/5–10cm wide, are single, semidouble, or double, and startlingly white, fading to creamy yellow before they drop. Mature gardenias may reach 4–6ft/1.2–1.8m indoors, but they are more usually bushy shrubs, often growing only 6in/15cm or so in a year.

FACT FILE

ORIGIN Southern China.

HEIGHT 2ft–6ft/60cm–1.8m indoors.

POTTING MIX Equal parts of peat-moss and leaf mold; must be lime-free.

REPOTTING Move into a pot one size larger every spring.

PROPAGATION Take 3-in/8-cm tip cuttings in spring or early summer and root them in a warm propagator.

KEEPING PLANTS Prune in late winter to maintain a good shape. The plant can last for many years under the right conditions.

PLANT CARE

Bright light, with some direct sunlight in winter. ● A constant temperature of 60°F/16°C when buds are forming; otherwise, normal room temperature. ● Water moderately with soft, tepid water in the period of active growth; less frequently in winter. ● Mist daily in warm weather with tepid rainwater but do not wet the flowers. ● Apply an "acid" liquid fertilizer every 2 weeks from early spring, when buds are forming, to late summer.

Yellowing leaves may mean that the plant's location is too shady.

Fumes from natural-gas appliances will cause the plant to wilt and die.

Flowers will fall early if the air around the plant is too dry.

Scale insects, mealybugs, aphids, and red spider mites all attack gardenias. If they are present, spray with insecticide and improve the humidity.

Foliage becomes pale and yellow if water has a high lime content. Use only lime-free water or rainwater, and apply sequestered iron every 2 weeks for a couple of months.

GERBERA JAMESONII
Compositae

African Daisy

The major attraction of this popular summer pot plant, also known as the Barberton or Transvaal daisy, is its large, showy flowers in shades of purple, crimson, red, orange, pink, yellow, cream, and white. Both single and double forms are available. The long-lasting flowers, measuring 2–4in/5–10cm across, have soft furry petals and are borne on stiff, gray-green leafless stems up to 2ft/60cm long.

Recent hybrids, with stems about half that length, are better suited to indoor cultivation. They are generally regarded as annuals and can produce up to six blooms at a time. The 6-in/15-cm-long lobed leaves are wooly on the undersides. Buy hybrid plants in bud in early summer.

Leaf spot fungus shows as large brown spots covered with tiny dots, and with a thin, violet-colored border. Eventually, the spots coalesce, and the leaves start to shrivel.

Aphids may attack gerberas; check regularly for signs of these pests.

Distorted stems and foliage, particularly with young growth, may be a symptom of infestation by tarsonemid mites.

FACT FILE

ORIGIN South Africa (Transvaal); Swaziland; hybrids.

HEIGHT To 18in/46cm.

POTTING MIX Peat-moss-based or soil-based.

REPOTTING In spring, when dividing plants.

PROPAGATION By division, or cuttings of nonflowering shoots; most hybrids will flower well the first year. Alternatively, sow seed in early spring. Plants grown from saved seed will revert to longer stems, but there are some seed strains available that will produce dwarf plants.

KEEPING PLANTS In a mild climate the plant is often used as a patio plant. Replace the plant after 2 or 3 years.

PLANT CARE

Bright light, with some direct sunlight. ● A temperature of 40°–70°F/4°–21°C when in flower. ● Allow to dry between thorough waterings. Do not mist. ● Feed flowering plants once a week with half-strength liquid fertilizer. ● Provide a good circulation of air around the plant.

GLORIOSA SUPERBA 'ROTHSCHILDIANA'
Liliaceae

Gloriosa Lily

A vigorous climbing plant that grows from elongated, fingerlike tubers, the glory lily has slender stems which bear shiny, lanceolate leaves with twining tendrils at their tips, by which the plant clings to its support. The flowers arise from the leaf axils near the top of the stems; they are carried singly on long stalks and look a little like a turk's cap lily, with reflexed, wavy-edged petals of bright red edged with yellow and with a yellow base. The prominent stamens are arranged like the spokes of a wheel below the petals. Flowers are carried throughout the summer, and after flowering the tubers should be dried off for the winter.

The glory lily is an unusual but spectacular indoor plant which is sometimes available from garden centres in flower, although it is more usual to buy dormant tubers from bulb specialists.

The reflexed petals have crimped and waved edges. Remove flowers once they begin to fade.

Provide the plant with a sturdy support for the tendrils to cling to.

The long, fingerlike tubers are brittle and must be handled carefully.

Water the plant freely during the flowering season, but make sure that drainage is good. Tubers will rot if the soil is too wet.

FACT FILE

ORIGIN Tropical Africa.

HEIGHT 4ft/1.2m or more.

POTTING MIX Soil- or peat-moss-based, with good drainage.

REPOTTING Handle tubers carefully and pot each in a 15cm/6in pot.

PROPAGATION By division of tubers formed during the growing season, or seed sown in spring.

KEEPING PLANTS After flowering, let the foliage die back; store tubers in a dry place no colder than 50°F/10°C until spring, then repot.

PLANT CARE

Bright light, but no direct midsummer sun. ● Warm room temperature no lower than 60°F/16°C in the active growing period. ● Water newly potted tubers sparingly until shoots emerge. Allow to dry between thorough waterings. ● Apply a high-potash liquid feed every 2–3 weeks when the plant is in active growth.

GREVILLEA ROBUSTA
Proteaceae

Silk Oak

In its native habitat, this grevillea makes a large tree, but as a pot plant it is seldom more than 6ft/1.8m in height and most plants are much smaller. The finely divided leaves are mid to dark green, slightly downy on top and silky beneath; they have a fernlike appearance but become less divided as they age. The mature foliage is less attractive than that of young specimens. The silk oak is fast-growing, and where there is room for it can make a striking indoor specimen tree.

A tolerant plant, *Grevillea robusta* thrives best in rather cool conditions. It does not flower in cultivation as an indoor plant.

FACT FILE

ORIGIN Australia.

HEIGHT To 6ft/1.8m.

POTTING MIX Ericaceous (lime-free).

REPOTTING In spring and also during the summer if roots can be seen emerging through the drainage holes in the base of the pot.

PROPAGATION By seed sown in spring and early summer, or by soft stem cuttings in summer.

KEEPING PLANTS The plant is often discarded after 2 or 3 years because the lacy fernlike young foliage becomes less finely divided on older plants and is less attractive.

PLANT CARE

Bright light with some sun, but not direct midsummer sun. Grevillea will also grow well in light shade. ● A minimum winter temperature of 45°F/7°C, with 55°–60°F/13°–16°C in summer. ● Keep the soil evenly moist in spring and summer. Allow the top 1in/2.5cm to dry out between waterings in winter. ● Mist the foliage occasionally, particularly in warm conditions. ● Feed with a balanced liquid fertilizer every 2 weeks in spring and summer.

The undersides of the leaves have a silky feel and appearance, giving the plant its common name.

Make sure that the growing points on young plants are not damaged when selecting one at a garden center or nursery.

Infestation by red spider mites is a sign that the atmosphere is too dry. Increase humidity by frequent misting and standing the pot on a tray of damp pebbles.

GYNURA 'PURPLE PASSION'
Compositae

PURPLE PASSION VINE

Thought to be a hybrid between *Gynura procumbens* and *G. aurantiaca*, this foliage plant produces ovate, toothed, more or less holly-shaped leaves on trailing or climbing stems. The plant is best displayed in a hanging basket or wall pot. The foliage is mid green and is covered with dense purple hairs, particularly on the underside. The stems are also hairy, which gives the whole plant an almost fluorescent, velvety appearance, and it is also known as the velvet plant. When purple passion vine is kept in bright light, the color is often particularly intense and can produce a quite startling effect.

Shaggy, orange-yellow, groundsellike flowers are produced in spring and should be removed, since they are not only unattractive but have an unpleasant smell.

The iridescent purple hairs are densest on young foliage and shoot tips, and the color is strongest on plants kept in bright light.

Mist the foliage with a fine spray only in warm conditions. The hairs trap the moisture, which can lead to rotting.

Stems are twining or semitwining, and can be trained up a trellis or left to trail.

FACT FILE

ORIGIN Hybrid.

HEIGHT Trailing stems up to 5ft/1.5m long.

POTTING MIX Soil- or peat-moss-based.

REPOTTING In spring move into a pot one size larger.

PROPAGATION By soft stem cuttings in spring and early summer.

KEEPING PLANTS Pinch off shoot tips to keep the plant compact. Cut back older plants to 4in/10cm in spring. Discard plants after 2 years.

PLANT CARE

Bright light for good coloration; some sun, but strong summer sun can scorch the leaves. ● Minimum winter temperature of 60°F/16°C. ● Water moderately in the growing season; less often in winter. ● Stand the plant on a tray of damp pebbles to increase humidity. ● Feed with a balanced liquid fertilizer every 2 weeks in spring and summer.

HAEMANTHUS HUMILIS 'WILSONII'
Amaryllidaceae

HAEMANTHUS

This lily with its pair of gray-green hairy leaves and stem is an unusual houseplant. In summer it produces a rather short-lived umbel up to 4in/10cm wide of pale pink or white flowers. The more commonly grown perennial bulb usually called *Haemanthus katherinae* is related, but it is now correctly known as *Scadoxus multiflora* ssp. *katherinae*. This bulb produces mid green, wavy-edged leaves up to 12in/30cm long on short stalks, which it retains during the winter. The bright red, showy flowers with prominent stamens are carried in a ball-like umbel at the top of a tall, fleshy stem that is often streaked or flushed with red at the base. The 8-in/20-cm-wide flowers appear in summer.

FACT FILE

ORIGIN Southern Africa.

HEIGHT Flower stems to 12in/30cm.

POTTING MIX Soil-based.

REPOTTING In spring, every 3–5 years, when the bulb is too large for the pot or roots can be seen through the base of the pot and on the surface of the soil. Otherwise, top-dress annually.

PROPAGATION Best from offsets. From seed it flowers in about 18 months; division is very slow.

KEEPING PLANTS Haemanthus flower best when undisturbed and may be kept in the same pot for several years.

PLANT CARE

Bright light with some direct sun. ● Average room temperatures, with a minimum of 50°F/10°C. ● Water freely in summer and let the surface of the soil dry out between watering; water less in winter. ● Give a high-potash liquid feed every 2 weeks during the growing season.

The globular flower head is usually about 4in/10cm wide.

Make sure the neck of the bulb is just above the surface of the soil when potting it.

HEDERA HELIX
Araliaceae

ENGLISH IVY

A well-known, fast-growing, climbing plant that is perfectly hardy and widely grown outdoors and also makes an excellent houseplant. The three- to five-lobed, roughly palmate leaves differ considerably in shape and size (from about ¾in/20mm to 4in/10cm) according to variety. Stems are tough and wiry, and progress upward, clinging to their support by means of aerial roots. Outdoors, they have no problem attaching themselves to brickwork, fences, and the like, but they usually need to be tied to stakes and supports in the home. In outdoor conditions, the growth of ivy changes to a mature form when the plant has reached the top of its climb. Stems become erect and bushy, leaves entire, and flowers are produced. This does not normally occur with plants grown indoors.

Dozens of varieties are suitable for growing as pot plants, many of them variegated. 'Glacier' has three-lobed leaves mottled gray-green, silver, and cream. 'Goldheart' has a large, irregular central blotch of creamy yellow against a dark green background. 'Sagittifolia' has an elongated central lobe, giving the leaves an arrowhead appearance; plain green and variegated forms are available. 'Ivalace' has curled and crimped leaf margins, that produce a lacy effect.

Hedera algeriensis *'Gloire de Marengo' has large leaves, pleasingly variegated with gray-green and white. It is a vigorous grower and, trained over a trellis, makes a good background to flowering plants.*

FACT FILE

ORIGIN Europe.

HEIGHT Most will climb as high as they are allowed to.

POTTING MIX Soil- or peat-moss-based.

REPOTTING Move small plants into larger pots when roots emerge through the base of the pot.

PROPAGATION In spring and early summer, take 3–4-in/8–10-cm tip cuttings and root them in water or soil.

KEEPING PLANTS Grow the plant up stakes or a trellis, and tie in the stems, or set several plants in a hanging basket or pot and allow the stems to trail. Pinch off the growing tips to keep the plant neat.

PLANT CARE

Bright light; variegated forms need some direct sun.
● Cool temperatures are required, ideally around 50°F/10°C. ● Allow the surface of the soil to dry out between waterings. ● Mist the foliage frequently.
● Apply a standard liquid fertilizer every 2 weeks in spring and summer.

ALSO RECOMMENDED
Hedera algeriensis, a larger-leafed species with shallowly lobed leaves up to 6in/15cm wide; 'Gloire de Marengo' is mottled gray-green with a white edge to the leaves.

Take care where you locate ivy. The aerial roots will cling firmly to walls and can spoil paintwork and furnishings.

Ivy is particularly prone to attack by red spider mites. Check the foliage for mottling or yellow flecking; mist the plants regularly, especially in warm conditions.

Cut out the all-green shoots that are sometimes produced on variegated ivies. Improve the light to maintain leaf coloration.

HEPTAPLEURUM ARBORICOLUM see
SCHEFFLERA ARBORICOLA

HIBISCUS ROSA-SINENSIS
Malvaceae

ℛOSE OF CHINA

Hibiscus is a shrubby evergreen plant, bearing dark green, ovate leaves with toothed edges. The species has large red showy flowers; those of the cultivars are shades of red, orange, yellow, and pink. All open out to flared trumpets, some 4–6in/10–15cm across, with a prominent column of fused stamens. On well-grown plants there will be a succession of flowers from spring to late summer. Single or semidouble varieties are available, and plants can sometimes be obtained trained as short standards, but they are expensive. *Hibiscus rosa-sinensis* 'Koenig' is an attractive double-flowered yellow variety; 'Golden Belle' has large, single, golden yellow flowers with ruffled petals, while those of 'Surfrider' are yellow with a red eye. The flowers of 'Paramaribo' are rich red; 'Rosalie' has flowers of a clear rose pink and sharply indented leaf margins. When conditions suit them, hibiscuses are long-lived plants, and they need regular pruning to keep them small enough indoors. Larger plants look good in a sunroom.

FACT FILE

ORIGIN Tropical Asia.

HEIGHT To 6ft/1.8m and more.

POTTING MIX Soil-based, with a little added peat moss or peat moss substitute.

REPOTTING In spring, into a pot one size larger. When the maximum desired pot size is reached, top-dress annually.

PROPAGATION In late spring and early summer, take 3–4-in/8–10-cm tip or heel cuttings.

KEEPING PLANTS Cut the stems back by half to two-thirds in early spring to keep indoor plants compact.

PLANT CARE

Bright light with some direct sun. ● Normal room temperature in the growing season; allow to rest at 60°F/16°C during the winter. ● Keep the soil thoroughly moist at all times in spring and summer; in winter allow it to dry out between waterings. ● Mist the foliage frequently and stand the pot on a tray of damp pebbles to increase humidity.
● Feed with a high-potash liquid fertilizer every 2 weeks in summer.
● Try not to move the plant while it is in bud or the buds may drop.

ALSO RECOMMENDED

Hibiscus schizopetalus, known as Japanese lantern or Japanese hibiscus, is a more graceful-looking plant with slender arching branches. The drooping pink flowers on long stalks have fringed, turned-back petals with a long stamen column; they can be more than 2in/5cm across.

Buds will drop if plants are moved to a place with a different temperature. Lack of humidity or allowing the soil to dry out may also cause buds to drop.

The large trumpet-shaped flowers will fall after a day or two, but more should be produced for a long succession of blooms.

Aphids sometimes attack the young foliage. Treat with a contact insecticide.

Hibiscus rosa-sinensis *'Koenig' has flowers with a double ring of bright yellow petals and, almost hidden within them, a red eye.*

HIPPEASTRUM **x** *ACRAMANNII* (SYN. *H.* **x** *ACKERMANNII*)
Amaryllidaceae

Amaryllis

The common name of this plant is a misnomer. The real *Amaryllis belladonna* is related, but is a quite different bulb. Hippeastrums are popular and readily available in a wide range of varieties. The big fleshy bulbs produce a tall, succulent, hollow green flower stem, usually in spring, although specially treated bulbs are available for winter flowering. Large, strong bulbs may sometimes produce two flowering stems, but one is more usual. The stem bears two to four large, colorful, lilylike trumpets, which have prominent curving stamens and last for several weeks. Flowers come in several colors—red, white, salmon, and pink; and they may be striped or flushed with a second color.

Normally the leaves follow the flower stem, although occasionally both are produced together. Leaves are long and strap-shaped, mid to dark green, and arise in opposite pairs that arch over. Hippeastrum bulbs must be given a rest in the fall and early winter if they are to flower successfully the following year.

FACT FILE

ORIGIN South and Central America; hybrids.

HEIGHT To 2ft/60cm.

POTTING MIX Soil-based.

POTTING Set the bulb in the soil with the top third above the surface. At the end of the rest period, repot the bulb in fresh soil in the same pot.

PROPAGATION Sow seed in spring, or pot up any offsets that appear around the base of the bulb; they will take several years to grow to flowering size.

KEEPING PLANTS A rest in fall and winter is important to bring plants into flower the following year. Bright light and adequate feeding until leaves die down in mid-fall are needed for the formation of flower buds.

PLANT CARE

Bright light with some direct sun. ● Fairly cool conditions will help the flowers last well; maximum temperature 65°F/18°C. ● Water sparingly until the flower bud appears, then increase watering, but allow the surface of the soil to dry out before rewatering. When flowers fade, gradually decrease watering until midfall. Then dry out the soil completely: bulbs need a dormant period of 8 weeks. ● Stand the pot on a tray of moist pebbles. Do not mist. ● Feed with a high-potash fertilizer every 10–14 days from the time the bud appears until the fall. ● The bud may drop if the plant is moved after the bud has emerged.

ALSO RECOMMENDED

Many hippeastrum cultivars are available for indoor cultivation. 'Appleblossom' is pale pink and white; 'Red Lion' is a strong, rich red; 'Picotee' is white with a fine red margin on the petals; and 'Bijou' has soft apricot-colored flowers. There are also double-flowered varieties such as 'Lady Jane,' with orange-pink and white flowers.

Hippeastrum *'Appleblossom'* bears blooms whose huge size is in marked contrast to their delicate pink-and-white coloration.

The huge flowers can make plants top-heavy, particularly if they are grown in peat-moss-based potting mix. For stability, use a pot that is as wide as it is tall.

Stake the flower stem if necessary, but be careful not to damage the bulb when inserting the stake.

Set the large fleshy bulb so that the top third is above the level of the soil. Buy only bulbs that are plump and not shriveled.

Plants that have not been well cared for during the previous season sometimes produce only leaves. This is unlikely to occur with commercially grown bulbs.

HOFFMANNIA REGALIS 'ROEZLII'
Rubiaceae

TAFFETA PLANT

The three species of hoffmannia used as houseplants are grown for their striking foliage. Although they do flower, the blooms tend to be insignificant and are hidden among the leaves. These plants are shrubby perennials which are usually fairly short-lived in the home.

Hoffmannia regalis 'Roezlii' has satiny puckered leaves some 6in/15cm long that are purplish green above and purple-red underneath. The leaves of *H. ghiesbreghtii* are lance-shaped and up to 12in/30cm long; they are a deep reddish green with the veins picked out in silver. The leaves of *H.g.* 'Variegata' are irregularly marked with dark green, pale silvery green, cream, and light pink. *H. refulgens* has rounded leaves of an almost iridescent coppery green, which are deeply veined, with a puckered, textured surface between the veins. The variety 'Vittata' has silvery veins.

The prominently veined foliage has an almost metallic sheen; the undersides of the leaves are purple-red.

Aphids may attack young leaves; treat the pests with a contact insecticide.

The short-stemmed flowers are quite attractive but are usually hidden among the leaves.

If the leaves droop, the temperature may be too low. Keep the plant in an evenly warm, draft-free location: it is an ideal resident for a sunroom.

FACT FILE

ORIGIN Mexico, Central America.

HEIGHT 1–2ft/30–60cm.

POTTING MIX Soil- or peat-moss-based.

REPOTTING Move into a pot one size larger in spring when roots can be seen emerging through the drainage holes in the base of the pot.

PROPAGATION Take stem cuttings in early summer. Some bottom heat in a propagator will improve rooting.

KEEPING PLANTS Discard plants when they become leggy; this is usually after about 5 years.

PLANT CARE

Bright diffused light. ● Warm conditions, with a minimum temperature of 60°F/16°C. ● Keep the soil just moist during the growing season; allow the surface to dry out between waterings. ● Mist the foliage occasionally with a fine spray. ● Feed with a balanced liquid fertilizer every 2 weeks in spring and summer.

HOWEA BELMOREANA
Palmae

SENTRY PALM

Still sometimes sold as kentia palms, howeas are popular, tolerant, slow-growing house plants; *Howea belmoreana* is also known as curly palm. Mature plants produce gracefully arching fronds with short leafstalks from the top of a short trunk. Indoors, each fan may be as much as 12in/30cm wide and 18in/46cm long on older specimens. The leaves of *H. forsteriana* have longer leafstalks and do not arch as gracefully as those of *H. belmoreana*. The former has a more spreading habit, but the two are so similar in appearance that they may be confused. Both make bold specimen plants.

FACT FILE

ORIGIN Lord Howe Island; South Pacific.

HEIGHT To 6ft/1.8m or more.

POTTING MIX Soil-based, with a little added peat moss.

REPOTTING Every 2 or 3 years move into a pot one size larger in spring.

PROPAGATION Sow seed in a heated propagator, but seedlings are slow-growing and propagation in the home is not really practical.

KEEPING PLANTS This long-lived palm will benefit from a spell outdoors in summer.

PLANT CARE

Bright, diffused light; the plant will tolerate shade. ● Normal room temperature, with a minimum of 55°F/13°C. ● Keep the soil moist during the growing season; allow the surface to dry out between waterings in winter. ● Mist the foliage regularly; stand the pot on a tray of moist pebbles. ● Feed with a standard liquid fertilizer every 2 weeks in spring and summer.

The dark green fronds are made up of many arching pinnae, or leaflets, about 1½in/4cm wide.

Refresh dull, dusty foliage by standing the plant under a gentle shower or outdoors in warm summer rain.

Leaf tips tend to turn brown even on healthy plants. Mist the foliage regularly with water to ensure high humidity. Scorch marks may be caused by bright, direct sunlight on the leaves.

Scale insects may attack this plant: look for dark brown oval scales firmly fixed to the undersides of the leaves. Remove them carefully with a thumbnail. If left, they can cause black sooty mold to develop.

HOYA LANCEOLATA SSP. *BELLA*
Asclepiadaceae

*M*INIATURE WAX PLANT

The long, slender stems of this plant (usually known just as *Hoya bella*), with their pale gray-green oval or lance-shaped leaves are upright at first, then arch over to trail gracefully. Flower heads, produced from the tips of the stems in summer, consist of a cluster of up to 10 starry, waxy, white flowers with a rose pink five-pointed center. The heads hang down, and the plant is best grown in a hanging basket so that the blooms can more easily be appreciated, or trained around a wire hoop and tied in at intervals with soft twine. The flowers are sweet-scented, and drops of sticky nectar often form on them. Do not move the plant when the buds are forming, since this will usually cause them to drop.

H. carnosa, wax plant, is generally easier to grow than *H. bella* and it climbs rapidly. The flowers, which are produced in summer, are similar to those of *H. bella*, but each flower head carries about twice the number of blooms. These are strongly fragrant, and another common name for *H. carnosa* is honey plant. The foliage is thick and fleshy, glossy and mid- to dark green; although several variegated forms are available, they are sometimes more difficult to bring into flower.

FACT FILE

ORIGIN India; Southeast Asia.

HEIGHT Stems trail to around 18in/46cm. *H. carnosa* can reach 15ft/4.5m or more.

POTTING MIX Peat-based; must be free-draining.

REPOTTING Plants flower best when slightly pot-bound, so move them into pots one size larger in late spring only every 2 years or so.

PROPAGATION Take 3–4-in/8–10-cm stem tip cuttings in late spring.

KEEPING PLANTS Do not remove faded flower heads; flowers will be produced from the same spur in subsequent years.

PLANT CARE

Bright light with some direct sun. ● Warm conditions, with a minimum of 60°F/16°C in winter and a temperature of 65°–70°F/18°–21°C in summer. ● Water moderately in summer, allowing the surface to dry out between waterings; in winter give only sufficient water to prevent the soil from drying out completely. ● Mist the foliage regularly, but avoid spraying the flowers. ● Apply a high-potash liquid feed every 2–3 weeks in the growing period.

ALSO RECOMMENDED

Hoya carnosa 'Variegata' has cream-edged leaves. *H. australis* has slightly smaller flowers with a honeysuckle scent.

Plant in a hanging basket or wall pot, so the drooping flower heads can be seen from below.

If stems are weak, leaves pale and widely spaced, and flowers few, move the plant to a lighter, sunny location. But protect plants from scorching caused by direct midsummer sun.

Pick off individual flowers when they fade, but do not disturb the spur from which the flowers arise.

Mealybugs may attack this plant. Remove them with a damp cloth and spray the plant with a suitable insecticide.

Hoya carnosa *produces heavy flower heads that may contain as many as 30 sweet-scented flowers. These start off white and soon turn pale pink with a white and rose center.*

HYACINTHUS ORIENTALIS
Liliaceae

*H*YACINTH

Most of the sweet-scented hyacinths that bloom indoors are grown from bulbs specially prepared for forcing, and they will flower several weeks earlier than their normal spring season outdoors. Leaves of *Hyacinthus orientalis* are long, strap-shaped, and mid green. A single flower spike arises from the bulb, with a fleshy stem and densely packed racemes of fragrant flowers. Many varieties are available in shades of blue, violet, red, pink, apricot, yellow, and white. Among the most popular are rose pink 'Anna Marie,' 'Delft Blue,' which flowers very early, and 'City of Haarlem,' a soft primrose yellow.

Plant treated bulbs as soon as you get them. Set them in a bowl of moist, peaty potting mix so that the noses show just above the surface. Keep them in cool (40°F/4°C), completely dark conditions for about eight weeks. When the shoots are about 2in/5cm high, bring them into the light and keep them at about 50°F/10°C. When the buds begin to show color, move the bulbs to their flowering position.

FACT FILE

ORIGIN Hybrid.

HEIGHT 10–12in/25–30cm.

POTTING MIX Peat-moss-based, rather than bulb fiber, if you want to keep the bulb to flower outside in future years.

REPOTTING None.

PROPAGATION Pot offsets from around the base of the bulb.

KEEPING PLANTS Cut down flower stalks after the flowers have faded, but water and feed the bulbs until the leaves die down. Bulbs are not suitable for indoor use again but can be planted outdoors.

PLANT CARE

Bright conditions for leaf and flower development. ● A maximum of 60°F/16°C in the bulbs' flowering position. ● Keep the soil just moist at all times. ● Give a balanced liquid fertilizer every 2 weeks from the time the flower buds are visible until the foliage dies down.

Use a thin stake to support the flowering stem if the large flower head is very heavy.

Malformed flower heads, or flower spikes that do not emerge properly above the leaves, are the result of keeping the bulbs too warm or not completely dark during the cold period.

Different varieties come into flower at different times. So for the best effect, plant bowls with several bulbs of the same variety, rather than mixing them.

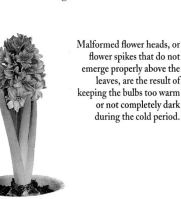

HYDRANGEA MACROPHYLLA (SYN. *H. HORTENSIS*)
Hydrangeaceae

*H*YDRANGEA

These hardy shrubs are usually treated as temporary pot plants, being discarded once the flowers fade. Several cuttings are usually grown in one pot to form a bushy plant. The hydrangea most commonly grown as a pot plant is the hortensia, or mophead, type. The large, globular flower heads are made up of sterile flowerets in shades of blue, pink, or white: the color is determined by the acidity of the soil. In alkaline soils the flowerets are pink. They turn blue in acid conditions; aluminum sulfate can be given to make sure the blue color is retained. Not all varieties change color successfully; some pinks turn a muddy purple. When you buy a plant in bloom from a florist or garden center, it is best to choose the color you want instead of trying to attain it.

If flower heads lose their blue color and begin to turn purple or pink, the soil has become alkaline. Treat with aluminum sulfate.

Foliage rapidly turns yellow and falls if the soil is allowed to dry out. Pots are usually tightly packed with roots, so water frequently.

FACT FILE

ORIGIN Japan.

HEIGHT To 2ft/60cm.

POTTING MIX Soil-based; acidic (lime-free) for blue varieties.

REPOTTING After flowering, if you wish to try the plant indoors for a second year.

PROPAGATION By cuttings in late summer; overwinter in a cold frame.

KEEPING PLANTS Plant outdoors if in good condition. Or after flowering, repot, cut back the stems by half, and continue to water and feed. Put in a cold frame or unheated greenhouse; move into warmer conditions in late winter to bring the plant into leaf and flower early.

PLANT CARE

Bright light but not direct sun. ● A maximum of 60°F/16°C will help the flowers last. ● Keep well watered during the growing season, using lime-free water. Water sparingly in winter. ● Give a high-potash liquid fertilizer every 1–2 weeks in the growing season.

HYPOESTES PHYLLOSTACHYA
Acanthaceae

Polka dot plant

A fast-growing foliage plant, the polka dot plant, also known as freckle face, has oval, pointed leaves about 1½in/4cm long. They are dark green, spotted, and splashed with pink. Plants in the 'Splash' series are the most commonly grown, and are so heavily marked that the leaves appear more pink with green flecks. In addition to the popular 'Pink Splash,' the deeper-colored 'Rose Splash' and 'White Splash' are available. The plant quickly makes a fairly open bush, and the growing tips should be pinched off regularly to keep it reasonably compact. It is usually discarded after it has become leggy, but soft stem cuttings are easily rooted to provide replacements. The pale lilac flowers are insignificant, and flower stems are usually pinched off as they appear.

Commercially grown plants are kept compact by the use of growth-regulating chemicals.

Hot summer sun may cause brown scorch marks on the foliage. Protect plants by filtering the sunlight with blinds or curtains.

Leaves may revert to all-green in poor light. Keep the plant in good, bright light for the best coloration and compact growth.

Pinch off any flower spikes that appear in summer, since they detract from the foliage.

FACT FILE

ORIGIN Madagascar.

HEIGHT Keep to about 12in/30cm by pinching off.

POTTING MIX Peat-moss-based.

REPOTTING Not usually required.

PROPAGATION Take soft stem cuttings in spring and summer; put several cuttings in a pot for a good display. Sow seed in early spring.

PLANT CARE

Bright light, with some direct sun, for good leaf color, but protect plants from scorching by very hot sun. ● Average room temperature, with a minimum winter temperature of 62°F/17°C. ● Keep the soil just moist during the growing season; allow the surface to dry out between waterings. Water more sparingly in cooler winter temperatures. ● Apply a balanced liquid fertilizer every 2–3 weeks during the growing season.

IMPATIENS WALLERIANA
Balsaminaceae

Impatiens

A popular and easily grown plant, impatiens or touch-me-not, has fleshy, succulent stems with lance-shaped to oval, toothed leaves. Flat-faced, usually spurred flowers, with a central eye, are carried in profusion in a wide range of colors: white, pink, red, carmine, salmon, orange, lavender, and bicolors. Plants may flower almost year-round.

There are many different varieties, some of which have larger flowers, darker bronze foliage, or double and semidouble flowers like miniature roses. The more compact, early, and free-flowering strains are most commonly produced commercially. New Guinea hybrids have attractive foliage, often with a central yellow stripe on the leaves. They produce plentiful flowers in summer, but they do not bloom so well during the wintertime.

FACT FILE

ORIGIN Warm temperate regions of Africa and Asia; New Guinea; hybrid.

HEIGHT To 18in/46cm.

POTTING MIX Peat-moss-based.

REPOTTING Repot only when the soil is filled with roots.

PROPAGATION In spring and summer, take soft stem cuttings, which root easily, or sow seed from early spring to early summer.

KEEPING PLANTS The plant is usually discarded when it becomes leggy. Bright light and regular feeding help to prolong its life.

PLANT CARE

Bright light but not direct hot summer sun. ● Normal room temperature, with a minimum of 55°F/13°C; for winter flowering 60°F/16°C or higher is necessary. ● Keep the soil moist at all times; reduce watering in winter. ● Give a high-potash liquid feed every 2 weeks in spring and summer to prolong flowering.

If the plant has a mass of foliage but few flowers, it has probably been overpotted. Wait until the soil is filled with roots before repotting, and avoid high-nitrogen fertilizers.

The plant flowers best when slightly potbound and so needs frequent watering, especially in warm conditions. Foliage wilts rapidly if the plant is short of water.

IRESINE HERBSTII
Amaranthaceae

Beefsteak Plant

The unusual color of the succulent stems and lance-shaped oval leaves of the beefsteak plant is caused by a pigment which masks the normal green chlorophyll of the leaf. Because this plant has such a vibrant color, it is also called the bloodleaf plant. Insignificant flowers are occasionally produced but are best pinched off because they detract from the colored foliage. In the variety 'Brilliantissima,' the veins are picked out in pink. 'Aureo-reticulata' has green leaves with yellow-marked veins, although stems and leafstalks are still red.

FACT FILE

ORIGIN Brazil.

HEIGHT To 2ft/60cm.

POTTING MIX Soil-based, with good drainage.

REPOTTING When roots emerge through the drainage holes in the bottom of the pot.

PROPAGATION By soft stem cuttings in spring and summer.

KEEPING PLANTS Pinch off the growing tips regularly to keep plants compact and bushy; discard them when they become leggy.

PLANT CARE

Bright light is essential to retain good leaf color, but shade from direct sun in midsummer. ● Normal room temperature, with a minimum of 55°F/13°C in winter. ● Keep the soil moist at all times in the growing season; reduce watering in winter. ● Mist the foliage occasionally in warm weather. ● Apply a standard liquid fertilizer every 2 weeks during the growing season.

The brilliant leaf color fades if the plant does not receive adequate light.

Watch out for aphid infestation of the soft young shoots. Treat with a contact insecticide when necessary.

Regular pinching off of the growing tips helps to keep plants compact. Once they become leggy, they can be replaced by cuttings, which are easy to root.

JASMINUM MESNYI
Oleaceae

Primrose Jasmine

This species was once known as *Jasminum primulinum* and is still sometimes sold under that name. It is a long-lived, scrambling, evergreen shrub with mid-green leaves divided into three leaflets. The bright yellow flowers are produced in spring and continue into the early summer; they are sometimes semidouble or double, and are carried singly in the leaf axils. Unlike those of the more popular members of the jasmine family, these flowers are unscented. The stems do not twine and need to be tied to thin stakes for support. If there is sufficient space, the plant will make a fine show trained on a wall trellis in a sunroom.

Tie the stems to thin stakes as they develop. This jasmine is an ideal plant for a sunroom or greenhouse, where it can be trained on a permanent wall trellis.

Trifoliate leaves are carried in opposite pairs on square stems and are evergreen in all but the coldest conditions.

FACT FILE

ORIGIN China.

HEIGHT To 10ft/3m.

POTTING MIX Soil-based.

REPOTTING In late spring move into a container one size larger. Once the maximum desired pot size has been reached, top-dress annually with fresh mix.

PROPAGATION Take stem cuttings between late spring and late summer; use soft tips in spring and semiripe wood later. You can improve the success rate by using a propagator with bottom heat.

KEEPING PLANTS This jasmine is long-lived and needs little attention other than tying in to its support and pruning to limit its size.

PLANT CARE

Bright light with some direct sun. ● Cool room temperature, with a range of 50°–65°F/10°–18°C. ● Keep the soil just moist at all times. ● Give a balanced liquid feed every 2–3 weeks during the period of active growth.

JASMINUM POLYANTHUM
Oleaceae

CHINESE JASMINE

This vigorous climber with wiry, branching stems is the most popular jasmine grown as a houseplant. Flowers are carried in winter and spring in large clusters arising from the leaf axils near the stem tips. They have a long tube and open to a small white star. The buds, tubes, and sometimes the reverse of the petals are deep pink. The intensely fragrant flowers—a single plant will scent a large room—are occasionally followed by small black berries. It may lose its leaves.

FACT FILE

ORIGIN China.

HEIGHT To 10ft/3m.

POTTING MIX Soil-based.

REPOTTING In summer as necessary; plants flower best when slightly pot-bound.

PROPAGATION Take semiripe cuttings in summer or soft stem cuttings in spring.

KEEPING PLANTS Cut out older, flowered stems in summer. Train new growth gently around a hoop to encourage prolific flowering.

PLANT CARE

Bright light with some direct sun. ● Normal to cool temperature, 50°–65°F/10°–18°C. ● Keep the soil moist in the growing season. Allow the surface to dry out between waterings in winter. ● Mist the foliage regularly. ● When the plants come into bud, apply a high-potash liquid fertilizer every 2 weeks.

Leaves may turn black if conditions are too cold in winter. Take off the affected leaves and move the plant to a position that is slightly warmer.

Repot only when the soil is filled with roots. Overpotting may cause lush, leafy growth and a failure to flower.

JUSTICIA CARNEA
Acanthaceae

BRAZILIAN PLUME

Also known as *Jacobinia carnea*, this is a shrubby plant with ovate or lance-shaped leaves up to 6in/15cm long. Leaves are often slightly furry and rather coarse in appearance. Flowers are produced in late summer and fall in dense plumes about 5in/13cm long. They are tubular and rosy pink with green bracts, and give the plant the common names pink acanthus and king's crown.

Tall plumes of shaggy rose pink flowers are carried in late summer and fall.

Growing tips should be regularly pinched off to keep the plant compact and bushy.

Take cuttings in spring from overwintered plants to provide replacements for those that are past their best.

Red spider mites can cause mottled, pale foliage with webbing visible around the young leaves. Increase the humidity by more frequent spraying.

FACT FILE

ORIGIN South America.

HEIGHT To 4ft/1.2m, but usually kept below this by pinching.

POTTING MIX Soil-based.

REPOTTING Whenever roots appear through the drainage holes in the base of the pot.

PROPAGATION Take stem cuttings in spring.

KEEPING PLANTS Cut stems back by half after flowering and give the plant a winter rest at about 55°F/13°C. Discard after 2 years.

PLANT CARE

Bright light with some direct sun, especially in winter. ● Minimum of 60°F/16°C in winter; otherwise, normal room temperature. ● Keep the soil thoroughly moist in the growing season; reduce watering in winter. ● Mist regularly while the plant is in active growth. ● Apply a balanced liquid fertilizer every 2 weeks from spring to fall.

CRASSULACEAE

KALANCHOES

This is an extremely varied group of plants, all of which are succulent to some degree; they are grown for either their foliage or their flowers. Because they all have more or less fleshy leaves, they are tolerant of a dry atmosphere and are good plants in heated houses; they will also thrive in a sunny spot where many other plants would wilt and fade. The leaves grow in pairs opposite each other, and the four-petaled tubular flowers are borne in panicles at the ends of the stems.

Probably the most popular species is *Kalanchoe blossfeldiana*, flaming Katy. Its natural flowering season is from late fall to early spring, but by cutting down the hours of daylight the plant receives in summer, growers can bring it into flower at almost any time of the year. It is a bushy plant with fleshy dark green leaves that are oval with a toothed margin and are often tinged with red at the edges and on the undersides. Small tubular flowers are carried in dense panicles on tall stems rising above the foliage.

Most of the kalanchoes grown as houseplants are fairly small, but some, such as *K. beharensis*, velvet-leaf, grow into specimens up to 4ft/1.2m tall. This species has triangular hairy leaves about 6in/15cm long. On the small *K. tomentosa*, the hairs are so fine and soft that they are more like fur. Most of the other species grown indoors have more typically succulent leaves with a smooth surface that is either shiny or has a waxy bloom.

Kalanchoe blossfeldiana hybrids produce dense panicles of up to 50 small flowers that are long-lasting and available in a good choice of colors. The most common is scarlet, but plants with yellow, white, orange, and pink flowers, like the hybrid 'Calypso' shown here, are easy to find.

Choose a plant with bright, fresh-looking leaves and flower stems with plenty of unopened buds.

Leaves are fleshy and succulent, and are usually flushed with red when the plant is kept in a sunny location.

ALSO RECOMMENDED

Kalanchoe manginii 'Tessa' is a good plant for a hanging basket. It has reddish wiry stems that bear loose panicles of flowers like dainty drooping bells. The flowers are usually salmon or pink with green tips.

Kalanchoe tomentosa, called panda plant or pussy ears, has rosettes of thick pointed leaves covered with silvery "fur." The leaf tips and margins are marked with brown.

Kalanchoe marmorata is commonly known as the penwiper because its blue-green, rounded fleshy leaves are blotched with purple-brown. Panicles of white flowers are sometimes borne.

Mealybugs commonly infest this plant. They appear as white, wooly patches, usually near the leaf stalk. Remove them with a damp cloth or cotton swab as soon as you see them.

The leaves are brittle and can be damaged by careless handling. Tips break away easily, leaving a brown line across the leaf.

Lower leaves will shrivel or turn yellow if the soil is allowed to become too dry.

If the plant droops and wilts for no explicable reason, take it out of its pot and check to see whether root mealybugs are the cause.

FACT FILE

ORIGIN Madagascar; tropical Africa.

HEIGHT 10–24in/25–60cm indoors; *Kalanchoe marmorata* will reach 4ft/1.2m outdoors.

POTTING MIX Soil-based with added sand or perlite.

REPOTTING In spring move plants that are not being discarded into pots one size larger.

PROPAGATION Take stem cuttings in spring. Kalanchoes can also be propagated from leaf cuttings and from seed. Home-propagated plants will flower in their natural season— late winter and spring—not necessarily the same flowering season as the plant you bought.

KEEPING PLANTS *K. blossfeldiana* is normally discarded after it has flowered, since it is difficult to bring it into flower again indoors. A second flowering can sometimes be achieved by giving the plant a rest period after flowering, then standing it on a bright windowsill. In mild conditions, stand the plant outdoors in a well-lit, lightly shaded spot for a spell to encourage it to flower again. Failure of the plant to flower at the expected time can be caused by exposing it to artificial light.

PLANT CARE

Bright light with some direct sun, especially in winter ● Normal room temperature, with a minimum of 50°F/10°C. Give plants grown especially for their foliage, such as *K. pumila*, a winter rest at 50°–55°F/ 10°–13°C. ● Water fairly sparingly, allowing the top 1in/2.5cm of the soil to dry out between waterings. Reduce watering in cooler winter temperatures when plants are resting. ● Apply a balanced liquid fertilizer every 3 weeks during the period of active growth and flowering.

PESTS & DISEASES

Kalanchoes may occasionally be attacked by tarsonemid mites, especially strawberry mites, but they are more commonly infested with mealybugs and root mealybugs. Otherwise, kalanchoes are largely trouble-free plants.

Kalanchoe pumila is a low-growing, branching plant. Its oval leaves have toothed edges and a white, waxy covering that gives them a bright, silver-blue appearance. Little lilac-pink flowers with deeper purplish lines on the petals are produced in clusters in late winter or early spring. It is displayed to best advantage in a hanging basket.

LANTANA CAMARA
Verbenaceae

Yellow Sage

The wrinkled, rather coarse, ovate, toothed leaves of this lantana are similar to those of sage, giving the plant its common name. But the flowers, which bloom between late spring and mid fall, are quite different, being more like those of the related verbena. They are carried in flattened or slightly rounded heads, and each flower is small and tubular, with a central eye. Buds open from the outside ring of the flower head. The plant shown here is the plain yellow 'Sundancer,' a spreading variety good in a hanging basket. But in 'Chelsea Gem,' the flowers start yellow, then darken through orange to orange-red. Thus as successive rings of flowers open toward the center, two or three distinct colors exist within each head. White, lilac, pink, red, and many bicolored varieties are also found.

The flowers are attractive to butterflies when the plant is grown in a place to which they have access.

Lantana is prone to attack by whiteflies. Spray several times with insecticide for good control.

Pinch off the growing points regularly to keep the plant bushy.

FACT FILE

ORIGIN Tropical America; cultivars.

HEIGHT To 6ft/1.8m, but usually kept to 12in/30cm in the home.

POTTING MIX Soil- or peat-moss-based.

REPOTTING In spring, only when the potting mix is tightly packed with roots; flowering is improved when plants are slightly pot-bound.

PROPAGATION Take soft stem cuttings in early summer.

KEEPING PLANTS Rest plants in winter in cool, dry conditions. Cut back stems to 4–5in/10–13cm in late winter, just before new growth begins. Stand plants outdoors in summer in mild sunny weather to improve their health.

PLANT CARE

Bright light with some direct sun, especially in winter. ● A temperature of about 50°F/10°C in winter, otherwise, normal room temperature. ● Keep the soil moist in the growing season; give just enough water to prevent the soil from drying out in winter. ● Stand the pot on moist pebbles to increase humidity from spring to fall. ● Apply a standard liquid fertilizer every 2 weeks in the period of active growth.

LITHOPS LESLIEI
Aizoaceae

Living Stones

This curious, long-lived succulent has the distinct appearance of grayish pebbles, hence the other common names stone plant and pebble plant. The fleshy, swollen leaves, arising from a short underground stem, are produced in pairs. But they are fused for virtually their entire length, having only a slit across the top that splits them into two parts, often of unequal size. Leaves are frequently gray with mottled, light brown markings, but other species have a range of stone colors. After two or three years, daisylike, bright yellow flowers with many shaggy petals are produced in fall. These emerge from the split between the leaves and are often larger than the leaves themselves. They rest on the leaf surface and may cover the plant completely. Once the flowers have faded, the leaves begin to shrivel, and a new pair pushes up through the split to replace them.

FACT FILE

ORIGIN South Africa.

HEIGHT 1–2in/2.5–5cm.

POTTING MIX Soil-based, with coarse sand added for good drainage.

REPOTTING After several years, when clumps become crowded. Use a standard-depth pot rather than a shallow pan, because this species forms relatively long taproots.

PROPAGATION Divide clumps in early summer, or grow from seed. Seedlings take several years to reach flowering size.

KEEPING PLANTS Lithops are best grown several together in a fairly large pan to help to keep the potting mix at a constant level.

PLANT CARE

Bright light, with several hours of direct sun. ● Minimum winter temperature of 50°F/10°C. ● Keep the soil barely moist from spring to fall; let the top half dry out between waterings. When the flowers have faded and the old leaves are shriveling, withhold water until the following spring. ● It is not necessary to feed lithops.

Lithops needs plenty of bright light and is an excellent plant for a sunny windowsill.

The large, daisylike flowers are fairly short-lived, but make a colorful sight when they appear.

The fleshy leaves vary in color, but are always natural stone shades. They are often mottled.

Overwatering causes the plant to rot. The fleshy leaves become wrinkled and shriveled after flowering. A new pair will replace them.

MAMMILLARIA BOCASANA
Cactaceae

POWDER-PUFF CACTUS

The cylindrical or globular stems of this cactus eventually form a large, rounded clump. Many silky white hairs arising from areoles (cushion-like bumps) on the stems cover the plant and give it its powder puff appearance. Each areole also bears one or more yellow-brown, hooked central spines, which are longer and stiffer than the silky hairs. The spines are sharp, so put the plant where people will not brush against it, hurting themselves and damaging the plant.

Like many mammillarias, this species blooms freely while it is still young. The flowers are produced in spring in a ring near the top of the stems and are yellow or creamy white and about ¹/₂in/13mm wide.

FACT FILE

ORIGIN Mexico.

HEIGHT To 2in/5cm.

POTTING MIX Soil- or peat-moss-based and grit in equal quantities.

REPOTTING After several years, when the clump is overcrowded. Handle the clump by means of a strip of newspaper to protect your hands and to cause minimum damage to the plant. A wide, shallow pan is most suitable.

PROPAGATION In spring and summer, remove offsets from the edge of a clump and pot up separately. Plants can also be grown from seed.

KEEPING PLANTS Plants will last for many years, given proper attention.

PLANT CARE

Bright, direct sunlight. ● Minimum winter temperature of 50°F/10°C. ● Water moderately from spring to fall, keeping the soil just moist but letting the top ¹/₂in/13mm of soil dry out between waterings. In winter, water just enough to prevent the soil from drying out completely. ● Apply high-potash fertilizer once a month during the growing season.

ALSO RECOMMENDED

Mammillaria zeilmanniana, the rose pincushion, produces large numbers of deep cerise flowers in summer.

More than 150 species of mammillaria are cultivated, most of which do not grow higher than 8in/20cm. Many start out as simple columnar plants, forming clusters and flowering only when they are 4 or 5 years old. But even without flowers, the plants are attractive, with their spiral pattern of spine-bearing areoles.

Stout hooked spines in the center of each areole catch easily on clothing, often causing damage to the plant's stem.

Too much water can cause the stems to rot and collapse from the base. Never let water remain on the surface of the soil, and water only around the outside of the clump.

Mealybugs—sap-sucking insects covered in waxy white wool— often lodge between the areoles under the spines and are difficult to control. Use a systemic insecticide to deal with them.

Mandevilla **x** *amoena* '**Alice du Pont**'
Apocynaceae

*M*andevilla

Many species of mandevilla used to be known as *Dipladenia*, and they are still often offered under that name. The most readily available plant is *Mandevilla* x *amoena* 'Alice du Pont,' a hybrid resulting from a backcross of *M. amabilis* and *M. splendens*. It has glossy, deep green, ovate leaves on twining stems and large, funnel-shaped flowers, which are carried throughout the summer. The scrolled buds open to pink, with a darker pink throat shading to yellow deep in the throat.

Mandevillas are handsome plants for a sunroom, where they can be grown in large tubs. They do well in borders, where they can be trained up a support against a wall. In pots they can be provided with stakes or a trellis, or the climbing shoots can be cut back after flowering to keep the plant bushy.

FACT FILE

ORIGIN Brazil; hybrids.

HEIGHT To 10ft/3m when allowed to climb.

POTTING MIX Free-draining, soil-based medium.

REPOTTING Annually in spring until the maximum desired pot size is reached, then top-dress with fresh soil.

PROPAGATION Not easy. Take soft stem cuttings in spring and root them in a propagator with bottom heat.

KEEPING PLANTS Cut stems back hard after flowering to keep growth bushy and promote flowering shoots the following year.

PLANT CARE

Fairly bright light, but no direct sun. ● Minimum winter temperature of 55°F/13°C. ● Water plentifully, allowing the surface of the soil to dry out between waterings. Water more sparingly in winter. ● Mist the foliage regularly. ● Give high-potash fertilizer every 2 weeks in the growing season.

Look out for scale insects on the undersides of the leathery foliage; if they are present, scrape them off with a fingernail.

The attractive pink flowers are often 4in/10cm or more wide.

Mandevilla does best in a large pot or tub, and when grown in a small pot the plant is often short-lived.

Manettia inflata
Rubiaceae

*F*irecracker vine

The freely branching, twining stems of this climber, occasionally sold as *Manettia bicolor* or *M. luteo-rubra*, bear lance-shaped, bright green leaves in opposite pairs. The plant can be trained up stakes or a trellis, and will also trail attractively when grown in a hanging basket. The colorful, tubular, hairy flowers, arising from the leaf axils on 1-in/2.5-cm stalks, are orange-red tipped with yellow and about ³⁄₄in/2cm long. They are produced in great profusion for most of the summer and sometimes well into the fall. This species is also known as the Brazilian firecracker.

FACT FILE

ORIGIN South America.

HEIGHT To 10ft/3m.

POTTING MIX Soil-based or peat-moss-based.

REPOTTING Move into a pot one size larger whenever roots appear through the drainage holes in the base of the pot.

PROPAGATION In spring and early summer, take soft stem cuttings from nonflowering shoots.

KEEPING PLANTS Cut back stems by half in spring to promote new growth and maintain the plant's shape.

PLANT CARE

Bright light with some direct sun. ● A minimum winter temperature of 55°F/13°C; otherwise, normal room temperature. ● Keep the soil moist throughout the growing season; water more sparingly in winter. ● Mist the foliage occasionally. ● Give a high-potash fertilizer every 2 weeks during the period of active growth.

The vigorous, slender, twining stems can be trained around stakes, up a trellis, or even allowed to trail.

Brightly colored tubular flowers are often carried in such large numbers that they almost obscure the foliage.

The oval leaves usually have short stalks but are sometimes stalkless.

MARANTA LEUCONEURA
Marantaceae

PRAYER PLANT

The brightly marked, attractively feathered foliage of marantas is similar to that of calatheas and ctenanthes, to which they are closely related. Marantas have earned their common name of prayer plant because of the way in which their leaves tend to fold up at night and unfold the following morning, sometimes with a distinct rustling noise. The blunt leaves are oval, strikingly veined, and patterned on the surface, often red below, with clasping leaf stalks. Three varieties of *Maranta leuconeura* are commonly grown.

FACT FILE

ORIGIN Brazil.

HEIGHT To 10in/25cm.

POTTING MIX Soil-based.

REPOTTING In spring, when roots appear through the drainage holes in the base of the pot, usually every other year. Marantas have a shallow rooting system and do best in a shallow pot or half pot.

PROPAGATION Divide clumps by pulling them apart carefully in spring.

KEEPING PLANTS Plants will last for several years provided they are repotted and fed regularly.

PLANT CARE

Moderate light with no direct sun; leaf colors fade and leaves curl in very bright conditions. ● Thrives in temperatures up to 75°F/24°C, with a minimum winter temperature of 65°F/18°C. ● Keep the soil moist throughout the growing season; water sparingly in winter. ● Mist the foliage regularly with lime-free water, and stand the pot on a dish of moist pebbles. ● Apply a balanced liquid fertilizer every 2 weeks during the growing season.

Maranta leuconeura erythroneura, the herringbone plant, with its shiny dark and pale green leaves with bright red veins, is the most colorful of the marantas.

ALSO RECOMMENDED

Maranta leuconeura leuconeura, which is often called *M.l. massangeana,* has dark, velvety green leaves with silver veins and a silver central section along the midrib.

M.l. erythroneura, herringbone plant, has dark green, satiny leaves with prominent red veins and irregular yellow-green patches behind the midrib. It is also sold as *M. tricolor.*

M.l. kerchoveana, rabbit tracks, has pale green leaves with lighter veins and irregular purple-brown blotches on each side of the midrib which give it its common name. It is much less striking than the other two varieties but is still popular.

Red spider mites attack the plant in warm, dry conditions. Increase humidity by frequent misting to combat these pests.

Dust the leaves lightly with a soft, dry cloth or feather duster to avoid spoiling the satiny leaf surface. Do not use a damp cloth to clean the leaves.

The leaves of most varieties naturally fold up and become more erect at night; this does not indicate that there is anything wrong with the plant.

Leaf tips and margins become papery and brown if the air is too dry; mist the plants regularly with lime-free water to make sure that chalky deposits do not spoil the appearance of the leaves.

MEDINILLA MAGNIFICA
Melastomalaceae

ROSE GRAPE

This is one of the most striking flowering plants grown indoors. It can become extremely large with an equally large spread, but it is not easy to keep and is normally treated as a short-term plant. It needs a big pot or tub and will do best if grown in a sunroom.

The angular stems carry pairs of leathery, glossy, dark green, ovate leaves that are stalkless and deeply veined. They are about 1ft/30cm long and half as wide. In late spring, long pendulous flower stalks, which can be up to 18in/46cm overall, are produced from the tips of the branches. The small, rosy pink flowers with yellow stamens are carried in long panicles beneath two or three tiers of bright pink bracts.

This plant is prone to attack by red spider mites, particularly in warm, dry conditions. Mist the foliage frequently to increase humidity.

The pendulous flower heads are spectacular in spring and early summer. Plants with deeper pink flowers are sometimes available.

Medinilla demands warmth and high humidity, and is difficult to grow well in the home. Sunroom conditions suit it better.

FACT FILE

ORIGIN Philippines.

HEIGHT To 4ft/1.2m.

POTTING MIX Soil-based, with added peat moss.

REPOTTING In spring every year until the maximum desired pot size is reached, then top-dress annually with fresh potting mix.

PROPAGATION Not practical by amateurs.

KEEPING PLANTS Cut back the shoots by about half after flowering and give the plant a winter rest in slightly cooler conditions. Reduce watering but continue to mist the foliage regularly.

PLANT CARE

Bright, filtered light with no direct sun. ● Warm conditions, about 70°F/21°C; a minimum winter temperature of 60°F/16°C. ● Keep the soil moist during the growing season, but allow the surface to dry out between waterings. Water sparingly in winter. ● Mist the foliage frequently and stand the pot on a tray of moist pebbles. High humidity is essential. ● Give a high-potash liquid feed every 2 weeks from the time the flower buds start to form until the autumn.

MONSTERA DELICIOSA
Araceae

SWISS CHEESE PLANT

A popular, tolerant foliage plant, monstera can become a large and striking specimen. It has a rather sprawling, scrambling habit and climbs by means of thick, fleshy aerial roots, which are freely produced from the stem. The young plant bears entire heart-shaped leaves, and if it receives adequate light as it develops, it will produce deeply cut adult foliage. Characteristic holes and deep splits from the margin almost to the midrib of the large, glossy, deep green leaves are responsible for its other common names split leaf and window plant.

'*Deliciosa*,' meaning pleasing, refers to the white spadix that on a mature plant may develop into an aggregate of white berries with a tropical fruit flavor, giving it the common names Mexican breadfruit and fruit salad plant.

Yellowing lower leaves are usually a sign of overwatering. Keep the soil just moist and do not allow the pot to stand in water.

Aerial roots low on the plant can be pushed into the soil, where they will help to provide nutrients and moisture. Higher roots can be removed or trained into a moss pole.

FACT FILE

ORIGIN Mexico.

HEIGHT To 10ft/3m.

POTTING MIX Soil-based, with some added peat moss.

REPOTTING In spring, when roots fill the pot—usually every other year.

PROPAGATION By small tip cuttings in spring, or air layering when the plant becomes too large.

KEEPING PLANTS A pole covered in moss is an ideal support for this plant; keep the moss moist and train the aerial roots to grow into it.

PLANT CARE

Fairly good light, but no direct sun. In shade, the leaves will be smaller and less perforated. ● A minimum winter temperature of 50°F/10°C; otherwise, 65°–75°F/18°–24°C. ● Water moderately in the growing season, but allow the surface to dry out between waterings. Give less water in winter. ● Mist the foliage regularly in warm conditions. ● Give a balanced liquid feed every 2 weeks from spring until fall.

NARCISSUS SPP.
Amaryllidaceae

DAFFODIL

Grown as houseplants during the winter, these bulbs are a wonderful harbinger of spring, when they flower naturally outdoors. There are dozens of varieties suitable for growing indoors, which can be bought in bud in winter or as specially treated bulbs. Bulbs can be planted from fall onward and will flower long before they would outside. Narcissus should be treated in the same way as hyacinth (see p. 98). They need a cold, dark period of about eight weeks after planting.

The foliage of narcissus is mid- to pale green, long, and strap-shaped. Flowers are in many shades of yellow or white and have several different forms. Perhaps most familiar is the trumpet daffodil, such as 'King Alfred' shown here, with its ring of petals backing a long, frilled trumpet (where the trumpet is as long as the petals, the variety tends to be commonly known as a daffodil; otherwise, it is called a narcissus). The trumpet, or cup, may be the same color as the petals or a contrasting shade. Other types have short, flared trumpets, or cups; in double varieties, the trumpets, or cups, are replaced by extra layers of frilly petals. Flowers may be carried singly on the stems or in bunches, and many varieties are sweetly scented. Size varies considerably, from tiny dwarf forms to large-flowered, tall hybrids.

FACT FILE

ORIGIN Temperate zones of Europe, Asia, and North Africa.

HEIGHT To 18in/46cm, depending on variety.

POTTING MIX Peat-moss-based potting mix, rather than bulb fiber if the bulbs are to be planted outdoors after flowering.

REPOTTING None. It is not worthwhile trying to grow treated bulbs indoors for a second year.

PROPAGATION By offsets produced around the base of the bulb.

KEEPING PLANTS Allow to dry off when the leaves die down, remove bulbs from the pot, and store in a cool, dry place until fall, when they can be planted out in the garden.

PLANT CARE

Keep bulbs in total darkness after planting until the shoots are about 3in/8cm high, then bring them into bright light out of direct sun.
● Keep bulbs at 40°F/4°C during the dark period; bring them into the light at about 50°F/10°C until the buds show color, then keep at a maximum of 60°F/16°C in their flowering positions. ● Keep the soil just moist until the leaves fade, then allow it to dry out. If you want to plant the bulbs outdoors, do not stop watering until the leaves begin to yellow. ● Apply a high-potash liquid fertilizer every 2 weeks until the leaves start to fade.

ALSO RECOMMENDED

Dwarf varieties are excellent for pot cultivation and include the cyclamineus hybrids 'February Silver,' 'February Gold,' and 'Tête-à-Tête,' the jonquil 'Baby Moon,' and the bunch-flowered tazetta narcissus 'Minnow.' Among the larger varieties, 'Paperwhite' is particularly easy to grow; it requires no cold, dark period and flowers 4 to 6 weeks from planting. 'Carlton' is a large, clear yellow; 'Ice Follies' is white with a creamy yellow cup, while 'Fortune' has soft yellow petals and a cup tipped with an intense orange.

Narcissus 'Paperwhite' is one of the Tazetta hybrids. It produce several flowers to a stem and is easy to grow, requiring no dark, cold period to bring it into bloom. It has a delicious sweet scent.

Excessive warmth will shorten the life of flowers and may cause buds to shrivel and turn brown, preventing them from opening.

The flowers may be a range of shades of white, cream, yellow, and orange; some varieties even have a pink tinge. Contrasting trumpet, or cups, are particularly attractive.

Keep the plants in a bright location to prevent the stems from becoming too tall and leggy. Support the flower stems of tall varieties with green split canes.

Bunch-flowered 'Soleil d'Or' and 'Paperwhite' can be grown in glasses of water or in wet pebbles. They will flower within 6 weeks with no cold, dark period necessary and are deliciously fragrant.

NEOREGELIA CAROLINAE 'TRICOLOR'
Bromeliaceae

*B*LUSHING BROMELIAD

The rosette-forming, strap-shaped leaves of this bromeliad can reach 12in/30cm or more long. They are glossy green, striped along their length with creamy yellow, which flushes pink as the leaves age, and have spiny-toothed edges. Just before flowering, the central leaves turn a brilliant, long-lasting rosy red; the flowers themselves are purplish blue and rather insignificant. The rosette dies back after flowering, but offsets are freely produced to take its place.

Scale insects are often found on the undersides of the leaves. Scrape them off carefully with a fingernail and treat the plant with a systemic insecticide if the infestation is severe.

The central foliage turns bright red just before the plant flowers. This red coloration and the cream and pink stripes on the foliage develop best in bright light.

Keep the center of the rosette half-full of water. Drain it once a month by tipping the plant carefully on one side, then refill the rosette.

The base of the plant may rot if the soil is overwatered. Keep the soil just moist during the summer: do not saturate it.

FACT FILE

ORIGIN Brazil.

HEIGHT 9–12in/23–30cm.

POTTING MIX Soil-based, with some added peat moss or leaf mold, or soil- and peat-moss-based in equal parts, both with coarse sand or shredded bark added for good drainage.

REPOTTING In spring as necessary. Do not overpot.

PROPAGATION Remove offsets in spring and pot up separately. If the offset does not have roots, root in a propagator with bottom heat.

KEEPING PLANTS Once the main rosette has completely died back after flowering, pot up the offsets that are produced to replace it.

PLANT CARE

Bright light with several hours of direct sun daily for good leaf color. ● Normal room temperature, with a minimum of 50°F/10°C. ● Keep the soil just moist, allowing the surface to dry out between waterings; top up the cup in the center of the rosette with water regularly. ● Mist the foliage daily in summer and stand the pot on a tray of moist pebbles. ● Apply a half-strength solution of balanced liquid fertilizer every 3–4 weeks in summer; pour it into the center of the rosette as well as on the soil.

NEPHROLEPIS EXALTATA 'BOSTONIENSIS'
Oleandraceae

*S*WORD FERN

Also known as Boston fern, this is the most commonly grown variety of nephrolepis. It produces a spreading rosette of broad trailing bright green fronds up to 4ft/1.2m long. These fronds are upright at first and arch over slightly as they grow. Brown spore cases can be seen on the undersides of the pinnae, or leaflets. The much divided fronds have given rise to another common name: ladder fern.

Wiry runners carry young plantlets that root readily to cover the surface of the soil. These ferns are best grown in hanging baskets or displayed on a pedestal where their graceful habit can be appreciated.

FACT FILE

ORIGIN Tropical and subtropical regions.

HEIGHT 9–12in/23–30cm.

POTTING MIX Peat-moss-based.

REPOTTING In spring, when roots emerge through the drainage holes in the base of the pot.

PROPAGATION Cut young plantlets away from the runners and pot up.

KEEPING PLANTS This fern will grow steadily all year-round, given the right conditions. When the plant has reached the maximum desired size, trim off some of the roots in spring and repot in the same pot.

PLANT CARE

Bright light but no direct sun; the fern will tolerate some shade. ● Normal room temperature, with a winter minimum of 50°F/10°C. ● Keep the soil thoroughly moist, but do not allow the pot to stand in water. If the temperature falls to near the minimum, reduce watering and let the top 1in/2.5cm of soil dry out before rewatering. ● Mist the foliage daily in summer and stand the pot on a tray of moist pebbles. ● Give a balanced liquid fertilizer every 2–3 weeks in summer.

Scale insects can be troublesome. Either scratch them off with a fingernail or treat affected plants with insecticide at about ¼ strength. Later, remove any residue by spraying with water.

Avoid brown tips to the foliage by regular misting to increase humidity around the plant.

The brown spore cases carried in two rows on the underside of each pinna are sometimes mistaken for scale insects.

Keep the soil moist at all times. If it dries out in the growing season, the fronds will yellow and die.

NERIUM OLEANDER
Apocynaceae

OLEANDER

An attractive sun-loving shrub for the home, oleander has dark green, narrow, lance-shaped leaves on woody, branching stems. The flat-faced, funnel-shaped flowers are carried at the ends of the stems in groups of eight or so and are up to 2in/5cm wide. Typically, flowers are rose pink, but there are also red, white, apricot, salmon pink, and yellow varieties, and some double-flowered forms. Oleander is a member of the periwinkle family, and some similarity can be seen in the flowers. All parts of this plant are poisonous. Do not grow if children or pets share the home.

The attractive pink, red, white, or yellow flowers are carried in groups at the tips of the stems. Some varieties are fragrant.

The baylike foliage and rose pink flowers give oleander its alternative common name of rose bay.

Established plants can make quite large, bushy shrubs; a sunroom is an ideal place for them.

Scale insects are a common problem. Remove scales found on the undersides of the leaves with a fingernail and spray the plant with insecticide if necessary.

FACT FILE

ORIGIN Mediterranean regions; Asia.

HEIGHT To 6ft/1.8m and more.

POTTING MIX Soil-based.

REPOTTING In spring, when roots emerge through the drainage holes in the base of the pot. Plants do best in large pots or tubs.

PROPAGATION Take stem cuttings in early summer.

KEEPING PLANTS After flowering, put the plant in a sheltered spot outdoors until fall to ripen the wood for good flowering the following year.

PLANT CARE

Bright light with several hours of direct sun. ● Normal room temperature, with a winter rest at 55°F/13°C and a minimum of 45°F/7°C. ● Keep the soil evenly moist in the growing season, especially when the buds are forming. Water more sparingly in winter. ● Apply a balanced liquid fertilizer every 2 weeks in summer.

NIDULARIUM INNOCENTII
Bromeliaceae

BIRD'S-NEST BROMELIAD

This bromeliad is closely related to neoregelia and has a similar appearance. The plant forms a rosette of 12-in/30-cm-long, strap-shaped leaves with spiny margins; they are purplish green, with a metallic sheen. In the center of the rosette, the leaves are much shorter and turn brick red just before the plant flowers in fall, producing white blooms carried in clusters. There are two striped varieties, 'Lineatum' and 'Striatum,' which are very similar, with white stripes running the length of the leaf; 'Striatum' tends to have broader stripes.

FACT FILE

ORIGIN Brazil.

HEIGHT 9–12in/23–30cm.

POTTING MIX Soilless with some added peat moss, or soil- and peat-moss-based in equal amounts, both with added coarse sand or shredded bark for good drainage.

REPOTTING In spring, only when roots fill the pot.

PROPAGATION Pot offsets individually in spring.

KEEPING PLANTS When it is 3–4 years old, nidularium flowers once only from each rosette, which then dies. Replace them with young offsets.

PLANT CARE

Bright light but without direct sun. ● Minimum winter temperature of 55°F/13°C, but preferably 60°F/16°C or above. Normal room temperature in summer. ● Keep the soil moist in the growing season, but allow the top to dry out between waterings. In winter, water sparingly. Keep the central cup filled with water; replace the water every 4 weeks. ● Apply half-strength balanced liquid fertilizer every 3 weeks in the growing season.

The undersides of the spiny-toothed leaves are flushed purple.

The center of the rosette turns bright red at flowering time, which can occur at any time of year, but most often in fall.

The natural home of nidularium is tropical rain forest, and it demands high humidity to grow well. Mist frequently and stand the pot on a tray of moist pebbles.

OCIMUM BASILICUM
Lamiacae

Sweet Basil

A popular aromatic herb for use in the kitchen, basil also makes an attractive houseplant. Among the many varieties available are 'Dark Opal' with purple-black foliage, 'Ruffles' and 'Purple Ruffles,' with large, strongly undulating and ruffled leaves in purple or green, and 'Crispum,' the lettuce-leaved basil, with large, undulating leaves up to 4in/10cm long.

Plants have the typical square stems of the mint family, with ovate leaves carried in opposite pairs. These are normally soft-textured, rather fleshy, and light green, with an intense, peppery, clovelike aroma. The plant is a fast-growing, small, lax bush. Heads of hooded white flowers are carried at the tips of the stems, but these are usually pinched off in bud to encourage the production of foliage. Keep the plant bushy by pinching off growing tips regularly.

FACT FILE

ORIGIN Asia.

HEIGHT To 2ft/60cm.

POTTING MIX Soil- or peat-moss-based.

REPOTTING When roots emerge from the holes in the base of the pot.

PROPAGATION Sow seed in early spring.

KEEPING PLANTS Basil is an annual, but plants can be kept through much of the winter by sowing seed in early summer and pinching off flower buds as soon as they are seen. Stand plants outdoors in warm summer weather.

PLANT CARE

Bright light, with 3–4 hours of sunshine; shade the plant from very hot sun, which will scorch the leaves. ● Normal room temperature. ● Keep the soil moist at all times. ● Apply a half-strength balanced liquid fertilizer every week during the spring and summer.

Pinching off the growing tips keeps plants bushy and compact. If the herb is used in the kitchen, this will happen as a matter of course.

If whiteflies are a problem, destroy affected plants and raise new ones from seed. Using an insecticide is not usually worthwhile.

Varieties with large leaves, ruffled edges, and unusual colors are attractive, but the plain-leafed type has the strongest flavor and aroma.

ODONTOGLOSSUM GRANDE
Orchidaceae

Tiger Orchid

The striking flowers of this odontoglossum, also known as *Rossioglossum grande,* are made up of petals and sepals of similar colors. Each large, egg-shaped pseudobulb produces a pair of mid green, lance-shaped leaves about 12in/30cm long. Flower stems are produced from late summer to spring and carry up to seven or eight clear yellow flowers with reddish brown stripes, which give the plant its most frequently used common name; it is also called the clown orchid. The lip of the bloom is white with brown bands. Each flower can be as much as 7in/18cm wide.

Although they originate in tropical America, odontoglossums grow at high elevations in cool mountainous regions and do not thrive if the temperature is too high.

Odontoglossums need high humidity, even though they like cool conditions. Mist the plant frequently and stand the pot on a tray of damp pebbles.

Egg-shaped pseudobulbs grow in clusters, and each one is up to 4in/10cm long. They produce leaves in pairs or occasionally threes.

Free drainage is important. Use a special orchid medium, and make sure there is a good layer of pebbles at the bottom of the pot.

FACT FILE

ORIGIN Mexico; Guatemala.

HEIGHT Flower stems to 12in/30cm.

POTTING MIX Special orchid medium, usually containing bark, perlite, and osmunda fiber or sphagnum moss in varying proportions.

REPOTTING Annually in spring or fall. Use a clay pot and place a good layer of pebbles in the base for drainage.

PROPAGATION Divide large clumps into groups of healthy pseudobulbs by cutting through the rhizome with a sharp knife.

KEEPING PLANTS Under the right conditions this orchid is long-lived.

PLANT CARE

Bright, diffuse light with no direct sun. ● A temperature range of 50°–65°F/10°–18°C. ● In the growing season, water thoroughly with lime-free water but let the surface dry out between waterings. Water less in the winter rest period. ● Apply a half-strength balanced liquid fertilizer as a foliar spray every 2 weeks in the growing season or use a commercial orchid fertilizer.

OPHIOPOGON JABURAN
Liliaceae

WHITE LILY-TURF

This is the only species of this plant that is grown as a houseplant. The grasslike foliage, rising directly from the roots, forms a good contrast with the more rounded shapes of other plants. The narrow leathery leaves, up to 18in/46cm long, arch over gracefully to make a fountainlike clump. In late summer or fall, from the center of each tuft, a flower stem arises. It bears tubular, creamy white or pale lilac nodding blooms, which are sometimes followed by violet-blue berries.

A variegated form with creamy stripes running the length of the leaf is most often seen as a houseplant. It may be offered as 'Variegatus,' 'Argenteo-variegatus,' or 'Javanensis,' all of which are synonymous with the variety 'Vittatus.' The stripes on the leaves of 'Aureo-variegatus' are a deeper yellow.

Ophiopogon planiscapus
'Nigrescens' is a striking plant with greenish black foliage and flowering stalks, which bear lilac flowers followed by black fruits.

The heads of nodding flowers are rather similar to those of the garden shrub pieris; they may be followed by colorful berries.

Clumps spread by underground rhizomes and will form a thick turf if given enough room. Although the leaves are grassy, the plant is a member of the lily family and is related to *Liriope muscari*, which it resembles.

FACT FILE

ORIGIN Japan.

HEIGHT To 20in/50cm.

POTTING MIX Soil-based, with a little added coarse sand.

REPOTTING Annually, in spring, when the clump has covered the surface of the soil.

PROPAGATION When the clump fills a 6-in/15-cm pot, divide it carefully in spring and pot up the divisions individually. Or sow seed in spring.

KEEPING PLANTS The plant requires bright light in order to flower. Keep it almost dry during the winter rest period.

PLANT CARE

Bright, diffuse light with no direct sun. ● Average warmth or relatively cool conditions, with a minimum temperature of 50°F/10°C. ● Keep the soil just moist throughout the growing period and water even more sparingly in winter. ● Mist the leaves regularly, especially in warm conditions. ● Apply a standard liquid fertilizer every 2 weeks during the growing season.

ALSO RECOMMENDED

Ophiopogon planiscapus 'Nigrescens' is a hardier plant than *O. jaburan* and can survive in lower temperatures. It is a good ground-cover plant for a large tub in a sunroom or a border in a greenhouse.

If plants fail to produce flowers, their location is probably too shady. Bright light is necessary for good flowering, but the foliage needs protection from direct strong sunlight.

ORCHIDACEAE

ORCHIDS

Prized for their exotic, long-lasting flowers, orchids are usually regarded as difficult plants that are suitable only for growing under controlled greenhouse conditions, but several species can be grown successfully in the home.

Some species of orchids are terrestrial, growing in soil, but most of those grown as indoor plants are epiphytic and in the wild grow on trees or sometimes rocks. In addition to roots at the base, these orchids usually have aerial roots and need a special medium and container if they are to do well in the home. There are two types of epiphytic orchids: monopodial orchids that produce a single stem from the roots at the base, and sympodial orchids that have many stems arising from a horizontal rhizome. The latter have pseudobulbs—variously shaped swollen stem bases that look like bulbs and store water and food for the plant. Among the best orchids for growing in the home are the epiphytic cymbidiums, cattleyas, coelogynes, dendrobiums, lycastes, miltonias, odontoglossums, and vandas. Phalaenopsis are the easiest to grow.

Orchid flowers come in an enormous variety of shapes, sizes, and colors, but they always have six petallike parts, three of which are true petals and three—the topmost one and the lower pair—sepals. The two upper petals are usually larger than the sepals, while the lower petal, or lip, is always a different shape and color from the others. The flowers are often luscious looking, with a waxy or velvety or sometimes lustrous texture to the petals.

Phalaenopsis **hybrid.** These flat-faced orchids are known as moth orchids because the numerous pale-colored flowers on arching stems look like moths in flight. Since they are monopodial orchids, aerial roots are produced from the stem, but there are no pseudobulbs. The leaves are thick and fleshy.

Each showy flower remains attractive for several weeks. Several flowers are borne on one stem, which may be erect or slightly pendulous.

ALSO RECOMMENDED

Cattleyas are probably the best-known orchids. They produce flowers singly or in small groups ranging from rose pink to white and pale lavender, and most have a deeper-colored curled, frilly lip.

Dendrobiums bear groups of flowers, often fragrant, on short stalks, which grow from tall, usually stemlike pseudobulbs. Flower color ranges from white to pink, lavender, and deep purple.

Miltonias, known as pansy orchids, have velvety, sometimes fragrant blooms in small groups on long stems. Flowers are fairly small and strikingly colored, with attractive markings on the large, lobed lip.

Colonies of aphids are attracted to young growth and flower stems. They can sometimes be removed with a damp cloth, or they can be treated with a contact insecticide.

f moisture is allowed to lie on the leaves, black spots will appear, and fungus infections may attack the plant.

Mealybugs, with their white waxy coating, can sometimes be found clustered at the base of leaves or flower stalks. A systemic insecticide is usually necessary to control them.

Brown scorch marks on the foliage are caused by direct sun falling on the leaves. Good light is essential, but it must be diffuse.

Unless a thick layer of stones is placed in the bottom of a conventional flowerpot, the soil will become waterlogged and sour, and the roots will rot. Good drainage is essential.

Oncidiums bear clusters of many small flowers on long slender stems that rise from the base of ovoid pseudobulbs. The large-lipped flowers vary from white to red, pink, yellow, green, and brown.

Paphiopedilums Slipper orchids are the only terrestrial orchids that do well in the home. They bear single flowers on long stems; flowers have a pouch-shaped lip and a streaked or spotted top sepal.

FACT FILE

ORIGIN Epiphytic orchids: most common in tropical regions of the world; hybrids.
Terrestrial orchids: most common in temperate zones; hybrids.

HEIGHT Up to 2ft/60cm.

POTTING MIX Special free-draining orchid medium.

REPOTTING Repot only when roots or clumps of pseudobulbs are almost bursting out of the pot.

PROPAGATION Divide clumps of pseudobulbs into smaller groups; cut through the rhizome that joins them with a sharp sterilized knife.

KEEPING PLANTS Some orchids flower in 18–20 months, others may take 5 or 6 years before they flower. Blooms usually last 3–6 weeks, but some may last up to 12 weeks. Cut off the flowers when they start to fade.

PLANT CARE

Epiphytic orchids: Bright light shaded from direct sun. ● Normal warm room temperature in summer, 50°–60°F/10°–16°C in winter. ● Moisten the medium thoroughly; allow the top ½in/13mm to dry out between waterings. Water less in cooler temperatures. Pseudobulbs will rot if the plant is overwatered. ● Apply a balanced liquid fertilizer every 2 weeks in the growing season. ● Mist foliage regularly and stand pots on a tray of moist pebbles. High humidity is important. ● Good ventilation is essential.

Terrestrial orchids: Medium light, but generally not direct sunlight. ● Normal room temperature. ● Water actively growing plants moderately; allow the top 1in/2.5cm to dry out before rewatering. Water sparingly for 6 weeks after flowering. ● Stand the pot on a tray of damp pebbles. Mist-spray daily in temperatures over 70°F/21°C. ● Apply a foliar feed every 2–3 waterings.

PESTS & DISEASES

Aphids and mealybugs may infest the plants, and if the atmosphere is too dry, red spider mites can be a pest. Orchids can be infected by viruses, especially cymbidium mosaic virus; this cannot be treated and plants must be destroyed.

OXALIS DEPPEI
Oxalidaceae

*L*UCKY CLOVER

The tuberous-rooted oxalis, called lucky clover or shamrock plant, is often a troublesome, invasive plant in the garden. But when confined to a pot it can be appreciated for its attractive flowers and foliage. The tubers of *Oxalis deppei* are reputed to be edible.

The leaves, which are carried on weak, slender stems, are typical four-leaf-clover leaves. Each lobed leaflet has a V-shaped purple-brown blotch at the base, and together these blotches form a ring in the center of these leaflets. The five-petaled flowers are pinkish red to purple, usually with a greenish yellow throat, and are held in loose umbels on long stalks in the summer. A white-flowered form also exists. Since this species requires plenty of warmth and sunlight, it makes a good windowsill plant.

The delicate, usually nodding umbels of flowers may be deep rose pink to purple. The white-flowered form is less popular.

Although oxalis is not a true clover, it is grown mainly for its "lucky" four-leaf-clover associations. It is also sometimes grown as shamrock, which it resembles.

Many fleshy, tuberous roots are produced. They spread rapidly if given sufficient room.

FACT FILE

ORIGIN Mexico.

HEIGHT 9–12in/23–30cm.

POTTING MIX Soil-based.

REPOTTING In spring, when the tubers fill the pot.

PROPAGATION Divide the clump carefully when repotting or sow seed in spring.

KEEPING PLANTS In time, the clump tends to sprawl, and growth becomes leggy and overgrown. The plant is often discarded at this stage, but dividing it and keeping it in good light will prolong its life.

PLANT CARE

Bright light with some direct sun. ● Cool conditions; a minimum winter temperature of 50°F/10°C. ● Keep the soil just moist in spring and summer; allow the surface to dry out between waterings. In winter, water more sparingly. ● Mist the plant from time to time. ● Apply a balanced liquid fertilizer every 3 weeks in summer.

PACHYSTACHYS LUTEA
Acanthaceae

*L*OLLIPOP PLANT

This branching, bushy plant has upright stems, woody at their base, which carry mid to deep green, lanceolate leaves in opposite pairs. The leaves are heavily veined, giving them a sculpted appearance. Tall flower spikes appear at the ends of the stems in spring and persist throughout the summer. Each white flower is hooded and lasts only a few days, but it is carried in a bright golden yellow, long-lasting bract. The blooms emerge through the bracts, starting from the base of the flower head and opening in succession. The flower heads themselves are reminiscent of those of aphelandra, and the two plants are sometimes confused, although they are, in fact, quite different.

FACT FILE

ORIGIN Tropical America.

HEIGHT To 3ft/90cm.

POTTING MIX Soil- or peat-based.

REPOTTING In spring, when roots show through the base of the pot.

PROPAGATION Take stem cuttings in early summer.

KEEPING PLANTS Pinch off growing tips from time to time to keep the plant bushy. Cut back the stems by a third or more when the plant starts into new growth in spring.

PLANT CARE

Bright light is necessary for flower production, but no direct sun. ● Minimum winter temperature of 60°F/16°C; cool to normal room temperature in summer. ● Keep the soil thoroughly moist in the growing season; water more sparingly in winter. ● Mist the foliage occasionally. ● Apply a high-potash liquid fertilizer every 2 weeks from spring until early fall.

The flower spikes, with their golden bracts and white flowers, are about 4in/10cm long, and are attractive from spring until early fall.

Plants often fail to flower if they do not get enough light. Move them into a bright location and apply a high-potash fertilizer to encourage flowering.

If the plant is allowed to dry out, the lower leaves will soon fall. Keep the soil constantly moist in the growing season.

Older plants become leggy in time and are best replaced with newly rooted cuttings.

PELARGONIUM x *HORTORUM*
Geraniaceae

Geranium

Easy to care for and colorful for long periods in summer, geraniums are among the most popular indoor flowering plants. *Pelargonium* x *hortorum*, the zonal geranium, is the most common type. Its stems branch freely and become woody and brittle with age. The zonal geranium carries rounded, lobed, scallop-edged leaves, which nearly always have a central brownish ring, or zone, which gives the plant its name. The foliage has a characteristic fragrance when handled. Flowers are carried in summer, in dense, rounded heads on top of sturdy, erect stems. Each individual flower is simple, five-petaled, or double, in a wide variety of shades of white, pink, salmon, scarlet, and purple; sometimes they are bicolored. Dozens of new varieties are bred every year and are available from specialist nurseries.

There are plenty of types with variegated leaves, such as 'Mrs. Henry Cox,' which has mid green leaves with a wide, red-flushed zone and creamy margin and bears single pink flowers.

FACT FILE

ORIGIN Warm temperate zones; South Africa.

HEIGHT To 3ft/90cm.

POTTING MIX Soil- or peat-moss-based.

REPOTTING In spring when roots show through the base of the pot. Flowering is improved if plants are slightly pot-bound.

PROPAGATION Take stem cuttings in spring and early summer. Zonal geraniums can also be raised from seed sown in early spring.

KEEPING PLANTS Overwinter in a cool room. To keep the plants reasonably compact and shapely, cut the stems back hard in early spring. This new growth is ideal for use as cuttings. Pinch off the growing tips regularly to encourage bushiness.

PLANT CARE

Bright light with full sun.
● Moderate to cool room temperature with a minimum of 45°F/7°C in winter.
● Water enough to make the soil thoroughly moist, then allow the top 1in/2.5cm to dry out before watering again. Water sparingly in winter.
● Apply a high-potash liquid fertilizer every 2 weeks during the growing season.

ALSO RECOMMENDED

Pelargonium x *domesticum*, the regal geranium. The leaves are larger than in zonals, lighter in color, and with a densely scalloped edge. Pinks, purples, white, and rose red are the usual flower colors. Individual flowers are large, with frilly edged petals, often marked with a different color. Rose red 'Grand Slam' has upper petals that are blotched strawberry black.

The zonal cultivar 'Robert Fish' is grown mainly for its red, yellow, brown, and green leaves. The plant produces small single flowers that are perhaps better removed, since they tend to detract from the foliage.

Lower leaves turn red or yellow in very dry or cool conditions. To some extent this is natural in winter, but be sure that the plant is receiving adequate warmth and moisture if a large number of leaves are lost.

Flower heads are composed of many individual flowers; the flower heads tend to shatter if brushed against or moved when in full bloom.

Overwatering will cause the main stem to rot at soil level. Always allow the soil to dry out slightly between waterings.

Pale circles on the leaf surface may indicate attack by the fungus disease rust; check the undersides of leaves for the characteristic powdery brown pustules. Rust is difficult to control; remove and burn affected leaves and spray the plant with an approved fungicide.

PELARGONIUM PELTATUM
Geraniaceae

*I*VY GERANIUM

This species has long, slender, brittle, trailing stems and fleshy, brittle, ivy-shaped leaves. Flowers are carried in small clusters and tend to appear more sparsely petaled than those of zonal geraniums, although there are double and semidouble varieties. The upper petals often have contrasting markings on them. There is a full range of flower colors in shades of red, orange, pink, salmon, white, and purple, and bicolored varieties such as the red-and-white 'Rouletta.'

Variegated leaves add to the attraction of these pelargoniums. 'L'Elégante' is a long-established variety, which has mid green leaves with cream edges that become flushed with purple in cool conditions. Some strains of ivy geranium, such as 'Summer Showers,' are now easily raised from seed.

FACT FILE

ORIGIN South Africa.

HEIGHT Prostrate, trailing to 3ft/90cm.

POTTING MIX Soil- or peat-moss-based.

REPOTTING In spring, when roots show through the base of the pot. Do not overpot.

PROPAGATION Take stem cuttings in spring and early summer or sow seed in early spring.

KEEPING PLANTS Overwinter in a cool room. Prune stems back hard in early spring to keep the plants reasonably compact and shapely. New growth is ideal for use as cuttings.

PLANT CARE

Bright light, full sun. ● Moderate warmth, with a minimum of 45°F/7°C in winter. ● Give enough water to make the soil thoroughly moist; allow the top 1in/2.5cm to dry out before watering again. Water very sparingly in winter. ● Apply a high-potash liquid fertilizer every 2 weeks from the time the buds form until fall.

High-nitrogen fertilizers given to young plants can cause lush leaf growth and a failure to flower. Do not feed plants until buds are forming; use a high-potash fertilizer.

The trailing stems of ivy geraniums are brittle and easily broken, so position the plants with care.

Corky growths on the leaf surfaces are caused by edema, the result of overwatering.

PELARGONIUM SPP.
Geraniaceae

*S*CENTED-LEAFED GERANIUMS

Although all pelargoniums have slightly aromatic foliage, a number of species have strongly fragrant leaves in a wide range of unusual scents, and the full fragrance is given off when the leaves are stroked or gently rubbed. The leaf shapes and plant forms are extremely variable, and the flowers are usually simple, rather sparse, and in pale colors. But it is for their foliage that these plants are grown.

Many types are available. *Pelargonium abrotanifolium* is a slow-growing, woody-stemmed plant with silver, finely cut foliage quite unlike other pelargoniums. *P. capitatum*, rose-scented geranium, has soft, furry leaves and pink flowers. *P. crispum*, lemon geranium, has small, scallop-edged leaves. *P. graveolens*, rose geranium, has gray-green, deeply lobed toothed leaves. *P. odoratissimum*, apple geranium, has tall, rather lax stems carrying small, softly hairy, wavy-edged leaves. *P. quercifolium*, oak-leaved geranium, is a tall, shrubby plant, with a strong, spicy, peppery scent. *P. tomentosum*, peppermint geranium, has large, lobed leaves, which are softly hairy and strongly scented.

Pinch off vigorous varieties frequently to prevent the stems from becoming too long. Use the shoot tips as cuttings.

Although many scented-leafed varieties bear flowers, they are usually fairly insignificant and can be removed if desired.

The fragrance is usually released by the slightest touch. Lemon-scented varieties, in particular, are intensely aromatic.

FACT FILE

ORIGIN South Africa.

HEIGHT To 3ft/90cm according to species.

POTTING MIX Soil- or peat-moss-based, with good drainage.

REPOTTING In spring.

PROPAGATION Take stem cuttings in spring and early summer.

KEEPING PLANTS Pinch off the shoot tips of strong-growing varieties regularly to encourage branching and maintain a bushy shape.

PLANT CARE

Bright light, full sun. ● Moderate warmth, with a minimum temperature of 45°F/7°C in winter. ● Make the soil thoroughly moist, then allow the surface to dry out before watering again. Water more sparingly in winter. ● Apply a standard liquid fertilizer every 3 weeks from spring to fall.

PEPEROMIA CAPERATA
Piperaceae

ℰMERALD RIPPLE

The heart-shaped, deep green leaves of this peperomia are borne on fairly long, red-tinged stalks. They are deeply veined and have an attractive, corrugated surface. Tall, white, pokerlike flower spikes, also with red stems, emerge above the mound of foliage in summer and early fall. 'Emerald Ripple' is a compact form that makes a dense mound of leaves. 'Variegata' has almost white leaves with a central splash of mid green, but the light and dark effect of the corrugated surface does not show up so well on the light-colored leaf.

FACT FILE

ORIGIN Brazil.

HEIGHT To 10in/25cm.

POTTING MIX Peat-moss-based.

REPOTTING In spring, move young plants into pots one size larger; it is not usually necessary to repot older plants every year.

PROPAGATION By leaf or stem cuttings in spring.

KEEPING PLANTS This is a long-lasting, usually trouble-free plant.

PLANT CARE

Moderate light, shaded from direct sun. ● A minimum winter temperature of 60°F/13°C; otherwise, normal room temperature. ● Water sparingly, especially in winter, allowing the top half of the soil to dry out before rewatering. ● Mist plants frequently and stand the pot on a dish of moist pebbles. ● Apply a balanced liquid fertilizer every 2 weeks from spring to fall.

Protect peperomias from strong sun; variegated types need brighter conditions than those with plain leaves.

The tall flower spikes are neither showy nor colorful, but they are produced in abundance and make a graceful addition to the plant.

If the lower leaves and base of the stems turn black, overwatering is the most likely cause. Water these plants sparingly at all times.

PEPEROMIA MAGNOLIIFOLIA
Piperaceae

𝒟ESERT PRIVET

This plant is often offered as *Peperomia obtusifolia*, but differs from it in that its growth tends to be more upright and it has more leaves. It forms a small, shrubby, branching plant with smooth, waxy, rather fleshy, rounded leaves that are carried alternately on the stems. Although growth is upright at first, the stems tend to bend downward as the plant gets older.

The variegated forms are most commonly grown. 'Variegata' has cream-and-green leaves, with the leaves often being almost entirely cream when young but turning a bright lime green as they age. The leaves of 'Green and Gold' are more irregularly marked, with light green centers, a creamy gold mid region and darker green margins, often with a feathered look.

Variegated leaf forms of this peperomia are most favored for growing as houseplants. Young leaves are often almost entirely cream and become marked with green as they age.

Edema, which causes corky swellings on the underside of the foliage, is the result of excessive watering. Keep the soil only just moist and never allow the plant to stand in water.

Lower leaves will fall if the conditions are too cold. Water plants sparingly in winter.

FACT FILE

ORIGIN South America; West Indies.

HEIGHT To 8in/20cm.

POTTING MIX Peat-moss-based.

REPOTTING Every 2 years or so, when the pot is filled with roots.

PROPAGATION By stem-tip cuttings in spring and early summer, or leaf stem cuttings in spring.

KEEPING PLANTS Under good conditions, this plant is long-lived.

PLANT CARE

Bright light but not direct sun. ● Normal room temperature with a minimum of 55°F/13°C; better at 60°F/16°C in winter. ● Keep the soil just moist in summer; allow the top 1in/2.5cm to dry out before rewatering. Water even more sparingly in winter. ● Mist the plant frequently and stand the pot on a tray of moist pebbles to increase humidity. ● Apply a balanced liquid fertilizer every 2 weeks during the growing season.

PEPEROMIA SCANDENS
Piperaceae

*C*UPID PEPEROMIA

The trailing forms of peperomia are much less common than the bushy species. *Peperomia scandens*, also known as *P. serpens*, has heart-shaped leaves about 2in/5cm long, which are carried alternately on pinkish stems that can trail up to 4ft/1.2m. The leaves are fleshy, with a waxy surface.

The form 'Variegata' is the one most commonly offered for sale. It has mid-green leaves with a wide, creamy yellow margin. The young leaves are often almost entirely cream, and the green centers develop gradually as the plant matures. Plants in containers do not often produce flowers.

FACT FILE

ORIGIN South America.

HEIGHT Stems trail or climb to 4ft/1.2m.

POTTING MIX Preferably peat-moss-based.

REPOTTING Repot only when the soil is filled with roots.

PROPAGATION Take stem tip cuttings in early summer. They should root in 4–6 weeks.

KEEPING PLANTS In good conditions peperomias last for several years.

PLANT CARE

Bright conditions, with shade from direct sun in summer. A little direct winter sunshine helps to intensify the variegation of the foliage. ● Normal room temperature, with a winter minimum of 60°F/16°C. ● Keep the soil just moist; allow the surface to dry out between waterings. Water less in winter. ● Mist frequently in summer and stand the pot on a tray of moist pebbles to increase humidity. ● Apply a balanced liquid fertilizer every 2 weeks in the growing season.

The foliage requires good, bright conditions to maintain its coloring. Some direct sunshine is beneficial in winter, but be careful not to scorch the fleshy leaves by overexposure to the sun.

Pinch off the shoot tips occasionally to promote branching, and cut the stems back hard in mid spring.

PHILODENDRON BIPINNATIFIDUM
Araceae

*T*REE PHILODENDRON

Unlike the more familiar philodendron species, this one does not climb. Instead, it is a sturdy spreading plant, which eventually develops a stout "trunk" and can form an impressive architectural specimen. Because of its spread—6ft/1.8m or more across—it needs plenty of space. It should not be confused with the somewhat similarly named *Philodendron bipennifolium*, horsehead philodendron, a climbing species with fiddle-shaped leaves.

The large leaves are a deep glossy green and are about 3ft/90cm long. When young, they are more or less heart-shaped, with indented margins. As they develop, the indentations become more deeply cut until the leaf appears to be divided into many slender leaflets and takes on an overall arrowhead shape. The leaves are carried on long stalks, arising in a rosette formation from the crown.

Direct sun falling on the leaves can cause brown scorch marks on the foliage.

To enhance the appearance of the leaves, carefully clean them with a damp cloth.

The long stems can be allowed to trail from a hanging basket or pot, but they can also be tied to supports to make the plant into a climber.

FACT FILE

ORIGIN Brazil.

HEIGHT To 4ft/1.2m.

POTTING MIX Soil-based with added peat moss.

REPOTTING Repot in spring or early summer when roots fill the current pot, usually every other year.

PROPAGATION Sow seed in spring in a heated propagator; do not cover the seed.

KEEPING PLANTS Provide a cane for support if needed.

PLANT CARE

Moderate light, shaded from direct sun. ● Average room temperature, with a winter minimum of 60°/16°C. ● Keep the soil moist at all times during the growing season. Water more sparingly in winter, and let the surface of the soil dry out between waterings. ● Mist the foliage occasionally. ● Apply a balanced liquid fertilizer every 2 weeks during the growing season.

PHILODENDRON ERUBESCENS
Araceae

ℬLUSHING PHILODENDRON

This strong-growing, climbing plant has leaves about 10in/25cm long, which are shaped like an arrowhead. They are a glossy deep green, with a coppery red underside and reddish margins, and are carried on long, purple-red leafstalks; the young stems are also red.

One of the most popular hybrids, 'Burgundy,' has *Philodrendron. erubescens* as one of its parents. 'Burgundy' is a slow-growing climber, whose long leaves are deep reddish green above and wine red on the undersides; it has glowing red leafstalks. 'Red Emerald' is another commonly grown variety with bright green foliage and red stems.

The wine-red tinge to the glossy, dark green foliage and stems is intensified by good light, but plants should be protected from direct, strong sun.

Lower leaves that turn yellow and fall usually mean the plant is being overwatered, particularly in winter. Do not let the pot stand in water; do allow the surface to dry out before rewatering.

The thick aerial roots should be carefully trained into a damp moss-covered pole. Use a piece of wire bent into a the shape of a hairpin to hold the roots in place.

FACT FILE

ORIGIN Colombia.

HEIGHT To 6ft/1.8m or more.

POTTING MIX Soil-based with added peat moss.

REPOTTING Repot in spring or early summer when roots fill the pot. Use a large, broad-based pot to prevent the plant becoming top-heavy.

PROPAGATION Take stem tip cuttings in early summer and root them in a mixture of half peat moss, half coarse sand.

KEEPING PLANTS Provide the plant with a pole covered in moss for support.

PLANT CARE

Good to moderate light, shaded from direct sun. ● Average room temperatures, with a minimum of 60°F/16°C in winter. ● Keep the soil moist at all times during the growing season. Allow the surface of the soil to dry out between waterings in winter. ● Mist the foliage occasionally. ● Feed with a balanced liquid fertilizer every 2 weeks in spring and summer.

PHILODENDRON SCANDENS
Araceae

ℋEARTLEAF PHILODENDRON

The most popular of the philodendrons, known also as the sweetheart plant, this one is undemanding and extremely easy to grow. The leaves are strongly heart-shaped and a bright, glossy mid-green; when the foliage is young, it has a bronze tinge. The leaves are normally 4in/10cm long, although they may double or treble in size as they mature. They are carried alternately on slender, twining stems, which will trail, or climb when given support. Trailing plants should have the tips pinched off occasionally to keep the plant bushy and encourage it to branch.

FACT FILE

ORIGIN Tropical America.

HEIGHT Climbs or trails to 4ft/1.2m or more.

POTTING MIX Peat-moss-based, or soil-based with added peat moss.

REPOTTING Repot in spring or early summer when the soil is filled with roots.

PROPAGATION Stem tip cuttings taken in spring and early summer will root very easily.

KEEPING PLANTS The plant can be trained on a trellis or up a pole covered in moss. In each instance, it will need to be tied in initially, although eventually the aerial roots will grow into the moss on the pole. Stems can also be allowed to trail from a hanging basket.

PLANT CARE

Bright light but no direct sun. ● Average room temperature, with a winter minimum of 60°F/16°C. ● Give enough water to keep the soil moist during the growing season; allow the surface to dry out between waterings in winter. ● Mist the foliage occasionally. If the plant is grown on a moss-covered pole, spray it every day. ● Apply a balanced liquid fertilizer every 2 weeks in the growing season.

Elongated, straggly stems show that the plant is not receiving enough light; move it to a brighter location, but not into direct sun.

Small aerial roots will attach themselves to a moist surface, such as a moss-covered pole. Stems must be tied in to the support when the plant is trained as a climber.

Young shoots are sometimes infested with aphids. If so, treat them with a contact insecticide.

PHOENIX ROEBELENII
Palmae

*P*YGMY DATE PALM

The arching, mid to deep green fronds on this slow-growing palm grow from a central crown. The fronds, which are divided into many slender pinnate leaflets, are soft, not spiky like those on other date palms. These spread out in a graceful fashion to give the plant a feathery appearance, more delicate than that of other members of the genus. The fronds are covered in a thin layer of white scales.

The slow-growing pygmy date palm makes a good specimen plant. It should be given enough room to spread up to 4ft/1.2m wide when it is several years old. The long panicles of yellowish flowers are not normally produced on indoor plants.

If the leaflets turn brown and crisp at the tips and margins, the air is too dry. Mist the plant regularly to maintain a humid atmosphere.

Scale insects often infect these plants. Check the undersides of the leaves and use a fingernail to remove any scales. Treat with systemic insecticide if the infestation is bad.

The fronds have a feathery appearance and arch outward, giving the plant a graceful outline.

FACT FILE

ORIGIN Laos.

HEIGHT To 4ft/1.2m or more; usually about 2ft/60cm indoors.

POTTING MIX Soil-based.

REPOTTING Repot in spring only when necessary, since this plant resents root disturbance. Take care not to damage the roots.

PROPAGATION Suckers are sometimes produced at the base of the plant and can be cut away carefully. Remove suckers with roots and pot them. Plants can also be raised from seed, but they take several years to achieve a reasonable size.

KEEPING PLANTS This palm needs a humid atmosphere. Stand the pot on a tray of moist pebbles and mist the foliage regularly.

PLANT CARE

Bright light; will tolerate some direct sun. ● A minimum temperature of 55°/13°CF in winter; normal room temperatures in summer. ● Keep the soil thoroughly moist during the growing season. Give just enough water in winter to prevent the compost from drying out, to give the plants a short winter rest. ● Apply a balanced liquid fertilizer every 2–3 weeks in summer.

PILEA CADIEREI
Urticaceae

*A*LUMINUM PLANT

A popular and easily grown plant, *Pilea cadierei* has ovate mid-green leaves about 3in/8cm long, which grow in opposite pairs on the rather fleshy stems. The leaf surface is textured, and the four rows of silvery raised patches between the veins give this pilea the other common name watermelon pilea. The undersides of the leaves have a reddish tinge; new foliage is lighter green in color.

The plant branches freely, forming a small bush, but it tends to become straggly after a couple of seasons. Frequent pinching off of the growing tips will help to keep it compact. Cuttings are easily rooted, so leggy plants can be regularly replaced. The variety 'Minima' is a dwarf form with smaller leaves.

FACT FILE

ORIGIN Vietnam.

HEIGHT Up to 12in/30cm before plants need to be replaced; 'Minima' grows to about 6in/15cm.

POTTING MIX Peat-moss-based.

REPOTTING Repot in spring as necessary.

PROPAGATION Stem tip cuttings taken in spring or summer root easily.

KEEPING PLANTS Plants are best discarded at the end of the season, and replaced with rooted cuttings. If plants are kept for a second season, cut the shoots back by half in spring.

PLANT CARE

Diffused light. ● Minimum of 60°F/16°C in winter; normal warm room temperature at other times. ● Keep the soil just moist during the growing season, allowing the surface to dry out between waterings. Water more sparingly in winter. ● Mist regularly to increase humidity, and stand the pot on a tray of moist gravel. ● Apply a balanced liquid fertilizer every 2 weeks in summer.

The foliage has an attractive quilted appearance, with strongly contrasting silver markings. Keep the plant in good light for the best coloration.

Aphids can often be found thickly clustered on the tips of the young shoots. Pinch out affected shoots or spray with a contact insecticide.

The lower leaves fall naturally, giving older plants a straggly appearance. This will be accentuated by both over- and underwatering.

PILEA PEPEROMIOIDES
Urticaceae

Pilea

This unusual pilea forms a mound of leaves, each of which rises directly from a shoot, unbranched stem. The oval, almost rounded leaves, up to 4in/10cm long, are fleshy and a bright mid green with a shiny surface. In summer small, fluffy, yellowish green flowers may be produced, but these are secondary to the foliage.

Another attractive species is *Pilea involucrata*, sometimes incorrectly called *P. spruceana*. This is a bushy, spreading plant with ovate leaves that are strongly textured and quilted on the upper surface. They are dark green with a reddish brown tinge and red undersides. One of the most popular forms is 'Moon Valley' (also sold as *P. mollis*), which has pointed, bright green, puckered leaves with dark bronze veins.

FACT FILE

ORIGIN West Indies.

HEIGHT To 12in/30cm.

POTTING MIX Peat-moss-based.

REPOTTING Repot in spring when necessary.

PROPAGATION Take stem tip cuttings in spring or summer.

KEEPING PLANTS In order to flower well, the plant needs a cool winter rest period. Discard the plant after 3 or 4 years when it becomes leggy.

PLANT CARE

Moderate to bright light, but shaded from direct sun. ● Warm room temperature, with a minimum of 55°F/13°C in winter. ● Keep the soil evenly moist during the growing season; allow the surface to dry out between waterings. Water more sparingly in winter. ● Apply a balanced liquid fertilizer every 2 weeks during spring and summer. ● Keep the plant out of drafts.

The foliage is brightly marked, especially in good light conditions.

Some leaves will fall naturally in winter, but cold conditions or overwatering may cause excessive leaf loss. Move an affected plant to a slightly warmer location and allow the soil to dry out between waterings.

PIPER ORNATUM
Piperaceae

Celebes Pepper

Although this climbing plant—sometimes incorrectly offered as *Piper crocatum*—has leaf forms similar to *Philodendron scandens*, the heartleaf plant, it is not as easy to find or to grow. It is, however, worth the search, since the heart-shaped leaves are more attractively colored, being olive green with silvery pink markings along the veins and red undersides. They are about 4in/10cm long and are carried alternately on slender pink wiry stems.

Also known as the ornamental pepper, the Celebes pepper belongs to the true pepper family, a group of plants that produce some of the world's most important commercial spices.

The heart-shaped leaves have a slightly puckered surface attractively marked with silvery pink.

Stems will trail gracefully if 2 or 3 plants are set in a hanging basket. Alternatively, the stems can be trained up stakes inserted into the pot and tied gently at intervals.

Plants will lose their leaves if the growing conditions are not to their liking. They need warm, humid conditions and resent sudden changes in temperature; do not expose them to drafts.

FACT FILE

ORIGIN Sulawesi.

HEIGHT To 5ft/1.5m.

POTTING MIX Peat-moss-based, or a mixture of peat-moss- and soil-based.

REPOTTING Repot in spring when the plant has become top-heavy, usually only every 2 or 3 years.

PROPAGATION By stem cuttings in late spring and summer. They are not easy to root, but a heated propagator will increase the success rate.

KEEPING PLANTS The plant is usually grown up two or three canes—stems must be tied in to the supports—or it can be allowed to trail.

PLANT CARE

Bright filtered sunlight. ● Evenly warm conditions, with a winter minimum of 60°F/16°C. ● Keep evenly moist, allowing the surface to dry out in winter between waterings. ● Mist the foliage regularly and stand the pot on a tray of moist pebbles. ● Apply a balanced liquid fertilizer every 2 weeks in spring and summer.

PLATYCERIUM BIFURCATUM
Polypodiaceae

STAGHORN FERN

One glance at this plant is enough to tell you how it got its common name—the fronds are large and distinctly antlerlike, dividing into lobes at their tips. It is also sometimes known as *Platycerium alcicorne* and commonly as elkhorn fern.

The plant has two types of frond. The sterile fronds at the base are more or less kidney-shaped, pale green becoming brown with age. And they clasp their support, which in the wild is normally a tree trunk, because the plants are epiphytes. These fronds are slightly curved, and the debris that falls and is trapped behind them rots down to form a source of nutrients for the plant. Fertile fronds up to 3ft/90cm long arise from the sterile fronds and are spreading or drooping, branching into antlerlike lobes. They are grayish green, covered with a white, felty scurf. Although the fern can be grown in a pot, it is better in a slatted basket or mounted on a piece of wood or bark, which more closely mimics its natural growing conditions. Wrap the rootball in damp sphagnum moss and tie it to the bark or a board with twine.

The large sterile frond will eventually cover the growing medium and clasp the sides of the pot, making it impossible to water the plant from above.

Handle the plant with care: the white scurf on the fronds is easily damaged.

FACT FILE

ORIGIN Australia; Polynesia.

SPREAD To 2ft/60cm.

POTTING MIX Moist sphagnum moss mixed with leaf mold or osmunda fiber or epiphytic mix.

REPOTTING The clasping sterile frond makes it difficult to repot a plant, so mount it or put it in a wooden orchid basket.

PROPAGATION Not practical in the home.

KEEPING PLANTS Mist the leaves frequently with tepid water, but do not allow water into the growing point; this may cause rot to develop.

PLANT CARE

Bright light with some direct sun, but not strong summer sun.
● Minimum temperature of 55°F/13°C. In summer 70°F/21°C is ideal.
● Water well, then allow to dry between waterings. Occasionally plunge the root area into water for several minutes, then drain. Water pot-grown plants from below; tip away water remaining after 15 minutes.
● Feed once a month in summer, either as a spray or in the plunging water.

PLECTRANTHUS COLEOIDES 'MARGINATUS'
Labiatae

CANDLE PLANT

Plectranthuses are easily grown plants, but not as common in garden centers as might be expected—probably because they are so simple to propagate that they tend to be passed from one gardener to another rather than bought. *Plectranthus coleoides*, today more correctly called *P. forsteri*, is a bushy plant with red stems that are upright at first, but soon trail. The ovate leaves are up to 2½in/6.5cm long with toothed margins, broadly edged white in the variety 'Marginatus,' which is the one used almost exclusively as an indoor plant. Pale lilac, nettlelike flowers are sometimes produced but are rather insignificant.

Common names for plants in this genus are confused. *P. oertendahlii*, a prostrate species whose rounded, bronze green leaves have creamy white or silver veins and red-tinted undersides, is known both as candle plant and Swedish ivy. And *P. australis* is called Swedish ivy in the United States.

FACT FILE

ORIGIN New Caledonia; Fiji.

HEIGHT Upright to 3ft/90cm, bends with weight to trail.

POTTING MIX Peat-moss-based.

REPOTTING In spring, but plants are usually replaced annually.

PROPAGATION By easily rooted stem cuttings from spring to fall.

KEEPING PLANTS Plants are usually replaced with fresh cuttings at the end of a year. Pinch off growing tips to maintain bushiness.

PLANT CARE

Bright light with some direct sun except in midsummer ● Minimum temperature 60°F/16°C: average room temperature in summer.
● Keep the soil thoroughly moist all through the growing season; frequent watering is usually necessary. Water more sparingly in winter.
● Mist the foliage occasionally. ● Feed with a balanced liquid fertilizer every 2 weeks in spring and summer.

Leggy stems, with long gaps between the leaves, are common on plants that do not get adequate light. Plants do, however, naturally grow straggly with age.

The toothed leaves are slightly aromatic when touched. A plain-leafed type exists, but the variegated form is more usual.

The trailing stems are best displayed in a hanging basket or a pot mounted on a pedestal. Pinch off the growing tips regularly to keep the plant bushy.

PLUMBAGO AURICULATA
Plumbaginaceae

CAPE LEADWORT

A rather straggling semi-climber, plumbago produces panicles of flowers throughout the summer. Both its common and scientific names refer to the fact that it was once thought to cure lead poisoning. It used to be known as *Plumbago capensis* and is still frequently offered under that name.

The mid green oval leaves are borne on slender stems, and the flowers, often a sky-blue, are carried in heads of up to 20 at the tips of young shoots. Flowers are tubular, opening to a star, each of the five petals having a thin dark line running down the center. 'Alba' is a white-flowered variety.

FACT FILE

ORIGIN South Africa.

HEIGHT To 4ft/1.2m.

POTTING MIX Soil-based.

REPOTTING In spring, in a pot one size larger until maximum desired pot size is reached; thereafter top-dress annually.

PROPAGATION Take stem cuttings of nonflowering shoots in late spring and summer, or sow seed in spring.

KEEPING PLANTS Cut stems back to about 6in/15cm just as the plant is starting into growth in spring—flowers are borne on the current year's growth. Tie the plant into a trellis or stakes, or train it around a hoop. Put the plant outdoors in summer where the climate is suitable.

PLANT CARE

Bright light with several hours of direct sun. ● Minimum temperature of 45°F/7°C in winter; can tolerate temperatures as high as 90°/32°C. ● Keep the soil moist at all times in spring and summer; water more sparingly in winter. ● Mist the foliage occasionally. ● Apply a high-potash liquid fertilizer every 2 weeks in spring and summer.

ALSO RECOMMENDED

Plumbago indica, scarlet leadwort, has foliage ranging from a soft pink to red. It is a tender species, originating in Southeast Asia, and needs bright filtered light with some sun, a minimum temperature of 60°–65°F/16°–18°C, and high humidity. As with *P. auriculata*, flowers are borne on the current year's growth if the plant is cut back in spring; left unpruned, it will bloom in late winter if the situation is warm enough.

If buds fall before the flowers open, conditions are too hot and dry for the plant. Move it to a cooler location, mist the foliage and see that the soil is moist.

Red spider mites can be a nuisance, by causing pale, flecked foliage with webbing on the underside. Spray plants with water regularly.

Most houseplants can be kept neat by training the stems around a hoop, but plumbago is ideal for a greenhouse, where it can be allowed to grow over a permanent trellis.

Plumbago indica *is a tender and unusual species that bears lax sprays of red or deep pink flowers in summer.*

PRIMULACEAE

PRIMROSES

Primula obconica is known as poison primrose because the hairs on the foliage can cause a skin irritation. The flowers come in a wide choice of colors.

The large primula family contains a number of popular houseplants that flower in winter and early spring. Like daffodils, they cheer us by anticipating the flowering of their outdoor relatives.

Among the most commonly grown is the robust *Primula obconica*, the poison primrose, so called because it contains the irritant chemical primin, although the 'Libre' series has been bred to be free of it. Most plants are available as unnamed varieties, but the 'Ariane' series has large flowers and compact foliage, and is available in purplish blue, orange, white, and red-and-white and blue-and-white bicolors.

Commercial varieties of *P. vulgaris* with larger flowers are available in yellow, purple, orange, red, pink, and white, all with pronounced yellow eyes. There are double varieties and bicolors. A hybrid of *P. vulgaris* and *P. veris* (the cowslip) is the polyanthus, *P. × tommasinii*. The foliage is similar to that of the primrose, but the flowers are carried in umbels on the top of stout, 4-in/10-cm-long stalks.

The species *P. sinensis* and *P. malacoides* are daintier and have smaller flowers. Those of *P. malacoides* are only about ¾in/2cm wide, but double-flowered and dwarf forms have also been developed. *P.* 'Kewensis' is a hybrid that comes true to seed and produces brilliant yellow, long-lasting flowers with a sweet scent from midwinter through to spring.

Flowers are 1in/2.5cm wide and have 5 heart-shaped petals. The indentation at the top of the petals makes it appear as though there are 10 of them. The flowers are borne in umbels on stems up to 12in/30cm tall.

Mid green, rather coarse rounded to heart-shaped leaves are covered in fine hairs.

ALSO RECOMMENDED

Primula denticulata, drumstick primula, is a vigorous upright plant. It has a round head made up of tightly packed mauve, purple, or purple-pink flowers on a stem up to 18in/46cm long.

Primula 'Kewensis' has wavy-edged, toothed leaves covered with a dusting of fine white powder. Whorls of bright yellow fragrant flowers with a long tube crown the 15-in/38-cm flower stalks.

Primula malacoides, the delicate-looking fairy primrose, has oval, toothed leaves. The small, fragrant flowers, arranged in 3–6 tiers on 18-in/46-cm stems, may be pink, purple, or white, with a yellow eye.

Aphids are sometimes found on the young foliage. Pick off affected leaves or spray the plant carefully with a contact insecticide. Not all insecticides are suitable for primulas; read the label carefully.

Limp, yellowing lower leaves may mean the plant has been overwatered. Keep the soil moist, but never let the plant stand in water.

The C-shaped grubs of vine weevils eat the roots, causing wilting and eventual collapse of the plant. By the time they have been discovered, it is usually too late to save the plant, but an insecticidal dust may help.

Hairs on the leaves can trap water, which leads to rotting of the foliage and gray mold. Do not mist the plant.

Primula sinensis, the Chinese primrose, has soft, hairy lobed leaves with toothed edges. The many-flowered stalks start short and lengthen as the frilly-petaled red, white, pink, or purple flowers open.

Primula vulgaris, the common primrose, forms a rosette of wrinkled leaves from the middle of which grow pale yellow flowers with deeper yellow eyes, each on a slender single stem.

FACT FILE

ORIGIN Mainly Northern Hemisphere, especially China.

HEIGHT 8–15in/20–38cm.

POTTING MIX Peat-moss-based.

REPOTTING Move *Primula obconica* and *P. sinensis* into a pot one size larger in early fall. Do not touch the foliage if you are allergic; use rubber gloves. The other primulas mentioned here should be discarded or, in the case of *P. vulgaris,* planted outdoors.

PROPAGATION Sow seeds in summer and fall according to type or species, or divide plants after they have finished flowering.

KEEPING PLANTS After flowering, keep plants of *P. obconica* and *P. sinensis* outdoors in a cool, sheltered, lightly shaded location. Water just enough to prevent the soil from drying out. In early fall remove yellow and dead foliage, repot the plants, bring them indoors, and gradually increase the amount of water.

PLANT CARE

Bright light with some direct sun, especially in winter. ● Cool conditions will extend the life of the flowers: 50°–60°F/10°–16°C is the ideal range. ● Keep the soil thoroughly moist at all times during the flowering period: water sparingly in summer. ● Apply a high-potash liquid fertilizer every 1–2 weeks during the flowering season, starting when buds appear ● Wear rubber gloves when handling plants of the hairy-leafed *P. obconica* and *P. sinensis.*

PESTS & DISEASES

Primulas are fairly free from pests and diseases, although vine weevils, aphids, and red spider mites may be a nuisance. Plants are more likely to suffer from botrytis and root rot, which are caused by poor cultivation and overwatering.

RHAPIS EXCELSA
Palmae

MINIATURE FAN PALM

Also known as bamboo palm and little lady palm, this is a neat, fairly compact palm of Oriental appearance. The leaves consist of a variable number of deep, glossy green, rather corrugated, deeply veined leaflets up to 12in/30cm long.

The plant forms clumps of slender, strongly upright stems covered with brown fiber. As the lower leaves fall, they leave smooth green scars on the stems, giving them a bamboolike appearance. A variegated form exists, with leaves striped creamy yellow or white.

FACT FILE

ORIGIN China.

HEIGHT To 10ft/3m.

POTTING MIX Soil-based.

REPOTTING In spring, every other year at most. Plants grow best when slightly pot-bound.

PROPAGATION Remove suckers—preferably with roots attached—from the base of the plant in spring and pot them up individually.

KEEPING PLANTS This is a slow-growing palm, and with proper care it should last for many years.

PLANT CARE

Filtered light. ● Normal to cool room temperature, with a minimum of 45°F/7°C in winter. ● Keep the soil constantly moist in spring and summer. Water less in winter; allow the top ½in/13mm to dry out between waterings. ● Mist the plant frequently, preferably with lime-free water, and stand the pot on a tray of moist pebbles. ● Apply a balanced liquid fertilizer once a month in the growing season.

Brown leaf tips are common. Increasing the humidity by more-frequent misting of the foliage will probably help.

Pale, mottled leaves with fine webbing under the tips are signs of red spider mite damage. A more humid atmosphere should discourage the mites.

The number of leaflets to each leaf differs widely. The variegated form tends to be slower-growing than the plain-leafed type.

RHIPSALIDOPSIS GAERTNERI
Cactaceae

EASTER CACTUS

The mid-green stems of this forest cactus are flattened and segmented, about 2in/5cm long and half as wide. The edges are scalloped and bear small areoles with tufts of yellow bristles rather than spines. The tip of each segment produces a new segment from its center, and the arching, trailing stems that result branch freely. In spring, the segments at the tips of the branches produce flowers with layers of colorful, reflexing petals and petallike sepals in shades of red or pink. The flowering season lasts for several weeks.

Rhipsalidopsis gaertneri, which has recently been reclassified as *Hatiora gaertneri*, is often confused with schlumbergera, the Christmas cactus (see p. 133), which is similar in appearance.

Do not move the plant when it is in bud, or the buds are likely to fall. Even turning the pot around can have this effect.

Dull, limp, wrinkled segments show the plant is short of water. Keep the soil thoroughly moist when the plant is in flower.

The trailing stems are brittle, and segments break off easily. Remove any that are damaged and use undamaged portions for propagation.

FACT FILE

ORIGIN Brazil.

HEIGHT To 12in/30cm, with a similar spread.

POTTING MIX Peat-moss-based with coarse sand in a ratio of 3:1; good drainage is essential.

REPOTTING In mid spring, after the rest period, when the soil is filled with roots. A hanging basket is ideal for this plant.

PROPAGATION Break off segments in spring and summer and insert the bases into soil, where they will root readily.

KEEPING PLANTS Give the plant a spell outdoors in a sheltered, shady location in summer.

PLANT CARE

Bright filtered sunlight. ● Normal room temperature, with a winter minimum of 60°F/16°C. Rest the plant in cool conditions after flowering for 2–3 weeks. ● Keep the soil moist while the plant is in bloom. For a month after flowering ceases, give just enough water to prevent the soil from drying out completely; then increase the amount of water but allow the surface of the soil to dry out between waterings. ● Mist the foliage frequently. ● Apply a high-potash liquid fertilizer every 2 weeks from the formation of the buds until flowering is over. Do not feed during the rest period, then give a balanced liquid feed every 4 weeks until flowering begins again.

RHODODENDRON SIMSII AND HYBRIDS
Ericaceae

*S*IM'S AZALEA

Although they are popular and colorful flowering plants in winter and early spring, many of these hybrid azaleas do not survive in the home for more than one season. They flower best when the roots are restricted, so any plant you buy is likely to be relatively pot-bound. This means that watering has to be frequent to keep the roots constantly moist, as the plant requires.

Azalea hybrids make small, spreading shrubs with leathery, dark green, oval leaves that are usually covered in silky, silvery hairs. The stems are woody and bear small clusters of colorful flowers at their tips. The flowers are usually about 1in/2.5cm across and are often double or semidouble, although there are single varieties that have prominent golden stamens. Some varieties have strongly ruffled petals. Colors includes shades of white, pink, and red, and some bicolors.

FACT FILE

ORIGIN China; Taiwan; hybrids.

HEIGHT To 2ft/60cm as a pot plant.

POTTING MIX Peat-moss-based, ericaceous (lime-free) medium.

REPOTTING Every 2-3 years after flowering; plants flower best when slightly pot-bound. Clay pots are preferable; ensure good drainage.

PROPAGATION Not practical in the home.

KEEPING PLANTS In summer sink the pot in the soil in the shade outdoors to prevent it from drying out and water it regularly.

PLANT CARE

Bright light but no direct sun. ● Cool conditions: 45°–65°F/7°–18°C. ● Water copiously with lime-free water, but do not let the pot stand in water. ● Mist the foliage frequently and stand the pot on a tray of moist gravel. ● Apply a high-potash liquid fertilizer every 2 weeks from spring to fall and sequestered iron occasionally.

Hot, dry air causes the flower buds to turn brown and papery and fail to open. It will eventually kill the plant.

If the plant dries out, it may wilt dramatically, with limp leaves and flowers. But if you act fast, you can usually revive it by plunging the whole pot into water.

Yellow leaves with green veins indicate a lime-induced nutrient deficiency. Use a fertilizer especially for lime-hating plants. Be sure that acid potting mix has been used. Water plants with rainwater in hard-water areas.

RHOEO SPATHACEA 'VARIEGATA'
Commelinaceae

*B*OAT LILY

Although this plant is now known as *Tradescantia spathacea* 'Vittata,' it is generally offered in nurseries and garden centers as *Rhoeo spathacea* 'Variegata' and sometimes even *R. discolor.* It is, however, much less common than the well-known tradescantia (see p. 144).

The long, fleshy, lance-shaped leaves grow in an erect or slightly spreading rosette from a short stem. The surface of the leaf is glossy green with yellow stripes along its length, and the underside is purple-red. At the base of the outer leaves, small, three-petaled, white flowers peep from within long-lasting, purple, boat-shaped bracts, giving rise to the plant's other common name, Moses-in-the-cradle. Flowering may occur at any time of year.

Avoid drafts or fluctuating temperatures, which slow the plant's development.

The yellow stripes on the surface of the leaves become more pronounced in bright light, but the plant will tolerate a shady location.

Purple boat-shaped bracts at the base of the leaves enclose numbers of small white flowers.

FACT FILE

ORIGIN West Indies; Mexico.

HEIGHT To 14in/36cm.

POTTING MIX Peat-moss-based or soil-based.

REPOTTING In spring when roots fill the pot, usually every 2–3 years.

PROPAGATION Remove offshoots, complete with a few roots, from the base of the plant and pot up individually. The plain-leafed form can be raised from seed.

KEEPING PLANTS Plants normally deteriorate after 4–5 years, but enough sideshoots should be produced to replace them regularly.

PLANT CARE

Moderate light with no direct sun. ● Minimum winter temperature 55°–60°F/13°–16°C; normal room temperature at other times. ● Keep the soil thoroughly moist throughout the growing season. Water less in winter; allow the top half of the medium to dry out between waterings. ● Mist the foliage frequently in summer and stand the pot on a tray of moist gravel. ● Feed with a balanced liquid fertilizer every 2 weeks in the growing season.

SAINTPAULIA SPP.
Gesneriaceae

AFRICAN VIOLET

Saintpaulias are one of the most popular of all flowering indoor plants. Hundreds of cultivars have been bred from the species, and new varieties come onto the market each year.

Plants usually form a low-growing rosette of rounded, hairy leaves with lightly scalloped edges, and long, fleshy leafstalks. Leaves are mid to dark green, often with a bluish tinge, and the undersides and leaf stalks may be red. Small clusters of star- or violet-shaped flowers with a pronounced yellow eye are held on stems which rise above the foliage; they may appear throughout the year, often in great profusion.

Modern varieties include doubles and semidoubles, and flowers with frilly-edged petals. Flower colors range from white and pale pink through all shades of violet and blue to rosy red; there are bicolors and flowers with a contrasting edge to the petals. The 'Chimera' strain has flowers with bold stripes in a variety of colors.

Less widely seen are the forms with variegated leaves. Some varieties are so striking that the flowers come a rather poor second to the foliage. There are also trailing varieties, with drooping stems, and miniature, and micro varieties, some of which are only 2in/5cm across when in full flower.

FACT FILE

ORIGIN Tanzania; hybrids.

HEIGHT To 6in/15cm, depending on variety.

POTTING MIX Peat-based; equal parts peat-moss and vermiculite.

REPOTTING In spring, when roots fill the pot. The plant flowers best when slightly pot-bound, so use a pot about one-third the diameter of the plant, up to 6in/15cm across.

PROPAGATION Take leaf stem cuttings or divide large clumps in spring and summer.

KEEPING PLANTS African violets will last for many years provided their special requirements are met.

PLANT CARE

A bright position with no direct sunlight. Filtered winter sunlight or additional fluorescent lighting in winter will encourage year-round flowering; position lights about 12in/30cm above the plants. ● An even temperature of 65°–75°F/18°–24°C. ● Water from below—moderately during the growing season—allowing the surface of the medium to dry out between waterings; water less in cooler winter temperatures. ● High humidity is essential, but the hairy leaves may be damaged by moisture. Stand the pot in a dish of moist gravel; spray foliage with a very fine mist only in warm conditions. ● Apply a dilute high-potash liquid fertilizer every 2 weeks when the plant is in flower and a standard liquid feed at other times.

ALSO RECOMMENDED

Among the best of the miniature hybrids, which seldom grow more than 5–6in/13–15cm wide, are *Saintpaulia* 'Little Delight,' with white flowers, edged with purple; 'Love Bug,' with semidouble, deep red flowers; 'Pip Squeak,' with tiny pale pink flowers, and 'Wee Hope,' whose flowers are white with a blue center.

Flower buds will not form when days are short, but extra artificial light from fluorescent tubes should promote winter flowering.

Remove damaged leafstalks and dead flower stalks by twisting them sideways, to break off the entire stalk. Do not cut them.

Soft, brown spots on the leaves can be caused by moisture lying on the foliage or by sun falling directly on the plant.

Fluffy, gray mold seen on dying flowers and leaves is botrytis, a fungus disease which starts on dead tissue. It is worst in cold, moist conditions. Remove all dead and damaged parts and move the plant to a slightly warmer location.

Use a long-spouted can to water the plant under the rosette of foliage, or stand the pot in water for 30 minutes. Overwatering will cause the leaves to rot at soil level.

Varieties with frilled petals, such as the large-flowered, pale pink 'Marguerite,' are among the most attractive saintpaulia hybrids for use in the home.

SANSEVIERIA TRIFASCIATA 'LAURENTII'
Agavaceae

Mother-in-law's tongue

This sansevieria is a popular house plant, well known for its longevity and tolerance of neglect. The fleshy leaves, which grow in a rosette from a thick rhizome, are sword-shaped, sharply pointed, stiff, and very tall; they are deep green, with horizontal bands of lighter gray-green in a pattern which gives the plant its other common name of snakeskin, or snake, plant. The margins of 'Laurentii,' which is the variety most commonly seen, are deep golden yellow. Sprays of small creamy white flowers appear only occasionally.

The second type of sansevieria is quite different. It is low-growing and forms a rosette of leaves that lie close to the surface of the soil, seldom growing taller than 6–8in/15–20cm.

FACT FILE

ORIGIN South Africa.

HEIGHT To 2ft/60cm.

POTTING MIX Soil-based.

REPOTTING Move in spring, only when the roots become too congested in the pot – sometimes they will even crack it. Use a clay pot to provide a stable base for the tall leaves.

PROPAGATION Divide the clump, or separate offsets from the base of the plant, using a sharp knife to cut through the rhizome, and pot them up individually. Otherwise cut a leaf into 2-in/5-cm strips and push these, right way up, into a mixture of soil-based compost and coarse sand in a ratio of 2:1. The new plants will not have the golden leaf margins of the parent.

KEEPING PLANTS Sansevieria grows slowly and will last for many years.

PLANT CARE

Bright light; this plant enjoys full sun.
● A minimum winter temperature of 55°F/13°C; average to warm room temperature at other times.
● Water moderately during the growing season; allow the top 1in/2.5cm of the soil to dry out between waterings. Give just enough water in winter to prevent the soil from drying out. Do not splash water into the center of the rosette of leaves, as it will cause them to rot.
● Apply a balanced liquid fertiliser every 4 weeks in the growing season.

ALSO RECOMMENDED

Sansevieria trifasciata 'Hahnii' forms a low-growing, compact, rather spreading rosette, with the relatively broad leaves reaching only about 6in/15cm long.
S.t. 'Golden Hahnii' has broad yellow leaf margins and stripes on the mid green leaves. The silvery leaves of *S.t.* 'Silver Hahnii' are mottled with dark green.

Yellow leaves may be caused by rotting at the base of the plant, which is nearly always a symptom of overwatering.

Do not repot plants until the clumps of stems are virtually bursting out of their pots.

A heavy, fairly wide container is necessary to balance the tall top growth; otherwise, the plant will topple over frequently, particularly in winter, when the soil must be kept fairly dry.

Sansevieria trifasciata *tends to sport, or deviate from the usual type, so many different cultivars exist; this is* S.t. 'Craigii,' *a mutant of* 'Laurentii.'

SAXIFRAGA STOLONIFERA
Saxifragaceae

Strawberry Begonia

This plant is ideal for a hanging pot, since its main feature of interest is the large number of baby plantlets it produces at the tips of long, slender runners. The rounded leaves, with lightly scalloped edges, are covered with silvery hairs. Leaves are deep olive green on top, with a network of silver veins, while the undersides and leafstalks are wine red. The variety 'Tricolor' has smaller leaves with an irregular, white, pink-flushed margin and is slower growing.

Plantlets grow on fine, threadlike red stolons, which can be 2ft/60cm or more long, and are generally produced in abundance. The plantlets root easily wherever they touch the soil and soon form a dense mat if allowed to do so. Small white star-shaped flowers, with rather lopsided petals, are carried on long spikes in late summer.

The red flush to the foliage is most pronounced when plants are grown in bright light, but shade the leaves from strong, direct sunlight.

Hang the pot in a well-ventilated location, but out of drafts.

The way the plants produce long runners, plus their rather geranium-like leaves, have given them an alternative common name of strawberry geranium.

FACT FILE

ORIGIN East Asia.

HEIGHT To 8in/20cm; stolons trail to 2ft/60cm.

POTTING MIX Soil-based.

REPOTTING In spring, move into a larger pot if roots are overcrowded.

PROPAGATION Peg down plantlets into pots of potting mix, where they will quickly form roots; they can be separated from the parent before or after they have rooted.

KEEPING PLANTS Replace plants with young plantlets after 2–3 years.

PLANT CARE

Bright light with some direct, but not very strong, sun to maintain leaf coloring. ● Cool conditions—50°–60°F/10°–16°C; a minimum winter temperature of 45°F/7°C. ● Allow to dry slightly between waterings. In winter, water just enough to prevent the soil from drying out. Do not mist. ● In a warm location, stand the pot on a saucer of moist gravel to increase humidity. ● Apply a balanced liquid fertilizer every 4 weeks in spring and summer.

SCHEFFLERA ARBORICOLA
Araliaceae

Umbrella Tree

Now available in a wide range of varieties, *Schefflera arboricola* is also known as *Heptapleurum arboricolum*. It forms a slender tree shape, the upright stem bearing fingered leaves with eight or so 4–6-in/ 10–15-cm-long oval leaflets, which are carried in a circle on leafstalks up to 6in/15cm long. The leaflets near the top of the circle are usually smaller than those at the base. If a tall plant is required, support the stem with a pole covered with moss; aerial roots are produced on mature plants, and these can be inserted into the moss. *S. actinophylla*, syn. *Brassaia actinophylla*, has more leaflets on longer stalks. These leaflets are darker green and can be 12in/30cm long.

FACT FILE

ORIGIN Southeast Asia.

HEIGHT To 6ft/1.8m; more usually 3ft/90cm in the home.

POTTING MIX Peat-moss-based.

REPOTTING In spring, when roots show through the drainage holes in the base of the pot. A large, unpinched plant will do better in a heavy clay pot; it will balance the top growth and add stability.

PROPAGATION Take stem tip cuttings in spring and summer.

KEEPING PLANTS Clean the large glossy leaves with a damp sponge.

PLANT CARE

Bright light with some direct sun except in midsummer. ● Normal room temperature, with a winter minimum of 45°F/7°C. ● Keep the soil moist but not wet in the growing season. Let the surface dry out between waterings in winter. ● Mist the plant regularly and stand the pot on a tray of moist gravel to increase humidity. ● Give a balanced liquid fertilizer every 2 weeks while the plant is in active growth.

Sponge the leaves with lime-free water every 2–3 weeks to remove the dust.

Pinch off the growing tips to produce a bushy, branching plant; an unstopped specimen will quickly become tall and need support.

The leafstalks are normally semierect but will droop if the plant is allowed to dry out. Keep the soil moist, but not waterlogged, from spring to fall.

SCHLUMBERGERA **x** *BUCKLEYI*
Cactaceae

CHRISTMAS CACTUS

The Christmas cactus is sometimes known as zygocactus and is related to the Easter cactus, rhipsalidopsis. Its parent is a forest cactus, valuable for its freely produced, colorful winter flowers.

It has flattened stems composed of segments, which have sharply toothed margins and small areoles surrounded by brownish bristles. New segments arise from the tips of existing ones, and eventually arching stems are produced. Flowers are borne at the tips of the stems in winter or early spring. Despite the common name, most varieties flower naturally rather later than Christmas. The flowers are tubular, about 2in/5cm or more long, with layers of swept-back petals and prominent stamens. They are generally magenta or rosy red; new varieties are constantly being bred.

Schlumbergera x *buckleyi*, also known as *S. bridgesii*, is a hybrid between *S. truncata* and *S. russelliana*.

FACT FILE

ORIGIN Hybrid.

HEIGHT To 2ft/60cm, with a similar spread.

POTTING MIX Peat-moss-based, with added coarse sand.

REPOTTING Every year, after the rest period, when the roots are showing through the drainage holes in the base of the pot.

PROPAGATION Segments root readily in a peat-moss-based mix for propagating cuttings.

KEEPING PLANTS Move to a sheltered, shaded location outdoors during the summer months to promote flowering the following winter.

The leaf segments have smoothly scalloped margins.

Although this plant is a cactus, its home is in humid forests, not deserts, so it needs growing conditions quite unlike those required for other cacti. Mist the plant regularly, preferably with lime-free water, to maintain humidity.

PLANT CARE

Bright light but no direct sun in summer; some winter sun.
● Normal room temperature, with a cooler rest period after flowering and a spell outdoors in summer. ● Keep the soil always moist when the plant is growing; after flowering, water sparingly for 8 weeks until new growth begins in spring, then increase watering. ● Mist the plant regularly and stand the pot on a dish of moist gravel. ● Apply a high-potash liquid fertilizer every 2 weeks during the growing season

ALSO RECOMMENDED

Schlumbergera truncata, known as Thanksgiving or crab cactus, is a parent of many of the hybrid schlumbergeras. Its stem sections have deeply indented edges with pointed "claws" at the ends—hence the name crab cactus. This plant bears large flowers with reflexed deep pink or red petals in the fall.

Schlumbergera truncata, *the crab cactus, has flowers that vary in shape and may be white, almost any shade of red or pink, or bicolored.*

Flowers are normally freely produced from year to year, but they will probably appear later in the season than when the plant was acquired.

SCINDAPSUS AUREUS see *EPIPREMNUM AUREUM*

SEDUM MORGANIANUM
Crassulaceae

*B*URRO'S TAIL

The sedum family is vast and includes many hardy outdoor plants as well as subjects suitable for the home. *Sedum morganianum* is one of the most popular of the indoor types. It is easy to grow and makes an excellent plant for a hanging pot. The long, trailing stems are covered with overlapping, fleshy pale green leaves with a gray-white bloom, each about 1in/2.5cm long and pointed-cylindrical in shape. A well-grown plant will completely cover the pot with a dense mound of stems. Small pink flowers are occasionally produced from the stem tips.

Sometimes the closely related *S. burrito* is available. This is a very similar plant, though the stems do not trail quite as pronouncedly and the leaves are rounder and more bean-shaped. It is easier to handle than *S. morganianum*, since the leaves are not so fragile.

FACT FILE

ORIGIN Mexico.

HEIGHT Stems trail to 2ft/60cm.

POTTING MIX Soil-based, with added coarse sand.

REPOTTING In spring, when the plant fills the pot, in a shallow pan or half pot one size larger.

PROPAGATION Take stem tip cuttings in spring and summer; remove the lower leaves to expose the stem and insert it in sandy potting mix.

KEEPING PLANTS Handle *S. morganianum* carefully so that leaves do not fall off and cause unsightly gaps on the stems.

PLANT CARE

Bright light with some direct sun; shade from strong summer sunshine. ● Keep reasonably cool in winter, with a minimum of 50°F/10°C; normal room temperature at other times. ● Water moderately during the growing season; allow the top ½in/13mm of the soil to dry out between waterings. Water sparingly in winter. ● Feed occasionally with a balanced liquid fertilizer; regular feeding is not necessary.

If leaves are shriveled, wrinkled, and dull-looking, see whether the soil is too dry. A large plant may need repotting.

Plants whose stems cover the soil completely may be difficult to water from the top. Be careful not to saturate the soil when watering from below: overwatering will cause the stems to rot at the base.

SELAGINELLA KRAUSSIANA
Selaginellaceae

*S*PREADING CLUBMOSS

This prostrate, mossy plant has tiny bright green leaves on creeping, branching stems and quickly forms a dense mat. Since selaginellas like humid conditions, they are most frequently grown in terrariums, but care must be taken that they are kept under control. The variegated and gold varieties grow rather more slowly than the plain-leafed type. Also popular is a rather different selaginella—*Selaginella lepidophylla*, the resurrection plant. This is completely dry and rolled into a ball when you buy it. Soak it in water to "resurrect" it to a fresh green rosette. Children love to watch it happen.

Plants can be grown in pots indoors provided they are not in a draft and are misted frequently with tepid water.

Dry air and drafts will quickly lead to the leaves becoming brown and shriveled. A terrarium provides the most suitable growing conditions for this plant.

The creeping stems root as they grow to form a spreading mat.

FACT FILE

ORIGIN South Africa.

HEIGHT Prostrate.

POTTING MIX Peat-moss-based, with added coarse sand.

REPOTTING Repot annually in spring in a shallow pan, until a pot size of 5–6in/13–15cm is reached.

PROPAGATION Take stem tip cuttings in spring.

KEEPING PLANTS Using sharp nail scissors, cut the stems back by up to half in spring when necessary to prevent the plant from becoming too large.

PLANT CARE

Moderate light or light shade, with no direct sun. ● Normal room temperature is suitable, but maintain a steady temperature at all times ● Water thoroughly to keep the soil constantly moist, but do not let the plant stand in water. ● Spray the plant daily with lukewarm water unless it is in a terrarium. ● Apply half-strength standard liquid fertilizer every 4 weeks.

SENECIO x *HYBRIDUS* (SYN. *PERICALLIS* x *HYBRIDUS*)
Compositae

Cineraria

Colorful, short-term flowering plants, cinerarias are especially popular in midwinter, although the main flowering season lasts until midspring. The large, hairy, coarse leaves are light green and roughly heart-shaped. Flowers may be single, semidouble, or double and are carried on long stalks above the foliage in dense, rounded heads up to 8in/20cm across. They are daisylike, with many petals and, usually, yellow centers, but the centers may match the petal color. The wide range of colors includes shades of blue, purple, pink, and red. Many varieties have a white band around the central eye; in some this is so pronounced that the petals appear white with colored tips.

A variety of forms in different sizes are available. The tallest, belonging to the Stellata group, reach a height of 24–30in/60–76cm and have markedly star-shaped flowers that grow in loose clusters. Plants of the Multiflora strain grow to 15–18in/38–46cm and have rounded flower heads, tightly packed with flat, daisylike flowers. Those of the Multiflora Nana group also have dense rounded flower heads, but the plants are more compact, barely reaching 12in/30cm in height. When buying, look for plants with just a few flowers open and plenty of buds to follow, as in the plant shown here. *Senecio* x *hybridus* is also known as *S. cruentus* and *Pericallis cruentus* and may be sold as such.

FACT FILE

ORIGIN Hybrid.

HEIGHT 2ft/60cm depending on variety. Many plants are artificially dwarfed with growth-regulating compounds.

POTTING MIX Peat-moss-based.

REPOTTING Not necessary.

PROPAGATION Sow seed, usually available in mixed color ranges, in summer to produce plants to flower the following winter.

KEEPING PLANTS Discard the plant once the flowers have faded.

PLANT CARE

Bright light, with some direct sun ● Keep the plant cool—preferably at a temperature of about 50°F/10°C—to prolong flowering. ● Water sufficiently to keep the potting mix just moist at all times. ● Feeding is not necessary.

ALSO RECOMMENDED

There is a lot of choice of different heights, flower size, profusion, and season. 'Chloe' is a popular early-flowering strain. 'Brilliant' has restricted leaf growth and large flowers in intense colors. 'Cindy' can be sown in succession for a long flowering season.

The daisylike flowers are available in a wide choice of bright colors and bicolors.

Cinerarias are particularly prone to attack by aphids. Check young foliage and buds regularly and treat with contact insecticide when necessary.

Plants collapse dramatically if the soil is allowed either to dry out or to become waterlogged. Water carefully to keep the soil just moist.

Flower colors range from deep purple and cerise to pale pink and lavender blue, with many varieties having a white central ring on the petals.

SENECIO ROWLEYANUS
Compositae

STRING-OF-BEADS

This unusual-looking foliage plant is quite different from its close relative, the bright-flowered cineraria. It is a creeping succulent with long slender stems, which carry many tiny ($^1/_5$–$^3/_8$in/5–12mm) almost spherical leaves; it is these that give the plant its common name. Small white flower heads that look like shaving brushes are borne in spring.

Several other senecios make good houseplants as well. Non-succulent *Senecio mikanioides*, German ivy, (also known as *Delairea odorata*) has mid- to dark green leaves about 3in/8cm long, which are carried alternately on long, trailing or twining stems. Each leaf has about seven lobes, the tips of which end in sharp points. Fragrant yellow groundsellike flowers are sometimes borne in small clusters.

Senecio macroglossus, the wax vine, is a similar plant, but the leaves have between three and five lobes. The form most commonly seen is 'Variegatus,' with irregular creamy yellow markings on a glossy, dark green background. The twining stems become woody with age.

FACT FILE

ORIGIN Namibia.

HEIGHT Trailing stems to 3ft/90cm.

POTTING MIX Soil-based, with coarse sand added in a ratio of 3:1.

REPOTTING Move into a larger pot in spring, when the plant fills the pot. A hanging pot allows the stems to trail gracefully.

PROPAGATION Take stem tip cuttings during spring and summer.

KEEPING PLANTS Flourishes under warm conditions, but flowers best after a cool early winter rest.

PLANT CARE

Bright light, with some direct sun except in midsummer. ● Warm conditions; a minimum of 50°F/10°C in winter. ● Keep the soil just moist during the growing season; allow the surface to dry out between waterings. Water only enough in winter to prevent the soil from drying out completely. ● Apply a balanced liquid fertilizer every 2 weeks during the growing season.

Watch out for aphids, which attack new shoots in summer, and for red spider mites.

Pinch off shoot tips occasionally to keep the plant compact.

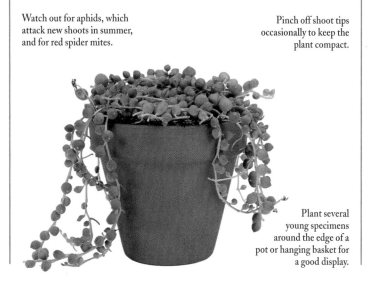

Plant several young specimens around the edge of a pot or hanging basket for a good display.

SETCREASEA PURPUREA
Commelinaceae

PURPLE HEART

Also known as *Tradescantia pallida* 'Purple Heart,' this is the variety nearly always found, since it is a tolerant, easily grown houseplant. The fleshy, succulent, jointed stems and the clasping, lance-shaped leaves are all a rich purple, set off in summer by three-petaled, bright purple-pink flowers that are produced in the leaf axils. Leaves are lance-shaped, about 4in/10cm long and 1in/2.5cm wide, and slightly hairy, the hairs giving them a glistening appearance.

The slender stems are about 16in/40cm long. They start upright but soon arch over the sides of the pot to trail, sometimes turning up slightly at the tips. This is an ideal plant for a hanging basket.

The fleshy, rather brittle foliage is quite delicate and easily damaged. Handle plants carefully, and do not place them where they will be brushed against.

Straggly stems with long gaps between the leaves may be a sign that the plant needs a brighter location, but it is natural for plants to become leggy after a few years.

Bright light, with plenty of direct sun, is essential for intense purple coloring in the leaves and stems.

FACT FILE

ORIGIN Mexico.

HEIGHT Stems trail to 2ft/60cm.

POTTING MIX Soil- or peat-moss-based.

REPOTTING Move into a larger pot as soon as roots show through the drainage holes in the base.

PROPAGATION Stem tip cuttings taken in the spring and early summer root easily.

KEEPING PLANTS Replace plants with newly rooted cuttings when they become straggly, usually after 2 or 3 years.

PLANT CARE

Bright light is essential for good leaf color. Some direct sun, but protect the plant from strong midsummer sun. ● 65°–70°F/18°–21°C is the ideal growing temperature, with a minimum of 50°F/10°C or a little lower in winter. ● Keep the soil moist at all times; allow the surface to dry out slightly between waterings. ● Apply a balanced liquid fertilizer every 2 weeks during the growing season.

SINNINGIA SPECIOSA
Gesneriaceae

Gloxinia

The brilliantly colored, flaring, trumpet-shaped flowers of this familiar pot plant are extremely showy. Hybrids are more commonly found than the species. The large, 8-in/20-cm-long leaves are more or less oval in shape, and velvety, with short, dense hairs. They grow in opposite pairs on short stems arising from a tuber.

Flower buds emerge from the leaf axils in summer. The flowers, which are about 3in/8cm across, are velvety and richly colored. They may be red, pink, purple, blue, or white; some are bicolored or have a picotee edge. The long throats of the flowers are often of a contrasting shade to the flared petals; in some varieties, the petals or throat are densely spotted, giving the blooms the appearance of a foxglove.

'Princess Elizabeth' is blue with a white throat, and 'Waterloo' is an intense scarlet. Seed-raised strains include the compact 'Glory' series, with flowers in blue, pink, red, and blue, and red with a white edge. 'Brocade' has double flowers in blue, pink, red, and red-and-white.

FACT FILE

ORIGIN Brazil; hybrids.

HEIGHT To 10in/25cm.

POTTING MIX Peat-moss-based; equal parts peat moss, perlite, vermiculite.

PROPAGATION Sow seed in spring. Plants can also be grown from leaf cuttings taken in late spring and early summer.

KEEPING PLANTS After flowering, continue to feed the plant but water more sparingly until the leaves die down. Let the soil dry out and overwinter the tuber dry in its pot at about 50°F/10°C. In spring repot in fresh soil with the tuber hollow side up. Water sparingly until new growth begins.

PLANT CARE

Bright light but no direct sun. ● Temperature of 60°F/16°C or above in a draft-free place. ● Keep the soil moist at all times, but do not overwater or allow water to lie in the hollow-surfaced tuber, or the plant will rot. ● Apply a balanced liquid fertilizer every 2 weeks during the growing season.

Plants can be obtained as dormant tubers. Pot them with the hollow surface upward and set the tuber level with the surface of the potting mix.

Fluctuating temperatures and dry air may cause the flower buds to drop before they open.

Stand the pot on a tray of moist gravel to provide extra humidity, but do not mist the hairy foliage or the flowers.

SOLANUM CAPSICASTRUM
Solanaceae

False Jerusalem Cherry

Two species of solanum are grown for their colorful winter berries, *Solanum capsicastrum* and *S. pseudocapsicum*. They are very similar and are often confused. *S. capsicastrum* makes a branching, twiggy plant with mid to dark green, lance-shaped leaves. The leaf surface is slightly hairy, and the leaf margins are gently waved. Small, starry white flowers with prominent stamens are carried in summer and are followed by round berries about ¹/₂in/13mm in diameter. These are green, turning pale green, then white, before ripening to orange-red. They are long-lasting, remaining on the plant throughout most of the winter. *S. pseudocapsicum*, the winter cherry or Jerusalem cherry, grows slightly taller, with larger, more brightly colored berries. Dwarf forms are often offered.

The fruits of both plants may be attractive to young children, but they are poisonous and should not be eaten.

Aphids often infest the young shoots. Spray with a contact insecticide.

Plants can be kept for a second year, but berries may fail to form. Ensure good flowering and berrying by placing the plant outside during the summer.

Hot, dry conditions will cause the berries to shrivel and fall prematurely.

FACT FILE

ORIGIN Brazil.

HEIGHT To 18in/46cm; usually about 12in/30cm.

POTTING MIX Peat-moss-based.

REPOTTING Move into a pot one size larger in late spring.

PROPAGATION Sow seed in early spring.

KEEPING PLANTS Once the berries have passed their best, reduce watering and cut the stems back by half. Repot the plant and place it in a sheltered, semishaded location outdoors when all danger of frost has passed. Bring it indoors in early fall, before the first frost.

PLANT CARE

A bright position in direct sun. ● Cool conditions for the berries to last well, ideally a maximum of 60°F/16°C. ● Keep the potting mix moist at all times; reduce watering in spring. ● Stand the pot on a tray of moist gravel and mist the plant frequently while it is flowering. ● Apply a balanced liquid fertilizer every 2 weeks.

SPATHIPHYLLUM WALLISII
Araceae

*P*EACE LILY

Also sometimes known as white sails, the long-lived peace lily is useful as a dual-purpose plant, with attractive foliage as well as flowers; it also tolerates lower light levels than many plants. The glossy dark green leaves, produced directly from rhizomes, are strongly veined and lance-shaped. They are about 6in/15cm long and are carried on long stalks, which arch outward elegantly. Arumlike flowers, which are produced during spring and early summer and sometimes into early fall, rise above the foliage on stiff stems. The white, saillike spathe surrounds a central spadix of creamy yellow. Flowers remain in good condition for several weeks, but when they are past their best, the flower stalks should be cut off as close to the base as possible.

Most of the popular varieties are of hybrid origin. 'Mauna Loa,' a vigorous cultivar with long leaves and large flowers, is perhaps the best known, but 'Cupido,' 'Illusion,' 'Petite,' and 'Sensation' are also grown.

The white flower spathes turn pale green as they age and remain attractive for several weeks.

Spathiphyllum is particularly sensitive to dry air, which causes the leaves to shrivel and fall prematurely. Mist the foliage daily in summer.

In hot, dry conditions, red spider mites often attack the plant. Increase misting and set the plant on a dish of moist gravel to raise humidity and help prevent infestation.

FACT FILE

ORIGIN South America; hybrids.

HEIGHT To 18in/46cm.

POTTING MIX Peat-moss-based.

REPOTTING Move into a pot one size larger in spring until the maximum convenient pot size is reached; thereafter top-dress annually.

PROPAGATION Divide large clumps in spring; pull the rhizomes apart carefully, and repot the sections individually.

KEEPING PLANTS Keep out of direct sun, which will scorch the foliage.

PLANT CARE

Bright, filtered light. ● Normal room temperature is suitable, with a minimum of 55°–60°F/ 13°–16°C. ● Keep the soil moist during the growing season but allow the surface to dry out before rewatering. Reduce the amount of water in cool conditions. ● Set the pot on a dish of moist gravel and mist the foliage frequently. ● Feed with a balanced liquid fertilizer every 2 weeks in spring and summer.

STEPHANOTIS FLORIBUNDA
Asclepiadaceae

*M*ADAGASCAR JASMINE

The beautiful, overwhelmingly fragrant flowers of stephanotis make this a much-coveted plant, but it is not among the easiest to grow. It is a strong climber, usually sold twined around a wire hoop.

The slender, light green young stems soon turn woody; they bear glossy, dark green, oval, pointed leaves about 4in/10cm long in opposite pairs. The flowers are carried in clusters from spring through summer; they are waxy, white, and tubular, opening into a five-petaled star about 1¼in/3cm across. One cluster of flowers is enough to perfume a whole room with a strong, intensely sweet fragrance. Stephanotis is also known as the wax flower.

FACT FILE

ORIGIN Madagascar.

HEIGHT To 15ft/4.5m or more, but usually kept to about 3ft/90cm.

POTTING MIX Soil-based or a mix of soil-based and peat-moss-based.

REPOTTING In spring, usually every 2 years, until an 8-in/20-cm pot is required.

PROPAGATION By semiripe stem cuttings in summer, but these are not easy to root. Hormone rooting powder and a heated propagator improve the chances of success. Or sow seed in spring.

KEEPING PLANTS Flowers are carried on new growth, so cut out old stems in winter and tie in young shoots as they form.

PLANT CARE

Bright light, but shade from direct midsummer sun. ● Evenly warm, draft-free conditions, ideally 65°–70°F/18–21°C, with a minimum of 55°F/13°C in winter. ● Keep the soil moist at all times in the growing season, but do not allow the plant to stand in water. In winter, let the top half of the soil dry out between waterings. ● Mist the foliage regularly and set the pot on a dish of moist gravel. ● Apply dilute high-potash liquid fertilizer every 2 weeks in spring and summer.

The fragrant, waxy, white flowers are popular for bridal bouquets.

Buds will drop before opening in fluctuating temperatures or if the plant is moved to a different position or if the soil is allowed to dry out during the growing season.

Scale insects may be found on the undersides of the leaves. Remove any scales seen with a fingernail and treat the plant with an appropriate insecticide.

STREPTOCARPUS **×** *HYBRIDUS*
Gesneriaceae

CAPE PRIMROSE

The foliage of the popular streptocarpus hybrids forms a rosette, with long, rather ungainly, wrinkled leaves like those of a primrose. Long flower stems arise from the rosette, carrying clusters of trumpet-shaped flowers in shades of red, pink, lavender, purple, and white. The flowers have a rather velvety texture, and their throats are often striped or marked with a contrasting color. Plants can be bought in bloom at virtually any time of the year.

The first popular hybrid, the violet-blue 'Constant Nymph,' was introduced some 50 years ago. Since then, hundreds of varieties have been bred, giving improved flower colors and more-compact foliage.

FACT FILE

ORIGIN South Africa.

HEIGHT To 10in/25cm.

POTTING MIX Peat-moss-based; or equal parts peat moss, perlite or vermiculite.

REPOTTING Repot annually in spring.

PROPAGATION Divide large plants or take leaf cuttings in spring and insert them into a coarse mixture of equal parts of peat moss and perlite or vermiculite. Small plants will grow from the base of the leaf; when they are 2–3in/5–8cm high, pot them individually.

KEEPING PLANTS In normal room temperature, the plant will grow all year-round.

PLANT CARE

Bright light but no direct sun. ● Average room temperature, with a minimum of 55°F/13°C in winter. ● Water moderately during the growing season to keep the soil just moist. In cooler winter temperatures, allow the top ½in/13mm of the soil to dry out before rewatering. ● Mist the foliage occasionally and set the pot on a dish of moist gravel, particularly in warm conditions. ● Feed with a high-potash liquid fertilizer every 2 weeks while the plants are growing.

ALSO RECOMMENDED

Streptocarpus 'John Innes' hybrids have flowers and foliage similar to 'Constant Nymph,' but the stems are slightly longer (about 8in/20cm). The choice of colors, includes pink, purple, and deep blue. *S.* 'Wiesmoor' hybrids have larger leaves and as many as 5 flower stems on a plant; these are up to 12in/30cm long and carry 3–4 flowers, which can be 3in/8cm across. Colors range from dark red through pinks to blue, often with darker markings on the lower lobes of the trumpet.

Small-flowered plants. Not all streptocarpus hybrids are large-flowered. Charming ones, such as the dainty 'Falling Stars,' have now been produced. They bear dozens of tiny flowers on semitrailing stems.

Flowers are sometimes followed by interesting, long, spirally twisted seed pods. But ideally dead flowers should be removed before seed sets, to avoid weakening the plant.

If the leaves suddenly become limp and droop, the plant may have been overwatered. Vine weevil grubs attacking the roots may also be responsible.

The plant will benefit from a fine mist spray over the foliage in the mornings, but keep moisture off the flowers, since it can cause unsightly brown spots.

The strap-shaped leaves are brittle and easily damaged, so take care when handling the plant.

Succulents

These plants—of which cacti form probably the best-known group—are able to store water very efficiently, so they are well adapted to dry conditions. They usually have fleshy leaves or stems, or both: cacti are those plants that have fleshy stems and small leaves or no leaves. Succulents are generally easy to grow and tolerant of neglect, but they can easily be killed by overwatering. Unlike most houseplants, the majority are happy on the brightest of sunny windowsills. They will withstand very hot conditions, while some can survive in temperatures as low as 45°F/7°C. They prefer cool conditions at night, and thrive in widely varying night and daytime temperatures.

There are two types of cacti, desert and jungle, but all are distinguished from other succulents by areoles, bumps, or indentations on the stems that bear spines, bristles, or hairs, and from which trumpet or bell-shaped flowers arise. Desert cacti have tiny leaves or no leaves. Their thick green stems conserve water and do the job of photosynthesis. Jungle cacti are mostly epiphytes; they grow in niches in trees and rocks that are often dry; hence their need for stems that can store water.

The plants known as succulents are not so easy to define. They do not all belong to a single family. Many families have some more or less succulent members, which store water in their leaves or have no leaves and store water in their stems. Others, such as several of the aloes, have little capacity to store water at all. The plants and their flowers differ widely in habit, shape, and size.

Opuntia microdasys, the prickly pear cactus, with oval flattened pads, is a popular houseplant. It tends to produce two new pads on the top of an existing one, giving it the appearance of a rabbit's head and the common name of bunny ears. Outdoors they can be invasive, and they are subject to strict controls in some countries.

Small, round tufts of yellow bristles grow symmetrically all over the pads. If the plant is touched, the bristles can break off and they irritate the skin; handle the plant with a folded newspaper when repotting it.

Opuntias flower and produce prickly fruits outdoors, but plants are unlikely to flower indoors.

ALSO RECOMMENDED

Crassula muscosa is a succulent with woody branches, hidden by a sheath of flat, pointed, gray-green leaves. It bears clusters of yellow-green flowers in summer.

Rhipsalis cereuscula originates in South America. It is a curious epiphytic cactus with two types of stem: long and cylindrical, and short, with branching clusters at the end. These clusters also branch and spread from the apex.

Schlumbergera truncata, crab cactus, is a forest cactus, so it likes shade and high humidity. The segmented stems have 2 forward-pointing "claws," and pink and white flowers are borne on the tips in winter.

Black marks at the base of the stem, followed by rotting and the top growth toppling over, are caused by overwatering.

Brown, shriveled patches on the pads often follow physical damage. Affected parts can be cut out and the exposed tissue treated with fungicidal powder to prevent the problem from spreading.

Mealybugs can be seen as patches of white, waxy wool on the surface of the pads. Remove them carefully with a cotton swab.

Slugs and some caterpillars, which seem impervious to the bristles, eat the stems, causing large holes.

Root mealybugs, a common pest of cacti, are difficult to control. Remove the plant from its pot and check for white, wooly bugs in the roots; if found, drench the roots with appropriate insecticide.

FACT FILE

ORIGIN Cacti: the Americas. **Succulents:** mainly arid regions worldwide.

HEIGHT Varies according to species; *Opuntia microdasys* will grow to about 18in/46cm indoors.

POTTING MIX **Cacti and succulents:** soil-based with sharp sand or perlite added for good drainage, or special cactus medium.

REPOTTING In spring, when the soil is filled with roots, move the plant to a pot one size larger.

PROPAGATION Some cacti and succulents produce offsets around the base of the plant. In others, single segments can be removed for use as cuttings. Let the base of the cutting dry out for a day or two before inserting it into sandy potting mix. Almost all can be raised from seed fairly easily.

KEEPING PLANTS Most cacti and succulents appreciate a spell outdoors in a sheltered but sunny location during summer.

PLANT CARE

Bright light to full sun (except jungle cacti in summer). ● Normal room temperature, with a minimum of 50°F/10°C for succulents and jungle cacti; desert cacti need a cool winter rest. ● Water all types fairly freely in the growing season, allowing the top 1/2in/13mm of soil to dry out between waterings. In winter give just enough water to prevent plants from shriveling. ● Feed established plants with a balanced liquid fertilizer (20-20-20) every 2–3 weeks in the growing season.

PESTS & DISEASES

Succulents and cacti do not suffer from many pests. Mealybugs and root mealybugs are the most troublesome, although red spider mites may be a nuisance if the air become too dry. Many species are, however, susceptible to infection by fungi and bacteria— often as a result of overwatering— which causes the stems to rot.

TAKE CARE

Cacti spines and bristles irritate when lodged in the skin. Keep plants out of the reach of children.

Echinocactus grusonii, golden barrel cactus, is a desert plant. The strongly ribbed stem is covered with spines up to 2in/5cm long. In summer it bears yellow flowers.

Gymnocalycium mihanovichii 'Red Cap' is a cultivar. The colored stem, which can be red, pink, or yellow, lacks chlorophyll and cannot survive on its own, so it is grafted onto a green cactus stock.

SYNGONIUM PODOPHYLLUM
Araceae

*A*RROWHEAD VINE

This plant is rather similar to a philodendron and makes a good climbing foliage specimen. The young leaves start off more or less heart-shaped, gradually become arrowhead-shaped (hence the name), then lobed and divided into segments as the plant matures; it is also called the goosefoot plant. Different types of leaves are carried on the plant at one time, adding to its interest. Young plants make a spreading bush, with climbing stems developing later.

The most popular varieties have different patterns of pale green, white, or cream marking the leaves. 'Butterfly' has deep green leaves with lighter veins, while 'Imperial White' has leaves marbled with white. 'Pixie' is a compact, small-leafed form.

FACT FILE

ORIGIN South America.

HEIGHT Climbs to 4ft/1.2m or more.

POTTING MIX Peat-moss-based or soil-based with added peat moss.

REPOTTING In spring, in a pot one size larger until a 12-in/30-cm pot is required, then top-dress annually.

PROPAGATION Take stem tip cuttings in early summer.

KEEPING PLANTS A moss pole makes an ideal support, since aerial roots are produced and can be encouraged to grow into the moss.

PLANT CARE

Bright light, especially for variegated types, but no direct sun.
● Normal room temperature, with a winter minimum of 60°F/16°C.
● Keep the potting mix moist in summer, allowing the surface to dry out before rewatering. Water less in winter; letting the top half of the potting mix dry out. ● Apply a balanced liquid fertilizer every 2 weeks during the growing season.

A bushy plant with juvenile foliage can be maintained by cutting out the climbing stems as soon as they form.

The leaves are usually variegated and change shape as the plant matures.

A hot, dry atmosphere may cause the foliage to shrivel and fall prematurely. Mist it regularly and place the pot on a dish of damp pebbles.

The stems can be allowed to trail from a hanging basket instead of being trained up a moss pole.

THYMUS VULGARIS
Labiatae

*W*ILD THYME

A strongly aromatic culinary herb, thyme is a useful plant to grow on a kitchen windowsill, especially in the winter. *Thymus vulgaris*, common thyme, shown here, makes a small, wiry-stemmed, spreading shrub, with tiny, scented, deep green, pointed leaves carried in opposite pairs. Small, pale lavender flowers are borne near the tips of the stems in summer, but not usually on indoor plants. 'Silver Posie' has attractive silver-variegated leaves.

Creeping thyme, *T. serpyllum*, forms a creeping mat, and has a fragrance and flavor similar to common thyme. 'Aureus' has yellow foliage. There are a number of hybrids, including *T.* x *citriodorus,* lemon-scented thyme, which has a popular golden variegated version, 'Doone Valley.' The low-growing species are probably best for indoor culture. They are hardy plants and should be given a spell outdoors whenever possible. Pinching off the growing tips for use in cooking should help to keep the plants compact.

The low-growing stems of creeping thyme will cascade over the sides of a pot.

Thyme grown indoors tend to have softer leaves and stems and a less pungent flavor than those grown outdoors.

Variegation adds to the interest of the plant, but good light is necessary to maintain the leaf coloration.

FACT FILE

ORIGIN Mediterranean regions.

HEIGHT To 12in/30cm when grown in a pot indoors.

POTTING MIX Soil-based.

REPOTTING Repot as necessary in spring. Older thyme should be planted outdoors; young specimens are best indoors.

PROPAGATION Take stem tip cuttings in early summer or sow seed in spring.

KEEPING PLANTS Place the plant outdoors in the summer and keep it watered. Bring it inside again in fall. When it becomes too large and straggly, replace it with a young plant.

PLANT CARE

Bright light, especially for variegated types, with as much direct sun as possible. ● Moderately cool room temperature (55°–65°F/13°–18°C). ● Water well, allowing the plant to dry between thorough waterings. Water sparingly in winter. ● Apply a balanced liquid fertilizer every 3 weeks during spring and summer.

TILLANDSIA IONANTHA
Bromeliaceae

$\mathcal{S}$KY PLANT

These plants have become popular as novelty plants in recent years and are found in a wide range of outlets. *Tillandsia ionantha* is one of the most common. It is a small plant, forming a tight, upright-growing rosette of stiff, silver, pointed leaves. The extremely fine tips usually curl over to give the whole plant the appearance of a small sea anemone. In late spring the center of the rosette turns red just before small violet flowers appear. The silver sheen on the leaves comes from the tiny, soft, furlike scales that cover the leaf surface and absorb moisture and nutrients from the atmosphere.

This tillandsia is an epiphyte, living not in soil but on the limbs of trees in its natural habitat. Like an epiphytic orchid, it can be grown in an open, free-draining medium of shredded bark or osmunda fiber, but it does best when mounted on wood or cork bark. Roots are usually produced to support the plant on its mount.

Mount this tillandsia on wood or bark to simulate the way it grows in its natural habitat. Ordinary potting mix will cause the base of the plant to rot.

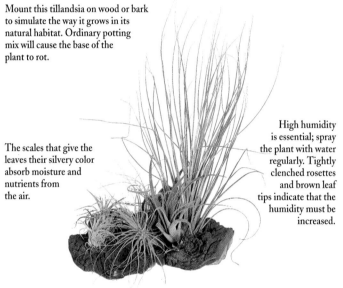

The scales that give the leaves their silvery color absorb moisture and nutrients from the air.

High humidity is essential; spray the plant with water regularly. Tightly clenched rosettes and brown leaf tips indicate that the humidity must be increased.

FACT FILE

ORIGIN South and Central America.

HEIGHT To 4in/10cm with a similar spread.

POTTING MIX Wrap the roots or base of a mounted plant in damp sphagnum moss. The plant can also be grown in orchid medium.

REPOTTING Not necessary.

PROPAGATION Detach the offsets that appear around the base of a mature plant with some roots, and establish them separately.

KEEPING PLANTS Most plants will benefit from a spell in a sheltered position outdoors during the summer.

PLANT CARE

Bright light, but not direct sun. ● Normal room temperature, with a minimum of 50°F/10°C. ● Mist the plant with water twice a week in summer, thoroughly wetting the leaves. In cooler winter conditions, mist once a week or once every 2 weeks. ● Add a half-strength solution of high-potash liquid fertilizer to the misting water every week in spring and summer.

TOLMIEA MENZIESII
Saxifragaceae

$\mathcal{P}$IGGYBACK PLANT

The main decorative feature of *Tolmiea menziesii* is the way in which young plantlets form at the base of the older leaves, giving the plant its common name; it is also sometimes known as mother-of-thousands and youth-on-age. The plant forms a mound of hairy, bright green, roughly heart-shaped leaves, which are lobed and have toothed margins. They are carried on long leafstalks, and where the leaf joins the stalk, small plantlets arise and eventually weigh the leaf down, inducing it to trail. The plantlets root where they touch the soil.

A yellow-splashed form, 'Variegata,' also called 'Taff's Gold,' which bears both variegated and plain leaves, is often grown. Tubular, greenish, rather insignificant flowers are occasionally borne in summer.

FACT FILE

ORIGIN Western North America.

HEIGHT To 10in/25cm; 15–20in/38–50cm in bloom.

POTTING MIX Peat-moss-based or soil-based.

REPOTTING At any time, when roots fill the current pot.

PROPAGATION Detach leaves bearing well-developed plantlets and set them in a pot so that their base is in close contact with the soil; roots will soon form. Take off the parent leaf only when it has dried up.

KEEPING PLANTS Tolmieas are good in a hanging pot. Put several young plants around the edge, and within 6 months they will cascade gracefully downward, forming an attractive plant.

PLANT CARE

Bright light with some direct sun, but shade from extremely strong midsummer sun, which will scorch the leaves. ● Cool room temperature (55°–65°F/13°–18°C), with a winter minimum of 45°F/7°C. ● Keep the soil moist during the growing season, watering more sparingly in winter. ● Mist the foliage occasionally. ● Feed with a balanced liquid fertilizer every 2 weeks in the growing season.

Brown, crisp, shriveled leaves indicate that the atmosphere is too hot and dry. The plant needs regular misting in warm conditions.

Leaves become pale and leafstalks elongated when the plant is not receiving enough light. Move to a brighter position.

TRADESCANTIA FLUMINENSIS 'VARIEGATA'
Commelinaceae

*W*ANDERING JEW

A member of the same family as setcreasea and zebrina, tradescantia is perhaps the best known of the group. It is popular for its rapid growth, colorful foliage, and tolerance of poor growing conditions. Most frequently called wandering Jew, it is also called spiderwort and speeding Jenny.

The plant produces long, fleshy stems set with succulent, clasping, alternate leaves about 2in/5cm long. These are light green, striped with cream, and have pale purple undersides. Small, three-petaled white flowers with a fluffy central boss of stamens are sometimes produced on well-grown plants. Another common variety is the fast-growing *Tradescantia fluminensis* 'Quicksilver,' which has white-striped leaves.

FACT FILE

ORIGIN South America.

HEIGHT Stems trail to 2ft/60cm and more.

POTTING MIX Peat-moss-based.

REPOTTING In spring, when the current pot is filled with roots. Put several rooted cuttings in the same pot for the best effect.

PROPAGATION By stem tip cuttings, which root readily at any time.

KEEPING PLANTS Pinch off the growing tips to create a bushy plant. After a few years, when older leaves fall and stems are bare, replace the plant with young rooted cuttings.

PLANT CARE

Bright light with some direct sun for good leaf coloration. ● Average room temperature, with a minimum of 45°F/7°C. ● Water freely during the growing season, keeping the potting mix moist at all times. In winter, allow the top 1in/2.5cm of medium to dry out before rewatering. ● Mist the foliage occasionally in warm weather. ● Apply a balanced liquid fertilizer every 2 weeks during the growing season.

Pinch off the tips of shoots regularly for a bushy plant.

Remove any all-green shoots from variegated plants. The stronger-growing green shoots will soon take over if they are allowed to do so.

Pinch off growing tips regularly and replace old straggly plants with newly rooted cuttings.

TRADESCANTIA PALLIDA see *SETCREASEA PALLIDA*
TRADESCANTIA SPATHACEA see *RHOEO SPATHACEA*
TRADESCANTIA ZEBRINA see *ZEBRINA PENDULA*

VRIESEA SPLENDENS
Bromeliaceae

*F*LAMING SWORD

Probably one of the easiest bromeliads to grow (see pp. 48–49), this vriesea makes a rosette of stiff, arching leaves about 12in/30cm long; these are dark green with purple-brown horizontal bands. A tall flower spike, topped with a series of flattened, bright scarlet bracts, grows from the center of the rosette. The yellow flowers that emerge from the bracts are short-lived, but the colorful bracts usually persist for several weeks.

Many vriesea hybrids have been bred to provide colorful flowering houseplants. Among them are *Vriesia × poelmannii* 'White Line,' with glossy green leaves that have a broad central yellow stripe; 'Marjan,' with yellow bracts flushed red at the base; and 'Margot,' with deep green leaves and a branching flower spike.

The brilliantly colored, swordlike flower spike may be produced at almost any time of year.

It is natural for the main rosette to die back after flowering. Offshoots at the base can be allowed to replace it, but they will not reach flowering size for 2 or 3 years.

When buying plants, look for specimens where the flower spike is only just emerging from the rosette of leaves.

Dull, speckled leaves may have been attacked by red spider mites: look for webbing under the arching tip. Provide high humidity to help prevent infestation.

FACT FILE

ORIGIN Tropical America.

HEIGHT To 2ft/60cm.

POTTING MIX Peat-moss-based.

REPOTTING In spring, only when the potting mix is filled with roots; usually every 2–3 years.

PROPAGATION Detach basal offsets carefully with a sharp knife, retain as much root as possible, and pot them up individually.

KEEPING PLANTS After flowering, the rosette dies back, but offsets are produced around the base of the plant to replace it.

PLANT CARE

Moderate to bright light with some direct sun, but protect plants from strong midsummer sun that may scorch the leaves. ● Average room temperature with a winter minimum of 60°F/16°C. ● Keep the potting mix just moist at all times and the central "vase" in the rosette of leaves filled with water. ● Mist the foliage occasionally in warm weather. ● Apply a half-strength solution of balanced liquid fertilizer through the central "vase" every 4 weeks in the growing season.

YUCCA ELEPHANTIPES
Agavaceae

Spineless Yucca

Yuccas are good architectural plants, tolerant of a wide range of conditions. *Yucca elephantipes* is usually available as a stout, woody trunk with one or two rosettes of long, sword-shaped, pointed leaves at the top. The edges of these leaves are toothed but spineless, and the leaves themselves are much softer than other houseplant yuccas such as the spiky *Y. aloifolia* (known with good reason as Spanish bayonet), making them safer plants where there are children. The leaves arch downward and can reach 4ft/1.2m in length. Plants are also available as a stemless or short-stemmed rosette in a pot. The panicles of creamy, bell-shaped flowers are not produced on indoor plants.

Several variegated varieties are available, including 'Silver Star,' 'Jewel,' and 'Variegata.'

FACT FILE

ORIGIN Mexico.

HEIGHT Varies according to the length of the prepared "trunk," usually 4–6ft/1.2–1.8m.

POTTING MIX Soil-based.

REPOTTING In spring, when the current pot is filled with roots. When the maximum convenient pot size is reached, top-dress annually.

PROPAGATION Basal offsets are sometimes produced and can be removed and potted up individually.

KEEPING PLANTS The plant will benefit from standing outdoors in summer in a sheltered, sunny spot.

PLANT CARE

Bright light with plenty of direct sun. ● Normal room temperature, with a winter minimum of 50°F/10°C. ● Keep the soil moist during the growing season. In winter give just enough water to prevent the soil from drying out. ● Yuccas are fairly tolerant of dry air, but mist the foliage occasionally in warm weather. ● Feed with a balanced liquid fertilizer every 2 weeks in spring and summer.

Plants may be produced either as a sawn-off trunk with one or two rosettes of leaves near the top, or as a single rosette in a pot.

The long, sword-shaped leaves are softer than the stiff-tipped varieties of yucca, making this a safer variety for the home.

Tall plants may topple over easily and should be potted in soil-based potting mix in a clay pot for extra stability.

ZEBRINA PENDULA
Commelinaceae

Silvery Inch Plant

A relative of tradescantia, and like tradescantia also sometimes called wandering Jew, *Zebrina pendula* is a fast-growing trailing plant with showy, glistening, colorful foliage.

The lance-shaped leaves are about 2in/5cm long, and their upper surface is banded with green and silver (giving rise to its name of zebra plant) and purple undersides. The variety 'Quadricolor' has green, silver, purple, and pink striped leaves. And 'Purpusii,' the bronze inch plant, has deep green leaves flushed with purple. It carries small, purple-pink, three-petaled flowers in spring and summer.

Pinch off the growing tips regularly to prevent stems from becoming straggly.

Brown, crisp tips and margins to the leaves indicate a hot, dry atmosphere, which will encourage attack by red spider mites. Spray to increase humidity and deter the pests.

Leaves may become dull or revert to all-green if they do not receive sufficient light.

The glistening leaves and stems are fleshy and break easily if handled carelessly. Pinch off damaged shoots at leaf nodes and use the top portion as a cutting.

FACT FILE

ORIGIN Mexico.

HEIGHT Stems trail to 3ft/90cm.

POTTING MIX Peat-moss-based or soil-based.

REPOTTING In spring, when roots fill the current pot, move to one a size larger. Plant several cuttings in a pot for the best effect. This is a good plant for a hanging basket, or it can be trained up a small trellis.

PROPAGATION By stem tip cuttings, which will root readily in spring and summer.

KEEPING PLANTS The plant will last for several years; when it becomes leggy, replace it with newly rooted cuttings.

PLANT CARE

A bright, sunny location to ensure good leaf color, although the plant is tolerant of shade. ● Normal room temperature, with a minimum of 55°F/13°C in winter. ● Keep the potting mix moist at all times during the growing season. Reduce watering in winter and allow the surface to dry out before rewatering. ● Mist the foliage occasionally to increase humidity. ● Apply a balanced liquid fertilizer from time to time during spring and summer; the plant does not normally need regular feeding.

ACORUS GRAMINEUS
Araceae

SWEET FLAG

The acorus most frequently grown as a houseplant is the form with the variegated leaves of a water margin plant from China and Japan. Its fine, grasslike arching leaves grow from a thin rhizome running just below the surface of the soil. They are some 4in/10cm wide and 12in/30cm long, and are narrowly striped with white. An insignificant pale green flower spathe, which is almost indistinguishable from the leaves, is borne in summer.

The plant looks good on its own but is perhaps better when grown in a bowl with several types of fleshy-leafed plants to provide a contrast.

FACT FILE

ORIGIN India; China; Japan.

HEIGHT To 12in/30cm.

POTTING MIX Soil-based.

REPOTTING In spring, when the clumps of leaves completely fill the surface of the soil, move into a pot one size larger.

PROPAGATION Divide overcrowded clumps in spring and pot up individually, ensuring that a piece of rhizome is attached to each portion.

KEEPING PLANTS Plants will last for several years, provided they do not suffer from lack of water or air that is too dry.

Acorus gramineus

PLANT CARE
Bright light with some direct sunlight. ● Normal room temperature with a winter minimum of 50°F/10°C. ● Water daily or sit plant in a water-filled tray. The plant must never be allowed to dry out. ● Apply a standard liquid fertilizer to actively growing plants at every two weeks.

ADROMISCHUS FESTIVUS
(SYN. *A. COOPERI*)
Crassulaceae

ADROMISCHUS

This is one of 50 species of small succulents which make good indoor plants, since their foliage is attractive all year-round. It has thick, fleshy, spoon-shaped leaves, about 2in/5cm long and half as wide. The blue-green foliage is splashed with purple-brown blotches, and the edges of the leaves are curiously wavy, which makes them look almost like clam shells; this is particularly noticeable at the tips.

During the summer, the plant sometimes sends up thin wiry stalks that bear insignificant bell-shaped reddish flowers ¼in/6mm long.

FACT FILE

ORIGIN South Africa (Western Cape).

HEIGHT To 5in/13cm.

POTTING MIX Soil-based, with added coarse sand for good drainage.

REPOTTING Move into a shallow pot one size larger in spring, when the plant has completely filled the current pot.

PROPAGATION Stem cuttings, leaf cuttings, or offsets all root easily if taken in spring or summer.

KEEPING PLANTS This small plant will remain attractive for years and will benefit from a spell outdoors in warm summer weather.

PLANT CARE
Bright light with some direct sunlight. ● Average room temperature from spring to fall, with a minimum winter temperature of 50°F/10°C. ● Water well during the growing season; allow the soil to dry out between waterings at other times. ● Do not mist the leaves. ● Feeding is not critical; feed plants once or twice in spring and summer with a standard liquid fertilizer. Do not feed newly potted plants for a year. ● Check the plant carefully from time to time for scale insects and mealybugs, which both attack it.

Agapanthus africanus

AGAPANTHUS AFRICANUS
Alliaceae

AFRICAN LILY

An evergreen with smooth, lance-shaped leaves, this plant produces tall, succulent flowering stems all summer long. The individual flowers are 1½in/4cm long and are borne in a rounded cluster at the top of the stem, forming a large inflorescence. As indoor plants, agapanthus are best suited to the sunroom.

Agapanthus africanus albus has flower heads of pure white, while the flowers of the Headbourne Hybrids may be blue or white. This is a group of hardy hybrids of garden origin, which make excellent large pot plants for the sunroom or greenhouse.

FACT FILE

ORIGIN South Africa.

HEIGHT To 2ft/60cm or more.

POTTING MIX Soil-based.

REPOTTING Only when the container is filled with roots or when the plant is divided.

PROPAGATION In spring, by division, every 4–5 years. Plants grown from seed may take 2–3 years to flower.

KEEPING PLANTS Agapanthus will benefit from a period outdoors in the summer.

PLANT CARE
Full sun is essential. ● Average room temperature, with a minimum of 50°F/10°C in winter. ● Keep the soil moist at all times in the growing season; water less in winter. ● Apply a standard liquid fertilizer every 2 weeks in spring and summer.

AGATHAEA COELESTIS see *FELICIA AMELLOIDES*

~

ALBIZIA JULIBRISSIN
Leguminosae

*S*ILK TREE

In mild climates this plant grows into a large shrub or small tree, with smooth pale grayish brown bark, and produces fluffy, globular heads of tiny pink flowers. When grown in a pot indoors, it is unlikely to flower and is most often grown for its ferny leaves which have oblong leaflets ¹/₄–¹/₂-in/ 6–13-mm-long. Seeds can be sown in early spring, and the resultant seedlings grown on and kept for a year.

FACT FILE

ORIGIN Asia, from Iran to Japan; naturalized in eastern and southern states of the US.

HEIGHT To 18in/46cm indoors, to 20ft/6m in the garden.

POTTING MIX Soil-based, with added coarse sand for good drainage.

REPOTTING Every second year, in late winter or early spring, move into a pot one size larger.

PROPAGATION Sow seeds in early spring. Alternatively, take 4-in/10-cm stem cuttings in summer, using hormone rooting powder.

KEEPING PLANTS Prune back to 5 or 6 buds in spring to control the plant's size and to prevent the lower stems from becoming bare. Albizia is best treated as a fairly short-term houseplant and discarded after 2 or 3 years.

Albizia julibrissin

Amaryllis belladonna

PLANT CARE

Direct sunlight, with shelter from hot midday sun. ● A minimum winter temperature of 45°–50°F/7°–10°C. ● Water liberally while the plant is in active growth, give less water in fall, and water sparingly in winter. ● Feed every 2 weeks during the growing period with a weak liquid fertilizer.

~

AMARYLLIS BELLADONNA
Amaryllidaceae

*B*ELLADONNA LILY

This is the only species in this genus and it is related to *Hippeastrum*. The bulb is large and produces a hollow, pale green flower stem up to 2ft/60cm long in late summer or early fall. At the top it carries an umbel 4-5in/10–13cm wide, consisting of 6 to 12 sweetly scented trumpet-shaped flowers on short stalks. The flowers range in color from pink to cerise and, occasionally, white.

The long strap-shaped leaves appear after the flower stalk and remain on the plant throughout the early summer following blooming; they should not be removed until they have died back naturally and are completely withered. The plant has a short rest period in midsummer.

FACT FILE

ORIGIN South Africa.

HEIGHT To 18in/46cm.

POTTING MIX Soil-based with added leaf mold and sand for good drainage.

REPOTTING Amaryllis flowers best when pot-bound. If necessary, move into another pot when dormant.

PROPAGATION Divide established clumps or remove offsets from the base of the plant when it is dormant and pot them up individually. They will take up to 3 years to flower well.

KEEPING PLANTS This plant is best grown in a large container in which it can remain for 5 or 6 years without disturbance.

PLANT CARE

Bright light with full sun; protect from the sun when in flower. ● Minimum temperature of 40°–45°F/4°–7°C. ● Water plentifully while the plant is in growth; water less as the leaves fade; keep dry in the rest period. ● When active, feed once a month with a balanced liquid fertilizer.

ANTHURIUM CRYSTALLINUM
Araceae

ℭRYSTAL ANTHURIUM

Known also as the strap flower, this plant is grown solely for its decorative foliage: the heart-shaped leaves are attached to 17-in/ 43-cm petioles and can be 15in/38cm long and 12in/30cm wide. When young, they are violet colored and metallic looking, turning a deep emerald green as they age, with the principal lateral veins and prominent midrib etched in shining silver. Between mid spring and early fall, green flower spathes about 3½in/9cm long appear, but they are quite insignificant compared with the foliage.

FACT FILE

ORIGIN Colombia; Peru.

HEIGHT To 18in/46cm.

POTTING MIX Peat-moss-based, with added leaf mold, or sphagnum moss; good drainage is essential.

REPOTTING In spring move into a pot one size larger every third year until maximum desired pot size is reached; top-dress thereafter.

PROPAGATION Divide the plant at repotting time; keep in humid conditions.

KEEPING PLANTS Cover aerial roots, which emerge from the stem, with sphagnum moss or insert them into the potting medium.

PLANT CARE

A bright position out of direct sun in winter; shadier in summer. ● Minimum winter temperature of 60°F/16°C; otherwise, normal room temperature. ● Keep the soil moist at all times. ● Mist leaves daily in summer. ● Apply a weak liquid fertilizer every 2 weeks from early spring to late summer.

～

ARISTOLOCHIA ELEGANS
(SYN. *A. LITTORALIS*)
Aristolochiaceae

ℭALICO FLOWER

A jungle plant native to Brazil, this vigorous, slender climber is capable of attaining 20ft/6m in a sunroom but can easily be kept smaller for use in the home. The heart-shaped leaves are smooth green above and gray-green beneath, and are about 3in/8cm wide. The flowers, which appear in summer and fall and are carried on long stalks, take the form of shallow heart-shaped bowls of deep black-purple with green-yellow marbling. In nature, aristolochias are pollinated by flies, so the flowers are usually foul-smelling to attract

their pollinators. Although the flowers of *Aristolochia elegans* lack the unpleasant smell typical of many other plants of this genus, the leaves are fetid when crushed.

The calico plant is also known as birthwort, although its relative *A. clematis* is the plant that has been used to relieve the pain of women in childbirth.

Aristolochia elegans

FACT FILE

ORIGIN Brazil.

HEIGHT To 20ft/6m.

POTTING MIX Soil-based with added peat moss.

REPOTTING Move to a pot one size larger when roots fill the current pot.

PROPAGATION In fall sow seed when ripe, or take cuttings in spring and raise them in a warm propagator.

KEEPING PLANTS The plant can become unmanageable, so provide support for the climbing stems and prune it to shape in late winter or early spring.

PLANT CARE

Full sun or partial shade. ● Warm room conditions, with a minimum of 60°F/16°C in winter. ● Water sparingly in winter and plentifully at other times. ● Apply a weak liquid fertilizer every 2 weeks when in active growth.

ARUNDINARIA VIRIDISTRIATA
(SYN. *PLEIOBLASTUS AURICOMA*)
Gramineae

ℬAMBOO

Several of the bamboos make excellent long-lived specimen plants in a large container. They are especially useful for a sunroom or greenhouse, or even a large hallway.

Arundinaria viridistriata is a particularly attractive species, with slender, hollow, purplish green canes rising from creeping underground rhizomes. The narrow, oblong leaves, 2–6in/5–15cm long, are slightly hairy and are striped along their length in green and brilliant yellow. The thickly growing leafy stems of a mature plant create a feathery effect.

FACT FILE

ORIGIN Japan.

HEIGHT To 4ft/1.2m.

POTTING MIX Soil-based.

REPOTTING In spring move into a pot one size larger until maximum desired size is reached, then top-dress instead.

PROPAGATION By division in spring; use younger sections from the edge of the clump.

KEEPING PLANTS Cut back old stems in early spring to encourage fresh young growth.

PLANT CARE

Indirect light to partial shade. ● Normal room temperature, with a minimum of 50°F/10°C. ● Water freely in the period of active growth; keep the soil moist but not water-logged. ● Stand the pot on a tray of moist pebbles to maintain humidity. ● Apply a standard liquid fertilizer monthly between spring and fall.

～

ASCLEPIAS CURASSAVICA
Asclepiadaceae

ℬLOOD FLOWER

A short-lived subshrub, this asclepias has lance-shaped leaves up to 6in/15cm long, which are carried in pairs. The flowers appear in summer and fall and are about ¾in/2cm wide and orange-red, with a deep yellow crown carrying the stamens; they are borne in umbels of 5 to 10.

The podlike fruits contain seeds that are crowned by long silky hairs for wind dispersal. The blood flower can become invasive in gardens in warm climates, so take care when disposing of it.

This is a good plant for the greenhouse which will be adequate in the home.

FACT FILE

ORIGIN Tropical South America.

HEIGHT To 3ft/90cm.

POTTING MIX Soil-based, with added peat moss or leaf mold.

REPOTTING Move to a pot one size larger each spring. A better show is achieved if plants are set 3 to a pot.

PROPAGATION Sow seed in spring, or take cuttings of young growth in late spring or summer. **Caution:** Take care when handling cuttings, since the plant bleeds copious amounts of a poisonous latex when cut.

KEEPING PLANTS After flowering, cut back the plant by up to half. Asclepias tends to become straggly and leggy with age, so replace the plant every 2–3 years.

PLANT CARE

Bright light with full sun where possible. ● Cool to warm room conditions. ● Water plentifully when in growth. Reduce watering after flowering and allow a dry rest period for about 2 months during winter. ● Give a dilute liquid fertilizer every 2 weeks from spring to fall.

~

ASPLENIUM BULBIFERUM
Aspleniaceae

*M*OTHER SPLEENWORT

Also known as the parsley fern and the hen-and-chickens fern, this plant produces much-divided mid green fronds, rather like carrot leaves, in a rosette shape. They grow on wiry black stalks. Tiny brown bulbils are borne near the tips of the fronds, and these develop into miniature replicas of the parent plant. This asplenium grows naturally in rain forests and requires high humidity indoors. The roots are fine and densely packed; a pot-bound plant will develop a deep, spongy layer on the top of the potting mix.

FACT FILE

ORIGIN Australasia; Malaysia.

HEIGHT To 18in/46cm, with spreading fronds as much as 3ft/90cm long.

POTTING MIX Peat-moss-based with added perlite.

REPOTTING Move into a pot one size larger every second year. Use a shallow pot or half-pot for a young plant, since aspleniums are shallow-rooting.

PROPAGATION In spring, detach and plant up the bulbils when they have developed 3 or 4 small fronds.

KEEPING PLANTS This easy-to-grow plant is fairly long-lived in the right conditions.

PLANT CARE

Bright filtered light or indirect light. ● Normal room temperature, with a minimum of 60°F/13°C. ● Water moderately during the period of active growth, but sparingly in winter. ● To increase humidity, stand the pot on a tray of damp pebbles. ● Apply a high-nitrogen liquid fertilizer every month from spring to fall.

ASTROPHYTUM MYRIOSTIGMA
Cactaceae

*B*ISHOP'S CAP CACTUS

The bishop's cap (or miter or monk's hood) cactus is a spherical cactus that becomes elongated with age. It is divided into four to eight (usually five) wide, thornless segments, covered with tufts of minute silvery hairs. Bright, shiny yellow daisylike flowers, each with a reddish center, emerge from the top of the plant in summer. This is a slow-growing plant best grown in a cactus garden or massed in a shallow bowl with gravel around it.

*Astrophytum
myriostigma*

FACT FILE

ORIGIN Mexico.

HEIGHT To 10in/25cm with a spread of 5in/13cm.

POTTING MIX Soil-based and coarse sand in a ratio of 2:1.

REPOTTING In spring, when the plant's roots have completely filled the current pot.

PROPAGATION From seed sown in spring.

KEEPING PLANTS The plant is long-lived and blooms only when it is 3 years old or more.

PLANT CARE

Full sunlight. ● A winter minimum of 50°F/10°C; otherwise, normal room temperature. ● Do not let the plant become waterlogged. Allow the top two-thirds of the soil to dry out before rewatering; water more sparingly during the winter rest period. ● Feed with a high-potash fertilizer once a month between spring and fall.

Asplenium bulbiferum

AUCUBA JAPONICA 'VARIEGATA'
Aucubaceae

GOLD DUST TREE

The plain green form of this plant, also known as Japanese laurel, was much used by the English in outdoor shrubberies and large greenhouses in Victorian times. This more frequently seen female variety with yellow-spotted leaves, and other modern hybrids, are considerably more cheerful. Most have leaves strongly marked with cream and yellow. Panicles of purplish flowers are borne in spring, and if male and female plants are grown together, bright red berries may follow. Indoors, plants can be hand-pollinated.

There are several varieties of variegated spotted laurel that make good houseplants. *Aucuba japonica* 'Crotonifolia' is a female form with broad leaves mottled with golden yellow. *A.j.* 'Fructu-albo' has leaves spotted with pale green and produces yellowish white berries in fall.

Spotted laurels tolerate a certain amount of neglect, poor light, and drafts and can be used in window boxes and in foliage arrangements for cool rooms.

FACT FILE

ORIGIN Cultivar.

HEIGHT To 3ft/90cm in a pot.

POTTING MIX Soil-based.

REPOTTING Move into a pot one size larger each spring; once plants are in 20-cm/8-in pots, top-dress instead.

PROPAGATION Sow seed in spring, or take 4–6-in/10–15-cm-long stem cuttings in late summer.

KEEPING PLANTS Cut old plants back hard in early spring if they become leggy or too large.

Aucuba japonica

PLANT CARE
Bright light or filtered sunlight. ● A cool room with a temperature of 50°–65°F/10°–18°C is ideal; the plant can withstand considerably colder temperatures, even down to 5°F/-15°C. ● Water copiously during the summer; give less water in winter. ● Apply a standard liquid fertilizer once a month from spring to fall. ● Clean leaves regularly with a damp sponge.

~

BERTOLONIA MARMORATA
Melastomataceae

BERTOLONIA

The chief ornamental value of this plant is provided by the velvety foliage: short, creeping stems bear green, quilted leaves up to 8in/20cm long, each irregularly streaked with white. The underside of the leaves is reddish purple and lilac-pink flowers are borne in summer.

Bertolonias are best in a group of other plants, where the increased humidity will benefit them, and are good plants for a bottle garden or terrarium. Only young plants are really attractive; older plants can become straggly.

The few named varieties are difficult to find, but they add a different dimension to a plant collection and are worth the search. *Bertolonia marmorata* 'Bruxellensis' has silvery leaves with rows of green spots between the main veins, while those of *B.m.* 'Mosaica' have a broader vein of silver and a pinkish tint.

FACT FILE

ORIGIN Brazil.

HEIGHT To 8in/20cm.

POTTING MIX Peat-moss-based with some added coarse sand.

REPOTTING When the stems cover the surface of the medium and hang over the edge of the container; probably about every 2 years.

PROPAGATION In spring sow seed, which bertolonias produce in quantity, or take stem or leaf cuttings.

KEEPING PLANTS When plants become straggly, replace them with new young plants.

PLANT CARE
Partial shade. ● Normal room temperature, with a minimum of 60°F/16°C. ● Water moderately throughout the year, but do not let water lie on the leaves, since it can cause unattractive brown spots. ● Increase humidity by placing the pot on a dish of damp pebbles. ● Apply a standard liquid fertilizer once a month between spring and fall.

BOUVARDIA LONGIFLORA
Rubiaceae

SWEET BOUVARDIA

A gloriously scented plant, this bouvardia bears trusses of white or pink star-shaped flowers from summer to midwinter. The plant flowers when it is quite young and makes an excellent bushy shrub for both the home and greenhouse. But even when it has had the most expert and loving attention, it lasts for only a couple of years.

Bouvardia ternifolia, the scarlet trompetilla, is not scented. But it makes up for this lack with its brilliantly colored flowers, which form a striking contrast with the plant's whitish gray bark.

Bouvardia longiflora

FACT FILE

ORIGIN Mexico.

HEIGHT To 3ft/90cm.

POTTING MIX Soil-based.

REPOTTING Move into a pot one size larger in spring.

PROPAGATION In spring, take stem cuttings or root cuttings.

KEEPING PLANTS Prune the plant vigorously in early spring and pinch out growing tips until late summer to make a bushy plant. Keep the plant fairly dry during the lengthy rest period in late spring and early summer.

PLANT CARE
Bright filtered light. ● A minimum of 55°F/13°C in winter; otherwise, warm room temperature. ● Water an actively growing plant freely; keep it fairly dry during the lengthy rest period in late spring and early summer. ● Apply a weak liquid fertilizer every 2 weeks while the plant is in flower. ● Bouvardia is susceptible to attack by whiteflies; check for these pests and spray with insecticide. Mealybugs may also infest the plant.

~

BOWIEA VOLUBILIS
Liliaceae

CLIMBING ONION

This is more of a curio and a talking point than an attractive plant to enhance a room. Thin stems emerge in late winter from a shiny, light green bulb that can be 6-8in/ 15–20cm wide; part of the bulb lies above the level of the potting mix. A few short-lived leaves and greenish white star-shaped flowers appear in late summer and fall, before the stems die down.

FACT FILE

ORIGIN South Africa.

HEIGHT Stems climb to 6ft/1.8m or more.

POTTING MIX Peat-moss-based with added sand.

REPOTTING Repot during summer or early fall, but only when offsets fill the pot.

PROPAGATION Divide offsets from the parent plant in summer or early fall or sow seed.

KEEPING PLANTS Plants are fairly long-lived in good bright conditions.

PLANT CARE

Bright light, but not direct sunlight. ● Cool room conditions, with a minimum of 50°F/10°C. ● Keep the potting mix just moist when the stems are actively growing. ● Apply a weak liquid fertilizer once a month from early fall until late winter. ● The small leaves naturally fall early, but the green stems carry on photosynthesis in their place.

BREYNIA NIVOSA (SYN. *B. DISTICHA*)
Euphorbiaceae

SNOW BUSH

The slender, angular branches of this plant are densely clothed in colorful green leaves marbled with white. The variety 'Rosea-Picta' is more popular than the species; its pink, white, and green leaves have a flower-like appearance, hence the plant's other common name of leaf flower. The actual flowers, which are insignificant and greenish, are sometimes produced.

Breynia nivosa, the only member of the genus commonly grown indoors, is slowly becoming more widely available. It is primarily a tropical garden plant, and as such it will grow into a shrub. Some years ago it was introduced as a houseplant, and in the house it tends to remain a small bush. It needs an extremely moist atmosphere.

FACT FILE

ORIGIN Tropical Asia; Pacific Islands; Australia.

HEIGHT To 4ft/1.2m.

POTTING MIX Soil-based.

REPOTTING Move into a pot a size larger every second spring.

PROPAGATION Take stem cuttings with a heel in summer, or root cuttings.

KEEPING PLANTS When breynia grows too large for the house, transfer it to a tub in the greenhouse or outdoors.

Breynia nivosa

PLANT CARE

Bright, filtered light with some sunshine. ● Average room temperature, with a minimum of 60°F/16°C. ● Keep the soil moist at all times. ● Stand the pot on a tray of damp pebbles and mist-spray regularly to maintain humidity. ● Apply a standard liquid feed every 2–3 weeks in the period of active growth.

BRODIAEA LAXA (SYN. *TRITELEIA LAXA*)
Liliaceae

GRASS NUT

Also known as Ithuriel's spear, this is equally good as a plant for the sunroom and as a temporary plant for the home, where it will thrive on a sunny windowsill. In any location, it increases and seeds itself freely.

An uncommon plant grown from a corm, the grass nut appeals to those who prefer small, dainty blooms. Plant the corms in late summer or early fall, in groups of five or six in a 15-cm/6-in pot. The large, loose umbels of deep blue or, rarely, white bell-shaped flowers appear during the following spring and early summer as the foliage dies back. The flowers are carried on stems up to 12in/30cm long and resemble those of alliums. The variety 'Queen Fabiola' has pale violet-blue flowers.

FACT FILE

ORIGIN USA (California; southern Oregon).

HEIGHT To 16in/40cm.

POTTING MIX Soil-based, leaf mold, and coarse sand in equal amounts for good drainage. The corms will rot if conditions are too wet.

REPOTTING In late summer, at the end of the dormant period.

PROPAGATION Remove and pot up offsets at planting time, or sow seeds in spring.

KEEPING PLANTS After flowering, store the pot in a warm, dry place until late summer, when the corms are ready to be repotted. Corms planted outdoors need protection from frost.

PLANT CARE

Full sun. ● Minimum winter temperature of 40°F/5°C. ● Water well once the plants have started to grow; after flowering, reduce watering. Do not water during the dormant period. ● Give 2 or 3 feeds of dilute general fertilizer after the bulbs have started growing and before flowering.

BRUGMANSIA x *CANDIDA* see
DATURA x *CANDIDA*

*Buddleia
madagascariensis*

BUDDLEIA MADAGASCARIENSIS
(SYN. *NICODEMIA MADAGASCARIENSIS*)
Loganiaceae

*B*UDDLEIA

The name of this plant is now correctly
spelt *Buddleja*, but it is still generally known
as *Buddleia*. It is a showy evergreen pot
plant for a large, bright sunny room or a
border plant for a greenhouse. Vigorous,
with an upright habit, it can easily reach
6–10ft/1.8–3m or more in height.

It has 5-in/13-cm-long lance-shaped
dark green leaves whose undersides are
covered with a downy white felt. The small,
bright yellow-orange flowers are borne in
slender, pyramid-shaped clusters between
late fall and spring. Unlike other buddleias,
which have fruits like dry capsules, the
flowers are followed by fleshy, berrylike
purple-blue fruits.

FACT FILE

ORIGIN Madagascar.

HEIGHT To 10ft/3m.

POTTING MIX Soil-based.

REPOTTING Only when roots completely fill
the current container.

PROPAGATION Sow seed in spring or take stem
cuttings in late summer.

KEEPING PLANTS Stems can be cut back by
about half after flowering, to keep the plant in
shape or to reduce its size. Flowers are produced
on the current year's growth.

PLANT CARE

Full sun or partial shade. ● Minimum
temperature of 45°F/7°C in winter. ● Water
moderately all year-round. Do not overwater,
but do not allow the plant to wilt, since that
can cause serious leaf loss. ● Feed every 2
weeks from spring to late fall with a dilute
standard fertilizer.

~

CALATHEA AMABILIS see *STROMANTHE
AMABILIS*

CALLIANDRA HAEMATOCEPHALA
(SYN. *C. INAEQUILATERA*)
Leguminosae

*P*OWDER-PUFF PLANT

The ball-like flowers of this plant, which
blooms in winter, are made up entirely of
stamens, and the bright red 3-in/8-cm-wide
"powder puffs" last for almost two months.
The dark green foliage is divided into
leaflets, each of which is about 2in/5cm
long. In time the plant will develop into a
bushy tree, but it will tolerate hard pruning,
so can be kept to 2–3ft/60–90cm by cutting
it back in spring. It can even be used as a
subject for bonsai.

Calliandra needs moist air, bright light,
and warmth, three conditions generally
found in a sunroom rather than in a living
room. But if these requirements can be
met, it will do well in the house. *Calliandra
tweedii* has smaller red flowers and its leaves
are feathery.

FACT FILE

ORIGIN Bolivia.

HEIGHT To 6ft/1.8m or more.

POTTING MIX Soil-based with some added leaf
mold and coarse sand.

REPOTTING In spring move into a pot one size
larger, until the plant has reached the desired
size, then top-dress annually.

PROPAGATION Take stem cuttings in spring.

KEEPING PLANTS This plant is tough and will
last for many years. Set the pot outdoors in
summer to ripen the wood and improve
flowering the following year.

PLANT CARE

Full sun except for the strongest summer
sunlight, or partial shade. ● Warm conditions,
with a minimum winter temperature of
16°C/60°F. ● Keep the soil damp at all times.
● Mist regularly to increase humidity. ● Feed
every 2 weeks from spring to fall.

CARICA PAPAYA
Caricaceae

*P*APAYA

Widely grown in tropical countries for its
fruit, the papaya makes an unusual
ornamental foliage plant. The straight stem
is usually unbranched and is topped by a
cluster of long-stalked, deeply lobed leaves,
which may reach up to 2ft/60cm wide on
large plants.

The fragrant trumpet-shaped flowers,
borne in summer, are cream or yellow and
up to 1in/2.5cm long. Male and female
plants in close proximity are required if
fruit production is the aim, although
bisexual plants that have both male and
female flowers, such as *Carica papaya* 'Solo,'
have been bred. When the papaya is grown
as a houseplant, pollination by hand may
be necessary.

The 5–12-in/13–30-cm-long melonlike
fruits are borne directly on the trunk, in the
leaf axils. They are green and turn yellow or
orange when ripe. The firm, fragrant flesh
is yellow to pinkish orange.

FACT FILE

ORIGIN Tropical America.

HEIGHT To 10ft/3m in a container.

POTTING MIX Soil-based with good drainage.

REPOTTING Move young plants into a pot one
size larger as they fill the container with roots.

PROPAGATION Seeds are frequently available
commercially and can be saved from fruits. Sow
in spring, in a temperature not lower than
75°F/24°C. They may not come true to type.

KEEPING PLANTS Replace the plant every 4
years or so.

Calliandra haematocephala

PLANT CARE

Full sun will help to ripen the fruits; as an ornamental, the plant will tolerate partial shade. ● Normal warm conditions, with a minimum winter temperature of 60°F/16°C. A temperature of at least 60°F/16°C is necessary to ripen fruit. ● Water well all year-round but do not overwater. If the soil becomes waterlogged, it will kill the plant within days. ● Apply a weak liquid fertilizer every 2 weeks during the period of active growth.

CARLUDOVICA PALMATA
Cyclanthaceae

PANAMA-HAT PLANT

This is one of a small group of short-stemmed palmlike perennials grown mainly for their leaves, although the brightly colored fruits are also attractive. The bright green, pliable, fan-shaped leaves are up to 3ft/90cm wide, with three to five main segmented divisions. Each lobe has a drooping ragged tip. In tropical regions the bleached leaves provide the material for Panama hats.

FACT FILE

ORIGIN Central America, south to Bolivia.

HEIGHT To 6ft/1.8m or more.

POTTING MIX Peat-moss-based with added sharp sand.

REPOTTING Repot only young plants, as they fill the container with roots.

PROPAGATION Sow seeds at any time of year.

KEEPING PLANTS This is a fairly long-lived plant in a warm sunroom or greenhouse.

PLANT CARE

Full sun. ● Minimum temperature of 60°F/16°C. ● Water plentifully when the plant is in active growth. ● Feed occasionally with dilute liquid general fertilizer.

CARYOTA MITIS
Palmae

BURMESE FISHTAIL PALM

Known also as the crested or tufted fishtail palm, this palm is distinguished from all others by its fronds. They are made up of roughly triangular segments, each of which is ragged at the edge, like a fish's tail. With age, the fronds arch over and develop their distinctive double division.

Indoors, *Caryota mitis* is unlikely to grow more than 6 to 10 fronds 3ft/90cm-long. The plant may reach a total height of some

Caryota mitis

6ft/1.8m, about a quarter of its potential height in the garden.

FACT FILE

ORIGIN Burma; Malaysia; Java; Philippines.

HEIGHT To 6ft/1.8m indoors.

POTTING MIX Soil-based.

REPOTTING Every other year, when the plant is starting into growth, move it into a pot one size larger until the maximum desired size is reached; the plant prefers to be slightly pot-bound.

PROPAGATION By sowing seed, in heat, during spring or summer; or by potting up offset divisions.

KEEPING PLANTS Move the palm outdoors in summer. It cannot be pruned and so should be discarded once it has outgrown its allotted space.

PLANT CARE

Bright indirect sunlight. ● Ideally, warm room temperature between 65°F/18°C at night and 85°F/29°C during the day. ● Water thoroughly, but allow the surface of the soil to dry out before rewatering. ● Increase humidity around the plant by standing the pot on a tray of moist pebbles. ● Apply a weak liquid fertilizer every 2 weeks while growth is active.

CEPHALOCEREUS SENILIS
(SYN. *PILOCEREUS SENILIS*)
Cactaceae

OLD-MAN CACTUS

The common name for this cactus is derived from the long, fine white hairs that shroud the fleshy columnar body and hide the sharp spines beneath them. The hairs serve to protect the plant from the sun, and the brighter the light, the denser they will be. When the hairs become discolored, they

may be washed in a weak solution of detergent, using a soft brush such as a shaving brush or paint brush. This will remove any dirt, but not the darkening of the hairs due to age.

The flowers, which are red and white, seldom form on potted plants and appear only on older specimens. These cacti are very slow growing, adding perhaps 1in/2.5cm a year.

FACT FILE

ORIGIN Mexico.

HEIGHT To 12in/30cm or more.

POTTING MIX Soil- or peat-moss-based with added perlite or coarse sand in the ratio of 2:1.

REPOTTING If roots have filled the pot, move the plant into a pot one size larger in spring. Older plants may be top-dressed instead.

PROPAGATION Only by sowing seed in spring.

KEEPING PLANTS These plants look best massed with other cacti in a cactus garden.

PLANT CARE

Direct sunlight. ● A minimum temperature of 40°F/4°C in winter; otherwise, normal room temperature. ● Allow the surface of the potting mix to dry out completely between waterings; water only enough during the winter rest period to prevent the plant shriveling. Be careful not to splash the hairs when watering. ● Apply a high-potash liquid fertilizer every 3 weeks between spring and fall.

Cephalocereus senilis

CEROPEGIA WOODII (SYN. *CEROPEGIA LINEARIS* SSP. *WOODII*)
Asclepiadaceae

ROSARY VINE

A long-lived tuberous succulent, this is the only ceropegia commonly grown indoors. It is a good plant for a hanging basket. The gray woody tuber, which can reach 2in/5cm across, rests on the surface of the soil, and from it spring several fine purplish flexible stems. Generally, these are about 3ft/90cm long, although they can become much longer.

Every 2–3in/5–8cm along the stem is a pair of 1-in/2.5-cm-long fleshy heart-shaped leaves, that give the plant its common names: hearts entangled, hearts-on-a-string, and chain of hearts.

The dark green leaves are marked with white on the upper surface and are purple underneath. Small tuberous growths are produced at intervals along the stem, and where they form, stems sometimes branch.

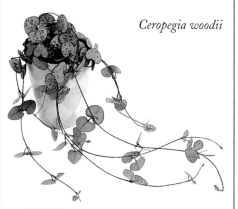

Ceropegia woodii

FACT FILE

ORIGIN South Africa.

HEIGHT Stems trail to 3ft/90cm or more.

POTTING MIX Soil-based and coarse sand or perlite in equal quantities; good drainage is essential.

REPOTTING In early spring move into a pot one size larger until a 4-in/10-cm pot is reached.

PROPAGATION At any time, remove stem tubers from the plant or take stem cuttings. Set several tubers around the edge of a hanging basket for a good display.

KEEPING PLANTS Keep ceropegia in a bright location; in poor light, leaf color will be poor and leaves will be widely spaced on the stem.

PLANT CARE

Bright light with at least 4 hours of direct sun daily. ● Normal room temperature, with a minimum of 55°F/13°C. ● Water actively growing plants moderately; water sparingly in the rest period from mid fall to early spring. ● Every 4 weeks apply standard liquid fertilizer to mature plants only.

CESTRUM AURANTIACUM
Solanaceae

CESTRUM

An evergreen semiclimbing shrub, cestrum makes a good plant for the greenhouse or sunroom, where it can be trained to a permanent support. It has oval leaves up to 3in/8cm long, which smell unpleasant. Flowers are borne in clusters in summer and they too have an odor that some find unpleasant; it is strongest at night. Each bright yellow-orange bloom has a 3/4-in/ 2-cm-long tubular corolla with five pointed petal lobes at the mouth. The flowers are followed by white berries.

Cestrum elegans 'Smithii' has apricot pink flowers and blooms all year-round; *C. nocturnum*, night-blooming jasmine, has white flowers.

FACT FILE

ORIGIN Guatemala.

HEIGHT To 10ft/3m.

POTTING MIX Soil-based with good drainage.

REPOTTING In spring, when the roots have filled the current pot, move a young plant into a pot one size larger.

PROPAGATION Sow seed in spring, or take stem cuttings with a heel in late summer.

KEEPING PLANTS Pinch off the growing tips of a young plant to encourage bushiness. And cut out a third or so of the oldest wood in the fall to ensure good flowering during the following year.

PLANT CARE

Bright, filtered sunlight. ● A minimum temperature of 50°F/10°C. ● Water well during the growing season and give less water for 4–6 weeks after flowering. ● Apply a weak liquid fertilizer every 2 weeks from spring to fall.

Cestrum aurantiacum

Clianthus puniceus

CLIANTHUS PUNICEUS
Leguminosae

PARROT'S BEAK

Also known as kaka beak and lobster claw, *Clianthus puniceus* has flowers with a large showy standard and a long pointed keel, from which it gets its common names. The flowers, which start off red and fade to pink as they age, are borne in clusters from summer to late fall. The thin stems of *C. puniceus* need support when it is grown as a free-standing shrub, and it is an excellent subject for training against a wall trellis in a cool room or greenhouse.

The closely related *C. formosus*, Sturt's desert pea or glory pea, is a relatively low-growing, trailing plant, with feathery leaves some 6in/15cm long. The stems may be pruned or trained in the fall when flowering is over, but the plant often declines at this time and it is best regarded as an annual.

FACT FILE

ORIGIN Australia; New Zealand.

HEIGHT To 6ft/1.8min a container.

POTTING MIX Soil-based with added grit.

REPOTTING Repot in spring, but only if the roots fill the current pot.

PROPAGATION Sow seed in spring.

KEEPING PLANTS Prune after flowering. Keep the plant well ventilated at all times.

PLANT CARE

Full sun or dappled shade. ● Cooler room temperatures of 50°–65°F/10°–18°C are best. ● Water well from spring to fall, but sparingly in winter. ● On hot, dry days, mist the plant with clean water. ● Apply a weak liquid fertilizer every 2 weeks during the period of active growth.

COCCOLOBA UVIFERA
Polygonaceae

SEA GRAPE

In its natural habitat on the coasts of South and Central America, coccoloba grows in almost pure sand. It is a shrubby plant whose leathery, circular to kidney-shaped leaves with red veins turn to ivory with age. The long trusses of white flowers, which are reluctant to form in room conditions, are followed by purple-red fruits ³⁄₄in/2cm long; these resemble grapes and give the plant its common name. In the wild, the leaves become so large that local people use them as picnic plates, and the fruits are used to make a jelly.

Because its leaves are leathery, this plant tolerates dry air fairly well and so is a good plant for heated houses.

FACT FILE

ORIGIN Tropical America; West Indies.

HEIGHT To 6ft/1.8m indoors; 20ft/6m in its natural habitat.

POTTING MIX Soil-based with added peat moss.

REPOTTING Move into a pot one size larger each spring. Once an 8-in/20-cm pot has been reached, top-dress instead.

PROPAGATION Take half-ripe tip cuttings in summer; sow seed in spring, or layer at any time of year.

KEEPING PLANTS Cut back just before the plant starts into growth in spring, to encourage branching. Discard after 3 or 4 years; young specimens are more attractive than older ones.

PLANT CARE
Good light but avoid direct sun. ● Minimum winter temperature of 60°F/16°C, with normal room temperature at other times. ● Keep the soil moderately moist at all times. ● Maintain a humid atmosphere by standing the pot on a tray of damp pebbles and misting the plant occasionally. ● Apply a weak liquid fertilizer every 2 weeks from spring to fall.

COFFEA ARABICA
Rubiaceae

ARABIAN COFFEE PLANT

It is not generally known that the coffee tree makes an excellent houseplant. It is evergreen and may grow to a height of 6ft/1.8m, although there is a compact form, *Coffea arabica* 'Nana,' that remains considerably smaller. From its third or fourth year it may even bear flowers and fruit. The uncooked beans can, however, be poisonous, and they must be properly

Coffea arabica

roasted before they can be made into coffee; this important process is best carried out by a professional.

The plant has shiny, dark green elliptical leaves with wavy edges; they can be as much as 6in/15cm in length and about 2in/5cm wide. The fragrant, star-shaped white flowers are followed by green fruits ½in/13mm long, which change to bright red and then to almost black as they ripen. The two seeds within the fruits contain caffeine.

FACT FILE

ORIGIN Tropical Africa; Arabia.

HEIGHT To 6ft/1.8m in a pot.

POTTING MIX Soil-based with added coarse sand; good drainage is essential.

REPOTTING Move into a pot one or two sizes larger each spring.

PROPAGATION Cuttings, taken in summer, do not root easily, but fresh seed can be sown in spring with reasonable success.

KEEPING PLANTS If necessary, prune the plant in spring to control its size and shape.

PLANT CARE
Bright light away from direct sunlight. ● Normal room temperature of 65°–70°F/18°–21°C, but the plant can stand slightly cooler temperatures in the dormant period between mid fall and late winter. Young plants up to 2 years old, with tender growth, prefer slightly warmer conditions. ● Water generously in summer, preferably with tepid water and from below; give only enough water in the rest period to prevent the soil from drying out completely. ● Apply a weak solution of lime-free fertilizer each week during spring and summer.

CONVALLARIA MAJALIS
Liliaceae

LILY OF THE VALLEY

This familiar plant, with delicate, highly fragrant bell-shaped flowers, is usually seen as a hardy specimen in woodland areas or in a shady spot in the garden. It grows from a creeping rhizome and so spreads quickly.

Convallarias are also easy to force and can be obtained as pot plants or as crowns at almost any time of year. The elliptical leaves grow from the rootstock, usually in pairs, and can be 8in/20cm long. Each flower stalk carries five to eight blooms.

In addition to the type, several good varieties are obtainable, among them *Convallaria majalis* 'Fortin's Giant' with large white flowers, which is most often used for forcing; *C.m.* 'Prolificans' with double flowers; and the less vigorous *C.m.* 'Rosea' with pale pink flowers.

FACT FILE

ORIGIN Europe; naturalized in America.

HEIGHT To 10in/25cm.

POTTING MIX Soil-based, leaf mold, and coarse sand in equal amounts.

REPOTTING Move into a pot one size larger each spring after flowering. Put 6–8 plants in a pot for the best effect.

PROPAGATION Sow seed in spring or divide plants when repotting.

KEEPING PLANTS Overwinter plants in a cold frame or cool greenhouse if possible. As they start into growth, increase watering and increase the temperature to about 70°F/21°C if you want to force them into early blooming.

PLANT CARE
Bright light but not direct sunlight. ● Cool room conditions will prolong the flowering period. ● Keep the potting mix moist at all times. ● Apply a weak liquid fertilizer once a month during spring and summer.

Convallaria majalis

COSTUS IGNEUS (SYN *C. CUSPIDATUS*)
Zingiberaceae

FIERY COSTUS

This plant is unusual in that the leaves spiral around the stem. Each leaf, which can be 6in/15cm in length, is oblong, glossy on the surface, and reddish below. The flowers, borne in summer, are 2–3in/5–8cm long, with an orange tube and a deep yellow lip.

Costus speciosus, Malay or crepe ginger, has white flowers; those of *C. spiralis* are red. *C. pulverulentus* (*C. sanguineus*) also has red flowers and decorative 4-in/10-cm-long pointed leaves, which are bluish green and accentuated with silvery central ribs.

FACT FILE

ORIGIN Brazil.

HEIGHT To 2ft/60cm.

POTTING MIX Soil-based.

REPOTTING In early spring, when the pot becomes overcrowded.

PROPAGATION Divide and repot the roots in spring, or take 4-in/10-cm-long stem cuttings at any time of year.

KEEPING PLANTS Cut out old canes at the base when new growth appears.

Costus igneus

PLANT CARE

Bright indirect light. ● Normal room temperature. ● Keep the soil moist at all times. ● Apply a weak liquid fertilizer once a month to actively growing plants.

~

COTYLEDON UNDULATA
Crassulaceae

SILVER CROWN

Cotyledons are shrubby succulents with fleshy, fan-shaped, stalkless leaves arranged in opposite pairs. Each leaf of this plant has an undulating edge and a dense covering of fine, silvery white powder. Although orange-yellow flowers may appear on older plants in summer, the plant is chiefly grown for its characteristic leaves. Mass several

Cotyledon undulata

plants together in a bowl on a low table for maximum effect.

Cotyledon orbiculata is slightly taller and has gray-green leaves edged with red, with just a little white mealy covering. Orange flowers appear in summer.

FACT FILE

ORIGIN South Africa.

HEIGHT To 20in/50cm.

POTTING MIX Soil-based with coarse sand added in a ratio of 2:1 for good drainage, which is essential for this plant.

REPOTTING Move the plant into a pot one size larger each spring; when a 6-in/15-cm pot is reached, top-dress instead.

PROPAGATION Take 3–4-in/8–10-cm tip cuttings in spring.

KEEPING PLANTS Avoid handling the plant, since the white mealy covering will rub off. When the plant eventually becomes leggy, cut off the leafy top and reroot it. The bare stem may then produce new growth, so it is worth caring for it for a while.

PLANT CARE

Full sunlight. ● Minimum winter temperature of 45°F/7°C, with normal room temperature at other times. ● Water copiously from spring to fall; give less water in winter. ● Apply a standard liquid fertilizer once a month between spring and fall.

~

CRASSULA COCCINEA see *ROCHEA COCCINEA*

~

CRINUM **x** *POWELLII*
Amaryllidaceae

SPIDER LILY

An elegant plant, this spider lily is a hybrid between *Crinum bulbispermum* and *C. moorei*, both of which originate from South Africa. During late summer or early fall, it bears bright pink trumpet-shaped flowers at the top of a thick, succulent stem up to 3ft/90cm high. The blooms are produced in succession, in clusters of five to eight, over about a month. Each "trumpet" can be up to 5in/13cm long and 6in/15cm wide. *C.* x *p.* 'Album' has pure white flowers.

The spectacular blooms and strap-shaped leaves, of which there are about 20 on a mature plant, arise from large bulbs, often as much as 6in/15cm in diameter. The leaves last for a year, dying only when there are new ones ready to replace them. Because of their relative longevity, they need attention to keep them looking attractive.

FACT FILE

ORIGIN Hybrid.

HEIGHT To 3ft/90cm.

POTTING MIX Soil-based, with plenty of coarse sand, leaf mold, and well-rotted manure added. Put plenty of pebbles or gravel on the bottom of the pot to ensure good drainage.

REPOTTING Crinums flower best when pot-bound, so top-dress annually and repot only every 3–4 years.

PROPAGATION Divide overcrowded clumps in spring by carefully separating the offsets from the parent bulb. For a month after potting up, water the offsets sparingly; thereafter, treat them as adult plants. Otherwise, sow fresh ripe seed singly in pots.

KEEPING PLANTS Picking off the flowers as they fade will help to prolong the blooming period.

PLANT CARE

Direct sunlight for 3–4 hours daily. ● A minimum temperature of 50°F/10°C during the winter rest period; at other times, normal room temperature. ● Water freely in summer but do not let the plant stand in water. Give only enough water in winter to prevent the soil from drying out completely. If necessary, mist the leaves at this time, to prevent them from wilting. ● Apply high-potash fertilizer every 3 weeks in spring and summer.

~

Cyanotis somaliensis

CYANOTIS SOMALIENSIS
Commelinaceae

*P*USSY EARS

Unlike the closely related tradescantia, cyanotis bears hairy leaves. The 2-in/5-cm-long shiny green leaves of *Cyanotis somaliensis* are edged with soft white hairs, which gives them an overall pale gray appearance. Three-petaled blue flowers sometimes appear between winter and spring. The plant looks good when growth is compact but unruly when the stems are weak and spindly, which they readily become if light is inadequate. This is a good plant for indoor hanging baskets.

C. kewensis, teddy bear vine, has fine, rust-colored hairs on its short creeping stems. Its small lance-shaped leaves are green on top and purple underneath. Violet-colored flowers are produced, but only rarely.

FACT FILE

ORIGIN Tropical Africa.

HEIGHT To 8in/20cm.

POTTING MIX Soil-based with added coarse sand or perlite in a ratio of 2:1.

REPOTTING A slow-growing plant, cyanotis does best in a shallow pot and rarely needs repotting.

PROPAGATION Take tip cuttings in spring; make sure that each cutting has three pairs of leaves.

KEEPING PLANTS The leaves develop brown tips if the air is too dry; stand the plant on a tray of moist pebbles to increase humidity.

PLANT CARE

Good light with some direct sunlight. ● Normal room temperature. ● Water well year-round, but allow the surface of the soil to become dry before rewatering. ● Apply a standard liquid fertilizer about 4 times between spring and fall.

CYPERUS PAPYRUS
Cyperaceae

*P*APYRUS

This exotic plant gets its name from the fact that the ancient Egyptians used its stems for making papyrus to write on. It grows in clumps and the smooth triangular stems can reach a height of 10ft/3m. The thin, rich green, grassy leaves are topped by a few bracts and a dense, umbrellalike tuft of pendulous stems that end in tiny brownish flowers.

This is a marsh plant in its natural habitat, so it is almost impossible to give it too much water. It is not always easy to find, but the miniature *Cyperus prolifer* (*C. isocladus*), also known as *C. papyrus* 'Nanus,' which grows to 2ft/60cm, is usually easier to come by.

FACT FILE

ORIGIN Tropical Africa.

HEIGHT To 10ft/3m.

POTTING MIX Soil-based with charcoal added to keep the soil fresh.

REPOTTING Move into a pot one size larger as soon as the roots fill the current container.

PROPAGATION Divide the plant in spring or root stem cuttings in water.

KEEPING PLANTS Do not allow cyperus to dry out, even for a short while, or the bracts will develop brown tips.

Cyperus papyrus

PLANT CARE

Full, bright sunlight or light shade. ● A minimum winter temperature of 55°F/13°C, with warm room temperature at other times. ● Keep the soil moist at all times: stand the pot in a bowl of water and keep it filled. ● Apply a weak liquid fertilizer once a month between spring and fall, or push fertilizing tablets into the soil around the roots.

~

CYRTANTHUS ELATUS see VALLOTA SPECIOSA

~

CYRTOMIUM FALCATUM
Aspidiaceae

*H*OLLY FERN

This handsome, long-lasting fern produces tufts of dark, scaly frond stalks up to 2ft/60cm in length. These bear shiny, dark green, pointed hollylike leaves, which are often as much as 3–4in/8–10cm long. An easy houseplant to grow, it even tolerates drafts and the warm dry air of heated homes. Occasional misting should keep the leaves clean, otherwise wipe them with a damp cloth or sponge, but do not use proprietary leaf shine.

Cyrtomium falcatum 'Rochfordianum' is more vigorous than the type. It has shorter but slightly broader fronds, the edges of which are wavy and distinctly toothed.

FACT FILE

ORIGIN South Africa; India; Korea; Japan; Hawaii.

HEIGHT To 2ft/60cm.

POTTING MIX Soil- or peat-moss-based.

REPOTTING In spring move the plant into a pot one size larger until maximum desired pot size is reached. Thereafter top-dress instead.

PROPAGATION In spring divide the rhizomes, ensuring each piece has a growing point and at least three fronds.

KEEPING PLANTS This plant is prone to attack by scale insects and mealybugs; keep a close watch for these pests.

PLANT CARE

Bright, indirect light, or semishade. ● A temperature of 65°F/18°C is ideal; if the level is much higher than this, it is essential to increase the humidity by spraying the foliage and standing the plant on a tray of moist pebbles. ● Allow the surface of the soil to dry out between waterings. ● Apply a weak liquid fertilizer every 2 weeks to plants that are actively growing.

Darlingtonia californica

DARLINGTONIA CALIFORNICA
Sarraceniaceae

CALIFORNIA PITCHER PLANT

A carnivorous bog plant, this darlingtonia has 12–20-in/30–50-cm-long tubular emerald green leaves with a conspicuous network of veins. The leaves curve over at the tip, so that the opening of the tube faces downward, preventing the entrance of rainwater, which would dilute the digestive juices. A two-lobed flap—green, dark brown, and purple—hangs near the opening of the tube. The tube, hood, and flap together resemble a snake's head, and it is easy to see why this plant is often called the cobra lily. The inside of the tubes is covered in downward-pointing hairs, which prevent insects from escaping. Every year a new rosette of leaves develops at the end of a short rootstock. The flowers have yellow-green sepals and petals, which are heavily veined in purplish red.

FACT FILE

ORIGIN USA (California; Oregon).

HEIGHT To 18in/46cm.

POTTING MIX Equal parts of peat moss, sphagnum moss, sharp sand, and charcoal.

REPOTTING Every 2 years in midsummer.

PROPAGATION By seed, or by division, in a bed of sphagnum moss, under glass.

KEEPING PLANTS Do not feed the plant; it contains enough chlorophyll to make its own food when there are no insects around.

PLANT CARE

Bright light but no direct sunlight. ● The plant needs cool room temperature all year-round. ● Never allow the medium to become dry. ● Humidity is vital, and the plant will do best as one of a group in a large shallow pan; mist the plant daily.

~

DATURA x CANDIDA
Solanaceae

ANGEL'S TRUMPET

Datura x *candida*, also known as *Brugmansia* x *candida*, is a plant that requires attention and plenty of space. It will easily grow to 6ft/1.8m in a container, with a similar spread, and is really best suited to the greenhouse or sunroom.

It bears magnificent trumpet-shaped flowers up to 10in/25cm in length, and has oval, mid green leaves about 9in/23cm long. The flowers, which are usually white, but can be pink or creamy yellow, have a strong, heady scent that some people find oppressive. *D.* 'Knightii' (*D.* x *candida* 'Plena') has white double flowers, one inside the other. After the flowers have faded, the stems can be pruned back, to encourage new growth.

Caution: All parts of the plant are poisonous. Do not grow if children or pets are present.

FACT FILE

ORIGIN Hybrid between *Datura aurea* and *D. versicolor*.

HEIGHT To 6ft/1.8m in a container.

POTTING MIX Soil-based with added peat moss.

REPOTTING Move into a pot one size larger each spring.

PROPAGATION Take stem cuttings in spring; young plants may flower the following fall.

KEEPING PLANTS Red spider mites can infest this plant; maintain high humidity to help to deter them. In a mild climate the plant will benefit from a spell outdoors in summer.

PLANT CARE

Full sun or light shade. ● Minimum winter temperature of 50°F/10°C, with cool room conditions at other times. ● Water generously between spring and fall; give less water in winter. ● Apply a weak liquid fertilizer once a week to actively growing plants.

Datura x *candida*

DICHORISANDRA REGINAE
Commelinaceae

QUEEN'S SPIDERWORT

Although not often seen, queen's spiderwort is worth the search. It is a close relative of the popular tradescantia, but it needs more careful attention if it is to do well.

With its erect stalks, lance-shaped dark green leaves with two silvery lengthwise stripes and a violet mid-rib, this is a very attractive plant. The lavender-colored flowers, about 1in/2.5cm wide, consist of three sepals, equal in size, and three contrasting petals.

The species *Dichorisandra thyrsiflora* bears clusters of deep blue-violet flowers striped with white in fall.

FACT FILE

ORIGIN Peru.

HEIGHT To 2ft/60cm.

POTTING MIX Peat-moss-based, with added loam; good drainage is necessary.

REPOTTING When roots fill the pot, move to a pot one size larger.

PROPAGATION In spring, by seeds, cuttings, or division.

KEEPING PLANTS A high degree of warmth and humidity is essential.

PLANT CARE

Medium light; no direct sunlight. ● Minimum winter temperature of 60°F/16°C; normal room temperature at other times. ● Water the plant moderately in summer; give less water in winter. ● Apply a balanced liquid fertilizer every 2 weeks from spring to fall.

Dichorisandra reginae

Dicksonia antarctica

DICKSONIA ANTARCTICA
Dicksoniaceae

TASMANIAN TREE FERN

A sizable fern, this plant is best grown in a greenhouse or sunroom, where it will thrive in a border or large container. Fronds grow from ground level on young plants. As the plant ages it develops a large trunk composed of red-brown matted roots, the surface of which looks like bark.

Fronds form a terminal crown, each frond being 4–9ft/1.2–2.7m long; on mature plants they arch over, giving an elegant lacy effect. The spores are carried at the ends of the veins near the margins of the undersides of the fronds, which reflex to protect them.

FACT FILE

ORIGIN Australia (Tasmania).

HEIGHT To 20ft/6m outdoors.

POTTING MIX Topsoil with added coarse sand, leaf mold, and shredded bark in a ratio of 1:2:3:1.

REPOTTING In spring, when roots fill the pot. When the plant becomes too large, top-dress it instead.

PROPAGATION Sow spores in spring, in a temperature of 65°F/18°C.

KEEPING PLANTS Spray the trunk with water regularly in hot weather to prevent the roots drying out.

PLANT CARE

Bright filtered sunlight. ● Average warmth; the plant may suffer in temperatures above 75°F/24°C. The palm can withstand a winter minimum of 45°F/7°C in shelter. ● Do not allow the soil to dry out. ● Apply a high-nitrogen liquid fertilizer every 2 or 3 weeks from spring to fall.

DROSERA ROTUNDIFOLIA
Droseraceae

COMMON SUNDEW

Although it is a difficult plant to grow, this sundew is a good species for a collector of carnivorous plants. It bears a rosette of deciduous, long-stalked leaves that are ½in/13mm wide and open in summer. The leaves are covered with red glandular hairs, or tentacles, which secrete terminal globules of sticky, glistening juice.

Small flies and other insects mistake the fluid for nectar and, once in contact with it, stick fast. The insect's struggles cause the surrounding tentacles to bend over, smothering it and pushing it down to the leaf surface. A digestive enzyme then breaks down the animal protein so that it can be absorbed by the plant.

FACT FILE

ORIGIN North America; northern Europe; northern Asia.

HEIGHT To 3in/8cm.

POTTING MIX Equal parts of peat moss and washed sharp sand; or pure live sphagnum moss.

REPOTTING Not necessary, since the plant has a remarkably small root system.

PROPAGATION Sow seed at any time of the year, or divide in spring.

KEEPING PLANTS Keep cold in winter, when the plant is resting.

PLANT CARE

Good light but not direct sunlight. ● Cool conditions; frost is tolerated. ● Never allow the medium to dry out; water from below. ● Every 4 weeks, apply weak liquid fertilizer to seedlings only; the mature plant will get its nourishment from insects.

DYCKIA FOSTERIANA
Bromeliaceae

DYCKIA

A rosette-forming bromeliad, dyckia—sometimes called miniature agave—has gray-green, elongated, arching leaves equipped with prominent, rather vicious, hooked spines along their margins. In spring, racemes of orange-yellow bell-shaped flowers are carried on tall stems. The rosettes do not die immediately after flowering as is the case with most bromeliads, and a spreading clump of several rosettes soon builds up.

Take care when handling these spiny plants; strong gloves are usually necessary for such tasks as repotting.

FACT FILE

ORIGIN Brazil.

HEIGHT To 6in/15cm; flower stems to 10in/25cm.

POTTING MIX Soil-based with added coarse sand or grit for good drainage.

REPOTTING In spring, move into a pot one size larger when the rosettes fill the current pot.

PROPAGATION Use a sharp knife to remove offsets when they are about 2in/5cm wide, and pot them individually in sandy soil mix.

KEEPING PLANTS Stand the plant outside in a sheltered position in full sun in summer.

PLANT CARE

Full sun. ● A minimum of 45°F/7°C, but will tolerate higher temperatures. ● Water fairly lightly in the growing season; allow the top third of the soil to dry out between waterings. Give just enough water in winter to prevent the soil drying out. ● Apply a balanced liquid fertilizer every 4 weeks in the growing season.

ECHEVERIA SECUNDA VAR. *GLAUCA*
Crassulaceae

BLUE ECHEVERIA

Although a succulent, this plant comes from cool and fairly moist mountainous regions. *Echeveria secunda* produces decorative rosettes of evergreen, overlapping, fleshy ovate leaves. Each leaf has a small point at the center and is of an intense blue-green shade.

The rosettes build up to form spreading clumps and may have short stems, although they are usually stemless. The foliage is brittle and easily damaged by careless handling. Arching racemes of red flowers on tall stems appear in spring.

Echeveria secunda var. *glauca*

FACT FILE

ORIGIN Mexico.

HEIGHT To 4in/10cm; flower stems to 12in/30cm.

POTTING MIX Soil-based with added coarse sand or perlite for drainage.

REPOTTING In spring move a small plant into a pot one size larger annually; move a large plant every 2 years or top-dress instead. Put a layer of gravel in the pot for drainage.

PROPAGATION Remove offsets from around the edge of the plant with a sharp knife and pot them up individually in gritty medium, or take leaf cuttings in spring and early summer.

KEEPING PLANTS The plant will benefit from a spell outdoors in summer.

PLANT CARE

Bright light with direct sunlight. ● Normal room temperature in the growing season; about 55°F/13°C in winter. ● Water growing plants sparingly; give just enough water to prevent the soil drying out completely in winter. ● Apply a balanced liquid fertilizer every 3 weeks during the period of active growth.

ECHINOPSIS EYRIESII
Cactaceae

SEA URCHIN CACTUS

The barrel-shaped stems of this cactus, with as many as 18 ribs, become cylindrical as they mature. The ribs bear areoles, each with 14 short, hard, dark brown spines. Large tubular, fragrant flowers, up to 10in/25cm long and 4–5in/10–13cm wide, are freely produced in early summer on three-to four-year-old plants that have had a winter rest. The flowers, with white petals and yellow stamens, open out flat at night and wilt within 24 hours. This plant is sometimes offered as *Echinocereus eyriesii*.

FACT FILE

ORIGIN South America.

HEIGHT To 10in/25cm.

POTTING MIX Soil-based and coarse sand or perlite in a ratio of 3:1.

REPOTTING Move into a pot one size larger in spring when the pot becomes overcrowded.

PROPAGATION In spring or summer, remove offsets from around the plant and press them into gritty medium in individual pots.

KEEPING PLANTS In good growing conditions, these cacti will survive for many years.

PLANT CARE

Full, direct sunlight. ● Normal room temperature in summer, but 45°–50°F/7°–10°C in winter to ensure good flowering. ● Water moderately in the growing season; give just enough water in winter to prevent the soil from drying out completely. ● Apply a weak solution of high-potash fertilizer every 2 weeks in the growing season to encourage flowering.

ERICA x *HIEMALIS*
Ericaceae

FRENCH HEATHER

This winter-flowering heather, which forms a small shrub, has erect stems with whorls of tiny deep green leaves. The ³/₄-in/2-cm-long tubular flowers are pink with white tips and are borne in clusters at the ends of the stems. *Erica carnea*, winter heath, is another popular winter-flowering houseplant. It has more slender stems, which are densely clothed in small, round rose-pink or purple flowers. Because they need cool conditions, winter heaths are difficult plants to keep in the home, and they should be discarded after flowering.

FACT FILE

ORIGIN South Africa (Cape Province); hybrids.

HEIGHT 12–18in/30–46cm.

POTTING MIX Ericaceous (acidic) medium.

REPOTTING Plants are usually discarded before repotting is necessary.

PROPAGATION By semiripe stem cuttings in late summer; these are difficult to root successfully in the home.

KEEPING PLANTS Ericas lose their leaves rapidly in a dry atmosphere and tend to be short-lived in centrally heated houses.

Erica × *hiemalis*

PLANT CARE

Bright light with some direct sun. ● Keep cool, preferably at a maximum of 50°F/10°C. ● Keep the medium moist at all times; never allow it to dry out. Use lime-free water where possible. ● Spray the plant frequently and stand the pot in a tray of moist gravel.

~

ERIOBOTRYA JAPONICA
Rosaceae

*L*OQUAT

Although grown for its edible fruit in warm climates, this plant is unlikely to flower and fruit in the home. It does, however, make an attractive foliage plant, with lance-shaped leaves up to 10in/25cm long and half as wide. Deep-set veins give the leaf surface a textured appearance, and the young foliage is covered with a silvery down. The plant grows into a small tree and is most suitable for a sunroom or large hallway.

FACT FILE

ORIGIN China; Japan.

HEIGHT To 10ft/3m in the home.

POTTING MIX Soil-based to give extra stability to the plant as it grows.

REPOTTING In spring move a young plant into a pot two sizes bigger; top-dress a large plant.

PROPAGATION By semiripe stem cuttings in late summer; a propagator with bottom heat will increase the chances of success. The plant can also be grown from the seeds in ripe fruits.

KEEPING PLANTS As loquats age, they begin to look leggy and ungainly and are best discarded.

PLANT CARE

Bright light with some direct sunlight.
● Normal room temperature during the growing season. Move to cooler conditions with a temperature of 50°F/10°C for a winter rest.
● Keep the soil moist at all times during the growing season; water sparingly in winter.
● Apply a balanced liquid feed every 2–3 weeks to an actively growing plant.

~

EUCHARIS × *GRANDIFLORA*
Amaryllidaceae

*A*MAZON LILY

A natural hybrid, this evergreen bulbous plant has broadly oval, deep green, stalked leaves about 12in/30cm long. The pendulous fragrant flowers, which are about 3in/8cm wide, appear in summer and sometimes again in fall or winter. They are carried in groups of three or more at the top of long, slender stems and look somewhat similar to white narcissus, but with a slender greenish tube. The central cup is flushed with green and sometimes has tendril-like outgrowths from the rim. The plant is also known as Eucharist lily and star of Bethlehem.

FACT FILE

ORIGIN Colombia; Peru.

HEIGHT Flower stalks to 2ft/60cm.

POTTING MIX Soil-based with added leaf mold and coarse sand.

REPOTTING In spring, every 3 years or so. Plant the bulb with the nose just covered.

PROPAGATION Detach offsets from around the bulb when the main plant is repotted, and pot them individually.

KEEPING PLANTS This lily thrives in a pot and will last for several years.

PLANT CARE

A bright position, shaded from direct sun.
● Minimum temperature of 50°F/10°C. ● Water newly potted bulbs sparingly until growth starts, and keep the soil moist at all times during the growing season. Reduce watering in early spring for about 6 weeks to encourage blooming.
● Apply a high-potash liquid fertilizer every 2–3 weeks during the growing season.

Eucharis × *grandiflora*

EURYA JAPONICA
Theaceae

*E*URYA

An evergreen bushy plant, most suitable for a sunroom or greenhouse where it can be allowed space to develop fully, eurya belongs to the same family as the camellia. The glossy, deep green, leathery leaves are lance-shaped, with toothed margins, and are about 2in/5cm long.

The small, rather unpleasant-smelling, white flowers, tinged with green, are followed by shiny black berries, but this plant is generally grown as a specimen for its beautiful foliage. *Eurya japonica* 'Winter Wine,' with leaves that turn deep red in fall, is smaller and has a more spreading habit of growth.

FACT FILE

ORIGIN China; Japan; South Korea; India.

HEIGHT To 4ft/1.2m.

POTTING MIX Soil-based.

REPOTTING In spring, when the plant has outgrown its pot.

PROPAGATION By seed from ripe berries or by semiripe cuttings in late summer.

KEEPING PLANTS Prune lightly after flowering if necessary, but be careful to retain the plant's characteristic herringbone growth habit.

PLANT CARE

Bright light with some direct sun or light shade. ● Cool conditions, with a winter minimum of 45°F/7°C. ● Water plentifully in the growing period, but allow the surface of the soil to dry out between waterings. Keep just moist in winter. ● Apply a balanced liquid fertilizer every 2–3 weeks when the plant is in active growth.

~

EUSTOMA GRANDIFLORUM
Gentianaceae

*P*RAIRIE GENTIAN

Often offered as *Lisianthus russellianus,* this is a relatively new houseplant. The large flowers, with satiny petals, appear in summer in clusters above gray-green, pointed leaves, and open into a wide poppy shape from spirally scrolled buds.

Eustoma is an annual or biennial grown from seed. Most popular is the 'Yodel' series in purple-blue, pink, and white. The 'Echo' series has double flowers in several shades of blue, as well as pink and white, and includes varieties that have a picotee edging to the petals. All eustomas make excellent cut flowers.

FACT FILE

ORIGIN Mexico; southern USA.

HEIGHT To 30in/76cm; compact varieties to about 15in/38cm.

POTTING MIX Soil-based, leaf mold, and coarse sand in a ratio of 2:1:1.

REPOTTING Not usually necessary.

PROPAGATION Sow seed in early spring. Plant seedlings 3 to an 8-in/20-cm pot to create a good show.

KEEPING PLANTS Plants are usually discarded after flowering.

PLANT CARE

Bright light with some direct sun. ● Fairly cool conditions with good ventilation. ● Water plentifully, but allow the surface of the soil to dry out between waterings. ● Apply a high-potash liquid fertilizer every 2 weeks from the time the buds start to form.

~

FELICIA AMELLOIDES
(SYN. *AGATHAEA COELESTIS*)
Asteraceae

*B*LUE MARGUERITE

This tender perennial makes a bushy plant with rounded, oval leaves. In summer, brilliant blue-mauve daisylike flowers with yellow centers are freely produced on long, slender stalks, but they will open only in a bright, sunny location. The plant will not thrive if the atmosphere is too hot and humid, and it will rot if conditions are too cold and damp.

FACT FILE

ORIGIN South Africa.

HEIGHT To 18in/46cm.

POTTING MIX Peat-moss-based with some added sand.

REPOTTING Repot as necessary in spring.

PROPAGATION From seed sown in late spring, or by stem cuttings in early spring.

KEEPING PLANTS Pinch off growing tips regularly and cut back hard after flowering, to keep the plant compact. Discard the plant when it becomes leggy and untidy.

PLANT CARE

Bright light is essential, with some direct sun. ● Fairly cool room temperature in summer, 45°–50°F/7°–10°C in winter. ● Water moderately in the period of active growth; keep almost dry in winter. ● Apply a high-potash liquid fertilizer every 2–3 weeks during spring and summer.

~

FEROCACTUS LATISPINUS
Cactaceae

*B*ARREL CACTUS

Also known as the fish-hook cactus and devil's tongue, this is a fiercely spined, slow-growing, globular specimen. The narrow ribs bear red or white radiating spines with clusters of four central spines about 1½in/4cm long. The lowest of these is larger and stouter than the rest and strongly hooked. The red or purple flowers are rarely produced in cultivation.

Felicia amelloides

FACT FILE

ORIGIN Mexico; southern USA.

HEIGHT To 12in/30cm after several years.

POTTING MIX Soil- or peat-moss-based with grit.

REPOTTING In spring allow a ½-in/13-mm space between the plant and the side of the pot.

PROPAGATION By seed sown in spring.

KEEPING PLANTS This cactus needs maximum light for the spines to develop properly.

Ferocactus latispinus

PLANT CARE

Bright light with plenty of direct sunlight. ● A minimum of 50°F/10°C in winter. ● Water sparingly in the growing season; give just enough water to prevent the medium drying out in winter. ● Apply a high-potassium liquid fertilizer every 4 weeks from spring to fall.

~

GENISTA x *SPACHIANA*
Leguminosae

Genista

This broom is grown for its strongly fragrant, bright yellow winter or spring flowers. They are of typical pea-flower shape and are carried in slender racemes at the tips of the branches. The leaves consist of three mid green leaflets that are covered with silky hairs, particularly underneath. The slender stems give the plant a graceful arching habit. The plant is also known as *Cytisus* x *spachianus* and *C. fragrans*.

FACT FILE

ORIGIN Hybrid.

HEIGHT To 3ft/90cm.

POTTING MIX Soil-based.

REPOTTING In fall, only when necessary: the plant resents root disturbance.

PROPAGATION Take stem cuttings in summer.

KEEPING PLANTS Cut back flowering stems once the flowers have faded, then stand the plant in a sheltered, sunny spot outdoors; bring it back indoors in fall.

Genista x *spachiana*

PLANT CARE

Bright light with 2 or 3 hours of direct sunlight in spring; otherwise, moderate light. ● Cool conditions, with a maximum of 60°F/16°C during flowering. ● Water freely from the time the buds appear to the end of the growing season; do not allow the pot to stand in water. Water more sparingly at other times. ● As soon as buds appear, give a high-potash liquid feed every 3 weeks.

~

GEOGENANTHUS UNDATUS
(SYN. *G. POEPPEGII*)
Commelinaceae

Seersucker plant

Related to *Dichorisandra*, *Tradescantia*, and *Zebrina*, this foliage plant produces a small number of erect, rather fleshy, unbranched stems, which bear rosettes of tough, oval leaves 3–5in/8–13cm long and 2–4in/ 5–10cm wide. The dark green leaves are strikingly marked with lengthwise silver stripes and the leaf surface is puckered, giving it the appearance of seersucker. The leaves are purple-red underneath.

In summer mature plants may produce small, fringed, purple flowers that last for only a single day.

FACT FILE

ORIGIN Brazil; Peru.

HEIGHT To 10in/25cm.

POTTING MIX Equal parts of peat moss, leaf mold, and perlite.

REPOTTING In spring, when roots fill the pot.

PROPAGATION Take stem tip cuttings in spring. Geogenanthus does not root as readily as many other members of the family.

KEEPING PLANTS The plant grows throughout the year, but most actively from spring to late fall.

PLANT CARE

Bright light but shaded from direct sun. ● The temperature must not drop below 60°F/16°C. ● Keep the medium moist in the growing season; water less in winter. ● Stand the pot on a tray of damp gravel to increase humidity. ● Apply a balanced liquid fertilizer every 2 weeks during the growing season.

Glechoma hederacea
'Variegata'

GLECHOMA HEDERACEA 'VARIEGATA'
Labiatae

GROUND IVY

Although generally regarded as a weed, this trailing plant is very attractive in its variegated form. The rounded, scallop-edged leaves are irregularly margined and splashed with white. They have a downy surface and are aromatic when crushed. In summer, pale lilac—or sometimes white or pink—flowers are produced in the axils of the leaves. Glechoma is a good plant for a hanging basket, easy to grow, and hardy.

FACT FILE

ORIGIN Europe.

HEIGHT Prostrate; stems trail to 10in/25cm.

POTTING MIX Soil- or peat-moss-based.

REPOTTING When the roots fill the pot.

PROPAGATION Stem cuttings root quickly in spring and summer.

KEEPING PLANTS Pinch off growing tips and cut stems back hard in early spring.

PLANT CARE

Bright light but not direct sun. ● Cool room temperature in summer; with a minimum of 50°F/10°C in winter. ● Keep the soil moist in summer; water sparingly in winter. ● Liquid-feed every 2–3 weeks in spring and summer.

GOMPHRENA GLOBOSA
Amaranthaceae

GLOBE AMARANTH

Often grown outdoors in beds to provide colorful flower heads for drying, this half-hardy annual can be grown as a houseplant for a sunny windowsill.

The rounded flower heads, which give the plant the name of bachelor's button, are composed mainly of brightly colored papery bracts in shades of red, pink, purple, white, yellow, or orange; seed is usually sold in mixed colors.

Some compact forms are available, such as the red-flowered 'Nana' and 'Buddy' with deep purple flowers, which both grow to 6–8in/15–20cm high.

FACT FILE

ORIGIN Old World Tropics.

HEIGHT To 2ft/60cm.

POTTING MIX Soil- or peat-moss-based.

REPOTTING Not usually necessary.

PROPAGATION By seed sown in early spring.

KEEPING PLANTS Discard the plant once it is past its best. The flower heads are good for dried-flower arrangements.

PLANT CARE

Bright light with some direct sunlight. ● Normal to cool room temperature. ● Keep the soil just moist at all times. ● Apply a high-potash liquid fertilizer every 2 weeks.

~

GRAPTOPHYLLUM PICTUM
Acanthaceae

CARICATURE PLANT

Although rarely seen, this evergreen shrub would prosper in the home, especially in a sunroom.

The laurel-shaped leaves, arranged opposite each other along the stalk, are up to 6in/15cm long. Each leaf is shiny deep green, marked in the center with a creamy white or yellow blotch that is sometimes thought to resemble a human face, hence the common name. There is occasionally a pinkish tinge along the central leaf vein. The 1½-in/4-cm-long tubular crimson or purple flowers open wide at the mouth.

FACT FILE

ORIGIN Australasia; Pacific Islands.

HEIGHT To 6ft/1.8m.

POTTING MIX Soil-based.

REPOTTING In spring, move to a pot one size larger.

PROPAGATION Take stem cuttings in late spring or summer.

KEEPING PLANTS Pinch off the growing tips regularly to encourage bushiness. Replace the plant after 3 or 4 years, when it becomes leggy.

PLANT CARE

Bright filtered light with some direct sun except on the hottest days. ● Average room temperature. ● Water thoroughly, particularly in summer. ● Apply a standard liquid fertilizer once a month between spring and fall.

~

GUZMANIA DISSITIFLORA
Bromeliaceae

GUZMANIA

Like other guzmanias, this unusual-looking plant has a rosette of long, semierect strap-shaped leaves that form a central vase. The long flower stalk, arising from the vase, is enclosed in bright red bracts and bears a flower head consisting of 7 to 15 flowers on short stems. These stems are also enclosed in bright red and yellow papery bracts, which are fused into a tube for the greater part of their length. The flowers themselves are small and white.

FACT FILE

ORIGIN Panama; Costa Rica; Colombia.

HEIGHT To 3ft/90cm in flower.

POTTING MIX Peat-moss-based.

REPOTTING Repot when the pot is overcrowded.

PROPAGATION Offsets can be detached from the base of the plant and potted up separately.

KEEPING PLANTS Warmth, shade, and humidity are essential. If they are provided, the plant will last for several years.

PLANT CARE

Bright light but shaded from direct sunlight. ● A minimum of 50°F/10°C; optimum temperature is above 65°F/18°C. ● Keep the soil just moist and top up the central vase occasionally. ● Spray the plant regularly to maintain humidity in the growing season. ● Apply a balanced liquid fertilizer every 2 weeks during the growing season. Foliar feed can be added to the misting water.

~

HAWORTHIA PUMILA
(SYN. *H. MARGARITIFERA*)
Liliaceae

PEARL PLANT

A succulent plant rather similar to an aloe, this haworthia forms a rosette of fleshy, triangular dark green or purple-green leaves with sharp tips, which tend to curve inward slightly. Pearly white "warts" on the back of the leaves make a striking pattern and give the plant its common name. Insignificant flowers may appear. Unlike most succulents, haworthias do not like direct sunlight, which causes the leaves to shrivel.

*Haworthia
pumila*

Guzmania dissitiflora

FACT FILE

ORIGIN South Africa (Western Cape Province).

HEIGHT To 6in/15cm.

POTTING MIX Soil-based, or peat-moss-based with some added grit.

REPOTTING Repot annually in spring. Use a shallow pot, since the root system is small.

PROPAGATION Remove offsets and pot them up individually in late spring and summer.

KEEPING PLANTS The plant needs a winter rest.

PLANT CARE

Bright indirect light but no direct sunlight. ● Normal room temperature with a rest period at about 50°F/10°C in winter. ● Water freely in the growing season; allow the top one-third of the soil to dry out between waterings; keep it almost dry in winter. ● Do not feed haworthias.

~

HEBE x *ANDERSONII*
Scrophulariaceae

HEBE

This almost hardy, evergreen shrub makes an attractive short-term houseplant; it is also suitable for a tub in the greenhouse or sunroom. The glossy, oblong leaves are about 4in/10cm long and mid to deep green. Very small flowers are carried all through the summer in dense, 6-in/15-cm-long, "bottle brush" racemes; they are pink or mauve, fading to white. The form 'Variegata' has smaller, lighter green leaves margined with cream.

FACT FILE

ORIGIN Hybrid.

HEIGHT To 5ft/1.5m but can be kept much smaller as a houseplant.

POTTING MIX Soil- or peat-moss-based.

REPOTTING In spring move into a larger pot as necessary.

PROPAGATION By semiripe stem cuttings in late summer.

KEEPING PLANTS The plant will benefit from a spell outdoors during the summer. In temperate climates, when it has become too large for a houseplant, it can be hardened off and planted in the garden.

PLANT CARE

Bright light, but protect the plant from strong midsummer sun. ● Keep moderately cool, with a minimum winter temperature of 40°–45°F/4°–7°C. ● Keep the soil moist at all times in spring and summer; reduce watering during the winter rest period. ● Give a high-potash liquid feed every 2 weeks in spring and summer.

~

HEDYCHIUM CORONARIUM
Zingiberaceae

BUTTERFLY GINGER

Because of its large size, this plant is best suited for a greenhouse or sunroom. Hedychium is a perennial that forms a dense clump of lance-shaped, pointed leaves. These rise from the rhizomatous rootstock and can grow up to 6ft/1.8m long. The flowers are carried in long spikes of about six strongly fragrant white blooms, which are tubular with a prominent lower lip. The plant is also known as garland flower and white ginger lily. In its natural habitat, this hedychium grows along the banks of streams, and it will tolerate standing in water.

FACT FILE

ORIGIN Tropical Asia.

HEIGHT To 4ft /1.2m or more.

POTTING MIX Soil- or peat-moss-based.

REPOTTING In early spring, when roots fill the current container.

PROPAGATION Divide overcrowded clumps in spring or sow fresh seed.

KEEPING PLANTS Cut out old spikes in winter, when the plant is dormant.

PLANT CARE

Moderately bright light but not direct sunlight. ● Minimum temperature of 60°F/16°C. ● Keep the soil moist in the growing season; water sparingly in winter, allowing the plant to become dormant. ● Give a high-potash liquid feed every 2–3 weeks in spring and summer.

HELICONIA SCHIEDEANA
Heliconiaceae

ℒOBSTER CLAWS

A magnificent perennial for the warm greenhouse or sunroom, heliconia is grown for its stately habit, its superb waxy flowers, and its handsome foliage, rather like that of a banana plant. The flowers resemble those of the exotic strelitzia, the bird-of-paradise plant. Since the tough, oblong leaves grow to 4½ft/1.4m in length, only young, relatively small plants are suitable for bringing into the house.

The upright floral bracts, which can grow to 14in/36cm, are slightly twisted when mature; they are red or orange-red, with yellow or, occasionally, green flowers emerging from them.

FACT FILE

ORIGIN Mexico.

HEIGHT To 10ft/3m.

POTTING MIX Peat-moss-based, or bark and leaf mold with added dried manure; must be moisture-retentive.

REPOTTING In spring, every 2 years.

PROPAGATION In spring sow seed or separate and pot up offsets, or divide the plant when repotting.

KEEPING PLANTS When stems have flowered, cut them away to encourage new growth. Watch out for red spider mites and scale insects, which can be a problem.

PLANT CARE

Semishade. ● A minimum temperature of 60°F/16°C. ● Water moderately at all times. ● Mist plants daily in warm weather. ● Feed with a high-potash foliar feed every 2 weeks during spring and summer.

Heliconia schiedeana

Hemigraphis colorata

HEMIGRAPHIS COLORATA
(SYN. *H. ALTERNATA*)
Acanthaceae

ℛED IVY

This low-growing, creeping plant, also known as red-flame ivy, gains its common names from the stems and the puckered leaves, which are strongly suffused with red. It needs high humidity and so is well suited to growing in a terrarium or large bottle garden. The upper surface of the oval leaves, which are some 3in/8cm long, is silver gray and quilted; the reverse is purple. In late summer hemigraphis bears spikes of rather insignificant white flowers, some ¾-in/2-cm long.

Hemigraphis repanda is very similar to *H. colorata*, but the leaves are more slender, purple-green above and deep purple underneath. The hybrid *H.* 'Exotica' has a bushier habit, with smaller white flowers.

FACT FILE

ORIGIN Malaysia.

HEIGHT To 12in/30cm.

POTTING MIX Soil- or peat-moss-based, with added leaf mold. Good drainage is essential.

REPOTTING Move to a pot one size larger every 6–8 weeks during the period of active growth.

PROPAGATION Take tip cuttings at any time.

KEEPING PLANTS Pinch off the growing tips regularly to promote bushy growth.

PLANT CARE

Bright filtered light but no direct sunlight. ● Average room temperature of 65°–75°F/ 18°–24°C all year-round. ● Keep the soil moist at all times; use with tepid soft water or rainwater. ● Feed at 2-week intervals during spring and summer.

~

HYMENOCALLIS LITTORALIS
Amaryllidaceae

ℐPIDER LILY

This frost-tender, evergreen bulbous plant is best grown in a warm greenhouse and brought indoors for flowering. Its fragrant, beautifully formed flowers have elegantly reflexed, narrow outer segments. These make the whole bloom appear spiderlike, and they give the plant its common name. They are white, with a greenish tinge to the base, and up to eight blooms may be carried in an umbel on each 30-in/76-cm-long flower stalk.

Hymenocallis littoralis

FACT FILE

ORIGIN Tropical America.

HEIGHT To 3ft/90cm.

POTTING MIX Equal parts of soil-based medium, leaf mold, and coarse sand.

REPOTTING At the end of the winter rest period, repot the bulb in fresh soil in the same pot.

PROPAGATION Separate and divide offsets when repotting, or sow seed in spring or summer.

KEEPING PLANTS Overwatering in winter when the plant is resting will cause the bulb to rot. Keep the soil just moist until new growth starts, then repot.

PLANT CARE

Bright, filtered light but no direct sunlight. ● Average warm greenhouse temperature, with a winter minimum of 60°F/16°C. ● Water plentifully when the plant is in active growth. In the winter rest period, keep the soil just moist. ● Liquid-feed every 2 weeks during the flowering period and for 2 months after the last flower fades.

~

HYPOCYRTA RADICANS **see** *NEMETANTHUS GREGARIUS*

~

Ipheion uniflorum
'Froyle Mill'

IPHEION UNIFLORUM
Liliaceae

*S*PRING STAR FLOWER

The beautiful star-shaped pale blue or white flowers, carried on slender 6-in/15-cm stems, are the main feature of this bulbous plant. As its name suggests, it blooms early in the year and is tolerant of cold weather, down to 14°F/-10°C.

The flower stalks grow through tufts of long, narrow, grasslike leaves, which smell of garlic when crushed, although the flowers themselves have a pleasant smell.

FACT FILE

ORIGIN Argentina; Uruguay.

HEIGHT To 8in/20cm.

POTTING MIX Soil-based with added grit to aid drainage.

REPOTTING The plant rests from late spring to late summer. Repot in early fall, after the plant has rested.

PROPAGATION Divide and replant the offsets every 2 or 3 years.

KEEPING PLANTS This is an attractive plant for a deep pot in a well-ventilated cold greenhouse and should be brought into the living room only at flowering time.

PLANT CARE

Full sun except during the hottest part of the day. ● Cool to average greenhouse conditions; cool room temperature. ● Water moderately during the growing season. ● Apply a standard liquid fertilizer once every 4 weeks during winter and early spring.

IPOMOEA TRICOLOR
Convolvulaceae

*M*ORNING GLORY

Ipomoea is an attractive frost-tender perennial climber that is more usually grown as an annual. It has heart-shaped pale green leaves 6–10in/15–25cm wide and freely produced flowers, which appear from midsummer to midfall. These are purple-blue with a white tube, and open to 5in/13cm wide in the morning, only to fade during the afternoon (hence the common name). 'Heavenly Blue' is a commonly seen cultivar, with sky blue flowers of a particularly vivid color.

FACT FILE

ORIGIN Tropical America.

HEIGHT Stems climb to 13ft/4m.

POTTING MIX Soil-based, with added peat moss.

REPOTTING Not required; the plants are discarded at the end of flowering each year.

PROPAGATION Sow seeds in heat, in spring. Nick the seeds or soak them in tepid water overnight to facilitate germination.

KEEPING PLANTS Deadhead daily to encourage flowering and prolong the flowering season. Discard the plant when flowering is over.

PLANT CARE

Full sun or light shade. ● Average to warm room and greenhouse temperature. ● Water well, but do not waterlog. ● Feed with a high-potash fertilizer every 2 weeks between spring and late summer.

IXORA COCCINEA
Rubiaceae

*F*LAME-OF-THE-WOODS

In its natural habitat, this handsome tropical evergreen shrub enjoys warm, humid conditions, and it will thrive in a well-heated greenhouse. Bring the plant into the home when it is in bloom.

The flat-topped flower heads, which appear from spring onward, are comprised of many individual tubular flowers, each up to $1^1/_2$in/4cm long. Cultivars are now freely available with flowers in a range of reds, oranges, and pinks. The 4-in/10-cm-long, broadly elliptic leaves are glossy and thick, and are arranged in pairs. New leaves have a bronze tinge, maturing to dark green.

FACT FILE

ORIGIN India; Sri Lanka.

HEIGHT To 4ft/1.2m in 4–5 years.

POTTING MIX Peat-moss-based, with added leaf mold, and coarse sand.

REPOTTING Move into a larger pot every spring until an 18-in/46-cm pot is reached; thereafter top-dress annually.

PROPAGATION Take 3-in/8-cm stem cuttings in spring or summer.

KEEPING PLANTS Protect the plant from drafts and do not water with cold water.

PLANT CARE

Full sun. ● Warm conditions with a minimum temperature of 60°F/16°C. ● When in growth, water freely with soft water or rainwater at room temperature; give less water in winter. ● Stand the pot on a tray of moist pebbles to increase humidity. ● Feed with a standard liquid fertilizer every 2 weeks in summer.

Ixora coccinea

JACARANDA MIMOSIFOLIA
Bignoniaceae

*J*ACARANDA

In the garden, jacaranda grows into a tree up to 40ft/12m high, and in Brazil it is the source of palisander wood. The foliage is doubly pinnate. And the leaves grow opposite along the stem and droop in spring, as some ferns do, so at first sight small specimens may be mistaken for them. Each leaf is composed of numerous tiny oblong pinnae, covered with downy hairs.

Outdoors, dense panicles of hyacinth blue flowers cover the tree in spring. These are reluctant to form on indoor plants until they reach a height of 1.5m/5ft or more. Generally, indoor plants are grown for their fine soft foliage.

FACT FILE

ORIGIN Argentina.

HEIGHT To 6ft/1.8m in a large container.

POTTING MIX Soil-based.

REPOTTING In spring, move into a pot one size larger, until maximum desired pot size is reached.

PROPAGATION From fresh seed sown in spring, or stem cuttings with a heel in early summer.

KEEPING PLANTS Prune the plant in spring if it becomes too large. After several years, when it become straggly, discard it.

PLANT CARE

Bright light with at least 3 hours of full sun daily. ● Average room temperature, with a winter minimum of 55°F/13°C, but the plant can tolerate temperatures down to 45°F/7°C. ● Water well from spring to fall; give less water in the winter rest period. ● Apply standard liquid fertilizer every 2 weeks during the period of active growth.

~

JATROPHA PODAGRICA
Euphorbiaceae

*G*OUT PLANT

An unusual succulent shrub, also known as tartogo, this is an easy plant to grow. It has a thick, bottle-shaped body, swollen with water-storage tissue, from which it derives its common name. From time to time it produces a few long-stalked shield-shaped leaves with three to five lobes, which can be up to 8in/20cm wide.

Bright red flowers in clusters up to 5cm/2in wide, which also have long stalks, are produced both in early spring before the leaves appear and at other times throughout the year.

Jatropha podagrica

FACT FILE

ORIGIN Central America.

HEIGHT To 3ft/90cm.

POTTING MIX Soil-based with added leaf mold and coarse sand; good drainage is essential.

REPOTTING In late winter, every 2–3 years, mainly to freshen the soil.

PROPAGATION Sow fresh seed or take cuttings in summer.

KEEPING PLANTS The plant should be kept dry during the winter, when most of the leaves fall.

PLANT CARE

Sunshine or semishade. ● Warm room temperature, with a winter minimum of 55°–60°F/13°–16°C. ● Water moderately in summer, hardly at all in winter. The plant must never stand in water. ● Feed twice a year, with a half-strength standard liquid fertilizer.

~

JUSTICIA PAUCIFLORA
(SYN. *J. RIZZINII*)
Acanthaceae

*J*USTICIA

This is another member of the genus that includes the very different-looking *Justicia carnea*. An attractive, many-branched, shrubby plant, with soft green stems and mid green leaves in pairs, *Justicia pauciflora* forms a small rounded bush. It is a cheerful addition to the list of winter-flowering plants, since from late fall to early spring, it is covered in clusters of 1-in/2.5-cm-long tubular flowers that are scarlet at the base and bright yellow at the tip.

FACT FILE

ORIGIN Brazil.

HEIGHT To 2ft/60cm.

POTTING MIX Soil-based.

REPOTTING Move the plant into a larger pot whenever roots show through the drainage holes; top-dress instead when the maximum desired pot size is reached.

PROPAGATION In spring take stem tip cuttings.

KEEPING PLANTS Pinch off the growing tips regularly to encourage bushiness. Replace when it becomes straggly, usually after about 2 years.

PLANT CARE

Bright filtered light or full sun with protection from the hottest sun. ● Normal room temperature, with a rest period at 55°F/13°C from the end of flowering until new growth appears. ● Keep the soil moist but not waterlogged in the growing season; give less water in the rest period. ● Above 55°F/13°C, stand the pot on a tray of moist pebbles to maintain humidity. ● Apply a standard liquid fertilizer every 2 weeks to an actively growing plant.

Justicia pauciflora

~

KOHLERIA ERIANTHA AND HYBRIDS
Gesneriaceae

*K*OHLERIA

All parts of this erect plant are hairy. The elliptic leaves are velvety green and wooly on the underside, with contrasting fine reddish hairs around the margins; the summer flowers are also hairy. They are tubular, some 2in/5cm long, and are usually carried in clusters of three or four. Cultivars range from shades of orange to red. The inside of the flowers' mouth is marked with yellow spots.

FACT FILE

ORIGIN Colombia; hybrids.

HEIGHT To 4ft/1.2m.

POTTING MIX Peat-moss-based with added sand or perlite, or equal parts of soil-based medium, peat moss, and perlite.

REPOTTING Move into a pot one size larger each spring.

PROPAGATION In spring divide the rhizomes or sow seed; take root tip cuttings in fall.

KEEPING PLANTS Be careful not to get water on the leaves; it will be trapped by the hairs and may scorch the leaves or cause botrytis. After flowering, cut the stems back to 1–2in/2.5–5cm.

PLANT CARE

Bright, filtered light. ● Normal room temperature. ● Water moderately during the growing season; give just enough water in winter to prevent the leaves from wilting. ● Feed with half-strength liquid fertilizer every 2 weeks in the growing season.

~

LACHENALIA ALOIDES
Liliaceae

CAPE COWSLIP

A good plant for a sunny windowsill, lachenalia has two or three arching fleshy leaves 12in/30cm long and about 2in/5cm wide. These spring from a bulb some 1½in/4cm round. The flower stalk is green or purple-brown, and racemes of tubular flowers appear in late winter and early spring. Several varieties are in cultivation: 'Aurea' has flowers of a soft deep yellow; those of 'Pearsonii' are apricot and red. 'Nelsonii' has golden yellow flowers with green tips. Lachenalia is sometimes called soldier boys, from the military look of the plants when grown in rows.

FACT FILE

ORIGIN South Africa (Cape Province).

HEIGHT To 12in/30cm.

POTTING MIX Soil- or peat-moss-based with added loam.

REPOTTING Every year in early fall.

PROPAGATION Sow seed in spring, or remove offset bulbs when repotting and plant them up separately; they will flower after 2 years.

KEEPING PLANTS As leaves wither, dry off the plant; keep almost dry when dormant.

PLANT CARE

Full sun or light shade. ● Cool temperatures in the range of 50°–60°F/10°–16°C. ● Water moderately in the growing period. ● Liquid-feed once a week from the time the flower stalks appear until the last flower dies.

LEEA COCCINEA
Leeaceae

WEST INDIAN HOLLY

This shrub is grown for its velvety wine-colored, 2–4in/5–10cm-long wavy-edged leaflets, which turn green as the plant matures. When still young, the plant will produce small grapelike flowers, which are red in bud, turning to pink. *Leea coccinea* 'Burgundy' has richer red leaves and needs better light to keep this coloring. *Leea coccinea* 'Green' produces mid green leaves.

FACT FILE

ORIGIN Burma.

HEIGHT To 6ft/1.8m.

POTTING MIX Soil-based.

REPOTTING In spring move into a pot one size larger until maximum desired size is reached.

PROPAGATION In spring sow seed, take stem cuttings or air-layer, all of which are difficult.

KEEPING PLANTS A healthy plant should last 5 or 6 years, but keep it out of drafts.

PLANT CARE

Bright indirect light. ● Minimum temperature of 60°F/16°C. ● Sensitive to both under- and over-watering; keep the soil moist, but not sodden, at all times. ● Mist the plant frequently and stand the pot on a dish of moist pebbles to maintain high humidity. ● Feed every 2 weeks in spring and summer with dilute liquid feed.

~

LILIUM SPP.
Liliaceae

TRUMPET LILIES

Although lilies are usually considered garden flowers, a few types make successful temporary plants for growing indoors. These include the trumpet lilies, the petals of which are fused together for part of the length of the flower to produce a basal tube.

There are dozens of hybrids from which to choose. Some of the most popular are the Mid-Century hybrids, derived from the Asiatic lilies. 'Pixie' is a typical example, with bright orange flowers.

Other good hybrids for growing indoors are 'Chinook,' which is also orange, and 'Cinnabar' with maroon-red flowers. 'Connecticut King' has golden yellow flowers, 'Destiny' has lemon yellow flowers, and those of 'Prosperity' are pale yellow.

Fall is the best time to plant lily bulbs for pot use. Buy plump, firm bulbs with no signs of wrinkling or softness. Plant each bulb in a 6-in/15-cm pot or larger, with at least 1in/2.5cm of potting mix above its head. Until growth begins, keep it cool, dark, and moist; when growth is visible, move it to a brighter position.

FACT FILE

ORIGIN Hybrid.

HEIGHT To 4ft/1.2m.

POTTING MIX Soil- or peat-moss-based, with good drainage.

REPOTTING Repot annually in fall. Lily bulbs should be planted in deep pots that are large enough to allow good root development. For example, only 3–4 medium-sized bulbs should be planted in a 12-in/30-cm pot, and there should be at least 1in/2.5cm between the bulbs and between the bulbs and the side of the pot.

PROPAGATION Separate bulblets when repotting; remove and plant bulb scales in winter, or sow stem bulbils (small black bulbs produced on the stem in the axils of the leaves) in late summer.

KEEPING PLANTS Overwatering and bad drainage can cause the bulb to rot. If the bulbs are not kept for another season's indoor flowering, plant them outdoors. Stake the stems to prevent them from toppling over.

PLANT CARE

Bright light but no direct sun. ● Overwinter the bulb in its pot at about 40°F/4°C; move it to a warmer place as growth begins in spring. ● Water well during the growing season. ● Feed with a weak liquid fertilizer once a month in spring and summer.

Lilium 'Pixie'

Liriope muscari

LIRIOPE MUSCARI
(SYN. *L. GRAMINIFOLIA DENSIFLORA*)
Liliaceae

*B*IG BLUE LILYTURF

Of the three or four species of liriope available, this is the most suitable for pot culture. When in flower, the plant closely resembles a large grape hyacinth with green foliage. It is an evergreen, stalkless plant with erect, conspicuously veined strap-shaped leaves 12in/30cm long and ½in/13mm wide. In late summer to fall, purple to violet flowers are produced in dense racemes, which are almost the same length as the leaves; they are followed by black berries. After flowering, cut off the flower stalks unless you require the berries.

There are several attractive cultivars, including 'Gold-banded,' which has wide, arching dark green leaves edged with gold, and the 18-in/46-cm-high 'Silvery Midget,' with white markings on the leaves and white flowers.

FACT FILE

ORIGIN China; Japan.

HEIGHT To 12in/30cm.

POTTING MIX Soil- or peat-moss-based.

REPOTTING Repot every couple of years, in spring.

PROPAGATION Divide in spring or sow seed in summer.

KEEPING PLANTS Keep the plant out of drafts; cold winds can damage the leaves.

PLANT CARE

Bright filtered light. ● Average to warm room temperature; keep at 40°–50°F/4°–10°C in winter. ● Keep the soil fairly moist, but the cooler the temperature, the drier the medium should be. ● Feed actively growing plants every 2 weeks with standard liquid fertilizer.

MIKANIA DENTATA (SYN. *M. TERNATA*)
Compositae

*P*LUSH VINE

This plant is grown chiefly for its unusual leaf coloring. It is really a jungle weed, with creeping, trailing, or slightly climbing red to purple stems. The hairy, compound leaves, up to 1½in/4cm long, are gray-green, with a violet-purple luster and violet veining. Small, fairly insignificant, groundsel-like yellow-white flowers appear in summer.

FACT FILE

ORIGIN Brazil.

HEIGHT To 6ft/1.8m.

POTTING MIX Soil- or peat-moss-based.

REPOTTING Repot in spring, in the same pot.

PROPAGATION Sow seed, take cuttings, or divide in spring. Young plants will grow well only if they are raised in warm greenhouse conditions.

KEEPING PLANTS Discard the plant after 2 years or so; older plants become unsightly.

PLANT CARE

Introduce the plant gradually to the light in spring, then set in full sun. ● Normal room conditions, with a minimum of 60°F/16°C. ● Water moderately all year round. ● Stand the pot on a tray of damp pebbles to maintain humidity, but do not spray the hairy leaves, since that may cause them to rot. ● Liquid-feed every 2 weeks during summer.

MILTONIA
Orchidaceae

*P*ANSY ORCHID

This epiphytic orchid has pseudobulbs, is evergreen, and grows all year-round. One to three long, narrow pale green leaves are borne at the tips of the pseudobulbs, and erect flower stems up to 18in/46cm long rise from the base. Each stem may carry as many as 10 flat-faced flowers, up to 4in/10cm wide, which look like pansies and account for the common name. The main flowering season is from late spring through summer, but there is sometimes a second flush of flowers in fall, each flower lasts four to five weeks.

Miltonia candida produces 3-in/8-cm-wide yellow flowers with chestnut brown patches and a white lip. *M. regnellii* has white flowers 3in/8cm wide, with a pink flush near the base. Numerous hybrids are available, and new forms are constantly being produced.

FACT FILE

ORIGIN Central and South America; hybrid.

HEIGHT To 2ft/60cm.

POTTING MIX Special orchid medium.

REPOTTING Repot in summer, only when essential; the plant flowers best when it is pot-bound.

PROPAGATION Divide the rhizome in summer, each section must have at least 2 pseudobulbs.

KEEPING PLANTS Remove wilting flowers and leaves at once; they can affect others. Watch out for thrips, which may infest the plant.

PLANT CARE

Medium light; in winter the plant needs bright light and 3 hours of sun. ● Keep within the range of 63°–70°F/17°–21°C at all times. ● Water generously in spring and summer; spray the foliage daily. ● In late spring and early summer give 2 or 3 feeds of standard liquid fertilizer at half strength.

MIMOSA PUDICA
Leguminosae

*S*ENSITIVE PLANT

This small shrub, which can grow like a weed in the wild, should not be confused with the yellow-flowered mimosa sold by florists. *Mimosa pudica* bears pale pink pompon flowers from midsummer through to early fall. The feathery leaves are composed of up to 25 pairs of small oblong leaflets; these fold up at night and the entire leaf stalk droops. The leaflets also fold up tightly if they are touched, if the plant is shaken, or if it is subjected to heat from a lighted candle or cigarette, indicating that heat might be the trigger.

The plant is most sensitive at high temperatures—between 75°F/24°C and 85°F/29°C. If left for a while, the leaves will slowly unfold and the stems will straighten.

Mimosa pudica

FACT FILE

ORIGIN Tropical America; naturalized in the tropics worldwide.

HEIGHT To 3ft/90cm.

POTTING MIX Peat-moss-based, or soil-based with added sand and leaf mold.

REPOTTING Repot throughout the season, whenever roots show through the base of the current pot.

PROPAGATION Sow seed in early spring.

KEEPING PLANTS *Mimosa pudica* is usually treated as an annual and discarded after flowering, since it loses its beauty as it ages.

PLANT CARE

Bright light with some direct sun to promote flowering. ● Normal room temperature. ● Allow the top of the soil to dry out before rewatering. ● Stand the pot on a tray of wet pebbles to increase humidity. ● Feed with a high-potash fertilizer every 2 weeks.

~

NEMATANTHUS GREGARIUS
Gesneriaceae

NEMATANTHUS

Also known as *Nematanthus radicans* and *Hypocyrta radicans*, this plant has trailing stems and is an ideal subject for a hanging basket. The stems are thickly clothed with 1¼-in/3-cm-long oval leaves, which are slightly fleshy and a glossy dark green.

In summer the plant bears waxy orange flowers with yellow lobes, the tubes of which bulge curiously at the base. This nematanthus needs a winter rest period.

FACT FILE

ORIGIN Brazil.

HEIGHT Stems trail to 2ft/60cm.

POTTING MIX Peat-moss-based.

REPOTTING Move to a pot one size larger either after flowering or after the dormant period.

PROPAGATION Take tip cuttings in summer or divide older plants.

KEEPING PLANTS In summer, after flowering, put the plant outdoors in a warm sheltered spot. Cut back a little each year to ensure flowering.

PLANT CARE

Bright light. ● Temperatures of 50°–55°F/10°–13°C during the winter rest period; normal room temperature at other times. ● Water moderately in summer; give less water in winter. ● Apply half-strength standard liquid fertilizer every 2–3 weeks during summer.

~

NEPENTHES **×** *HOOKERIANA*
Nepenthaceae

PITCHER PLANT

A large plant for the heated, shaded greenhouse, where the atmosphere is humid, this epiphytic carnivorous plant is not very easy to grow, but it is intriguing and worth the effort. The oblong leaves are mid green, about 12in/30cm long, with a tendril at the tip; this usually develops into a liquid-filled pitcher, topped with a "lid." Insects are attracted by the scent produced by nectar glands at the mouth of the pitcher, only to fall into the liquid it contains, where they die and are digested.

The plant produces climbing stems to 10ft/3m or more. The pale yellow-green pitchers, which are broadly oval, some 5in/13cm long and 3in/8cm wide, are heavily marked with purple-brown spots or blotches. Plant nepenthes in lattice or wire baskets to ensure good drainage.

Nepenthes **×** *hookeriana*

FACT FILE

ORIGIN Borneo; Sumatra; Malaysia.

HEIGHT To 10ft/3m.

POTTING MIX Peat-moss-based with added moss and perlite in the ratio of 1:2:1; or sphagnum moss with charcoal added to prevent it from turning sour.

REPOTTING Repot in spring, but be careful because the delicate roots break easily.

PROPAGATION Air-layer, or take leaf cuttings in spring. Root them in sphagnum moss with bottom heat; rooting may take up to 8 weeks. Spray with fresh water daily.

KEEPING PLANTS Prune old plants heavily in spring to encourage new growth.

PLANT CARE

Avoid bright sunshine at all times; in winter place the plant near a window but out of direct sun. ● A minimum of 65°F/18°C all year-round. ● Water well with lime-free water during the period of active growth. ● Spray the plant daily. ● Occasionally during the growing season, drop a few insects into the pitcher if there are none flying around.

~

NERINE BOWDENII
Amaryllidaceae

NERINE

This frost-tender bulbous plant is grown for its long-lived flowers, which appear in late summer and early fall. The oval bulb, about 2in/5cm in diameter, produces umbels of 6 to 12 flowers on stalks up to 18in/46cm long. The trumpet-shaped flowers are some 2½in/6.5cm long and vary in color from bright candy pink to soft rose pink and, rarely, white. The petals have a wavy edge, which gives the umbel a spidery appearance. Arching, deep green, strap-shaped leaves some 12in/30cm long emerge after the flowers have bloomed and last throughout the winter and well into the following spring. Nerines are best raised in a greenhouse and brought into the house just before they flower.

Nerine bowdenii 'Fenwick's Variety' is an early-flowering, vigorous form with cyclamen pink flowers. *N.b.* 'Zeal Giant' has large deep pink flowers, and 'Alba' produces white flowers with a hint of pink.

FACT FILE

ORIGIN South Africa.

HEIGHT Flower stems to 18in/46cm.

POTTING MIX Well-drained, soil-based mix with added leaf mold.

REPOTTING In summer, at the end of the dormant period.

PROPAGATION Sow fresh ripe seed in late winter or early spring, or remove offsets when repotting and pot them individually.

KEEPING PLANTS Allow bulbs to dry after flowering, then store them during the summer when they are dormant. Repot for flowering in fall or plant the bulbs out in the garden in frost free areas.

PLANT CARE

Bright light, with some direct sun. ● Cool greenhouse temperature and cool room conditions; the plant can stand a temperature as low as 5°F/-15°C provided conditions are dry. ● Water well during the period of active growth; do not water during the dormant period. ● Liquid-feed every 2 weeks from the time the buds appear until the leaves begin to die down.

Nertera granadensis

NERTERA GRANADENSIS
Rubiaceae

BEAD PLANT

This curious-looking but attractive creeping plant has tiny fleshy green intertwining leaves, on stems up to 10in/25cm long, that grow into a thick mat. In early summer it bears small greenish white flowers in the leaf axils. These are followed by long-lasting orange-red berries some ¼in/6mm in diameter which can be so numerous that they completely hide the foliage. The plant is also known as coral moss. When it is not covered with berries, the plant's small leaves closely resemble those of *Soleirolia soleirolii*, baby's tears.

Nertera is shallow rooting, so it is best grown in a shallow pan or half-pot, which will display the berries well. Keep the plant in an airy situation, since poor ventilation may hamper the formation of berries.

FACT FILE

ORIGIN South America; Tasmania; New Zealand.

HEIGHT To 3in/8cm.

POTTING MIX Peat-moss-based with added leaf mold and sand or grit for good drainage.

REPOTTING Move into a larger pot in spring only when necessary.

PROPAGATION When repotting, divide clumps into 3 or more pieces and pot these up individually, or put 3 or 4 around the edge of a large shallow pan. Alternatively, sow seed or take tip cuttings in spring.

KEEPING PLANTS If possible, stand the plant outdoors in a sheltered spot with some sun in spring. Leave it there until the berries start to form, then bring it indoors.

PLANT CARE

Bright light with some sun. ● Cool room temperature with a maximum of 62°F/17°C; in very warm rooms the plant will produce leaves instead of berries. ● Water well, but allow the surface of the soil to dry out before rewatering. ● Increase humidity by standing the plant on a saucer of damp pebbles, and spray it daily from the time the flowers begin to open until the berries have formed. ● Apply weak liquid fertilizer once a month in summer and fall, while the berries are forming and are on the plant.

~

OLEA EUROPAEA
Oleaceae

OLIVE

The olive tree has become popular as a houseplant in recent years, since it is very tolerant of a dry atmosphere. In Mediterranean climates this plant forms a tree up to 20ft/6m high; indoors it can be kept far smaller.

The branches are covered with short-stalked, narrow, gray-green leaves 1–3in/2.5–8cm long, the undersides of which are covered with white or rust-colored hairs. Yellow-white flowers are borne in clusters at the tips of the stems in summer, but the fruits do not ripen until the winter.

Several other higher-yielding varieties are available commerically, but they are no more ornamental for the home than the species is.

FACT FILE

ORIGIN Mediterranean region.

HEIGHT To 10ft/3m in a container.

POTTING MIX Soil-based with added coarse sand; good drainage is essential.

REPOTTING Move to a pot one size larger each spring; once an 18-in/46-cm pot has been reached, top-dress annually instead.

PROPAGATION Sow seeds in spring or summer or take half-ripe tip cuttings with a heel in summer; however, cuttings do not root easily.

KEEPING PLANTS The plant needs at least 2 months at a temperature below 50°F/10°C to produce flowers, and it will benefit from a spell outdoors in summer. Weighting the branches so that they droop may encourage fruiting. Prune after fruiting, but only if it is necessary to control the plant's size and shape.

PLANT CARE

Full sun or bright light. ● Average to warm temperature, with a winter minimum of 40°F/4°C. ● Water moderately all year-round. ● Feed actively growing plants every 2 weeks.

~

OPLISMENUS HIRTELLUS
Gramineae

BASKET GRASS

The wiry, creeping stems make this an attractive plant for a hanging basket, since the stems will trail. It has yellowish green lance-shaped leaves, 2–6in/5–15cm long, with sharply pointed tips and a slightly undulating, or wavy, surface. *Oplismenus hirtellus* 'Variegatus' has white, green, and rose-red striped leaves. Pinch off the insignificant flowers as soon as they appear.

FACT FILE

ORIGIN Southern USA; West Indies; Mexico; Argentina.

HEIGHT To 3ft/90cm.

POTTING MIX Soil- or peat-moss-based.

REPOTTING Move in spring, if plants are kept for a second year.

PROPAGATION The long runners root spontaneously; detach and pot up the resulting plantlets. Take tip cuttings in spring.

KEEPING PLANTS As it ages, this plant loses some of its leaves and becomes straggly; cut it back severely or replace it after a year or two.

PLANT CARE

Bright light, but direct sun only in winter. ● Normal room temperature. ● Keep the soil moist at all times. The plant will lose its leaves if the soil is allowed to dry out. ● Liquid-feed every 4 weeks in summer; overfeeding is detrimental to the appearance of the plant.

~

OREBEA VARIEGATA see STAPELIA VARIEGATA

OSMANTHUS HETEROPHYLLUS 'VARIEGATUS'

Oleaceae

VARIEGATED FALSE HOLLY

Also known as *Osmanthus ilicifolius* (holly-leafed osmanthus), this dense, woody-stemmed shrub has prickly, glossy leaves that are arranged in pairs. The leaves of 'Variegatus' are about 2½in/6.5cm long and have creamy white markings, sometimes with a tinge of pink at the margins. The shape of the leaves varies, even on the same plant. Some may be almost egg-shaped with smooth edges and a single spine at the tip, while others may be elliptic, with a number of large spiny teeth, including a long spine at the tip. Plants grown indoors only rarely produce small, white, scented flowers in fall.

FACT FILE

ORIGIN Japan; cultivar.

HEIGHT To 6ft/1.8m in a container.

POTTING MIX Soil-based.

REPOTTING Move into a pot one size larger each spring.

PROPAGATION Take tip cuttings, with a heel, in spring or summer.

KEEPING PLANTS Pinch off growing tips regularly to prevent the plant becoming lanky.

Osmanthus heterophyllus

PLANT CARE

Full sun. ● Cool temperature, ideally between 55°–65°F/13°–18°C at all times. ● Water moderately throughout the year. ● Feed actively growing plants every 2 weeks.

~

PANDANUS VEITCHII

Pandanaceae

VEITCH'S SCREW PINE

The best known of the five or so commonly grown pandanuses, the screw pine is a stately plant, especially when it grows older. It has leaves up to 3ft/90cm long, the lower ones arching, with coarse spines along the margins. A feature of the foliage is the lengthwise creamy white striping. Mature plants develop beautiful stiltlike aerial roots. This pandanus enjoys very humid air and warmer temperatures. It is, therefore, better suited to a greenhouse, but properly looked after it will thrive in the living room.

FACT FILE

ORIGIN Polynesia.

HEIGHT To 7ft/2m.

POTTING MIX Soil- or peat-moss-based with good drainage.

REPOTTING Young plants may require repotting more than once a year, but after the plant is a year old, repotting each spring will be sufficient.

PROPAGATION Remove suckers from older plants and pot these up individually.

KEEPING PLANTS High humidity is essential for luxuriant leaf growth.

PLANT CARE

A well-lit location; no full sun. ● Minimum temperature of 65°F/18°C. ● Water moderately, using water at room temperature; keep the soil a little drier from midfall until midspring. ● Stand the pot on a tray of moist pebbles and spray the plant daily. ● Feed every 2 weeks from spring to fall.

~

PAPHIOPEDILUM SPP.

Orchidaceae

LADY'S SLIPPER ORCHIDS

Several species of this orchid, particularly *Paphiopedilum callosum* and *P. sukhakulii*, and some of the smaller hybrids will do well in a living room, preferably near a window that does not receive too much sunlight. Wherever slipper orchids are sited, they require plenty of humidity as well as good ventilation during the hotter months. Paphiopedilums do not require a dormant

Paphiopedilum

season, but if the temperature drops in winter, the water supply must be decreased.

The blooms of these popular orchids have a striking sepal, usually called the flag; the lip of the flower is called the "slipper" because its pouchlike shape resembles a house slipper. Many hybrids are available from specialist suppliers, and new ones are being added constantly.

FACT FILE

ORIGIN Tropical Asia; hybrids.

HEIGHT To 15in/38cm.

POTTING MIX Special orchid medium.

REPOTTING Repot annually in late winter. Always provide excellent drainage in the bottom of the pot. *P. callosum* should be kept completely dry for a few weeks after being repotted.

PROPAGATION Divide when repotting.

KEEPING PLANTS High humidity (65–75%) and a daytime temperature some 9°F/5°C above the night temperature are needed.

PLANT CARE

Bright light, but full sun only in winter. ● Normal room temperature, but not below 65°F/18°C at night. ● Water once a week throughout the year. ● Spray the plant daily and stand the pot on a tray of moist gravel to maintain humidity. Never allow water to lie on the leaves or in the center of the growth; this will encourage botrytis and cause the plant to rot. ● Apply a weak foliar feed once a month from spring to fall.

PASSIFLORA CAERULEA
Passifloraceae

COMMON PASSION FLOWER

The common, or blue, passion flower grows in tropical conditions, clinging by tendrils to the trunks of jungle trees. Indoors it needs heat, sun, and good ventilation in order to do well.

The handlike leaves are large and glossy dark green. The 3-in/8-cm-wide flowers, give the plant its name. They have five white petals, five white sepals, and fine purple-blue filaments surrounding prominent gold anthers. Jesuit missionaries who discovered the plant in Brazil in the 18th century likened its white petals and sepals to the Ten Apostles who witnessed Christ's crucifixion. The anthers were seen as the five wounds, the rays of the corona of filaments as His crown of thorns, and the three stigmas as the nails that pinned Him to the Cross.

Passiflora caerulea

FACT FILE

ORIGIN Brazil to Argentina.

HEIGHT To 16½ft/5m; but as a houseplant it is frequently sold trained around a hoop.

POTTING MIX Soil-based.

REPOTTING Repot in spring for 2 or 3 years, then top-dress instead; the plant flowers best if its roots are restricted.

PROPAGATION Take 7-in/18-cm tip cuttings in summer.

KEEPING PLANTS Pruning does the plant no harm. Each spring, cut the stems of a young plant down to about 9in/23cm. Prune an older plant to keep it within bounds; cut side branches back to 3–4in/8–10cm.

PLANT CARE

Full sun; the plant will not flower if the light is not bright enough. ● A temperature of about 70°F/21°C in summer, 50°F/10°C in winter. ● Water freely in summer; in winter water just enough to prevent the soil drying out. ● Feed with standard liquid fertilizer every 2 weeks in summer.

~

PELLAEA ROTUNDIFOLIA
Sinopteridaceae

BUTTON FERN

A native of the temperate forests of New Zealand, the button fern produces a mass of thin dark stems that, close-up, are seen to be covered with brown scales and hairs. From these stalks arise small, arched fronds of leathery green leaflets, which trail over the edge of the pot, making it ideal for a hanging basket. Unlike most ferns, pellaea tolerates relatively dry conditions.

FACT FILE

ORIGIN New Zealand; Australia.

HEIGHT Fronds to 1ft/30cm long.

POTTING MIX Soil-based, with added peat moss and sand.

REPOTTING Use a shallow pot and repot only when roots fill the current container.

PROPAGATION In spring divide the plant into 2 or 3 sections with roots and top growth.

KEEPING PLANTS Mist when the temperature rises above 70°F/21°C; if the soil becomes waterlogged, the plant will die. If conditions are right, it will grow year-round, with no rest period.

PLANT CARE

Bright light but not direct sunlight. ● Normal room temperature, as constant as possible. ● Water freely in summer but allow the surface of the soil to dry out before rewatering. ● Feed once a week in summer with a weak solution of standard liquid fertilizer.

Pellaea rotundifolia

PELLIONIA DAVEAUANA (SYN. *P. REPENS*)
Urticaceae

WATERMELON BEGONIA

Although this exotic creeper grows in tropical forests, it adapts well as a houseplant and looks especially good in a hanging basket. It produces a profusion of succulent stems that carry fleshy, elliptic leaves up to 2in/5cm long. These are bronze to olive green with a pale green band in the center. This creeper enjoys plenty of light, warmth, high humidity, and a protected position.

Pellionia pulchra, satin pellionia, has green stems with a pink tinge and pale gray-green leaves marked with brown-black veins.

FACT FILE

ORIGIN Burma; Vietnam; Malaysia.

HEIGHT To 2ft/60cm.

POTTING MIX Soil-based.

REPOTTING Move to a pot one size larger each spring until a 5-in/13-cm pot is reached.

PROPAGATION In summer, by division; make sure that each section has some roots. Or take 2-in/5-cm-long stem cuttings at any time.

KEEPING PLANTS The plant should live for several years, but divide it every 2–3 years to prevent it becoming spindly.

PLANT CARE

Bright light or partial shade; no direct sunlight. ● Warm room temperature, 65°–85°F/18°–29°C. ● Water well all year. ● Humidity is essential; stand the pot on a dish of moist pebbles and mist the plant daily. ● Apply weak liquid fertilizer every 2 weeks from spring to fall.

~

PENTAS LANCEOLATA (SYN. *P. CARNEA*)
Rubiaceae

EGYPTIAN STAR CLUSTER

An upright shrubby plant with pale green, hairy oval leaves 2–4in/5–10cm long and 1in/2.5cm wide, this is the most common species grown as an indoor plant. It thrives best in a heated greenhouse where the air is not too dry. And it should really be regarded as only a temporary plant in the home.

The flowers, which appear in late summer and fall, grow in terminal clusters on the many branches. They come in shades of pink, lilac, and carmine red to mauve and blue, and, occasionally, white. The corona has a narrow, ¾-in/2-cm-long tube, widening slightly toward the top and ending in a five-lobed star.

FACT FILE

ORIGIN Tropical East Africa; Arabian Peninsula.

HEIGHT To 3ft/90cm.

POTTING MIX Soil- or peat-moss-based.

REPOTTING Move into a pot one size larger in spring.

PROPAGATION In spring or early summer, take 2–3in/5–8cm stem cuttings.

KEEPING PLANTS Pinch off the growing tips from time to time to encourage bushiness.

PLANT CARE

Good light with 4 hours of direct sunlight. ● Normal warm room temperature, but never allow the level to drop below 50°F/10°C. ● Water moderately in the growing period; give less water when flowering is over. Overwatering causes the leaves to turn yellow, and they will not recover. ● Feed every 2 weeks in summer.

~

PHALAENOPSIS SPP.
Orchidaceae

Moth Orchid

A free-flowering epiphyte, the moth orchid blooms throughout the year. Its branched spikes bear up to 30 flowers at a time. Individual blooms can be as much as 5in/13cm wide, but in many varieties they are smaller. The flowers vary in color from white through pinks to red and yellow, often with stripes or spots. The moth orchid tends to suffer if conditions are too cool. The movement of air from an electric fan, combined with a humid atmosphere while the plant is in bloom, will help. Numerous hybrids are available, and the number is increasing each year.

FACT FILE

ORIGIN Asia; Australasia; hybrid.

HEIGHT Foliage to 8in/20cm; flowers to 4ft/1.2m.

POTTING MIX Special orchid medium.

REPOTTING About every 2 years, when the current pot becomes crowded.

PROPAGATION Not applicable.

KEEPING PLANTS These orchids grow well in wooden or wire baskets that have been lined with sphagnum moss.

PLANT CARE

Bright filtered light or partial shade. ● Normal room temperature, with a minimum of 70°F/21°C. ● Water well all year-round. ● Apply a special orchid fertilizer once a month all year-round; overfeeding will produce leaves at the expense of flowers.

PIPER NIGRUM
Piperaceae

Black Pepper

This climbing member of the pepper family is suitable for the warm greenhouse; it spreads extensively and needs support. It is an interesting plant to grow and produces fruits some ¼in/6mm round, which ripen to red, then black, and are the source of the culinary spice. The 4-in/10-cm-long heart-shaped leaves are dark green with strongly marked veins.

FACT FILE

ORIGIN South India; Sri Lanka.

HEIGHT To 13ft/4m.

POTTING MIX Peat-moss-based.

REPOTTING In spring move the plant into a pot one size larger.

PROPAGATION Sow seed in spring or take semiripe cuttings in summer.

KEEPING PLANTS Support the plant on a wire or trellis to show it to its best advantage. Prune annually in late winter or early spring, before growth starts, to remove weak, congested stems.

PLANT CARE

Bright indirect light. ● Minimum winter temperature of 50°F/10°C. ● Water moderately when in growth. ● Feed every 2 weeks from spring to fall.

~

PISONIA UMBELLIFERA '*VARIEGATA*'
Nyctaginaceae

Bird-Catcher Tree

Although the plain form of pisonia, also known as para-para, grows into a tree in the wild, this attractive form with variegated foliage makes a good houseplant. The 16-in/40-cm-long leaves, marbled with pale green, have cream-colored margins that are faintly pink when young. In the cultivated form, small pink or yellow flowers bloom in clusters.

FACT FILE

ORIGIN Australia; New Zealand; Mauritius.

HEIGHT To 10ft/3m in a container.

POTTING MIX Soil-based.

REPOTTING Repot young plants in late winter or spring; top-dress older plants.

PROPAGATION Take stem cuttings, or air-layer, in summer.

KEEPING PLANTS The plant may quickly outgrow its space, but it can be pruned to maintain size and shape when it is repotted. Set the plant outdoors in summer in mild climates.

PLANT CARE

Full sun or partial shade; the plant loses its color if the light is not bright enough. ● Warm room or greenhouse conditions, with a winter minimum of 50°F/10°C. ● Water moderately when in growth, sparingly in winter. ● Feed every 2 weeks from spring to fall.

~

PITTOSPORUM TOBIRA
Pittosporaceae

Japanese Pittosporum

Increasingly used by interior decorators, this glossy-leafed small tree, also called Australian laurel, will survive fairly inhospitable indoor conditions. It is a flat-topped plant with dark green leaves up to 4in/10cm long. The leaves of *Pittosporum tobira* 'Variegatum' are a soft gray-green, with a creamy margin. In spring clusters of fragrant, tubular, starry white flowers are carried at the ends of the stems on both varieties, but only on plants that receive good light. Each bloom is ½in/13mm wide. A cool period is required in winter.

Pittosporum tobira

FACT FILE

ORIGIN China; Japan.

HEIGHT To 4ft/1.2m in a container.

POTTING MIX Soil-based.

REPOTTING Move into a pot one size larger each spring.

PROPAGATION Take tip or stem cuttings in spring; these can be difficult to root, so use hormone rooting powder and bottom heat.

KEEPING PLANTS Prune in spring to restrict size and to remove any straggly growth.

PLANT CARE

Bright light; avoid direct sunlight. ● Although it is hardy, as an indoor plant it needs normal room temperature, with a winter minimum of 40°F/4°C. ● Water well in the growing period, but sparingly in winter. ● Feed every 2 weeks with a general fertilizer from spring to fall.

PLUMERIA RUBRA (SYN. *P. ACUMINATA*)
Apocynaceae

FRANGIPANI

Other common names for this popular shrub include temple tree, nosegay, West Indian jasmine, and pagoda tree. Because it likes warm conditions and grows quite large, it is well suited to the greenhouse and is a rarity in the home. It is well worth growing, however, if the right conditions can be provided.

The glory of the plant is the large clusters of heavily scented flowers carried at the ends of the branches in summer and fall. Each 2-in/5-cm-wide flower comprises five thick overlapping petals, which are often pink but can be white, yellow, bronze, salmon, or red, invariably with yellow-stained centers. The pointed oval leaves can be as much as 12in/30cm long.

FACT FILE

ORIGIN Central America.

HEIGHT To 10ft/3m in a container.

POTTING MIX Soil- or peat-moss-based.

REPOTTING In spring, every second year.

PROPAGATION By stem cuttings in late spring.

KEEPING PLANTS Watch out for infestation by red spider mites, particularly in dry conditions.

PLANT CARE

Bright light with some direct sun. ● Warm temperatures, with a winter minimum of 55°F/13°C. ● Water well during the growing period and sparingly in winter. ● Feed every 2 weeks from spring to fall with a general houseplant fertilizer.

~

PODOCARPUS MACROPHYLLUS
Podocarpaceae

BUDDHIST PINE

If this slow-growing plant is to live successfully indoors, it must be kept in an unheated room; since it will tolerate a drafty situation, it is ideal for a cool hall or passageway. The upright stems bear narrow, straplike, glossy 3-in/8-cm-long leaves, but the catkinlike flowers are not produced indoors.

The plant is also known as Japanese yew or Kusamaki; indeed, the variety most frequently seen as a houseplant is 'Maki`' whose growth is compact and whose leaves are only ½in/13mm long.

Podocarpus macrophyllus

FACT FILE

ORIGIN Japan.

HEIGHT To 6ft/1.8m in a container.

POTTING MIX Soil- or peat-moss-based.

REPOTTING In spring, when roots have filled the current container.

PROPAGATION In late spring or summer, take stem cuttings or sow seeds (the latter is the more difficult of the two methods).

KEEPING PLANTS The plant's slow-growing habit means that it requires little attention, but it can be kept compact by regular pruning.

PLANT CARE

Bright light to partial shade. ● Cool to normal indoor conditions, with a winter minimum of 40°F/4°C. ● Keep the soil moist at all times; water sparingly in winter. ● Mist the plant regularly during hot weather. ● Feed once a month from spring to fall with a standard liquid fertilizer.

~

POLYSCIAS SCUTELLARIA '**BALFOURII**'
Araliaceae

MING ARALIA

Previously known as *Polyscias balfouriana*, this is an excellent specimen plant when placed in a decorative container. The dark green, rounded leathery leaflets, up to 3in/8cm wide, are carried on stems speckled with a pale green or gray. It is not an easy plant to grow in normal room conditions

and in a less than ideal environment will readily drop its leaves. Large plants are prohibitively expensive, so it is better to buy a small plant and look after it well.

FACT FILE

ORIGIN New Caledonia.

HEIGHT To 6ft/1.8m in a container.

POTTING MIX Soil-based.

REPOTTING Repot every spring in a pot one size larger until maximum desired pot size is reached; thereafter, top-dress annually.

PROPAGATION By stem tip cuttings or pieces of stem in summer. Cuttings root readily in a closed environment with bottom heat.

KEEPING PLANTS Humidity is essential, so mist the plant daily in warm weather and stand the pot on a tray of damp pebbles.

PLANT CARE

Bright light, but no direct sunlight. ● Normal to warm room conditions with a minimum of 65°F/18°C. ● Water moderately during the growing season; give less water in winter. ● Apply a standard liquid fertilizer every 2 weeks when the plant is in active growth.

Polyscias scutellaria 'Balfourii'

PSEUDERANTHEMUM ATROPURPUREUM
Acanthaceae

*P*SEUDERANTHEMUM

Sometimes still sold under the name of *Eranthemum atropurpureum*, this small erect shrub is grown chiefly for its brightly colored oval leaves. These are dark green marked with purple or wine red, about 5in/13cm long. The varieties 'Variegatum' and 'Tricolor' have splashes of pink, cream, and purple on the leaves. The plant requires warmth and high humidity, and if conditions are right a mature specimen will produce tubular purple-eyed white flowers ³⁄₄in/2cm wide in late spring and summer.

Pseuderanthemum atropurpureum

FACT FILE

ORIGIN Polynesia; naturalized in tropical America.

HEIGHT To 1.2m/4ft.

POTTING MIX Soil- or peat-moss-based.

REPOTTING In spring, but only when roots fill the container.

PROPAGATION Take tip or stem cuttings in spring or summer.

KEEPING PLANTS Cut the plant back if necessary to maintain its shape and size.

PLANT CARE

Bright light; partial shade. ● Warm room conditions, with a minimum winter temperature of 60°F/16°C. ● Allow the surface of the soil to dry out between waterings. ● Mist the plant daily and stand the pot on a tray of moist pebbles. ● From spring to fall, feed every 2 weeks with a standard liquid fertilizer.

Pteris cretica

PTERIS CRETICA
Adiantaceae

*T*ABLE FERN

Also known as Cretan brake and ribbon fern, this long-lived plant should thrive in most indoor situations, provided it is never allowed to dry out. Its main feature is the elegant, compact fronds that die back from time to time; but if they are cut back to the base, new ones will form. Do not use leaf shine.

Two good varieties are *Pteris cretica* 'Albolineata,' variegated table fern, with deep green leaf edges and a broad white central stripe, and *P.c.* 'Alexandrae,' cristate table fern, which has lighter green pinnae tipped with a cockscomb of leaflets.

FACT FILE

ORIGIN Old World tropics; subtropics.

HEIGHT To 3ft/90cm.

POTTING MIX Soil-based with low acidity.

REPOTTING Repot in spring only when pots become congested; the plant grows best when pot-bound. Do not bury the crown of the plant.

PROPAGATION Divide large plants into two or three pieces in spring.

KEEPING PLANTS Fronds will turn yellow if the air is too warm and dry; mist regularly to maintain high humidity.

PLANT CARE

Bright indirect light. ● Average temperatures, ideally 60°–75°F/16°–24°C. ● Keep the soil moist, but not sodden, at all times. ● Feed every week in spring and summer with a dilute standard liquid fertilizer.

PUNICA GRANATUM 'NANA'
Punicaceae

*D*WARF POMEGRANATE

This compact and shrubby plant, with masses of 1-in/2.5-cm-long evergreen leaves, is not difficult to care for. The tubular scarlet flowers, borne in summer, hang from the plant rather like those of fuchsia, but they are not as plentiful. If the blooms are pollinated with a soft brush, there is a good chance that small orange-red fruits will develop; these are not edible, but are interesting and attractive to look at.

FACT FILE

ORIGIN Eastern Mediterranean to Himalayas.

HEIGHT To 90cm/3ft.

POTTING MIX Soil-based.

REPOTTING In spring, but only when roots have filled the pot.

PROPAGATION Take stem cuttings in summer, or sow seed in spring (named varieties do not come true).

KEEPING PLANTS To encourage flowering, shorten outward-growing shoots when the buds are breaking in early spring, and prune out old or weak wood in late spring or summer.

PLANT CARE

Bright light with some direct sun. ● Normal room temperature, with a winter minimum of 50°F/10°C. ● Keep the soil moist at all times. ● Feed every 2 weeks from spring to fall with a high-potash fertilizer.

Punica granatum 'Nana'

RADERMACHERA SINICA
(SYN. *STEREOSPERMUM SINICUM*)
Bignoniaceae

$\mathcal{E}$MERALD TREE

This treelike plant succeeds indoors because of its tolerance of the dry atmosphere in most homes. It has shiny, pointed, veined leaves up to 2½in/6.5cm long. In its natural habitat, it has sweetly scented, yellow bell-shaped flowers—hence its other common name, Asian bell tree—but these are not usually produced on young plants grown in the home.

FACT FILE

ORIGIN China.

HEIGHT To 4ft/1.2m.

POTTING MIX Peat-moss-based.

REPOTTING Repot in spring, but only if roots have filled the pot.

PROPAGATION Take stem cuttings in summer.

KEEPING PLANTS Keep away from open fires and smokers: a smoky atmosphere will make the leaves drop. Prune after flowering to keep the plant compact. Put the plant outdoors in summer in a protected spot.

PLANT CARE

Bright, indirect light. ● Normal room temperature, with a minimum of 50°F/10°C in winter. ● Keep the soil moist at all times. ● Mist frequently to maintain humidity. ● Feed every week in spring and summer.

~

REBUTIA MINUSCULA
Cactaceae

$\mathcal{R}$ED CROWN CACTUS

All rebutias are beautiful in the spring flowering period, and this quick-growing species is particularly good. The individual heads of this solitary or clustering cactus are globular, sometimes with a flattened top, and reach a height of only 2in/5cm or so. The short white spines form a neat pattern against the green stem, and in spring each head is surrounded by 1½-in/4-cm-wide crimson-scarlet flowers, which give it its other name, Mexican sunball. In the home, as in its natural habitat, rebutia needs plenty of sunshine, so it will be happiest standing on a sunny windowsill.

Rebutia minuscula

FACT FILE

ORIGIN Northern Argentina.

HEIGHT To 2in/5cm.

POTTING MIX Soil- or peat-moss-based with added coarse sand or grit for good drainage.

REPOTTING In summer every 2 years in a wide, shallow pot.

PROPAGATION Remove offsets in summer and pot them up individually, or sow seed in spring.

KEEPING PLANTS Watch out for mealybugs, which may be a problem, especially on new growth.

PLANT CARE

Full sun, but protect from hot midsummer sun. ● Normal to warm room temperature, with a winter minimum of 45°F/7°C. ● Water freely during spring and summer, but never overwater. Do not water in winter. ● Feed every 2 weeks with a high-potash fertilizer from the time the buds form and throughout the period of active growth.

~

RHIPSALIS BACCIFERA (SYN. *R. CASSUTHA*)
Cactaceae

$\mathcal{M}$ISTLETOE CACTUS

One of the epiphytic forest cacti, this plant hangs from trees in its natural habitat. Indoors, its long, light green, cylindrical branching stems trail over the rim of the pot. Insignificant greenish flowers about ¼in/6mm wide appear in winter and spring, and are followed by slightly smaller, translucent whitish fruits, which look rather like the berries on mistletoe.

Radermachera sinica

FACT FILE

ORIGIN Brazil; Peru; USA (Florida); Africa; Madagascar; Sri Lanka.

HEIGHT Stems trail to 6ft/1.8m indoors.

POTTING MIX Slightly acid epiphyte-type medium composed of equal parts of organic and inorganic matter.

REPOTTING Repot annually in a small pot, after the spring blooms have faded.

PROPAGATION Take cuttings in summer, or sow seed in spring.

KEEPING PLANTS The stems are fragile and may break off at the joints if this plant is roughly handled.

PLANT CARE

Bright light, but shade from direct sunlight, which causes stems to shrivel and turn reddish. ● Normal to warm room temperature, with a cool winter rest at a minimum of 50°F/10°C. ● In spring and summer; allow the surface of the potting mix to dry out before watering; water less in winter. ● Mist frequently; otherwise, the stems will dry out and become soft. ● Apply a high-potash fertilizer every 2 weeks from the time the buds form until the end of flowering; once a month at other times.

~

ROCHEA COCCINEA (SYN. *CRASSULA COCCINEA*)
Crassulaceae

Rochea

A small shrubby bush, rochea carries masses of leathery, oval, pointed leaves 1in/2.5cm long in pairs along the many-branched stems. In summer, showy clusters of scented tubular red flowers, each about 1in/2.5cm long, appear at the ends of the stems. The varieties 'Alba,' with white flowers, and 'Bicolor,' with red-and-white flowers, are also popular.

FACT FILE

ORIGIN South Africa (Cape Province).

HEIGHT To 18in/46cm.

POTTING MIX Soil-based.

REPOTTING In spring, but only if necessary.

PROPAGATION By stem cuttings in spring or summer. Allow the cuttings to dry for 2 days before inserting them into fresh potting mix.

KEEPING PLANTS *Rochea coccinea* needs plenty of ventilation, light, and water in summer, and a period outdoors in a sheltered spot. Watch out for mealybugs and scale insects.

PLANT CARE

Bright light with some direct sunshine. ● Cool to normal room temperature. ● Water well during the growing season; give less water in winter. ● Feed every 2 weeks with a standard liquid fertilizer in the period of active growth.

Rosa

***ROSA* SPP.**
Rosaceae

Miniature Rose

These roses are invariably hybrids from *Rosa chinensis* 'Minima' and have all the qualities of a good temporary houseplant, yet they are seldom seen indoors. There are dozens of excellent varieties, with flowers in all colors, from white, pink, and cream through oranges, reds, and yellows. Plants may bloom indoors from early spring to late summer, depending on variety, but they should be treated as outdoor plants.

After the leaves have fallen, give the plant a two-month rest period and in late winter prune it, cutting stems back by about one-third. Then bring it indoors and leave it in an unheated room for a week or two before moving it into the warmth to start it into growth. Put the plant in a brightly lighted location, give it plenty of water when it is flowering, and deadhead it to prolong the flowering season.

FACT FILE

ORIGIN Hybrid; cultivars.

HEIGHT To 15in/38cm.

POTTING MIX Soil-based.

REPOTTING In fall, in a pot large enough to accommodate the roots. Overwinter the plant in a cool greenhouse or shed or on a balcony, or bury the plant in the pot outdoors.

PROPAGATION Take tip cuttings in spring; they do not, however, always come true to type.

KEEPING PLANTS Miniatures are prey to all the usual rose pests and diseases; deal with them as you would for other rose types.

PLANT CARE

Full sun or bright light while the plant is actively growing. ● Normal room temperature during the period of active growth. Keep below 45°F/7°C for 2 months during the rest period. ● Water well in the growing period; keep the soil just moist at other times. ● Mist the leaves regularly and stand the pot in a tray of damp pebbles, but make sure that ventilation is good, since roses are prone to fungal diseases. ● Feed every 2 weeks from early spring to late fall with a standard rose fertilizer.

~

RUELLIA MAKOYANA
Acanthaceae

Monkey Plant

A pretty plant, this ruellia has velvety oval leaves up to 3in/8cm long. They are soft olive green, tinged with purple, and have prominent silver veins and purple edges; the undersides of the leaves are also purple. In fall and winter, beautiful 2-in/5-cm-long-trumpet-shaped carmine flowers, which flare out to some $2^1/2$in/6.5cm wide, grow singly from the axils of the leaves.

Ruellia makoyana is an excellent plant for indoor hanging baskets and is sometimes known as trailing velvet plant.

FACT FILE

ORIGIN Brazil.

HEIGHT Stems trail to 18in/46cm.

POTTING MIX Soil-based and leaf mold in equal quantities, with some added grit or perlite.

REPOTTING In spring, when roots fill the current container, move the plant to one size larger.

PROPAGATION Take 3–4in/8–10-cm-long tip cuttings in spring or summer; alternatively sow seed or divide mature plants in summer.

KEEPING PLANTS Pinch off the growing tips regularly to encourage bushiness. The plant should last for 2 or 3 years. Watch out for aphids, which often infest the plant.

PLANT CARE

Bright indirect sunlight. ● Normal room temperature. ● Water well during the flowering period, but allow the surface of the soil to dry out before rewatering. Water just enough to keep the plant from drying out for 6–8 weeks after flowering. ● Mist the plant frequently to maintain humidity. ● Apply a standard liquid fertilizer every 2 weeks between spring and fall.

SALPIGLOSSIS SINUATA
Solanaceae

PAINTED TONGUE

Salpiglossis is an annual that makes an outstanding pot plant for the greenhouse or sunroom and, although not often seen in the home, it makes a good temporary houseplant. The beauty of the individual flowers is often lost when it is grown outdoors, and the five-pointed star-shaped blooms, some 2in/5cm wide, should really be examined closely. They come in a choice of colors, including yellow, orange, red, and lilac, with velvety petals heavily veined and overlaid in contrasting colors.

FACT FILE

ORIGIN Chile; hybrids.

HEIGHT To 2ft/60cm.

POTTING MIX Peat-moss-based.

REPOTTING Move seedlings into larger pots as they grow, until a 5-in/13-cm pot is reached.

PROPAGATION Sow seed in spring for summer flowering, or fall for early spring blooming.

KEEPING PLANTS Stake stems as they grow, to prevent them from falling over and breaking.

PLANT CARE

Bright light with some full sun. ● Cool to normal room conditions. ● Water well, but allow the top of the potting mix to dry out before rewatering. ● Feed every 2 weeks until early fall with a standard liquid fertilizer.

SANCHEZIA SPECIOSA (SYN. S. NOBILIS)
Acanthaceae

SANCHEZIA

A striking plant best grown as a small shrub in the sunroom or greenhouse, sanchezia will, however, thrive as a houseplant if the humidity is high enough. The 12-in/30-cm ovate leaves are pointed, with yellow and ivory veins. They provide the main display, although attractive yellow flowers are borne in upright clusters above the foliage in early summer. High humidity is essential.

FACT FILE

ORIGIN Ecuador; Peru.

HEIGHT To 5ft/1.5m.

POTTING MIX Soil-based, with added grit or perlite.

REPOTTING Annually in spring.

PROPAGATION Take stem cuttings in spring or summer.

KEEPING PLANTS Prune the plant in spring to keep it bushy and within bounds; it can easily be kept to half its potential growing height.

PLANT CARE

Bright light, but not direct sunlight in summer. The plant will, however, also tolerate low light. ● Normal room temperature, with a minimum of 55°F/13°C in winter. Make sure that there is adequate ventilation. ● Water liberally when the plant is in active growth, but allow the top ½in/13mm of the soil to dry out before rewatering. ● Stand the pot on a tray of moist pebbles to increase humidity. ● Feed every 2 weeks from spring to fall with a standard liquid fertilizer.

Sarracenia flava

SARRACENIA FLAVA
Sarraceniaceae

YELLOW PITCHER PLANT

Known also as the huntsman's horn, this is a carnivorous plant for a cool room or greenhouse. Like *Darlingtonia californica*, the cobra lily, the leaves are fused into a pitcher shape, with the top slightly bent over to act as a lid. Insects falling into the liquid contained by the pitcher are unable to escape, and they are then absorbed by the plant's juices.

The leaves are bright yellow-green, often with red veining on the lid, and in summer the plant produces yellow flowers up to 4in/10cm wide.

FACT FILE

ORIGIN USA (Virginia to Florida and Louisiana)

HEIGHT To 2ft/60cm in a container.

POTTING MIX Sphagnum peat, sand, and leaf mold in a ratio of 2:1:1.

REPOTTING Only when the pot becomes overcrowded.

PROPAGATION By division when repotting, or by seed in spring.

KEEPING PLANTS Remove leaves from the base of the plant as they die off.

PLANT CARE

Bright light with some direct sun. ● Cool room temperature, with a winter minimum of 40°F/4°C at night and 50°F/10°C in the daytime. Water copiously with soft water when it is in active growth. ● Stand the pot on a dish of moist pebbles, but do not let water stagnate around the roots.

SCHIZANTHUS PINNATUS
Solanaceae

POOR MAN'S ORCHID

Usually only hybrids of this plant, also called butterfly flower, are available. This is an annual plant which buds in spring and is discarded when flowering is over—often in late fall. The 2-in/5-cm-wide flowers resemble those of an orchid and come in shades of red, pink, mauve, and white with a yellow center, which is often marked with purple. The foliage is fernlike, and the stems are somewhat sticky.

Schizanthus pinnatus

FACT FILE

ORIGIN Chile; hybrids.

HEIGHT To 3ft/90cm.

POTTING MIX Peat-moss-based.

REPOTTING Pot seedlings as they grow, ending with a 5-in/13-cm pot for dwarf varieties, and a 7-in/18-cm pot for taller forms.

PROPAGATION Sow seed in spring for summer flowering, or fall for an early spring.

KEEPING PLANTS Pinch off growing tips to encourage bushiness. Stake the stems to prevent them from toppling over and splitting.

PLANT CARE

Full sun. ● Cool or normal room temperature. ● Keep the potting mix moist at all times. ● Feed every 2 weeks until flowering is over.

~

SCILLA SIBERICA
Liliaceae

SIBERIAN SQUILL

A hardy spring-flowering bulb, this scilla makes an attractive pot plant. The strap-shaped shiny leaves are about 6in/15cm long. Pendant, intensely blue bell-shaped flowers appear in late winter or early spring, in clusters of three or more on 4-in/10-cm stalks. The deep blue, early flowering 'Spring Beauty' is commonly offered; 'Alba' is a white-flowered form.

Once the bulbs have been potted up, leave them in a sheltered location outdoors until the shoots are well developed; then bring them into a cool room to flower.

FACT FILE

ORIGIN Turkey; the Caucasus.

HEIGHT To 6in/15cm.

POTTING MIX Free-draining, peat-moss- or soil-based.

REPOTTING Set the bulbs close together in a shallow pan or half-pot in early fall, with the noses of the bulbs just covered with soil.

PROPAGATION Take offsets when the foliage dies back.

KEEPING PLANTS Feed and keep moist until the leaves die down, then plant the bulbs outdoors in the fall.

PLANT CARE

Bright light, but not direct sunlight while flowering. ● Keep pots of bulbs in a sheltered spot outdoors until ready to flower. Keep the plants in a temperature of about 50°F/10°C to prolong flowering. ● Keep the soil just moist at all times. ● Apply a balanced liquid fertilizer every 2 weeks after the plants are brought indoors.

Sedum sieboldii

SEDUM SIEBOLDII
(SYN. *HYLOTELEPHIUM SIEBOLDII*)
Crassulaceae

STONECROP

The variety of this sedum that is usually grown is the hardy, long-lived 'Medio-variegatum.' It has slender stems, which begin to grow upright but soon arch over. They trail to about 10in/25cm, making this a good plant for a hanging basket.

The fleshy round leaves, with lightly scalloped edges, are carried in whorls of three; they are steely blue-gray tinged with pink and have a cream central splash or stripe. Heads of small pink flowers are borne at the ends of the stems in late summer or early fall.

FACT FILE

ORIGIN Japan.

HEIGHT To 4in/10cm; stems trail to 10in/25cm.

POTTING MIX Soil- or peat-moss-based, with added perlite or coarse sand for good drainage.

REPOTTING Move to a pot one size larger in spring.

PROPAGATION Take stem tip cuttings in spring or summer. Remove the leaves to expose about 1in/2.5cm of the stem and allow it to dry for 1–2 days before inserting it into soil.

KEEPING PLANTS Watch out for mealybugs and aphids, which both attack this plant.

PLANT CARE

Bright light with plenty of direct sunshine. ● Cool to moderate temperatures: 40°–60°F/ 4°–16°C. ● In summer allow the top ½in/ 13mm of the soil to dry out between waterings; water more sparingly in winter. ● It is not necessary to feed this plant.

SIDERASIS FUSCATA
Commelinaceae

BROWN SPIDERWORT

Although related to the easy-to-grow tradescantia, this plant needs high humidity and is best grown in a bottle garden. The broad leaves form a low rosette; on the surface they are deep green with a central silvery stripe, and their undersides are deep purplish red. The whole plant is covered with fine rust-colored hairs. Purple flowers, about 1in/2.5cm wide, emerge from the center of the rosette in summer, and have the typical three-petaled shape of those of the *Tradescantia* genus.

FACT FILE

ORIGIN Brazil.

HEIGHT Usually less than 8in/20cm.

POTTING MIX Soil-based and peat-moss-based in equal amounts.

REPOTTING Move into a pot one size larger in spring; this is not usually necessary every year. Put a layer of gravel or pot shards in the pot to ensure good drainage.

PROPAGATION Divide the clumps of rosettes as they become crowded.

KEEPING PLANTS If the plant is not being grown plant in a bottle garden or terrarium, it should stand on a tray of moist pebbles to maintain high humidity, which is essential.

PLANT CARE

Partial shade. ● Warm temperatures of 70°–85°F/21°–29°C are essential. Protect from drafts. ● Water moderately; allow the surface of the soil to dry out between waterings. ● Keep the humidity high at all times. ● Apply a balanced liquid fertilizer every 4 weeks.

SINNINGIA CARDINALIS
Gesneriaceae

CARDINAL FLOWER

This plant belongs to the same genus as gloxinia, but the two have little in common except that both grow from fibrous tubers and bear rather coarse, hairy leaves and brightly colored flowers. The mid green leaves of sinningia have rather darker veins and are up to 6in/15cm long.

The scarlet flowers open in clusters at the tips of the stems in summer. They are long and tubular, and the top of the corolla juts out over two distinct lower lips. This gives the flowers the appearance of a helmet with an open visor, hence sinningia's other name of helmet flower.

FACT FILE

ORIGIN Brazil.

HEIGHT To 10in/25cm.

POTTING MIX Peat-moss-based.

REPOTTING Set the dormant tubers level with the surface of the potting mix in spring. Move into a larger pot only after several years.

PROPAGATION Take cuttings of young shoots in late spring. A heated propagator will improve the success rate.

KEEPING PLANTS Sinningia has a short dormant period after flowering; keep the tuber dry and store the pot on its side.

PLANT CARE

Bright light with no direct sun. ● Keep at about 70°F/21°C during the growing period; 50°F/10°C or less when the tubers are dormant. ● Water sparingly after potting until growth is evident, then keep the medium constantly moist until flowering has finished. Gradually reduce watering as the stems die back, and keep the tubers dry while dormant. ● Apply a high-potash liquid fertilizer every 2 weeks from the time flower buds form until the leaves die down.

~

SMITHIANTHA HYBRIDS
Gesneriaceae

TEMPLE BELLS

Several species of smithiantha have been crossed to produce a race of free-flowering plants. They have heart-shaped, velvety-textured, deep green leaves topped with panicles of long-stalked, tubular blooms that resemble penstemon flowers. The flowers are carried between late summer and early spring and come in shades of bright orange, yellow, or pink. Plants grow from fleshy rhizomes and become dormant once they have flowered.

FACT FILE

ORIGIN Mexico.

HEIGHT To 12in/30cm.

POTTING MIX Peat-moss-based, with a little added lime to reduce the acidity of the peat moss.

REPOTTING In late winter, set 2 or 3 rhizomes in a pot; barely cover them with potting mix.

PROPAGATION By division when repotting.

KEEPING PLANTS Store dormant tubers in cool conditions in the pot or in dry peat moss.

PLANT CARE

Light shade. ● In the growing season, about 70°F/21°C; cooler in the dormant period. ● Let the top ½in/13mm of the medium dry out before rewatering in the growing season. Reduce watering after flowering; keep dormant tubers dry. ● High humidity is necessary; stand the pot on a tray of moist pebbles, but do not spray the hairy leaves. ● Feed with high-potash liquid fertilizer every week in the growing season.

~

SOLEIROLIA SOLEIROLII
Urticaceae

MIND-YOUR-OWN-BUSINESS

The common name of this evergreen creeping plant derives from its fast-growing, mat-forming habit: it can become a weed in gardens in mild areas or in terrariums indoors. The tiny round leaves, which give it another of its names, baby's tears, are carried alternately on slender, fragile stems. They are silvery green in the variety 'Argentea,' while 'Aurea' has pale yellow foliage. It was formerly known as *Helxine soleirolii* and is still sold under that name.

FACT FILE

ORIGIN Corsica; Sardinia.

HEIGHT To 2in/5cm; prostrate.

POTTING MIX Soil-based, with added leaf mold and grit for good drainage.

REPOTTING Move in spring, into a wide shallow pot.

PROPAGATION Divide plants into smaller clumps by pulling them apart carefully.

KEEPING PLANTS Soleirolia makes an attractive groundcover under taller pot plants.

PLANT CARE

Bright filtered light; direct sun will scorch the foliage. ● Normal to cool room temperature. ● Keep the soil moist at all times. ● Feed occasionally with dilute liquid fertilizer.

SONERILA MARGARITACEA
Melastomataceae

PEARLY SONERILA

This plant is not easy to grow: it demands even warmth and a humid atmosphere. It is a good candidate for a terrarium, where these conditions can be easily provided. The upper surface of the highly decorative lance-shaped leaves is puckered, and they are heavily marked with silver which gives the plant a frosted or metallic appearance. Small rosy pink, three-petaled flowers appear in summer.

FACT FILE

ORIGIN Java to Burma.

HEIGHT To 10in/25cm.

POTTING MIX Peat-moss-based, with added leaf mold and coarse sand for good drainage.

REPOTTING Move into a pot one size larger each spring; a shallow pot is most suitable.

PROPAGATION Take stem cuttings in spring and summer. A heated propagator will aid rooting.

KEEPING PLANTS Older, larger plants tend to lose their bottom leaves and are best replaced with cuttings when they begin to get leggy.

PLANT CARE

Bright, filtered light all year-round; no direct sun. ● A minimum of 65°F/18°C in winter; 70°F/21°C and more in the growing season. ● Keep the soil just moist during active growth; water more sparingly in winter. ● Mist the foliage often and stand the pot on a tray of moist gravel. ● Apply a balanced liquid fertilizer every 2 weeks in spring and summer.

~

Soleirolia soleirolii

Sparmannia africana

SPARMANNIA AFRICANA
Tiliaceae

AFRICAN HEMP

Also known as the indoor linden, or linden tree, this plant quickly forms a tree shape when grown in a large container. It has 5–6-in/13–15-cm-long, downy, pale green heart-shaped leaves with toothed edges. In late winter and early spring, umbels of white-petaled flowers, with a central boss of purple-tipped golden stamens, are borne at the ends of the stems.

FACT FILE

ORIGIN South Africa.

HEIGHT To 3ft/90cm in a container.

POTTING MIX Soil-based.

REPOTTING Move into a larger pot whenever the roots fill the current pot.

PROPAGATION Take stem cuttings of young shoots in spring.

KEEPING PLANTS Replace large, untidy plants by cuttings. Cut stems back after flowering and pinch off growing tips to encourage bushiness.

PLANT CARE

Bright light; protect from direct sun in summer. ● Best at about 60°F/16°C. ● Water freely in spring and summer, give less water in winter. ● Apply high-potash liquid fertilizer every 3 weeks from the time flower buds appear until the fall.

STAPELIA VARIEGATA
Asclepiadaceae

CARRION FLOWER

Although striking in appearance, the flowers of this unusual plant smell unpleasantly of rotting meat to attract pollinating flies. The upright stems are thick and fleshy. They tend to sprawl as the plant ages, and the leaves are then reduced to spinelike protuberances. In summer, flowers may be produced either singly or in small groups at the base of the stems. The star-shaped flowers are pale yellow with purplish brown blotches and are up to 3in/8cm wide.

Stapelia variegata

FACT FILE

ORIGIN South Africa.

HEIGHT To 8in/20cm.

POTTING MIX Soil-based with some added coarse sand.

REPOTTING Move into a pot one size larger in spring or whenever the stems appear crowded.

PROPAGATION Sow seed or take stem cuttings in spring and summer. Allow the base of the cuttings to dry before inserting them into a sandy medium.

KEEPING PLANTS Warm, dry air is essential.

PLANT CARE

Direct sunlight. ● A minimum of 55°F/13°C in winter. ● Water from below to moisten the soil thoroughly, then let the top half of the soil dry out before watering again. ● Apply a high-potash liquid fertilizer every 4 weeks in the growing season only.

~

STENOTAPHRUM SECUNDATUM 'VARIEGATUM'
Graminae

ST. AUGUSTINE GRASS

Also known as buffalo grass, this plant looks a little like chlorophytum. The pale green leaves are long and straplike, blunt-tipped, with a broad cream band down the center. The creeping stems produce clumps of leaves from the nodes and will root easily wherever they touch the soil. The flowers are inconspicuous and are not often produced on plants grown in containers.

This is a good plant for a hanging basket that allows the stems to trail.

FACT FILE

ORIGIN Southern USA; tropical America.

HEIGHT To 8in/20cm.

POTTING MIX Soil-based.

REPOTTING Move into a larger pot whenever the roots appear crowded; use a half-pot or other shallow container.

PROPAGATION Separate rooted clumps from the parent plant and pot them up individually.

KEEPING PLANTS When leaves lose their color and die back, gently pull them off the plant. This will not damage the plant.

PLANT CARE

Bright light with 3 or 4 hours of direct sun daily to help keep the variegation of the leaves. ● Normal room temperature, with a winter minimum of 50°F/10°C. ● Water freely in spring and summer; more sparingly in winter. Never let the plant stand in water. ● Apply a balanced liquid fertilizer once a month during the period of active growth.

Strelitzia reginae

PLANT CARE

Bright light with 3–4 hours of direct sun daily. ● Normal room temperature in the growing season; about 55°F/13°C in the winter rest period. ● Let the surface of the soil dry out between waterings in spring and summer; water sparingly in winter. ● Give a high-potash liquid feed every 3 weeks when in active growth.

~

STREPTOSOLEN JAMESONII
Solanaceae

MARMALADE BUSH

In summer, at the tips of the branches, streptosolen produces plentiful clusters of bright orange and yellow, tubular, flared flowers, which give it its other common name of fire bush. A scrambling shrub, with ovate, deep green, rather wrinkled leaves, it can be grown as a trailer, but is probably best in a sunroom or greenhouse where it can be trained against a wall.

Streptosolen jamesonii

STRELITZIA NICOLAI
Strelitziaceae

WHITE BIRD-OF-PARADISE

This is a tall-growing species with woody stems carrying glossy, deep green, ovate leaf blades up to 4ft/1.2m long. The white or pale blue flowers are held in a long, brown, boat-shaped bract.

FACT FILE

ORIGIN South Africa.

HEIGHT To 6ft/1.8m in a container.

POTTING MIX Soil-based.

REPOTTING Repot in spring until the largest desired pot size is reached; thereafter top-dress.

PROPAGATION In spring, divide the clumps of rooted suckers.

KEEPING PLANTS Patience is required when growing strelitzias, since they do not flower until they are about 6 years old.

PLANT CARE

Bright light with some direct sun. Shade from midsummer sun. ● Normal room temperature in the growing period, about 55°F/13°C in the winter rest period. ● Allow the surface of the growing medium to dry out before rewatering in the growing season. Water sparingly in winter. ● Give a high-potash liquid feed every 3 weeks in the period of active growth.

STRELITZIA REGINAE
Strelitziaceae

BIRD-OF-PARADISE

Also known as crane flower, this spectacular plant has flowers that look like the head of the exotic crested crane. The slender green bracts, some 8in/20cm long, are sharply pointed and held horizontally, giving the appearance of a beak. Bright orange-and-blue-petaled flowers emerge from the bracts to form a colorful "crest." Flowers are borne on plants 5 to 6 years old in early spring and summer and sometimes to late summer. Individual flowers last for about a week, but each spathe produces several, which open in succession.

The oblong, leathery leaves up to 18in/46cm long, on stalks almost twice as long, rise directly from the base of the plant.

FACT FILE

ORIGIN South Africa.

HEIGHT To 3ft/90cm.

POTTING MIX Fertile, well-drained, soil-based.

REPOTTING In spring, move into a larger pot until a 10-in/25-cm pot is reached; thereafter top-dress annually.

PROPAGATION In spring, by seed or division.

KEEPING PLANTS Strelitzias need sunlight; they will not flower if the light is not bright enough.

FACT FILE

ORIGIN Colombia; Ecuador; Peru.

HEIGHT To 6ft/1.8m.

POTTING MIX Soil-based.

REPOTTING Repot after flowering, or top-dress a large plant.

PROPAGATION Take stem cuttings in late spring or early summer.

KEEPING PLANTS Cut back the stems of old plants by half in late winter. Pinch off growing tips to promote bushiness.

PLANT CARE

Bright light with some direct sun, but shade from hot midsummer sun. ● A minimum of 50°F/10°C in winter. ● Keep the soil moist in the growing season; give less water in winter. ● Apply a high-potash liquid fertilizer every 3 weeks while the plant is actively growing.

Strobilanthes dyeranus

STROBILANTHES DYERANUS
Acanthaceae

$\mathcal{P}$ERSIAN SHIELD

This is an attractive, erect, evergreen foliage plant with lance-shaped leaves. The pointed oval leaves, about 6in/15cm long, have a metallic, silvery purple surface with green margins and deep purple undersides; the color becomes lighter as the leaves age.

FACT FILE

ORIGIN Burma.

HEIGHT To 2ft/60cm.

POTTING MIX Soil-based with added leaf mold.

REPOTTING Whenever roots fill the pot.

PROPAGATION Take stem cuttings in spring; root them in a propagator with bottom heat.

KEEPING PLANTS Replace the plant by a cutting when it becomes straggly, usually after a year.

PLANT CARE

Bright, filtered light. ● A minimum of 60°F/16°C. ● Let the surface of the soil dry out between waterings. ● Apply a balanced liquid fertilizer every 2 weeks to a plant that is actively growing.

STROMANTHE AMABILIS
Marantaceae

$\mathcal{S}$TROMANTHE

This plant is also known as *Ctenanthe amabilis* and is a member of the same family as maranta and calathea. It was formerly included in those genera and may be offered under those names. It has typical feathered herringbone markings on oblong, gray-green leaves and forms a compact clump.

FACT FILE

ORIGIN Brazil.

HEIGHT To 10in/25cm.

POTTING MIX Peat-moss-based.

REPOTTING In spring, when the pot appears crowded with foliage.

PROPAGATION Divide clumps in spring.

KEEPING PLANTS Stromanthe does not like to stand in a draft, so be careful where you site it.

PLANT CARE

Moderately bright light out of direct sun. ● Normal to warm room temperature with a winter minimum of 60°F/16°C. ● Water moderately; allow the top 1in/2.5cm of the soil to dry out between waterings. ● Give a balanced liquid fertilizer every 3 weeks during the growing season.

SYAGRUS WEDDELLIANA
Palmae

$\mathcal{W}$EDDEL PALM

Rather similar to *Chamaedorea elegans*, the parlor palm, this is a slow-growing, graceful plant with feathery fronds on arching stems. It is not as robust as the parlor palm and is more difficult to grow successfully, requiring higher temperature and humidity. The tips of the fronds will quickly turn brown and crisp in dry conditions. It is also known as *Microcoelium weddellianum* and *Cocos weddelliana*.

Syagrus weddelliana

FACT FILE

ORIGIN Brazil.

HEIGHT To 4ft/1.2m in a container.

POTTING MIX Soil-based.

REPOTTING In spring, only when essential; usually not more often than every 3 years.

PROPAGATION Plants are raised from seed, but this is not practical in the home.

KEEPING PLANTS This palm will remain small for many years, so is a very suitable houseplant.

PLANT CARE

Bright light, but shaded from direct sun. ● Does best at 70°–75°F/21°–24°C, with a minimum of 60°F/16°C in winter. ● Water moderately; allow the top $^1\!/_2$in/13mm of soil to dry out before rewatering. Water more sparingly in cooler conditions. ● Stand the pot on a tray of moist gravel and mist the foliage frequently to increase humidity. ● Apply a balanced liquid fertilizer every 4 weeks in the growing season.

TETRASTIGMA VOINIERANUM
Vitaceae

$\mathcal{C}$HESTNUT VINE

Related to the more popular grape ivy and kangaroo vine (*Cissus* genus), tetrastigma is a large and vigorous climber that needs plenty of space. The deep green leaves, composed of five leaflets, are shaped rather like a horse chestnut leaf and can be more than 12in/30cm wide. The leaf edges are toothed, and the undersides are covered with reddish brown hairs. Strong, wiry tendrils cling firmly to any support, and the stems will rapidly cover a wall or trellis.

FACT FILE

ORIGIN Southeast Asia.

HEIGHT Climbs to more than 6ft/1.8m.

POTTING MIX Soil-based with good drainage.

REPOTTING Move into a pot two sizes larger in spring; when maximum desired pot size is reached, top-dress annually instead.

PROPAGATION By stem tip cuttings in late spring and summer.

KEEPING PLANTS This vigorous, large-leafed plant needs a sturdy trellis or similar support. Prune in spring, removing overcrowded stems.

PLANT CARE

Bright light, shaded from direct sun; will tolerate partial shade. ● Ideally, a range of temperatures of 60°–80°F/16°–27°C, with a winter minimum of 55°F/13°C. ● Keep the soil moist in the growing season; water more sparingly in winter. ● Apply a balanced liquid fertilizer every 4 weeks in spring and summer.

THUNBERGIA ALATA
Thunbergiaceae

ℬLACK-EYED SUSAN

Generally grown as an annual, this fast-growing climber is easily raised from seed. The slender, twining stems bear light green, arrowhead-shaped leaves with indented margins. In summer, daisylike flowers with a tubular throat appear; the species has orange petals, but there are varieties with yellow or white petals, and all have a deep chocolate brown center. Provide stakes around the edges of the pot for the plant to twine around, or train it over a trellis or similar support; it also makes a good candidate for a hanging basket.

FACT FILE

ORIGIN Tropical Africa.

HEIGHT To 6ft/1.8m.

POTTING MIX Soil-based.

REPOTTING Move the plant into a larger pot when roots can be seen through the drainage holes in the bottom.

PROPAGATION By seed sown in early spring.

KEEPING PLANTS Discard after flowering.

PLANT CARE

Bright light with some direct sun. ● Normal room temperature. ● Keep the soil moist at all times. ● Apply a high-potash liquid fertilizer every 2 weeks from the time the flower buds start to form.

~

TRACHYCARPUS FORTUNEI
Palmae

𝒲INDMILL PALM

When they first appear, the leaves of this hardy palm are attractively pleated and covered with fine hairs, but these fibers curl away from the edges as the leaves gradually open out into wide, deeply segmented fans. As the plant ages, a stout stem develops, covered with coarse brown fibers from decomposing leaf sheaths.

FACT FILE

ORIGIN Southeast Asia.

HEIGHT To 8ft/2.4m in a container.

POTTING MIX Soil-based.

REPOTTING In spring, move into a pot one size larger.

PROPAGATION By seed, but seedlings are so slow-growing, this is not practical for an amateur.

KEEPING PLANTS This palm will benefit from a spell outdoors in summer, but keep it out of heavy winds, which can shred the leaves.

Trachycarpus fortunei

PLANT CARE

Bright light with plenty of direct sun. ● Normal room temperature, with a winter minimum of 40°F/4°C in winter. ● Water moderately throughout the growing season, but sparingly in cooler temperatures. ● Give a balanced liquid feed every 2–3 weeks in spring and summer.

~

TULIPA HYBRIDS
Liliaceae

𝒯ULIPS

Tulips are less commonly grown indoors than hyacinths or narcissi, but several varieties make good short-term pot plants. The early-flowering single and double types are best. Singles include scented yellow 'Bellona'; red 'Christmas Marvel'; salmon pink 'Apricot Beauty'; and 'Flair,' which is golden yellow with red feathering. Good doubles include orange-yellow 'Maréchal Niel'; white 'Schoonoord'; and rose pink 'Peach Blossom.'

Also attractive are varieties of the low-growing *Tulipa greigii*, with mottled foliage, and *T. kaufmanniana*, the water-lily tulip, with wide, open blooms.

Treat tulip bulbs like those of hyacinth and narcissus and give them a cool, dark period after planting so they will develop an adequate rooting system. Plunge the pot in the ground outdoors under a covering of peat moss or enclose it in a black plastic bag and stand it in a cool place.

FACT FILE

ORIGIN Turkey; East Asia; hybrid.

HEIGHT To 2ft/60cm, depending on variety.

POTTING MIX Peat-moss-based or bulb medium.

REPOTTING Set bulbs close together in a pot in fall, with their noses just covered.

PROPAGATION Not practical for the amateur. Seedlings take 5–7 years to flower. Mature bulbs increase slowly by offsets.

KEEPING PLANTS Plant bulbs outdoors once flowering is over; it is not worth growing them for indoor use again.

PLANT CARE

Give bulbs a cool, dark period of about 10 weeks after planting; bring them into the light when they have about 2in/5cm of top growth. Keep in a bright location during flowering. ● About 40°F/4°C for 10 weeks after planting; increasing gradually to about 55°F/13°C for flowering. ● Keep the medium just moist at all times. ● Give a balanced liquid feed every 2 weeks.

~

VALLOTA SPECIOSA
(SYN. *CYRTANTHUS ELATUS*)
Amaryllidaceae

𝒮CARBOROUGH LILY

This evergreen plant produces tall stems topped by clusters of brightly colored, trumpet-shaped flowers from summer to fall. Although the flowers are not as large as those of hippeastrum, to which the plant is related, they are showy. The leaves are strap-shaped and about 12in/30cm long. The flower stems rise above the foliage and bear groups of four to eight scarlet, white, or salmon pink flowers.

FACT FILE

ORIGIN South Africa.

HEIGHT To 2ft/60cm.

POTTING MIX Soil-based.

REPOTTING In spring set the bulb in a 5-in/13-cm pot, half burying it in the soil. Plants flower best when undisturbed, so top-dress annually and repot only every 3 to 4 years.

PROPAGATION Remove offsets in spring or early summer and pot up individually.

KEEPING PLANTS The plant needs a rest period in cool conditions in the winter.

PLANT CARE

Bright light with some direct sun. ● Normal room temperature in summer, but a cooler period in winter at about 50°F/10°C. ● Water sparingly until growth starts in spring; keep the soil just moist during the growing season. ● Apply a high-potash liquid fertilizer every 2 weeks from spring until flowering ceases.

Washingtonia filifera

WASHINGTONIA FILIFERA
Palmae

DESERT FAN PALM

One of only two species of washingtonia, this palm is a tall, handsome plant with spiny leafstalks some 18in/46cm long supporting grayish green fan-shaped leaves up to 2ft/60cm wide. The leaves are split about halfway down into many narrow segments, from the tips of which hang fine, dry, brown fibers.

In the wild, the tapered red-brown trunk is densely clothed in dead foliage, which is generally cut away on cultivated plants. This fringe of dead leaves gives the plant its name of petticoat palm.

In their arid natural habitat, these palms are a sure sign of subterranean water, into which they send down long, deep roots. Since they thrive in hot, dry regions, the palms do well in centrally heated homes.

FACT FILE

ORIGIN USA (California; Arizona).

HEIGHT To 10ft/3m; to 80ft/24m in the wild.

POTTING MIX Soil-based with added peat moss or leaf mold in a ratio of 2:1.

REPOTTING Move into a pot one size larger when roots appear on the surface of the soil—every 2 or 3 years—and then only when the plant is in active growth. Plant the palm firmly, but be very careful not to damage the brittle roots, especially the larger, thicker ones.

PROPAGATION From seed in considerable heat; this is generally not practicable for the home gardener.

KEEPING PLANTS The palm will benefit from a spell outdoors in a sheltered spot during the summer. Bring it indoors again in the fall before the first frost.

PLANT CARE

Bright light with plenty of direct sun. ● Warm or hot rooms, with a minimum of 50°F/10°C. ● Water plentifully in the growing period, more sparingly in winter. ● Stand the pot on a tray of damp pebbles in very dry conditions. ● Apply a standard liquid fertilizer every 2 weeks in the growing period.

~

ZANTEDESCHIA AETHIOPICA
(SYN. *Z. AFRICANA*)
Araceae

WHITE CALLA LILY

In late spring the stately white calla, or white arum, lily produces its golden, club-shaped spadix surrounded by a pure white spathe. The tall stem stands above the large, shiny, dark green arrowhead-shaped leaves, which are strongly veined and arise on long leafstalks directly from the rhizome.

Many varieties have been developed that are more compact and free-flowering than the species. 'Childsiana' is a compact form. 'Green Goddess' has white spathes tipped and streaked with green; those of 'Little Suzie' are tinged with pink. *Zantedeschia rehmannii* has slender pink spathes and long leaves, and *Z. elliotiana* has extremely large, lush, dark green leaves spotted with white, and golden yellow spathes.

FACT FILE

ORIGIN South Africa (Cape Province, Natal, Transvaal); Lesotho.

HEIGHT To 3ft/90cm.

POTTING MIX Soil-based.

REPOTTING Move into a pot one size larger in early fall, when roots fill the current pot.

PROPAGATION Divide clumps when repotting.

KEEPING PLANTS The plant usually has a short rest period after flowering. Set the pot in a sheltered place outdoors in summer.

PLANT CARE

Bright light with some direct sun. ● Cool to average room temperature to prolong the life of the blooms. ● Water sparingly until growth starts, then plentifully throughout the flowering season; do not let the soil dry out. Reduce watering as the leaves begin to die back, and water sparingly from midsummer. ● Apply a balanced liquid fertilizer every 2 weeks in the growing season.

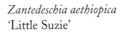

Zantedeschia aethiopica
'Little Suzie'

CARING FOR PLANTS

ALL PLANTS REQUIRE CERTAIN conditions for healthy growth, and a good understanding of a plant's basic needs will set you on the right road to correct cultivation.

Every plant needs light in order to photosynthesize (manufacture food from sunlight), but the quality of light each plant demands varies from species to species. Ideal temperature ranges vary too, as does the quantity of water required. The Plant Directory gives you details of the requirements of individual plants, and this chapter aims to help you understand the role played by these variables in the existence of all plants. Most houseplants are grown in conditions very different from those of their natural habitat, but with a little help, the majority of them can adjust to the environment in our homes.

There is no substitute for experience and observation. Trying out different types of plants, and learning to observe them closely, will do more than anything else to help you acquire that coveted green thumb. People who complain that they just can't get plants to grow often simply fail to pay enough attention to them. Learn to look at your plants carefully, checking for healthy young growth, noticing yellowing foliage or the early signs of pests or disease. Turn the leaves over to look at the undersides; that's where many pests hide.

To help you to decide whether the plant needs water, prod the surface of the soil with a finger and try the weight of the pot to judge the moisture content. Check the color and size of the leaves to estimate whether a plant is running short of nutrients. It takes only a few minutes every few days, and you will soon find that your plants begin to speak to you.

When buying a plant you have not grown before (or have tried and failed with), seek advice from the seller. At any reliable garden center or nursery, there should be qualified people who can help you with any queries.

Give a new plant time to adjust to the conditions in your home. Don't keep moving it from room to room because it doesn't look happy. Find a suitable care regime and stick to it. Resist the temptation to overwater and overfeed an ailing plant for the sake of doing something to help, when all it really needs is to be left alone for a while to get over the move.

Finally, do not expect miracles. Some plants were never intended to do more than provide a little color and cheer for a few weeks; others are notoriously difficult to grow well, and you should not be too disappointed if you fail.

The golden rule is never to spend more on buying a plant than you feel happy about, unless you are certain you can keep it alive long enough to get your money's worth from it.

Any corner of a garden shed or utility room (left) *can be equipped to provide a place where you can deal with your houseplants. All you need is good light, a bench, some shelves to store your equipment on, and easy access to water.*

COMPARING PLANTS: HEALTHY VS. UNHEALTHY

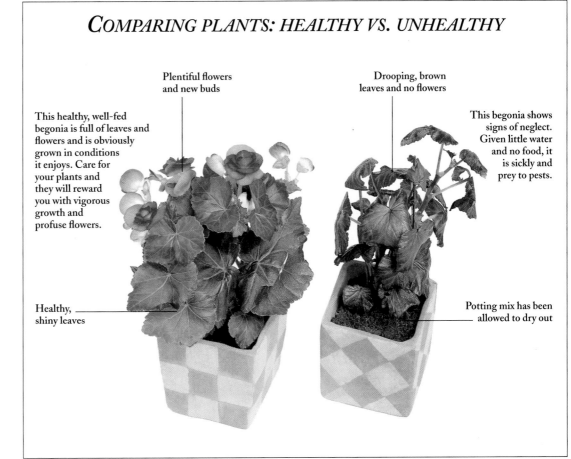

Plentiful flowers and new buds

Drooping, brown leaves and no flowers

This healthy, well-fed begonia is full of leaves and flowers and is obviously grown in conditions it enjoys. Care for your plants and they will reward you with vigorous growth and profuse flowers.

This begonia shows signs of neglect. Given little water and no food, it is sickly and prey to pests.

Healthy, shiny leaves

Potting mix has been allowed to dry out

PLANT ANATOMY

THE FORM OF PLANTS VARIES GREATLY, but as the simplified diagram below shows, the major parts of a typical specimen can be observed on almost every kind of plant.

APICAL BUDS
These are the growth buds at the tips of the shoots.

AXILLARY BUDS
Buds in the leaf axils (the upper point where the leaves join the stem) may develop into either shoots or flowers.

FLOWERS
The reproductive organs of the plant are carried in the flowers. Their form differs tremendously, but a typical flower has brightly colored petals, which serve to attract pollinating insects, and sepals, which cover the bud; these may also be colored and are often green. Both petals and sepals are modified leaves.

The female reproductive organs are the ovary, usually hidden by the petals, from which emerges the style (stalk) topped by a stigma, which receives pollen grains from another flower. The three parts are known collectively as the pistil. The male organs are the filament, which is topped by pollen-bearing anthers; together they make up the stamen.

LEAVES
The plant's food manufacturing process normally takes place in the leaves, which may or may not have stalks. Again, the leaves are extremely variable in form, but they tend to be thin, with a

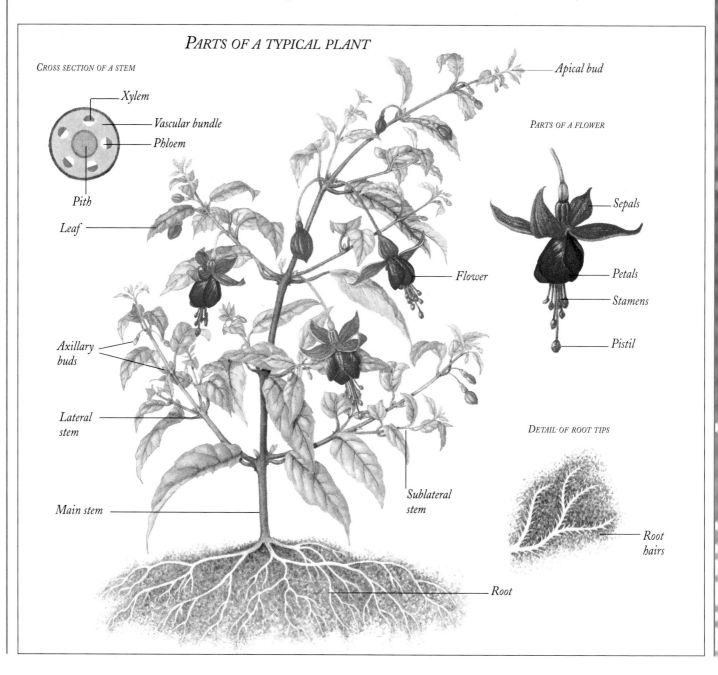

PARTS OF A TYPICAL PLANT

CROSS SECTION OF A STEM

Xylem

Vascular bundle

Phloem

Pith

Leaf

Axillary buds

Lateral stem

Main stem

Apical bud

PARTS OF A FLOWER

Sepals

Petals

Stamens

Pistil

Flower

Sublateral stem

DETAIL OF ROOT TIPS

Root hairs

Root

large surface area to absorb maximum sunlight. In some plants green stems take on this role.

STEMS

While the stems of many plants grow upright, others are prostrate, trailing, or climbing. There may be one main stem with laterals (side stems) branching off it and sublaterals branching off those, or there may be several stems arising from soil level. Throughout the stems, shoots, and roots are vascular bundles, which act rather like a system of veins and arteries, transporting food and water to all parts of the plant. Xylem carries water from the roots, while phloem transports nutrients from the site of manufacture, which is generally in the leaves and stems. The center of the stem is woody pith, which provides support.

ROOTS

Water and dissolved nutrients from the soil are absorbed largely through very fine root hairs found toward the tips of the rootlets. A plant may have a fibrous root system with a mass of equal-size roots, or a taproot that branches in much the same way that stems do. It may have tuberous roots or aerial roots that grow above the soil. In addition to absorbing food and water, roots anchor and support the plant.

TYPES OF PLANTS

The plant kingdom contains an astounding range of plants, from single-celled algae found in pond water to ancient, towering trees. Along the way are plants of all shapes and sizes, some wonderfully adapted to their natural habitats. Among the many species we grow as houseplants can be found a good selection of different types.

Annuals grow from seed, flower, and die in one season, persisting only as seeds for future years. Perennials persist from year to year (although many are short-lived and die after only a few years). Most houseplants are perennials, but exacums, schizanthuses, and ipomoeas are among the annuals grown in the home.

Perennial plants may be deciduous, losing their leaves during the fall and winter, or evergreen, keeping their leaves year-round. The distinction between evergreen and deciduous plants is somewhat blurred when it comes to houseplants, since the artificially warm conditions indoors can make evergreens of plants that would normally shed their leaves in a more natural environment.

The majority of foliage houseplants are evergreen—monsteras, peperomias, ficuses, dieffenbachias, and many others. Caladiums are among the few deciduous foliage plants; they die right back below soil level in winter.

Plants are split into further categories according to their habit of growth. Herbaceous plants produce soft, nonhardy stems and foliage, whereas shrubby plants produce woody stems that tend to persist from one year to another. Ficuses, camellias, and fuchsias are among the shrubs or sub-shrubs grown indoors. Several of the plants we grow would become trees if given enough room for both roots and top growth to expand naturally, but by confining them in containers, we can keep their size to more manageable proportions. Some plants, such as one or two of the palms, are slow-growing and would take many years to achieve the height and spread of trees; others, such as eucalyptus, will reach 20ft/6m or more in a very short time when planted outdoors.

Bulbs, corms, and tubers are plant storage organs that hold food reserves for the following year's growth: cyclamens, hyacinths, narcissus, hippeastrums, and freesias are popular examples. All these plants have a dormant period after the flowers and foliage have died down.

Some plants have highly specialized systems to help them overcome problems encountered in their natural environment. Epiphytes, such as several orchids and bromeliads, cope with the lack of light beneath the tree canopy in the dense tropical and temperate rain forests by growing high on the branches of trees where the light is better. They absorb moisture and nutrients from the humid atmosphere through their leaves.

Cacti and succulents from hot, arid regions store water in fleshy stems and are often covered with dense hair to protect them from scorching by the sun. Carnivorous plants obtain nutrients by trapping passing animal life, rather than relying on the impoverished soil in which they grow. A number of ingenious traps allow the plants to lure and capture insects, which they then digest, making them fascinating, if rather gruesome, plants to cultivate in the home.

Tubers are large, often branching, storage organs; some begonias grow from tubers.

Bulbs are specialized shoots in which the swollen leaves, or scales, are folded over each other—tightly in narcissus (below) and loosely in some lilies.

Corms are solid, swollen stems with a bud at the top. Crocuses and some irises have corms.

The term bulb *is commonly used to cover all plants that grow from bulbs, corms, rhizomes, and tubers. Although these are botanically quite different, they are all organs for storing food for the plant, and many common houseplants grow from one or another of these organs.*

THE IMPORTANCE OF LIGHT

PLANTS NEED GOOD-QUALITY LIGHT in order to manufacture their food through photosynthesis. The amount of light in a typical room (*below right*) is extremely variable: it depends not only on the size and location of windows, but also the season, weather, and trees or buildings outside, which may block the light.

EAST WALL
An east-facing window receives direct sun in the morning and moderately bright light for the rest of the day. It is a suitable position for plants that like only a few hours of direct sunlight.

The area on each side of the fireplace in the illustration, particularly to the left, receives little or no direct light, and could be a difficult place for plants. White or light-colored walls or mirrors will help to reflect what little light there is.

SOUTH WALL
Patio doors or French windows take full advantage of the sun falling on a south-facing wall. The area directly in front of the window receives good light all day, but the intensity of the light falls off quickly the farther away from the window you are. The areas on each side of the window are relatively dark.

This is a good place for a floor-standing group of sun-loving plants; it is especially suitable for taller subjects, which can make maximum use of the floor-to-ceiling brightness.

WEST WALL
The windows on this wall receive good light throughout the day, with direct sun in the afternoon. (The amount of direct sun east and west windows get will vary according to the time of year and the height of the sun in the sky; no sun may fall through the windows for some weeks at the height of summer.) Here you can grow plants similar to those on the east wall. Plants that need bright but diffuse light can be protected by a sheer curtain or translucent blind at the window that will filter the sun falling on the foliage.

NORTH WALL
Although this area may appear fairly bright to our eyes because it faces the

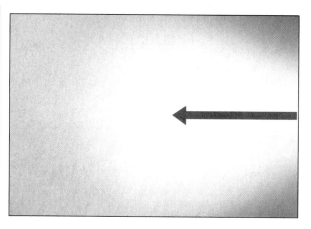

Where direct sunlight enters a room, the level of the light is almost constant. As you go farther from the source of the light, the brightness decreases until, at the opposite end of a large room, light levels are low. There are also unexpected darker corners at each side of the window. You should bear these facts about light levels in mind when deciding where to locate your plants.

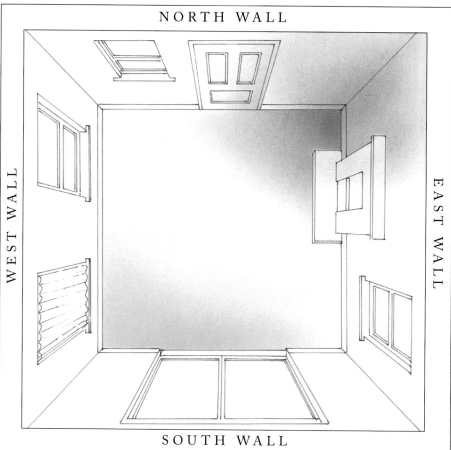

NORTH WALL

WEST WALL

EAST WALL

SOUTH WALL

large window area in the south wall, the quality of light penetrating this far into the room is much reduced. The small, high window receives no direct sunlight, but does give an even level of light during the day, which is suitable for plants that like moderately bright conditions without direct sun.

To the right of the interior door (*above*) is one of the darkest areas in the room, a corner with no immediately adjacent windows. Even the most shade-tolerant plants would struggle to thrive here. To widen the selection of plants that can be grown here, you can add artificial light. A special plant table, with a fluorescent tube suspended above the plants, makes an attractive feature. (See p. 211 for more information about using supplementary lighting.)

NORTH WALL

The dark area on the right of the doorway is an excellent place for growing plants under artificial light.

Incandescent bulbs give off too much heat to be suitable, but twin 40-watt fluorescent tubes about 10–24in/25–60cm above the tops of the plants are excellent.

Plants raised under artificial light will grow continuously. This is acceptable for most tropical foliage plants, and flowering plants will bloom more regularly and for longer periods.

EAST WALL

The area each side of the fireplace receives little or no direct light. Pale-colored walls and mirrors help to reflect what light there is.

The east-facing window receives morning sun and provides suitable light for plants that like just a few hours of direct sunlight.

Saintpaulias, fuchsias, and tradescantias will thrive on the windowsill, and sansevieria will do well on floor on the right of fireplace. *Philodendron scandens* would be suitable in a wall-mounted pot close to the window.

WEST WALL

The windows on this wall receive good light all day, with direct sun in the afternoon.

Clivias, chrysanthemums, codiaeums, cacti, and succulents will all thrive in the warmth and bright, direct light on the windowsill.

Plants such as nephrolepises, pachystachyses, *Piper ornatum*, aphelandras, columneas, and cyclamens, which need bright diffuse light, can be protected by a sheer curtain or blind.

SOUTH WALL

Although the area directly in front of the doors receives some direct sun and good light all day, it is an impractical place for houseplants. The area needs to be clear so that people can move in and out.

This is a good place for a floor-standing group of plants that revel in plenty of light, such as pelargoniums, jasmines, hibiscuses, and cordylines.

A tall specimen plant—a fatsia, gardenia, or *Aucuba japonica*, for instance—would be quite at home in the corner near the doors.

TEMPERATURE AND HUMIDITY

To DISCOVER THE TYPE OF GROWING conditions a particular indoor plant requires, it is useful to know where in the world it originated. That will give you a good idea of the conditions under which it grows naturally and which you should try to imitate to make it feel at home. But you should also remember that in many instances a great deal of selective breeding of plants has taken place to produce varieties that are suited to growing in conditions rather different from those of their natural habitat.

Most houses are heated and ventilated to suit their human occupants, and few people are going to make drastic alterations just for the sake of their indoor plants. But while plants, by and large, have to fit in with people, you can still make sure that they have the most congenial environment that is reasonably possible.

Most houseplants probably originated in tropical regions, particularly evergreen foliage plants such as philodendrons and monsteras. In tropical forests the atmosphere is hot and very humid; dense tree canopies mean that, at best, only dappled sunlight penetrates to the places where these plant species grow. In the home, the ideal conditions for these plants are even warmth, with no drafts or sudden temperature fluctuations, and frequent spraying or moist pebble trays to increase humidity. As a rule, plants should also be kept out of direct sunlight, which will scorch the leaves.

Cacti, most of which originate in extremely hot and dry desert regions, are well adapted to arid conditions, and frequent watering and regular misting would soon cause them to rot and die.

Plants from more temperate regions, like cyclamens, and bulbs such as narcissus and crocuses, prefer cooler conditions than the average home can easily provide. Too much heat leads to pale, drawn stems and foliage, weak, spindly growth, and short-lived flowers.

Houseplants come from virtually every continent. The temperate regions of Asia have provided us with chrysanthemums, camellias, and aspidistras, which thrive in cool rooms. Warm, damp areas of India have given us several species of ficuses, which are common plants in many tropical and subtropical regions of the world. From parts of Australia that have warm summers and fairly good summer or winter rainfall come eucalyptuses, callistemons, and grevilleas.

The hot arid regions of Africa are home to many species of succulents, such as lithopses and haworthias, as well as most of the aloes, and these plants need dry conditions and well-drained soil to do well in the home. A wide variety of foliage plants, such as dracaenas, peperomias, and begonias, which all need humidity in the home, come from the tropical areas, as do the popular African violets. From the Cape mountains of South Africa, which have wet winters, hot dry summers, and well-drained soil, come streptocarpuses, and bulbs such as ixias and hippeastrums.

The Americas supply a great wealth of indoor plants. Some of the most popular species of cacti come from arid areas of the southern US and Mexico, which also produces *Euphorbia pulcherrima*, the common poinsettia, achimenes, and dozens of other plants. Many species of

In the mountainous regions of the Eastern Transvaal in South Africa (left), with its well-drained soil, lilies bloom along the roadside in the early fall. Summers are warm and rainy, winters are cool and dry, and there is plenty of sunshine to bake the bulbs and ripen them for good flowering the following season.

Hot, humid rain forests, such as those of Costa Rica (right), are home to a wide variety of large-leafed foliage plants, bromeliads, and ferns that have become common plants in the home. It is often a challenge to provide the growing conditions these plants enjoy in their natural habitat and still demand when you grow them indoors.

bromeliads grown as houseplants are from the hot, humid rain forests of Central and South America.

Europe has provided relatively few plants for indoors. *Campanula isophylla,* the bellflower, comes from Italy; *Chamaerops humilis,* the European fan palm, and oleander are from Mediterranean regions, with hot dry summers and wet winters; *Hedera helix,* common ivy, is widespread across Europe.

MINIMUM AND MAXIMUM TEMPERATURES

The temperatures that are comfortable for people (65°–75°F/18°–24°C) are also, fortunately, comfortable for most indoor plants. Within their preferred temperature range, plants will grow and develop steadily, provided they have enough light. If temperatures drop below the preferred range, growth slows down, and at a certain point it will stop altogether. If the temperature drops too low, plants will die.

Most houseplants, even the hardy species, will be killed by frost because their growth will be soft and susceptible, since they have been grown in warm, indoor conditions. Such extremely low temperature damage is not common in most homes, but in cold areas plants in unheated rooms are at risk, as are plants on windowsills. When curtains are closed at night, these plants may be cut off from the warmth of the room, and in cold spells the temperature on the windowsill can drop to freezing. Either move the

plants off the windowsill in the evening or open the curtains before going to bed.

Most low-temperature damage is not as dramatic as this. There may be localized damage to leaves and growing points after an unexpected cold snap or when the heating system fails. And if conditions are consistently too cool for a particular species, the plant may simply fail to thrive and gradually fade away.

Widely fluctuating temperatures should be avoided, although many plants will cope with temperatures a few degrees outside their preferred range as long as it is steady. A fall in temperature at night is, however, normal and acceptable as long as it is not too pronounced.

Temperatures that rise above the plant's preferred range pose different problems. Warm air is capable of containing a lot more moisture vapor than cool air: as the temperature rises, moisture is drawn into

Desert areas of the western United States and Mexico are home to a huge variety of cacti. A miniature version of the fish-hook cactus shown here is a common houseplant.

A native to the meadows and woodlands of western and southern European countries, the pale yellow common primrose, Primula vulgaris *(left), is the source of the brightly colored spring-flowering plants often seen indoors.*

the air from any available surface, including plant foliage. As long as the atmosphere is humid enough (and the potting mix is kept sufficiently moist), most plants can tolerate temperatures a bit above their ideal. To be comfortable, plants generally need 50–60 percent relative humidity; in most modern heated homes, the humidity is nearer 15–20 percent. Placing dishes of water near radiators can help, but increasing the humidity directly around the plants is preferable. Misting and setting pots on wide dishes of moist pebbles or gravel are the easiest ways to increase humidity. Grouping plants helps to create a humid microclimate in which they can flourish.

If the temperature is markedly above a plant's preferred range, growth will be soft and drawn, making the plant leggy, and any flowers will have a very short life.

WATERING

ALL PLANTS NEED WATER TO GROW and develop, but the amount of water they require varies considerably from species to species.

In addition to providing the necessary turgor (stiffness) to keep the plant upright, water is essential for many chemical processes within the plant. It is generally taken up from the soil through the roots, although epiphytic plants (such as some orchids and bromeliads) absorb water through their leaves rather than their roots. Water is distributed throughout the plant by a network of water-conducting tissues.

Water vapor is given off into the atmosphere, in a process known as transpiration, from all the above-ground surfaces of the plant, but mainly from the leaves. This sets up a suction effect, whereby water is constantly being pulled up through the plant from the soil.

The most practical piece of equipment for watering plants is a watering can with a long spout, but many ingenious devices have been produced both to detect when plants need watering and to water them when you are unable to do so yourself.

The drier and warmer the atmosphere is around the plant, the more water is lost from the leaves, and the more water is therefore required at the roots to replace it. The soil must always contain adequate reserves of water to supply the needs of the plant.

But roots also need air, which should be present in the gaps between the particles of soil. If these gaps are kept constantly filled with water—in other words, if the soil is saturated—the roots will be killed and will rot away. So watering any plant necessitates maintaining a delicate balance, which is even more pronounced with houseplants in pots. They have only a small volume of soil around the roots, which allows little room for mistakes to be rectified.

A watering can with a long spout is the easiest vessel to use when watering plants. If you put a sprinkler on the spout, you can wash dust off the leaves as well. Use soft water—hard water leaves lime spots on the leaves.

Capillary matting is useful for watering plants when you go away. Fill the sink with water and put the matting on the drainboard, with about half of it in the water. The mat is made of thick felt or felt rubber that absorbs water, and plants standing on it take up the water they need by capillary action. It works best with plastic pots; with clay pots, too much of the water is absorbed by the pot itself.

Use a mister to spray the leaves of plants in order to increase humidity.

An irrigator (left) is a way to water plants when you are away. Fill the plastic bag with water, insert the green paper strip into the soil, then attach the bag to the pot by pushing the plastic pin through the tab and into the soil. Water seeps through the paper strip into the soil.

These tabs help to prevent over- or underwatering. Push one into the pot so that the bottom of the green area is just below the soil surface. Water the plant from the bottom until the yellow can and water drops turn green; give more water when they begin to revert to yellow. The spot at the top right remains yellow for comparison.

HOW TO WATER

For the majority of plants, the soil should be kept just moist throughout the growing season. Apply water until it starts to seep through the drainage holes of the pot, let it stand for 10–30 minutes, then throw away any water that remains in the saucer. Do not water again until the surface of the soil is dry to the touch: since the surface will dry out first, the soil will still be slightly moist below. More frequent watering will be necessary in warm conditions. In winter, watering should be reduced for most plants. They will be growing more slowly, if at all, so less water is required, and roots are more liable to rot in cool conditions.

Some species need frequent watering and should never be allowed to dry out; indeed, some plants such as cyperuses are adapted to growing with their roots standing in water at all times. Other plants, like cacti, are adapted to dry conditions and require watering only sparingly. Such exceptions are noted in the Plant Directory.

The simplest way to water house-plants is to apply water directly to the surface of the soil with a long-spouted can. But, like cyclamens, many plants do not like water being splashed onto the crown, where it can cause rotting. If the plant is difficult to water from above, pour water into the saucer and let the plant stand in it for not more than 30 minutes before emptying away any remaining water. If the soil is very dry, immerse the plant in a bucket of water up to the pot rim (water should not flow into the pot) until the soil has been completely moistened. Let the plant drain well before replacing it on its saucer.

WATERING SPARINGLY

1 Let the top half to two-thirds of the soil dry out before watering a plant that needs little water. Test with a stick.

2 Pour water on the surface so that it seeps down through the soil but does not run into the saucer.

3 Test it again with the stick. Make sure the soil is just damp throughout; add a little more water if necessary.

WATERING MODERATELY

1 Water a plant that needs a moderate amount of water when the top ½in/ 13mm of the soil feels dry to the touch.

2 Pour water on the surface of the soil until the entire mixture is thoroughtly wet but not sodden.

3 If water percolates through into the saucer, stop watering and drain the saucer. Do not let the plant stand in water.

WATERING LIBERALLY

1 Water a plant that needs plenty of water when the surface of the soil feels dry to the touch and the pot feels light.

2 Pour plenty of water on the surface of the soil and let it flood out through the drainage holes in the bottom of the pot.

3 When water ceases to flow through the drainage holes, empty the saucer and replace the plant on it.

FEEDING

A LTHOUGH PLANTS MANUFACTURE their own food from sunlight, they need various minerals to start this manufacturing process working. The minerals occur naturally in the soil, and because pot plants have only a limited volume of soil to draw on, we generally have to supply some extra nutrients in the form of fertilizers.

PLANT NUTRIENTS

The elements required by plants in the largest quantities are nitrogen, phosphorus, and potassium (often referred to by their chemical symbols N, P, and K). These are known as the macronutrients. Very small amounts of other minerals, called micronutrients or trace elements,

are also needed. Among the most important of these are iron, zinc, magnesium, and manganese.

The nutrients are required for a range of different processes within the plant. But to simplify, we can say that nitrogen is needed for leafy growth, phosphorus for healthy root development, and potassium for general hardiness and the production of flowers and fruits.

Most fertilizers contain a mixture of nutrients in varying proportions. Houseplant fertilizers are generally formulated either as fertilizers for foliage plants (high in nitrogen) or as fertilizers for flowering plants (high in potassium).

Fertilizers that are rich in trace elements may be formulated as fast-acting foliar

feeds. A deficiency of trace elements is often shown by yellowing of the leaf veins or of the area between the veins, while the rest of the leaf stays green.

TYPES OF FERTILIZER

Food of all types is always taken up by the plant in solution, but it does not need to be applied in that way: dry fertilizers, for instance, will dissolve in the moisture in the soil and so become available to plants. Fertilizers for houseplants can be obtained in a wide variety of forms.

Most houseplants need only a standard fertilizer, in liquid or solid slow-release form, but special fertilizers are available for all types of plants from cacti to orchids.

High-potassium fertilizers like those used for tomatoes are best for flowering plants.

Standard liquid fertilizers are suitable for most houseplants. All of them contain nitrogen, phosphorus, and potassium; and many are highly concentrated, so they must be diluted.

Fine granular fertilizer must be dissolved in water before it is used on plants. Some coarser granules are merely sprinkled on the surface of the soil.

Feeding spikes usually contain balanced quantities of the macronutrients, which are slowly released into the surrounding soil.

Fertilizing pills can be inserted into the soil. The tip of the container can be used to make a hole in the soil in which to insert the tablet.

Liquids

These fertilizers may be ready to use but are more usually found as concentrates, which require dilution before they are applied to the soil. Because the nutrients are already dissolved, the fertilizers are fast-acting. Liquids are probably the most popular types of fertilizers that are used with houseplants.

Powders

This type of fertilizer generally needs to be dissolved in water before use. It is sometimes recommended that pinches of dry fertilizer should be applied directly to the soil in the pot, but there is a risk of scorching the roots with an over-concentration of fertilizer in this way. Powders are often good value for money.

Granules

These are usually mixed with the soil when plants are potted, or they are scattered on the surface of the soil around established plants. Because the granular formulation is slow to break down, there is less risk of scorching the roots than with powdered fertilizers.

Some granular fertilizers are formulated as slow-release. This means that they are manufactured to break down slowly and release small amounts of fertilizer gradually over a long season so that only one application is necessary. The breakdown rate is faster in warm, moist conditions, so the rate of nutrient release is highest when the plants are growing most strongly.

Fertilizer pills and sticks

This is another way of making a single fertilizer application last a long time. Powdered fertilizers are compressed into tablet or stick form and are pushed down into the soil in the pot. The stick or tablet dissolves gradually, releasing fertilizer to the plant as it does so. These types are useful for people who are are busy and likely to forget to feed their plants on a regular basis, and for those who find it difficult to do so.

Foliar feeds

Although the roots are mainly responsible for taking up nutrients, the leaves can also absorb them, and this is an extremely quick way of getting food to work in the plant. The majority of fertilizer formulations would scorch the foliage if they were applied to the leaves, but some fertilizers are specifically made to be applied in this way. Most foliar feeds contain trace elements.

WHEN TO FEED

Overfeeding a plant is potentially more damaging than not feeding it, and an excess of fertilizer can quite easily kill it. Plants need feeding only when they are growing actively, and for most this means between spring and fall. In winter, when temperatures and light levels are lower, plants generally need less water and fewer nutrients than in spring, summer, and fall. Plants that bloom in winter should, however, be fed during the flowering period.

All soil contains some plant nutrients, and a newly potted plant does not usually need any additional fertilizer for several weeks. Peat-moss-based (or peat substitute) potting mix contains a much lower level of nutrients than soil-based ones. Consequently, houseplants set in a peat-moss-based mix will need feeding sooner and more frequently than will plants in a soil-based potting mix.

As a general rule, the faster-growing the plant, the more frequently it will need feeding. Every 2–3 weeks is a good rule of thumb for the majority of plants, but always check the pack recommendations for the particular fertilizer you are using. The Plant Directory gives feeding guidelines for all the plants featured in this book.

METHODS OF FEEDING PLANTS

Sticks of concentrated powdered fertilizer should be pushed fairly deeply into the soil near the edge of the pot. Watering the plant will dissolve them over time.

Push pills containing slow-release fertilizer almost to the bottom of the pot, using a pencil or stick. Be careful not to damage the roots of the plant as you do so.

Liquid fertilizers in solution are the most common type of fertilizer and may be applied either from on top or from below. Do not make the solution too strong or you may kill rather than feed the plant.

Spraying with foliar feed is a good way to feed plants such as bromeliads, which have a small rooting system, and large-leafed plants like philodendrons. This will also quickly revive a plant that has been starved of nutrients.

REPOTTING

THE CULTIVATION AND GROWTH OF a plant in a pot differ markedly from those of a plant growing outdoors. The container restricts the spread of the roots, which in turn restricts the size of the top growth. Thus many indoor plants, while perfectly healthy, are in effect stunted by their containers.

A pot of any size holds only a small volume of soil compared with an outdoor situation, and this affects the plant in a number of ways. First, the supply of nutrients available to the plant is limited and may be exhausted quite quickly. The supply of water is also limited. But para- doxically, because the drainage is not as efficient as in an outdoor situation, plants in containers are frequently damaged by waterlogging.

The potting mixes for houseplants are sterile. This eliminates competition from weed seedlings and potential damage by harmful organisms and pests in the soil, but the many beneficial effects of the flora and fauna of natural soil are also absent. As a consequence, the indoor gardener must exercise caution when caring for container-grown plants.

REMOVING A PLANT FROM A SMALL POT

1 Place your hand over the surface of the soil with the main stem or stems of the plant between your fingers.

2 Turn the pot upside down and gently but firmly knock it against the edge of a bench or table to loosen the plant.

3 Remove the plant with the rootball intact from the old pot. Tease out the old soil from around the roots and repot.

REMOVING A PLANT FROM A LARGE POT

1 To remove a plant from a large pot, first ease the soil away from the edge of the pot, with a large knife or spatula.

2 Lay the pot on its side. Turn it as you tap it with a piece of wood to loosen the soil. Hold the plant with one hand.

3 Make sure the plant is loose before trying to remove it from the pot. If the plant is large, you may need some help.

REMOVING A CACTUS FROM A POT

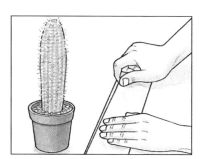

1 The best way to remove a cactus or other prickly plant from a pot is to protect your hands with thickly folded newspaper.

2 Wrap the paper around the plant, making sure that it is long enough to give you something to hold on to.

3 Grip the paper firmly in one hand and then gently ease the pot away from the soil with the other hand.

POTTING MIXES

There are many different brands of house-plant mediums, each with its own devotees, but the main choice you need to make is between peat-moss-based and soil-based potting mix. Although some plants are said to do better in loam-based (soil-based) soil and some in loamless (peat-moss-based) mixes, which of these is used is generally determined by what the gardener feels happier with. Nearly all plants adapt quite well to either.

Different brands of potting mix have different formulations, however slightly they may vary, and it will be a matter of trial and error to find one that suits you and your plants.

The medium for seeds and cuttings contains only small amounts of nutrients and is suitable mainly for propagation. Potting mix contains more fertilizer and is suitable for growing plants.

LOAM-BASED POTTING MIX
This type of potting mix was originally based on turf with specified quantities of added fertilizer. It looks, feels, and handles like good garden soil. Plants should be firmed moderately when potting, but care is needed not to damage roots by over-firming.

ADVANTAGES
Provides a long-lasting nutrient supply. ● Creates a stable base for large plants and pots. ● Available in different strengths for different types and sizes of plant.

DISADVANTAGES
Heavy to transport, both in pots and in the bag. ● Messier to use than loamless potting mix. ● Quality is variable, since it depends on the quality of loam used by the supplier.

LOAMLESS POTTING MIX
These mixes were formerly based on only peat-moss, but with the growing controversy over the ecological damage said to be caused by harvesting peat moss, several substitutes are now available. These include coir, made from coconut husks. It is still too early to assess how successful these substitutes may prove to be. Meanwhile, peat-moss-based potting mix is still widely available and very popular. Plants need to be firmed-in only lightly when they are potted in loamless mix.

ADVANTAGES
Lightweight. ● Clean to handle. ● Standard quality, with only fairly minor differences between brands.

DISADVANTAGES
Soon runs out of nutrients, so supplementary feeding is necessary from an early stage. ● Large plants can become top-heavy and topple over. ● Can be difficult to rewet if allowed to dry out.

SPECIAL MEDIUMS
Some plants do best in a more specialized medium. The most commonly found is orchid medium, which is suitable for epiphytic plants such as orchids and some bromeliads. This is an open, free-draining mixture usually consisting of pieces of bark, osmunda fiber, sphagnum moss, and polystyrene plastic chips.

Ericaceous mixes, which are suitable for lime-hating plants such as ericas and azaleas, are acidic and contain no free lime.

It is also possible to buy cactus mediums, which are particularly free-draining.

Loamless, or peat-moss-based, potting mix consists of peat moss or peat moss substitutes such as coir with added nutrients.

Loam-based, or soil-based, potting mix has a base of superphosphate, hoof and horn meal, and sulfate of potash in a ratio of 2:2:1, added to varying amounts of loam, peat moss, and sand.

Cactus medium consists of two-thirds of any general commercial potting mix and one-third of grit or coarse sand by volume.

Orchid medium consists of sphagnum moss, bark chips or osmunda fiber, and coarse peat moss in a ratio of 2:2:1 by volume.

ℛEPOTTING (continued)

POTTING ON

Plants are usually bought or obtained at an immature stage of growth because they are less expensive and easier to transport and market while they are relatively small. As they develop in the home, most will need moving on into progressively larger pots, a process known as repotting, or potting on.

While it might seem sensible to pot the plant immediately into the largest size pot it is likely to need and skip the intervening stages, this does not lead to healthy growth. Plants should generally be moved into a pot just one size larger than the one they are in (quick-growing species can be moved into pots two sizes larger). This means that the fresh soil around the existing rootball will soon be penetrated by new roots. If there is a large expanse of potting mix that does not contain roots, it is likely to become waterlogged and stale.

Plants that resent root disturbance or are in pots of the biggest practical size should be topdressed, not repotted.

GETTING THE TIMING RIGHT

With experience it becomes quite easy to tell when a plant needs repotting. The most obvious sign is when roots cover the surface of the soil or emerge from the drainage holes in the base of the pot. When the latter is very evident, turn the plant out of its pot to check the state of the rootball.

If the rootball holds together and the soil appears full of roots, the plant is ready for repotting, but if the soil falls away, place the plant carefully back in the same container, lightly firm the soil around it, and leave the plant for a little while longer.

The best time for repotting is at the beginning of the period of active growth, which is generally spring, although plants that bloom in winter will need to be repotted in early fall, after their dormant period.

TWO WAYS TO REPOT A PLANT

1 Put a layer of pebbles or broken china in the bottom of a clean pot one size larger than the old one. Cover it with potting mix and set the plant in the pot.

2 Fill the gap between the plant and the side of the pot with mix. Dribble it in carefully by hand to avoid damaging the plant and press it down quite firmly.

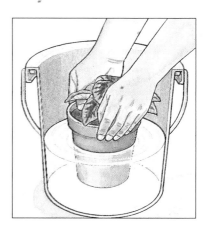

3 Finally, water the plant thoroughly, using a sprinkler head on the watering can, or plunge the pot into a bucket of water to soak the mix. Then drain the pot.

4 Alternatively, use the old pot as a mold. Add drainage layer as instructed in Step 1. Set the plant in the pot and check that it will sit at the same level in the new pot.

5 Remove the plant. Put the old pot inside the new one and make a mold in which to set the plant by filling the space between the two pots with potting mix.

6 Insert the plant and fill any gaps with mix, firming it down to make sure that the plant is well supported. Water the plant as described in Step 3 above.

REPOTTING A PLANT IN THE SAME SIZE POT

1 **Repot plants** that prefer to be slightly pot-bound in the same size pot. Crumble away some of the old mix and, if necessary, cut off part of the rootball.

2 **Put layers of pebbles and mix** on the bottom of the pot and set the plant in it. Fill in around the edges of the rootball with new mix. Water thoroughly.

TOP DRESSING

1 **With an old dinner fork** or similar instrument, gently scrape away the top 2–3in/5–8cm of mix, taking care not to damage the roots.

2 **Fill the pot** to the old level with the right type of new potting mix, to which slow-release fertilizer has been added. Firm the mix down and water the plant.

MAKING A BROMELIAD TREE

Epiphytic plants, such as some bromeliads, which have few or no roots, will grow readily on a tree branch as they do in nature, provided they are kept thoroughly moist. Choose a forked branch with attractive bark.

PREPARING A PLANT FOR A BROMELIAD TREE

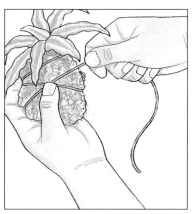

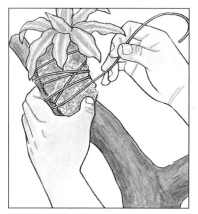

1 **Turn an epiphyte out of its pot** and wrap a mixture of potting mix and sphagnum moss around the rootball, attaching it with fine plastic-coated wire.

2 **Put the plant in a tree fork** or remove a piece of bark to provide a niche for it. Wire the plant to the branch and mist the moss frequently until the roots have taken hold.

TRAINING

A NUMBER OF HOUSEPLANTS WITH lax stems or with very large, heavy flowers benefit from the unobtrusive support of slender stakes. But the climbing and scrambling plants need serious attention paid to their training. A well-trained plant is not only neater and easier to care for, it is usually more attractive, since it permits you to show off its flowers or foliage to advantage.

Some plants are true climbers with clinging tendrils, and they will rapidly attach themselves to a support. Many others are scramblers in their natural habitat, making their way over and through the mass of vegetation that surrounds them and using it to hold themselves up. In the home, they need to be encouraged to use a support and to be tied into it at intervals. (See p. 27 for more detail on supports.)

Climbing plants all produce long, lax stems. They may also have tendrils that arise either from the stems or from the tips of the leaves and that coil tightly around any object they come into contact with. Or they may have aerial roots, which need a damp surface to which they can attach themselves.

TENDRILS
Plants with tendrils, such as *Cissus antarctica* and *Gloriosa superba*, do not need much help to climb. A simple trellis will provide ample support. And the only training necessary will be to keep the shoots within the bounds of the support by pinching, and occasionally to thread in the tips of the shoots so that all parts of the trellis are evenly covered.

AERIAL ROOTS
Aerial roots can be a problem. Plants such as monsteras and philodendrons, which produce thick, fleshy roots, prefer a moss pole—a sturdy stake covered with moss that is kept constantly moist—into which the roots can be trained. The lower roots on these plants can be trained down into the soil.

Roots of this type can be brittle, and they need careful handling. Use pieces of fine wire bent into a hairpin shape and then pushed through the moss, to hold them in the right position.

The aerial roots will not support the upper stems of the plant, which are generally wound loosely around the pole and kept loosely but securely in place with similar loops of bent wire.

Ivy, *Hedera*, produces a quite different type of aerial root: small pads of fringe-like roots are formed at intervals along the stems. These are very effective at supporting the plant on brick walls or tree trunks, but they cling extremely tightly and are not usually welcome in the home because they can damage walls, furniture, and fixtures. Ivies are, therefore, usually treated as plants that need to be given a means of support.

SCRAMBLERS AND TRAILERS
These plants, which include hoyas, jasmines, passion flowers, and stephanotises, do not have the means of attaching themselves to a support. They can be grown up trelliswork and tied in at intervals with soft twine in a figure-eight loop, but they are often trained around hoops made from wire or cane.

The hoop is inserted firmly into the mix (see p. 27), and the stems are simply

PINNING DOWN AERIAL ROOTS

1 To pin the aerial roots of large plants such as *Monstera deliciosa* into a moss pole, first make sure that the moss is thoroughly moist by spraying it with water. Then secure the roots with hoops of fine wire.

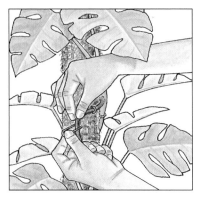

2 Wind the long, heavy stems around the moss pole, tying them in at intervals, or pin them to the pole with wire hoops in the same way as the roots. Always keep the moss on the pole damp.

COILING SHOOTS AROUND A SUPPORT

1 To train an ivy plant around a hoop, first push the "legs" of the support firmly into the mix over the top of the plant. Then twist the stems around the hoop or use soft twine to tie them firmly in place.

2 As the plant grows, gently weave the new stems around the hoop. When a stem reaches the end of the hoop, turn it back on itself. That way, the plant will form an attractive bushy shape.

twisted gently around the wire while they are still young and supple. They may need tying into place at first, but as a framework of stems builds up, they will stay in position more easily. When the tip of the stem reaches the surface of the potting mix on the other side of the hoop, it can be turned back gently.

PINCHING AND PRUNING

Most houseplants do not need regular pruning, but many require some form of pinching back or stopping to keep them shapely. Removing the growing tip from a stem stimulates several buds in the leaf axils below it into growth. In this way,

not only is the stem kept short, but it branches outward as well. The process is known as stopping or pinching off, and results in bushy, compact plants that are generally more desirable in the home. Such plants will have a more pleasing shape, and they will often bear more flowers than plants that have not been stopped.

Because it is generally the soft tips of stems that are removed, this job is normally easily carried out with finger and thumb. But if the stems are too tough for this to be done cleanly, use a very sharp knife or a single-edged razor blade. Pinch the stem just above the first

or second node, the point at which the leaves join the stem.

For some plants, regular pinching is required all through the growing season; others are stopped once or twice at the beginning of the season only. Care must be taken with plants that carry their flowers at the ends of the stems, since too-frequent pinching out could prevent flowering altogether.

Plants that are more drastically pruned back at the end of the season or after flowering should also be cut just above a node where possible; use sharp shears. Details of pruning and pinching, where applicable, are given for individual plants in The Plant Directory.

DEADHEADING

It is nearly always recommended to remove dead flowers, a process known as deadheading. Dead and fading flowers look unattractive, and they can encourage attack by the fungus disease botrytis. If flowers are allowed to set seed, the plant's energy is wasted. And setting seed signals to the plant that the flowering season is over, preventing further flushes of bloom that might otherwise have occurred. Once again, try to remove stems just above a node.

PINCHING OFF GROWING TIPS

1 Many plants produce trailing stems that can become lank and unattractive, with long gaps between the leaves. Shorten such stems by pinching off the growing tips with your finger and thumb.

2 Pinching off the tips of soft stems encourages the plant to put out new growth, and the new leaves will grow closer together. It is also a good way to keep a plant looking shapely.

Deadheading flowering plants like chrysanthemums regularly will enable plants to produce more blooms and continue to flower for far longer. Pick off any dead or fading flowers with your finger and thumb.

PRUNING TO ENCOURAGE BUSHINESS

1 Cut back woody plants and fast-growing plants that have become too large for the space at the end of the growing season. Stems can usually be reduced by up to two-thirds without damaging the plant.

2 Pruning plants in this way reinvigorates them and encourages them to put out plenty of strong new growth. To keep the plant's bushy shape, pinch off the growing tips as described above.

Obviously, flowers should not be removed from plants that are grown for their fruits, such as capsicums and solanums, and care should be taken with hoyas, since the following season's flowers will arise from the same spurs.

PROPAGATION METHODS

MOST HOUSEPLANTS ARE BOUGHT as young or established plants from garden centers and nurseries. Even so, it is advisable to have a supply of young plants ready to replace the originals once they are past their prime. You may also wish to have several specimens of a particular plant around the house, or to have spare plants to give to friends. If this is so, you needn't buy more plants—it is quite easy to increase your stock of many specimens by a variety of means.

No specialized equipment is needed for propagating the easier species, although a seed tray with a clear plastic lid is cheap to buy and always worth having. A propagator with bottom heat will certainly help you to increase your stock of some of the more difficult subjects.

CUTTINGS

Probably the method most often used to increase houseplants is to take cuttings. A cutting is taken from the parent plant and encouraged to make its own roots (or sometimes shoots). Two types are used to propagate houseplants: stem cuttings and leaf cuttings.

Stem cuttings.
These are generally taken in spring or early summer. Snap a healthy young shoot, preferably without flower buds, from the parent plant. If it will not snap cleanly, use a sharp knife and cut just above a node.

The length of the cutting will vary, but it should have at least three or four pairs of leaves or leaf nodes (joints) between the tip and the base.

Use a sharp knife to trim the base of the cutting to just below a node and remove the bottom leaves to give a clear portion of stem. Rooting powder is recommended for some species, athough most do just as well without it. If it is used, a light dusting of powder on the base of the stem is all that is needed.

Fill a shallow pot or seed tray with moist rooting medium and press it until it is firm. Scatter a thin layer of sharp sand on top. With a pencil or dibble, make holes in the medium for the cuttings, and insert them into it, making sure the base of the cutting is in good contact with the medium. Firm the medium lightly.

Space the cuttings so their leaves do not touch and water the completed tray or pot, using a sprinkler head on the can. Put a plastic cover over the tray and place it in a warm (68°F/20°C), bright location out of direct sun.

The time the cuttings take to root will vary, but eventually they will start to look fresh and to grow from the center. They can then be potted up individually.

Leaf cuttings
Some fleshy-leafed plants can be propagated from their leaves. The new plants are produced from either the plant's leafstalks or from the veins.

Saintpaulias, the African violets, for instance, are generally increased from leaf stem cuttings. With a sharp knife or razor blade, cut off a fully opened, healthy leaf at the base of the leafstalk. Trim the stalk to 1–1½in/2.5–4cm long, dip the base in hormone rooting powder, and insert it, at an angle, into moist rooting medium close to the edge of a small pot; bury about two-thirds of the stalk. Firm the medium gently and then place the pot in a warm location in light shade. Keep the medium just moist, and plantlets will appear within about eight weeks. Once they have grown into strong young plants that can be handled easily, remove them from the pot, tease the plants apart carefully, and pot them individually. Saintpaulias will also root quite easily in water.

Some plants—streptocarpuses and begonias, for example—can be propagated by leaf vein cuttings, which are taken in one of two ways.

Remove a healthy, fully formed leaf cleanly from the parent plant. Cut the leaf horizontally into three or four sections, or split it lengthwise straight up

TAKING SOFT STEM CUTTINGS

1 **Plants with soft stems,** such as pelargoniums, can be rooted from the tip of a healthy stem. Cut a stem with 3 or 4 leaf nodes between the tip and the base.

2 **Remove the lower leaves** from the stem and with a sharp knife trim it cleanly to just above a leaf node.

3 **Dip the end of the cutting** into hormone rooting powder and shake off any excess. (It is not essential to use rooting powder.)

4 **Fill a small pot** with rooting medium and make a hole in it with a pencil or dibble. Insert the cutting and gently firm the medium around it.

TAKING LEAF STEM CUTTINGS

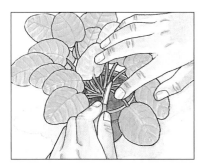

1 Choose a strong, healthy leaf, and with a sharp knife, cut it away from the plant at the base of the stalk. Trim the stalk to about 1½in/4cm long.

2 Holding the leaf gently between your fingers, dip the cut end into hormone rooting powder. Several cuttings can be taken at one time.

3 Insert the leafstalks into rooting medium near the rim of the pot. If you push the stems in at an angle of 45°, they will have underground support.

TAKING CUTTINGS FROM LEAF SEGMENTS

1 Plants like streptocarpuses can be rooted from small pieces of the leaf. To take a cutting from a leaf, first cut off a good healthy mature leaf at the base.

2 Cut the whole leaf horizontally into strips about 1in/2.5cm wide. Dip the base of each cutting (the end nearest the stalk) in hormone rooting powder.

3 Insert the base of the pieces of leaf into a tray of rooting medium, and gently firm the medium around the cuttings with your fingers.

the center of the midrib. Use a razor blade or sharp knife to make the cuts. If you cut the leaf into horizontal sections, make sure you know which is the top and which the base (the part nearest the leaf-stalk) of each section.

Dust the bases or the split midribs with rooting powder and insert them to about one-third of their depth in moist rooting medium in a pot or seed tray. Plantlets will be produced in the same way as with leaf stem cuttings.

OFFSETS

Several plants naturally produce small plantlets around the outer edge, which can be carefully removed and potted. This is an easy way to propagate succulents such as echeverias, bromeliads, some cacti, and bulbous plants.

Wait until the offsets are a reasonable size and can be handled easily; remove the plant from its pot, then carefully separate the offsets from the parent plant; you may need to use a sharp knife to cut through the rootstock. Keep as many roots on the offset as possible. If there are none, keep the newly potted offset in a warm, humid atmosphere and treat it like a cutting. Roots should form within a few weeks. (*Continued on p. 208.*)

PROPAGATING BY OFFSETS

1 Many plants produce offsets around the base. Remove the plant from its pot and detach a good-sized offset, preferably with roots, from the parent.

2 Pot up the offset in rooting medium to the same depth as it was on the parent. When the root system is established, treat it as a mature plant.

DIVISION

Plants such as saintpaulias, sansevierias, many ferns, spathiphyllums, calatheas, and several others are suitable for division. This is usually done when the plant has outgrown its pot.

Take the plant out of its pot and carefully crumble away the soil until you can see the best way to split the plant. Every portion should have a healthy growing point and plenty of roots. Tease the sections apart carefully with as little damage to the root system as possible. Pot the portions individually in moist potting mix and keep the pots just moist and out of direct sun until the plants have become established.

LAYERING

The technique whereby a new plant is induced to form roots while still attached to the parent is known as layering. One of the most common examples is chlorophytums, which produce young plantlets on long stems in great abundance. When the base of a plantlet comes into contact with the soil, it will rapidly produce roots and can soon be separated from the parent. A piece of wire bent into a hairpin shape is useful for pinning the plantlet down to keep it in close contact with the soil while roots form.

Many climbing and trailing plants, such as the ivies, increase naturally by layering, and as indoor plants they can be layered simply by pinning a section of stem firmly into a pot of soil. If the stem is woody, first scrape off a little bark from the underside with a sharp knife; roots will form at this point.

PROPAGATING BY DIVISION

1 Take the plant out of its pot, crumble or wash away some of the soil, and lever or cut the sections apart. Be sure that each part has plenty of roots and a growing tip.

2 Pot up the divisions to the same level as they were in moist soil in a pot a little larger than the rootball. Water sparingly until new growth can be seen.

Air layering is slightly different. Here the stems cannot be brought down to soil level, so the soil is brought up to them. Plants that have stiff, woody stems or that have grown too tall and leggy are often treated in this way; *Ficus elastica* is a common candidate.

A ring of bark is carefully removed from the stem just below the lowest leaf. Alternatively, a sloping cut is made about one-third of the way through the stem. It is dusted with hormone rooting powder and wedged open with a matchstick or wad of sphagnum moss.

Moist sphagnum moss is then packed around the wounded area, and a piece of plasic is wrapped firmly around it and taped top and bottom. (Peat-moss-based potting mix can be used instead of the moss, but it is not so easy to handle.)

Care for the plant being layered in the normal way while roots slowly form

within the moss: if clear plastic is used, they can be seen developing. Once they are well grown, cut off the rooted portion with a sharp knife or shears and pot it. Cut back the stump of the original plant and water it sparingly until new growth has appeared.

SEEDS

Only a relatively small number of houseplants are raised from seed, but cyclamens, cinerarias, capsicums, primulas, coleuses, fuchsias, and many cacti, among others, are not difficult to grow this way. A heated propagator and a greenhouse will make it easier to raise some species, but others will germinate quite easily in a dark warm place.

Seeds can be obtained from most major seed merchants, as well as a number of smaller, specialist companies. If you save seeds from your own plants,

PROPAGATING BY LAYERING

1 Some plants, such as ivy, are easy to layer. Lightly scrape the underside of the stem to be buried, or make a nick in it, to check the flow of sap and stimulate rooting.

2 Fill a small pot with potting mix and anchor the stem firmly to the soil by pegging it down with small hoops of fine wire; otherwise, cover the stem with soil.

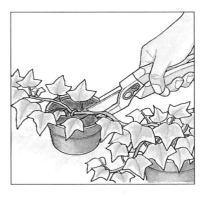

3 Cut the layered plant away from the parent when new growth is evident. Be careful to preserve the shape of the original plant.

remember that the chances are they will not produce plants of the same variety as the parent. Many seeds from seed merchants are also potluck mixtures that produce unpredictable colors and forms.

Fill a shallow pan or seed tray with rooting medium and firm it with a small flat piece of wood. Water the medium with a fine sprinkler head on the can or a sprayer and let it drain.

Sow the seeds thinly and evenly on the surface of the medium; very small seeds can be mixed with fine sand as a carrier to aid even sowing. Cover the seeds to their own depth with potting mix (such as a mixture of sharp sand and peat-moss); take care not to bury them too deeply. Some fine seeds, such as those of orchids, are best left uncovered.

Place a clear plastic propagator cover on the tray (a plastic bag supported by thin stakes can be used instead) and leave it in a warm place at a temperature between 68°F and 80°F/20°C and 27°C,

depending on the species. Bring the tray into diffuse light when most of the seedlings are visible. Keep the plastic cover on the tray for the time being, but open the vents to allow fresh air to circulate around the plants. Once the plants are growing strongly, remove the cover. Keep the soil just moist.

When the seedlings can be handled easily, prick them out into another container to give them extra space. Handle them by the seed leaves (the first pair of leaves they produce), never by the stems. Keep them in good, bright but diffuse light. As the young plants develop, prick them out into other trays and finally into individual pots.

Fern spores

Ferns produce spores instead of seeds, and they are challenging plants to raise. Spores are sown on the surface of the soil in a way similar to seeds, but the potting mix is kept more thoroughly moist. Cover the tray or pan with a propagator

top and keep it in a warm, light location. After several weeks, a green mossy growth will gradually cover the soil surface; this contains the plant's male and female organs, and fertilization takes place at this stage. Eventually tiny ferns will develop and can be potted up, first in groups, then separately as they develop. Be prepared to be patient, since the whole process is very slow.

LEAF EMBRYOS

A small number of plants produce tiny, complete plantlets on their leaves and are very easy to propagate. Some, such as *Kalanchoe daigremontiana*, can be a real nuisance, since large numbers of plantlets can take root among other plants, wherever they happen to fall. *Tolmiea menziesii* and *Asplenium bulbiferum* also produce plantlets on their leaves. All that is necessary for propagation is to make sure that the base of the plantlet comes into contact with moist soil.

PROPAGATING BY SOWING SEEDS

1 Put a thin layer of gravel on the bottom of a seed tray to provide good drainage and cover it with rooting medium. Press it down gently to firm it.

2 Scatter larger seeds thinly on the surface of the rooting medium. If you mix small seeds with sand, they will be much easier to handle.

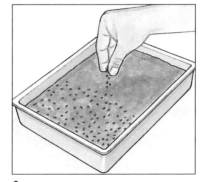

3 Cover the seeds with a thin layer of rooting medium and spray it with water until it is thoroughly moist. Remember that some seeds should not be covered.

4 Put a specially made plastic top on the seed tray, or cover it with glass or a plastic tent. This will create a humid atmosphere and induce the seeds to germinate.

5 Thin out the seedlings so that the space between them is about the same as their height. When they are well grown, prick them out into another tray.

6 When the seedlings have at least two true leaves in addition to the first pair of seed leaves, lift them carefully from the tray and transfer them to individual pots.

SPECIALIST GROWING METHODS

HYDROPONICS

Plants do not need soil or another potting mix in order to grow, they require merely a source of nutrients and water. Houseplants can be grown by a method of soilless culture known as hydroponics, or hydroculture. Its advantages are that it is clean and convenient and takes away the worry of over- or underwatering (both common causes of houseplant death).

The simplest method of hydroculture is a bulb glass containing a fertilizer solution; this is suitable for such bulbs as hyacinths. In a single container (right), the plant roots are anchored in aggregate, some of which is covered by water. In a double container (center), the roots grow through a small pot filled with aggregate into the fertilizer solution in the large outer pot.

A gauge is often used to indicate the depth of the fertilizer solution. It is inserted into the pot, and as the cross-section on the right shows, a marker moved by a float drops as the level falls.

The substrate used to support the plant's roots can be pebbles, glass beads, vermiculite, or several other substances, although the most common is light-weight expanded clay aggregate (Leca). This is a byproduct of the building trades and consists of extremely light, porous, round granules. Hydroculture plants are usually grown in mesh pots full of Leca, which are set in an outer container filled with nutrient solution. Water and fertilizer are added through a tube that contains a gauge to show exactly how much water is needed.

While ready-potted hydroculture plants can be bought, plants can be converted to

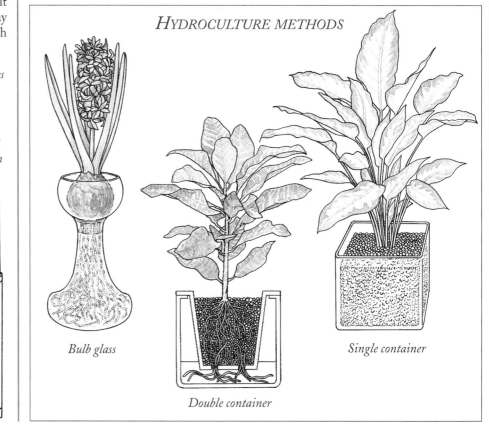

HYDROCULTURE METHODS

Bulb glass

Double container

Single container

TRANSFERRING A PLANT FROM POTTING MIX TO HYDROCULTURE

1 Remove the plant from its pot carefully so that the rootball does not suffer any damage. Soak the plant in a bucket of water for half an hour.

2 Hold the plant firmly in one hand and gently tease apart the rootball. Remove as much of the potting mix as you can without harming the roots.

3 Wash the roots under tepid running water to get them clean. Put the plant into a pot of aggregate and give it warmth and high humidity while roots adapted to hydroculture form.

the method in the home. The best way is to take cuttings and root them in water, but healthy young plants growing in potting mix can often be successfully transferred to the hydroculture system.

Remove the plant from its pot and place the rootball in a bucket of water to soak for half an hour, then gently wash the soil off the roots under a tap. Pot the plant in soaked Leca granules (or similar material) in much the same way as if it were being repotted conventionally. A plastic cover or inflated plastic bag placed over the top of the plant will help to keep the atmosphere humid and prevent the plant wilting while new roots form.

ARTIFICIAL LIGHT

Although a heated room may provide summertime warmth in midwinter, plants will not grow as well as they do in summer because of the difference in light levels. Not only are the days shorter, but the intensity of the light is less. Even in midsummer, the light intensity in a room is a small fraction of that outside: on overcast winter days, it is hardly surprising that many plants indoors merely hang on and barely exist.

Artificial lighting can supplement natural daylight or replace it altogether, keeping plants growing and sometimes flowering throughout the winter months. Special lamps, such as high-pressure mercury-vapor lamps, can be used to stimulate plant growth. These lamps provide the correct wavelengths of light (the blue and red parts of the spectrum are most important for photosynthesis). However, ordinary fluorescent tubes, including the compact types, are quite satisfactory for most indoor plants. The normal incandescent light bulb is not suitable, since it gives off too much heat in relation to the intensity of light.

The source of light must be quite close to the plants; generally a maximum of 2ft/60cm above the top of the foliage. Some flowering plants, such as saint-paulias, should be as close as 9in/23cm for the best results. If the lamp cannot easily be moved (an adjustable light fixture is particularly useful), the plants themselves can be raised and lowered.

Artificial lighting is generally used for between 8 and 12 hours a day, but flowering plants may need up to 18 hours for the initiation of buds and for their development.

The fluorescent lights, commonly found in the kitchen, will keep plants in good condition, and even in flower, during the short days of winter. Fluorescent tubes provide a high level of light without the heat that is generated by ordinary incandescent lightbulbs.

DAY LENGTH AND FLOWERING

For some plants the time of flowering is controlled by day length: this response is known as photoperiodism. While many plants flower when days are long, for some the signal to initiate their buds is the shortening of day length: kalanchoes, poinsettias, and chrysanthemums are common examples. Each species has its own critical day length, and these have been used by commercial growers to manipulate flowering times to suit specific markets.

As far as the indoor gardener is concerned, the importance of this response is that plants may fail to flower if subjected to artificial light in fall and winter. For although ordinary lightbulbs may not provide enough light to promote plant growth, it can easily be enough to interfere with bud initiation. Exposure to sodium street lighting can have the same effect on plants.

So-called short-day plants, such as *Euphorbia pulcherrima*, poinsettia, can be brought into flower as required by blacking them out for certain periods each day, but this is difficult to carry out satisfactorily in the home. A better method is to keep the plants in a room that is not used at night—perhaps a spare bedroom—so that they receive only natural daylight. Remember that accidentally switching on the light for even a short period can break the cycle and delay or prevent flowering.

REST PERIODS

In their natural environment, most indoor plants from tropical regions will continue to grow vigorously all year. Others, from temperate zones, will have a marked seasonal response. Growth stops in late fall, the plant becomes more or less dormant during the winter, and then starts into growth again in spring.

Most homes are heated to a comfortable level throughout the year so that there is little, if any, seasonal temperature change for the plants. The amount and intensity of light does, however, change in winter, as we have seen. This presents the plant with a confusing set of conditions, since the warmth stimulates growth, which then becomes leggy and drawn because of poor light.

When days shorten, it is a good idea to give many plants a rest period. Move them into a room with cooler conditions if necessary, stop feeding them, and cut down on the watering. Growth will slow down or stop, and the plants will become dormant or continue to plug along slowly until spring. The Plant Directory gives more detail on the winter requirements of individual plants.

The rest period does not always coincide with winter. Some winter-flowering plants, such as cyclamens and spring-flowering bulbs like narcissus and crocus, have their rest period during the late spring and early summer or even through to fall.

PESTS AND DISEASES

HOUSEPLANTS ARE SUBJECT TO attack by a surprisingly large number of pests and diseases, not quite as many as outdoor plants perhaps, but more than enough for most plant owners. Constant vigilance is the answer.

PREVENTING PROBLEMS
Most pests and diseases arrive with new plants, so always inspect any potential purchase (or gift) thoroughly before putting it with your existing houseplants. When buying plants, reject those with obvious signs of disease or infestation, and quarantine new plants for a week or two, keeping them apart from your other plants until you are sure that they are free from pests or diseases.

The correct cultivation techniques will keep your plants strong and robust. It will not make them immune to attack, but it will increase their ability to cope with it. Inspect all your plants regularly and deal promptly with any pest or outbreak of disease. They are much easier to control at an early stage, and you may prevent the problem from spreading.

PEST AND DISEASE CONTROL
While garden centers have an impressive array of pesticides, it is not always necessary to use them. Indeed, there are several ways of dealing with problems.

Physical
A localized outbreak can often be literally nipped in the bud by removing and destroying the affected part of the plant. Pinch off a shoot tip infested by aphids or pick off a single caterpillar on a leaf, and that may be the end of the problem.

Pinch off the affected part of the plant.

Cultural
Several pests and diseases are encouraged by specific conditions. Red spider mites, for instance, thrive in hot, dry air; lowering the temperature and misting the plant regularly with plain water will help to prevent attacks.

Basal rot on succulent plants is usually a sign of overwatering, and gray mold (botrytis) is prevalent in excessively cool, damp conditions.

Biological
The use of natural parasites and predators to control pest species is more feasible in the controlled atmosphere of a greenhouse than in the home. Whiteflies, red spider mites, mealybugs, and aphids all have natural enemies, which can be obtained from specialist suppliers. If an affected plant can be moved to a greenhouse for treatment, it will have a better chance for success.

Chemical
Modern pesticides are usually effective, and when used correctly, they are harmless to plants, pets, and people. However, they often contain potentially damaging substances, so take care when using them.
- Choose the right product for the problem.
- Read the label and follow the instructions.
- Use the correct dose.
- Spray outside, if possible, in a sheltered position.
- Spray plants inside a large plastic bag when using aerosol sprays, and leave them for 20 minutes.
- Remove pets (especially fish) from the room where treatment is taking place.
- Keep pesticides away from children and animals.

Alternative remedies
Various home remedies, using homemade brews or household products such as dishwashing liquid are often recommended for the control of pests and diseases on plants.

Sometimes considered preferable to commercial insecticides, they may be ineffective. In some countries their use is discouraged because they have not been officially tested for safety or efficacy.

HOUSEPLANT PESTS

APHIDS

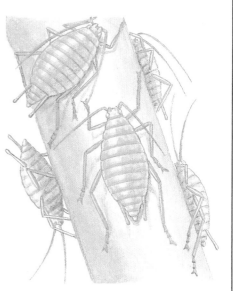

There are in fact many different species of aphids, some are known as greenflies, but all are treated in the same way. Females give birth to live female young, which can mature within one week. Since they reproduce without the need for fertilization by a male, colonies increase at an amazingly rapid rate.

Aphids feed by sucking sap from the plant, weakening it and sometimes spreading virus diseases. They excrete a sticky honeydew which is a nuisance when it drops on furniture. In severe attacks, it also encourages the growth of powdery black sooty mold on the leaves of the plant.

Infestations are usually concentrated on soft young growing shoots and around flower buds, and aphids may be present in such numbers that they cause distorted growth. They cast off their skins as they grow, and the presence of the white shed skins is sometimes more noticeable than the creatures themselves.

Nonchemical control
Caught at an early stage, colonies can be removed by pinching off affected shoots or gently washing off the aphids with tepid water. Alternatively use Safer's soap or oil sprays.

Suitable insecticides
Use selective insecticides such as pyrethrum or pyrethrins which have a short residual life.

CATERPILLARS

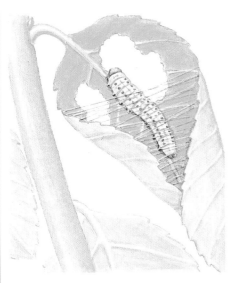

Caterpillars are the larval stage of various insects, and they have voracious appetites. One of the more common caterpillars found on houseplants is that of the variegated cut worm that feeds on plants such as carnations. While they feed, these small, yellow-green grubs climb the plants, chewing the young buds and leaves.

The caterpillar of the carnation tortrix moth, shown above, is a small grub that forms a web at the tips of shoots, pulling the edges of the leaves together.

Nonchemical control
Pick off individual caterpillars or any infested shoots.

Suitable insecticides
Apply diazinon to the soil prior to planting or spray with serin.

CYCLAMEN MITES

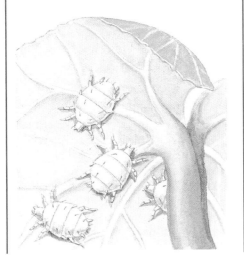

Also called strawberry mites, cyclamen mites belong to a group known as tarsonemid mites. They can attack a wide range of indoor plants besides cyclamens, as well as some outdoor plants.

The mites, which usually congregate in buds and at the tips of shoots, are too tiny to be seen with the naked eye. But if affected plants are studied with a magnifying glass, mites and their eggs can sometimes be seen as a dustlike layer. They feed on plant tissue, causing distorted, puckered growth, often with light brown scabs. The plant's development is generally stunted, shoots and flower buds may wither and die, and flowers that do open are discolored.

In the warm conditions of homes and greenhouses, the mites breed extremely rapidly, and populations continue to increase during the winter. Insecticides have relatively little effect on them, and infested plants are best destroyed as soon as the mites or their eggs are seen. This will help to prevent the spread of the mites to neighboring plants.

LEAF MINERS

These larvae eat their way between the two outer layers of a leaf, leaving a characteristic, winding, silvery-beige trail. Chrysanthemums and cinerarias are the most commonly affected houseplants. Affected leaves are unsightly, but the plant seldom suffers greatly from an attack. Since these are both short-term,

disposable plants, it is not generally necessary to take any action.

Nonchemical control
Remove and destroy all affected leaves.

Suitable insecticides
Neem oil or other horticultural oils such as sunspray oil.

MEALYBUGS

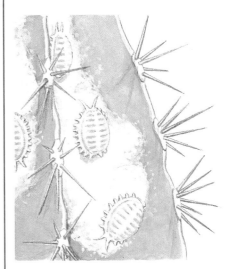

These sap-sucking pests are rather like wood lice in appearance, but they have a white, waxy, fluffy-looking coating that helps to protect them from insecticidal sprays. They can move around the plant but tend to remain immobile, and are often found clustered in the leaf axils. Cacti are particularly prone to attack by mealybugs.

Root mealybugs present a greater problem, since they are not normally visible, although they may be suspected where a plant fails to grow properly. White wooly masses can be found among the roots when a plant is turned out of its pot. Again, cacti and succulents are particularly at risk.

Nonchemical control
These pests can be removed by lifting them off with a moist cotton swab. Or spray plants with a mixture of equal parts of rubbing alcohol and water. If the plant is infested with root mealybugs, wash the soil and pests from the roots and cut away damaged parts before the plant is repotted into fresh potting mix.

Suitable insecticides
It is usually necessary to use systemic insecticides such as dimethoate to overcome the water-repellent effect of the pests' waxy coating.

RED SPIDER MITES

Almost invisible to the naked eye, red spider mites form colonies, usually at the tips of shoots. Fine webbing may be seen on the undersides of leaves, and under a magnifying glass, the yellowish red mites can be observed scurrying back and forth within it.

These sap-sucking pests cause fine yellow speckling on the leaves, which take on a dried-up appearance and eventually fall. Red spider mites overwinter in woodwork and in other nooks and crannies away from the plants, so infestations may be troublesome from year to year, particularly in greenhouses. A hot, dry environment provides ideal conditions for them.

Nonchemical control
Remove infested shoots and increase the humidity around plants by frequent misting with plain water.
Suitable insecticides
Kelthane.

SCALE INSECTS

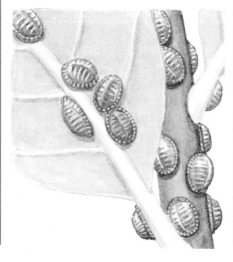

In infestations by these pests, smooth, brown, oval, limpetlike scales can be found attached to the undersides of leaves, usually along the midrib. Thick leathery leaves are most commonly attacked. There are several different stages in the life cycle of the scale, but this immobile, unlifelike stage is the most noticeable. Honeydew, produced as they feed, often attracts sooty mold.
Nonchemical control
Scrape off scales with a fingernail or wipe them off firmly with a damp cloth.
Suitable insecticides
Horticultural oil, insecticidal soap, or the more toxic malathion.

SCIARID FLIES

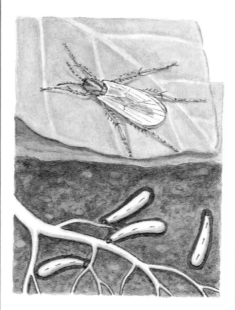

Also known as fungus gnats, these tiny, grayish black insects are a nuisance rather than a serious problem on indoor plants.

They live in the soil, and when the plant is disturbed or watered, can be seen flying up a short distance, sometimes in considerable numbers. The larvae feed on organic matter in the soil and may sometimes damage young roots.
Nonchemical control
Sciarid fly infestation is usually a sign of overwatering and sodden soil. Let the surface of the soil dry out between waterings.
Suitable insecticides
Drench the soil with malathion to rid the plant of this pest.

THRIPS

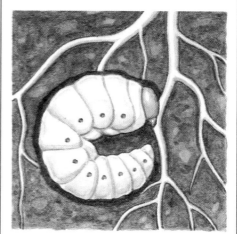

These small, long-bodied creatures with fringed wings, sometimes called thunderflies, are abundant in homes and outdoors in spells of hot weather. They feed on plant tissues and cause a characteristic silvering and mottling of stems, foliage, and flowers. They are usually present in large numbers and can often be seen hopping around the plant. A large number of houseplants may be affected.

Damage on plants is worst in hot, dry atmospheres.
Nonchemical control
Make sure that plants are being given adequate water and increase humidity.
Suitable insecticides
Thrips can be controlled by spraying with most contact insecticides.

VINE WEEVILS

The larvae of the vine beetle, these relatively large, creamy white grubs live in the soil and eat plant roots. Often the total collapse of the plant is the first sign that anything is amiss. The 1-in/2.5-cm-

long gray-black adult beetles are active at night and can sometimes be seen crawling over the soil surface or biting notches out of leaf margins.

Cyclamens are particularly prone to attack. By the time damage is noticed, it is usually too late to save the plant.

Nonchemical control

Pick off and destroy adults whenever they are seen. Destroy grubs found in the roots of plants to prevent the pests from spreading. Biological control is available in the form of a parasitic nematode, which can be used both as a preventive and a treatment.

Suitable insecticides

Drench the soil of plants at risk with gamma-HCH or mix a dust formulation of this chemical with soil when potting susceptible plants.

WHITEFLIES

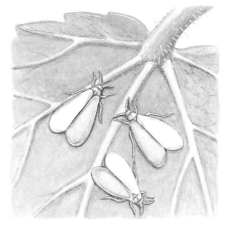

These small, white, mothlike creatures can occur in large numbers, rising up from affected plants in a cloud when they are disturbed. They suck sap, debilitating the plant, secreting honeydew, and attracting sooty mold. They are usually more of a problem in greenhouses than in the home.

Whiteflies have a complex life cycle in which only the adult stage is susceptible to insecticides. So spraying must be repeated regularly to catch each generation as it matures.

Nonchemical control

Yellow sticky cards can be hung near the plants to trap the adults as they fly.

Suitable insecticides

Use Enstar, insecticidal soap, and horticultural oils.

HOUSEPLANT DISEASES

BOTRYTIS

Usually known as gray mold, this fungus prevails in damp, cool conditions and is less common in the home than in greenhouses. It starts on dead tissue and may spread to the rest of the plant. Affected parts become covered in fluffy gray mold.

Nonchemical control

Remove dead and damaged parts of a plant promptly. Keep the atmosphere warmer and drier.

Suitable fungicides

Most are effective.

POWDERY MILDEW

This disease, in which powdery white patches form on foliage, is encouraged by hot, dry conditions.

Nonchemical control

Adjust the temperature and humidity.

Suitable fungicides

Use a sulfur-based spray, but not in air temperatures above 80°F/27°C.

RUST

Pelargoniums and chrysanthemums are often affected. Pale spots form on leaf surfaces, and brown concentric rings of spores appear on their undersides.

Nonchemical control

Pick off and burn affected leaves. Destroy heavily infected plants.

Suitable fungicides

Use a sulfur-based spray, but not in air temperatures above 80°F/27°C.

SOOTY MOLD

Although this fungal disorder is not a disease in itself, it develops on the honeydew excreted by various sap-sucking pests such as scale insects, whiteflies, and aphids. Leaves become coated in a thick, black deposit, which is unsightly and interferes with photosynthesis, checking plant growth.

Nonchemical control

Wipe the black deposit from foliage with a damp cloth.

Suitable insecticides

Control any pests with an appropriate insecticide to get rid of the mold.

*B*UYER'S GUIDE

PLANT	COMMON NAMES	FEATURES	SHAPE	WATERING	LIGHT	IDEAL INDOOR TEMPERATURE	SPECIAL POINTS
A							
Abutilon pictum 'Thompsonii'	Spotted flowering maple	Flowers and foliage	Upright/ bushy	Moderate; sparingly in winter	Bright: direct sun	60°–70°F/16°–21°C	Prune to shape in early spring
Acalypha hispida	Red-hot cat's-tail, chenille plant	Tassellike flowers	Upright	Plentiful; sparingly in winter	Bright, filtered	70°–75°F/21°–24°C	High humidity required
Acalypha wilkesiana	Copper leaf	Colored foliage	Upright	Plentiful; sparingly in winter	Bright, filtered	70°–75°F/21°–24°C	Bright light is essential for well-colored foliage
Achimenes hybrids	Cupid's bower, hot-water plant	Flowers	Bushy/ trailing	Plentiful in growth; keep dry when dormant	Bright	65°F/18°C	Dormant rhizomes are started into growth in spring
Acorus gramineus	Sweet flag	Foliage	Grassy	Plentiful	Medium; some direct sun	55°–65°F/13°–18°C	Never allow the potting mix to become dry
Adiantum raddianum	Delta maidenhair fern	Foliage	Arching	Moderate	Bright light or light shade; no direct sun	65°–70°F/18°–21°C	High humidity essential
Adromischus festivus (*A. cooperi*)	Adromischus	Foliage	Rosette-forming	Moderate; sparingly in winter	Bright; some direct sun	60°–70°F/16°–21°C	Pot in free-draining potting mix
Aechmea fasciata (*Billbergia rhodocyanea*)	Urn plant, silver vase plant	Flowers and foliage	Upright/ arching	Moderate; keep the central "vase" filled with water	Bright filtered light or direct sun	75°–80°F/24°–27°C	The rosette dies after flowering but is replaced by offsets
Aeonium arboreum 'Atropurpureum'	Purple tree aeonium	Foliage	Rosette-forming	Moderate; very sparingly in winter	Direct sun	65°–75°F/18°–24°C	Direct sun required for good foliage color. Individual rosettes die after flowering
Aeschynanthus lobbianus	Lipstick plant	Flowers	Trailing	Plentiful while flowering; moderate at other times	Bright light with a small amount of direct sun	60°–75°F/16°–24°C	High humidity required
Agapanthus africanus	African lily	Flowers	Upright	Moderate to plentiful, less in winter	Full sun	60°–70°F/16°–21°C	Best in a greenhouse
Agave americana	Century plant	Foliage	Rosette-forming	Sparing to moderate	Direct sun	60°–75°F/16°–24°C	Beware of the very sharply tipped leaves
Aglaonema 'Silver Queen'	Painted drop tongue, Chinese evergreen	Evergreen foliage	Bushy foliage	Moderate	Moderately bright; no direct sun	60°–75°F/16°–24°C	Plain green varieties are tolerant of subdued light
Albizia julibrissin	Silk tree	Foliage	Bushy	Moderate; sparingly in winter	Bright; some direct sun	55°–65°F/13°–18°C	Best discarded at the end of the season
Allamanda cathartica	Golden trumpet	Flowers	Scrambling	Moderate	Bright; some direct sun	70°–75°F/21°–24°C	Provide support for climbing stems
Alocasia sanderiana	Elephant's-ear	Foliage	Upright/ bushy	Moderate; sparingly in winter	Bright; no direct summer sun	70°F/21°C	High humidity required
Aloe barbadensis (*A. vera*)	Medicine aloe	Flowers and foliage	Rosette-forming	Moderate; sparingly in winter	Bright; some direct sun	65°–75°F/18°–24°C	Sap has been used for healing burns
Aloe variegata	Partridge-breast aloe	Flowers and foliage	Rosette-forming	Moderate; sparingly in winter	Bright, filtered	65°–75°F/18°–24°C	Tolerant of dry air
Amaryllis belladonna	Belladonna lily	Flowers	Upright	Plentiful in growing season; reduce as leaves fade and keep dry in rest period	Bright; direct sun except when in flower	60°–70°F/16°–21°C	Provide a short rest period in midsummer
Ananas bracteatus var. *tricolor*	Red pineapple	Foliage	Rosette-forming	Moderate; sparingly in winter	Direct sun	65°–75°F/18°–24°C	Leaves have sharply saw-toothed edges
Anthurium andreanum	Flamingo lily	Flowers	Bushy	Moderate; sparingly in winter	Medium to bright	60°–70°F/16°–21°C	High humidity essential

PLANT	COMMON NAMES	FEATURES	SHAPE	WATERING	LIGHT	IDEAL INDOOR TEMPERATURE	SPECIAL POINTS
Anthurium crystallinum	Crystal anthurium	Foliage	Upright	Plentiful while in growth; sparingly at other times	Moderate, filtered light or light shade	70°F/21°C	Very high humidity required
Anthurium scherzerianum	Flamingo flower	Flowers and foliage	Bushy	Plentiful while in growth; sparingly in winter	Moderate, filtered	70°F/21°C	Even temperatures required; keep free from drafts
Aphelandra squarrosa 'Louisae'	Zebra plant, saffron spike	Flowers and foliage	Bushy	Plentiful while in growth; sparingly at other times	Bright; no direct sun	65°–70°F/18°–21°C	Remove flower stems after flowering
Aporocactus flagelliformis	Rat-tail cactus	Flowers and foliage	Trailing	Plentiful while in growth; moderate to sparingly at other times	Direct sun	65°–70°F/18°–21°C; 45°–50°F/7°–10°C during rest period after flowering	Good drainage is essential
Araucaria heterophylla (*A. excelsa*)	Norfolk Island pine	Foliage	Treelike	Plentiful; moderate in winter	Moderate to bright	60°–75°F/16°–24°C	Hot dry air causes needles to fall
Ardisia crenata	Coral berry, marlberry, spiceberry	Berries, flowers, foliage	Upright/ bushy	Plentiful; moderate in winter	Bright; some direct sun	45°–60°F/7°–16°C	Berries will fall prematurely in hot, dry air
Aristolochia elegans (*A. littoralis*)	Calico flower, birthwort	Flowers and foliage	Climbing	Plentiful in growing season; sparingly in winter	Bright to moderate	55°–65°F/13°–18°C	Provide support for the climbing stems
Arundinaria viridistriata (*Pleioblastus auricoma*)	Bamboo	Foliage	Upright	Moderate; plentifully during growth	Bright or indirect	60°–75°F/16°–24°C	Needs humidity
Asclepias curassavica	Blood flower	Flowers	Upright	Plentiful in growing season; sparingly in winter	Full sun	55°–70°F/13°–21°C	Provide a cool, dry rest period in winter
Asparagus densiflorus 'Sprengeri'/ 'Myers'	Asparagus fern (both) Foxtail fern ('Myers')	Foliage	Spreading ('Sprengeri'); upright ('Myers')	Plentiful during active growth; moderate at other times	Bright; no direct sun	60°–70°F/16°–21°C	Leaves will fall if the potting mix is allowed to dry out
Aspidistra elatior	Cast-iron plant	Foliage	Upright	Sparing to moderate	Medium; no direct sun	50°–70°F/10°–21°C	Very tolerant of poor conditions
Asplenium bulbiferum	Mother spleenwort, hen-and-chickens fern, parsley fern	Foliage and baby plants	Rosette-forming	Moderate; sparingly in winter	Medium; no direct sun	60°–70°F/16°–21°C	High humidity required
Asplenium nidus	Bird's-nest fern	Foliage	Rosette-forming	Plentiful during active growth; moderate at other times	Moderate; no direct sun	65°–75°F/18°–24°C	Foliage easily damaged by handling. Needs humidity
Astrophytum myriostigma	Bishop's cap cactus	Flowers, succulent stems	Globular	Sparing	Full sun	60°–70°F/16°–21°C	Free-draining potting mix required
Aucuba japonica 'Variegata'	Gold dust tree, Japanese laurel	Foliage	Shrubby	Plentiful in growing season; moderate in winter	Bright	50°–65°F/10°–18°C	Tolerant of shade

B

PLANT	COMMON NAMES	FEATURES	SHAPE	WATERING	LIGHT	IDEAL INDOOR TEMPERATURE	SPECIAL POINTS
Beaucarnea recurvata (*Nolina recurvata*)	Ponytail plant, bottle palm, elephant foot	Foliage and swollen stem base	Arching	Moderate	Bright; preferably full sun	60°–70°F/16°–21°C	Do not overwater
Begonia: fibrous rooted, e.g., *B.* 'Corallina de Lucerna'	–	Flowers and foliage	Upright/ bushy	Moderate; sparingly in winter	Bright; some direct sun	65°–75°F/18°–24°C	Provide stakes for the tall stems

PLANT	COMMON NAMES	FEATURES	SHAPE	WATERING	LIGHT	IDEAL INDOOR TEMPERATURE	SPECIAL POINTS
Begonia: foliage types, e.g., *B. rex*, *B. masoniana*	Painted leaf begonia	Foliage	Spreading/ bushy	Moderate; sparingly in winter	Bright or light shade; little or no direct sun	65°–75°F/18°–24°C	High humidity required
Begonia: tuberous e.g., *B.* x *biemalis*, *B.* x *tuberhybrida*	Winter-flowering begonia	Flowers	Bushy	Moderate; no water in dormant period	Bright, filtered	60°–65°F/16°–18°C	Store dormant tubers in dry peat moss
Beloperone guttata (*Justicia brandegeana*)	Shrimp plant	Flowers	Bushy	Moderate; sparingly in winter	Bright; some direct sun	70°F/21°C	Pinch off growing tips to encourage bushiness
Bertolonia marmorata	Bertolonia	Foliage	Low-growing	Moderate	Bright; no direct sun	60°–70°F/16°–21°C	High humidity essential; good candidate for a terrarium
Billbergia nutans	Queen's tears, friendship plant	Flowers and foliage	Arching	Moderate	Bright	50°–70°F/10°–21°C	Very tolerant of cold temperatures
Bougainvillea glabra	Paper flower	Flowers	Climbing	Moderate; very sparingly in winter	Bright light; some direct sun	65°–75°F/18°–24°C; below 60°F/16°C for winter rest	Bright light is necessary for flowers to be produced
Bouvardia longiflora	Sweet bouvardia	Scented flowers	Bushy	Plentiful during active growth; sparingly during rest period	Bright; no direct sun	60°–70°F/16°–21°C	Tends to be short-lived
Bowiea volubilis	Climbing onion	Flowers, stems	Climbing stems	Moderate in growing season; keep dry in summer	Bright; no direct sun	50°–60°F/10°–16°C	Grown as a curiosity rather than for its beauty
Breynia nivosa (*B. disticha*)	Leaf flower, snow bush	Foliage	Shrubby	Moderate	Bright; no direct sun	60°–70°F/16°–21°C	High humidity essential
Brodiaea laxa (*Triteleia laxa*)	Grass nut, Ithuriel's spear	Flowers	Bushy	Moderate; reduce after flowering and let corms dry out when leaves yellow	Full sun	50°–60°F/10°–16°C	Plant corms in late summer or early fall for spring flowers
Browallia speciosa 'Major'	Sapphire flower, bush violet	Flowers	Bushy/ trailing	Moderate	Bright; some direct sun	60°–70°F/16°–20°C	Discard once flowering is over
Brunfelsia pauciflora (*B. calycina*)	Yesterday-today-and-tomorrow	Flowers	Shrubby	Moderate; sparingly in winter	Bright; some direct sun	65°–75°F/18°–24°C	Pinch off growing tips to keep plant bushy. Mist regularly
Buddleia madagascariensis (*Nicodemia madagascariensis*)	Buddleia	Flowers	Shrubby	Moderate	Full sun or partial shade	55°–70°F/13°–21°C	Best suited to a sunroom or greenhouse

C

PLANT	COMMON NAMES	FEATURES	SHAPE	WATERING	LIGHT	IDEAL INDOOR TEMPERATURE	SPECIAL POINTS
Caladium x *hortulanum*	Angel wings, elephant's-ear	Colored foliage; deciduous	Bushy	Moderate; keep tubers virtually dry over winter	Bright, diffused; no direct sun in rest period	At least 70°F/21°C; 80°F/27°C is ideal	High temperature and humidity essential
Calathea makoyana	Peacock plant	Variegated foliage	Bushy	Moderate; more sparingly in winter	Bright: no direct sun	65°–75°F/18°–24°C	High humidity essential; mist foliage regularly
Calceolaria x *herbeohybrida*	Slipper flower	Flowers	Bushy	Plentiful	Bright; no direct sun	50°F/10°C	Needs high humidity. Discard after flowering
Calliandra haematocephela (*C. inaequilatera*)	Powder-puff plant	Flowers and foliage	Bushy/ treelike	Plentiful to moderate	Bright; some direct sun	65°–75°F/18°–24°C	Prune to restrict size in spring
Callisia repens	Callisia	Foliage	Trailing	Moderate; sparingly in winter	Bright; some direct sun	65°–70°F/18°–21°C	Replace straggly plants with fresh cuttings after two or three years
Callistemon citrinus	Crimson bottle brush	Flowers	Shrubby	Plentiful in summer; sparingly in winter	Bright; some direct sun	65°–70°F/18°–21°C	Stand plants outside during summer
Camellia japonica	Camellia	Flowers	Shrubby	Moderate to plentiful while flowering; sparingly afterward	Bright; no direct sun	45°–60°F/7°–16°C	Mist regularly while buds are forming

PLANT	COMMON NAMES	FEATURES	SHAPE	WATERING	LIGHT	IDEAL INDOOR TEMPERATURE	SPECIAL POINTS
Campanula isophylla	Star of Bethlehem, bellflower, falling stars	Flowers	Trailing	Moderate	Bright; no direct sun	50°–60°F/10°–16°C	Keep cool in winter
Capsicum annuum	Ornamental or Christmas pepper	Fruits	Bushy	Moderate to plentiful	Bright; some direct sun	55°–60°F/13°–16°C	Discard when berries shrivel
Carex morrowii 'Variegata'	Japanese sedge grass	Foliage	Grassy	Moderate	Bright; some direct sun	60°–65°F/16°–18°C	Mist regularly to increase humidity
Carica papaya	Papaya	Foliage	Treelike	Moderate	Bright, some direct sun; will tolerate light shade	65°–75°F/18°–24°C	Never allow the potting mix to become waterlogged
Carludovica palmata	Panama-hat plant	Foliage	Bushy	Plentiful when in active growth	Full sun	65°–75°F/18°–24°C	Best suited to a sunroom or greenhouse
Caryota mitis	Burmese fishtail palm, crested (tufted) fishtail palm	Foliage	Bushy/upright	Moderate	Bright; no direct sun	65°–80°F/18°–27°C	Discard plants when they outgrow their space
Catharanthus roseus	Madagascar periwinkle	Flowers	Bushy	Moderate	Bright; some direct sun	60°–75°F/16°–24°C	Discard after flowering
Cattleya spp.	Cattleya	Flowers	Upright	Moderate to plentiful in growing period; sparingly after flowering	Bright; no direct sun	65°–75°F/18°–24°C	Use special orchid-fiber growing medium
Cephalocereus senilis (*Pilocereus senilis*)	Old-man cactus	Succulent stems	Upright, columnar	Sparing	Full sun	50°–70°F/10°–21°C	Spines are sharp: take care when handling
Ceropegia woodii (*C. linearis* ssp. *woodii*)	Rosary vine, hearts entangled, hearts-on-a-string	Foliage	Trailing	Sparing	Bright; some sun	60°–70°F/16°–21°C	Produces round stem tubers among the leaves
Cestrum aurantiacum	Cestrum	Flowers	Semi-climbing	Plentiful	Bright; no direct sun	60°–70°F/16°–21°C	Cut out some of the oldest stems in fall
Chamaedorea elegans	Parlor palm	Foliage	Bushy/upright	Moderate; sparingly in winter	Moderately bright	65°–75°F/18°–24°C	Humid atmosphere required
Chamaerops humilis	European fan palm	Foliage	Bushy/upright	Moderate	Bright; some direct sun	65°–70°F/18°–21°C	Tolerant of light shade
Chlorophytum comosum 'Vittatum'	Spider plant	Foliage	Grassy, with arching trailing plantlets	Plentiful; sparingly in winter	Bright; occasional direct sun	60°–70°F/16°–21°C	Bright light is necessary for well-variegated leaves
Chrysalidocarpus lutescens	Butterfly palm	Foliage	Upright	Moderate; sparingly in winter	Bright, filtered	65°–75°F/18°–24°C	High humidity required
Chrysanthemum x *morifolium*	Florists' chrysanthemum	Flowers	Bushy	Moderate	Bright; no direct sun	55°–60°F/13°–16°C	Discard after flowering
Cissus antarctica	Kangaroo vine	Foliage	Climbing	Moderate	Bright; no direct sun	55°–60°F/13°–16°C	Provide sturdy supports
x *Citrofortunella microcarpus*	Calamondin	Foliage, flowers, fruits	Treelike	Moderate	Bright; some direct sun	65°–70°F/18°–21°C	Stand plant outdoors in summer
Clerodendrum thomsoniae	Bleeding-heart vine	Flowers	Climbing/trailing	Moderate; sparingly in winter	Bright light; no direct sun	65°–70°F/18°–21°C	Prune stems back by half in spring
Clianthus puniceus	Parrot's beak, kaka beak, lobster claw	Flowers	Lax, bushy	Moderate; sparingly in winter	Full sun or dappled shade	55°–65°F/13°–18°C	Best discarded after flowering
Clivia miniata	Clivia	Flowers	Bushy	Moderate; very sparingly in winter	Bright light; some direct sun	65°–70°F/18°–21°C	Provide a cool, dry winter rest period
Coccoloba uvifera	Sea grape	Foliage	Bushy	Moderate	Bright; no direct sun	60°–70°F/16°–21°C	Tolerant of dry air
Codiaeum variegatum pictum	Croton, Joseph's coat	Colored foliage	Upright	Moderate; sparingly in winter	Bright light; some direct sun	65°–75°F/18°–24°C	Needs bright light for well-variegated leaves
Coelogyne cristata	Coelogyne	Flowers	Bushy	Moderate to plentiful; very sparingly during rest period	Bright, filtered	55°–60°F/13°–60°C	Provide a winter rest period of about six weeks

PLANT	COMMON NAMES	FEATURES	SHAPE	WATERING	LIGHT	IDEAL INDOOR TEMPERATURE	SPECIAL POINTS
Coffea arabica	Arabian coffee plant	Foliage	Treelike/ bushy	Plentiful in summer; more sparingly in winter	Bright; no direct sun	60°–70°F/16°–21°C	Flowers and fruit may form on older plants
Coleus blumei	Flame nettle	Colored foliage	Bushy	Moderate to plentiful	Bright; direct sun except very strong summer sun	60°–70°F/16°–21°C	Discard when leggy and replace with cuttings
Columnea x *banksii*	Goldfish plant	Flowers	Trailing	Moderate to sparingly, especially in winter	Bright; no direct sun	65°–75°F/18°–24°C	High humidity required
Convallaria majalis	Lily of the valley	Scented flowers	Bushy	Moderate to plentiful	Bright; no direct sun	50°–60°F/10°–16°C	Cool conditions will prolong flowering
Cordyline australis	Cabbage tree, palm lily, grass palm	Foliage	Upright/ bushy	Moderate; sparingly in winter	Bright; no direct sun	60°–70°F/16°–21°C	Will tolerate light shade
Cordyline terminalis	Good luck plant, ti tree	Foliage	Upright/ bushy	Moderate; sparingly in winter	Bright; no direct sun	60°–70°F/16°–21°C	Bright light is required for well-colored foliage
Costus igneus (*C. cuspidatus*)	Fiery costus, crepe ginger	Flowers	Upright	Moderate	Bright; no direct sun	60°–70°F/16°–21°C	Best suited to a sunroom
Cotyledon undulata	Silver crown	Foliage	Upright	Plentiful in growing season; sparingly in winter	Full sun	60°–70°F/16°–21°C	The attractive mealy leaf covering is damaged by handling
Crassula arborescens (*C. cotyledon*)	Chinese, or silver, jade plant	Foliage	Treelike	Plentiful in spring and summer; sparingly in winter	Bright; some direct sun	60°–70°F/16°–21°C	Benefits from a spell outdoors in summer
Crassula muscosa	Crassula	Succulent stems and leaves, flowers	Upright, then scrambling	Moderate to plentiful in growing season; sparingly in winter	Bright; some direct sun	60°–70°F/16°–21°C	Prone to mealybugs and scale insects
Crassula ovata (*C. portulacea*)	Jade tree, money tree	Foliage	Treelike	Moderate to plentiful in growing season; sparingly in winter	Bright; some direct sun	60°–70°F/16°–21°C	Mature plants produce white flowers in spring
Crinum x *powellii*	Spider lily	Flowers	Bushy/grassy	Plentiful in summer; very sparingly in winter	Bright; some direct sun	60°–70°F/16°–21°C	Repot only when essential
Crocus hybrids	Dutch crocus	Flowers	Grassy	Moderate	Bright; no direct sun	50°–60°F/10°–16°C	Corms need a cold, dark period after planting
Crossandra infundibuliformis	Firecracker flower	Flowers	Bushy	Moderate to sparingly	Bright, filtered	70°F/21°C	Replace plants when they deteriorate after two years
Cryptanthus acaulis	Green earth star, starfish plant	Foliage	Rosette	Moderate, preferably with rainwater	Bright	75°F/24°C	High humidity and good drainage are required
Cryptanthus bivittatus	Cryptanthus	Foliage	Rosette	Moderate in growing season; sparingly in winter	Bright	75°F/24°C	High humidity; good for a terrarium
Ctenanthe oppenheimiana 'Tricolor'	Never-never plant	Foliage	Bushy	Plentiful in spring and summer; moderately in winter	Bright filtered or light shade	65°–75°F/18°–24°C	High humidity required
Cuphea ignea (*C. platycentra*)	Cigar flower	Flowers	Bushy	Moderate; sparingly in winter	Bright; some direct sun	60°–70°F/16°–21°C	Replace plants when they become straggly and deteriorate
Cyanotis somaliensis	Pussy ears	Foliage	Trailing	Moderate	Bright; some direct sun	60°–70°F/16°–21°C	Good light required to keep stems compact
Cycas revoluta	Japanese sago palm	Foliage	Rosette	Moderate	Bright; no direct sun	60°–70°F/16°–21°C	Tolerates dry atmosphere
Cyclamen persicum	Cyclamen	Flowers	Bushy	Moderate; keep dry in rest period	Bright	55°–65°F/13°–18°C	Do not splash the tuber when watering
Cymbidium hybrids	Cymbidium	Flowers	Bushy	Plentiful in summer; sparingly at other times	Bright, filtered	55°–65°F/13°–18°C	Provide a rest period for 4–6 weeks in fall
Cyperus alternifolius	Umbrella plant	Foliage	Grassy	Plentiful	Adaptable; direct sun or light shade	60°–70°F/16°–21°C	Stand the pot in a saucer of water

PLANT	COMMON NAMES	FEATURES	SHAPE	WATERING	LIGHT	IDEAL INDOOR TEMPERATURE	SPECIAL POINTS
Cyperus papyrus	Papyrus	Foliage and flowers	Grassy	Plentiful	Adaptable; direct sun or light shade	65°–75°F/18°–24°C	Stand the pot in a saucer of water
Cyrtomium falcatum	Holly fern	Foliage	Bushy	Moderate	Bright light or semishade	65°F/18°C	Tolerant of dry air

D

Darlingtonia californica	California pitcher plant, cobra lily	Insect-catching pitchers	Upright	Moderate to plentiful	Bright; no strong direct sun	60°–70°F/16°–21°C	High humidity essential
Datura x candida (*Brugmansia x candida*)	Angel's trumpet	Scented flowers	Bushy/ upright	Plentiful in the growing season; sparingly in winter	Full sun or light shade	50°–60°F/10°–16°C	All parts are poisonous
Davallia fejeensis	Rabbit's-foot fern	Foliage, furry rhizomes	Upright/ bushy	Moderate; sparingly in winter	Bright; no direct sun	60°–70°F/16°–21°C	Creeping, furry rhizomes growing over the edge of the pot are a feature
Dendrobium spp.	Dendrobium	Flowers	Upright	Moderate in the growing season; keep almost dry in winter	Bright, filtered	60°–70°F/16°–21°C; lower during winter rest period	Mist-spray daily
Dichorisandra reginae	Queen's spiderwort	Foliage	Upright	Moderate; sparingly in winter	Medium; no direct sun	60°–70°F/16°–21°C	High humidity essential
Dicksonia antarctica	Tasmanian tree fern	Foliage	Upright	Moderate	Bright; little or no direct sun	60°–70°F/16°–21°C	High humidity required. Best in a sunroom or greenhouse
Dieffenbachia maculata (*D. picta*)	Dumb cane, leopard lily	Foliage	Bushy/ upright	Plentiful in spring and summer; sparingly in winter	Bright; no direct sun	65°–75°F/18°–24°C	Sap is poisonous; take care when handling
Dimorphotheca sinuata (*D. aurantiaca*)	Star of the veldt	Flowers	Rosette- forming	Sparing	Full sun	65°–75°F/18°–24°C	Best discarded after flowering
Dionaea muscipula	Venus's-flytrap	Foliage; insect- catching traps	Rosette- forming	Plentiful to moderate	Bright; no direct sun	60°–70°F/16°–21°C	Feed with dead insects or meat over winter
Dizygotheca elegantissima	False aralia, finger aralia	Foliage	Upright/ treelike	Moderate	Bright; no direct sun	65°–75°F/18°–24°C	High humidity required
Dracaena fragrans 'Massangeana'	Corn plant	Foliage	Upright/ treelike	Moderate; sparingly in winter	Bright; some direct sun	60°–75°F/16°–24°C	Protect from drafts
Dracaena marginata	Madagascar dragon tree	Foliage	Upright/ treelike	Moderate; sparingly in winter	Bright; no direct summer sun	60°–70°F/16°–21°C	Bright light is necessary for good leaf color
Dracaena sanderiana	Belgian evergreen, ribbon plant	Foliage	Upright	Plentiful in summer; sparingly in winter	Bright; no direct sun	60°–70°F/16°–21°C	Repot only when essential
Drosera rotundifolia	Common sundew	Insect-catching traps	Rosette- forming	Plentiful to moderate	Bright; no direct sun	50°–60°F/10°–16°C	Do not overpot; the root system is very small
Dyckia fosteriana	Dyckia, miniature agave	Flowers and foliage	Rosette- forming	Moderate to sparingly	Full sun	50°–75°F/10°–24°C	Sharp spines: take care when handling the plant

E

Echeveria secunda var. *glauca*	Blue echeveria	Succulent foliage and flowers	Rosette- forming	Sparing	Full sun	60°–70°F/16°–21°C; 50°–60°F/10°–16°C in winter	Delicate foliage is easily damaged by handling
Echinocactus grusonii	Golden barrel cactus	Spines and flowers	Globular	Moderate in growth; sparingly in winter	Full sun	60°–70°F/16°–21°C; 50°F/10°C in winter	Very slow-growing
Echinocereus pectinatus	Hedgehog cactus	Flowers/stems	Columnar	Sparing	Direct sun all year	60°–70°F/16°–21°C; 50°–60°F/10°–16°C in winter	Full sun is required for reliable flowering
Echinopsis eyriesii	Sea urchin cactus	Flowers/stems	Cylindrical	Moderate to sparing; very sparingly in rest period	Full sun	60°–70°F/16°–21°C; 50°–60°F/10°–16°C in winter	Cool winter rest is necessary for flowering

PLANT	COMMON NAMES	FEATURES	SHAPE	WATERING	LIGHT	IDEAL INDOOR TEMPERATURE	SPECIAL POINTS
Epiphyllum ackermannii	Orchid cactus	Flowers	Trailing	Plentiful during active growth; sparingly otherwise	Bright; no direct summer sun	60°–70°F/16°–21°C; 50°–60°F/10°–16°C in winter	Flowers best if slightly pot-bound
Epipremnum aureum	Devil's ivy, golden pothos, taro vine	Foliage	Climbing	Moderate	Bright; no direct sun	60°–70°F/16°–21°C	Provide a moss-covered pole or similar support
Episcia cupreata	Flame violet	Foliage and flowers	Low, creeping	Plentiful; sparingly in winter	Bright; no direct sun	60°–70°F/16°–21°C	Free-draining potting mix is required
Erica x *hiemalis*	French heather	Flowers	Bushy	Plentiful	Bright; some direct sun	45°–50°F/7°–10°C	Discard after flowering
Eriobotrya japonica	Loquat	Foliage	Treelike	Moderate; sparingly in winter	Bright; some direct sun	60°–70°F/16°–21°C; 50°F/10°C in winter	Discard plants when they become leggy
Eucharis x *grandiflora*	Amazon lily, Eucharist lily, star of Bethlehem	Scented flowers	Grassy	Plentiful while growing; keep bulb virtually dry when leaves die back	Bright; no direct sun	65°–75°F/18°–24°C	Water newly potted bulb sparingly until growth starts
Euphorbia milii var. *splendens*	Crown of thorns	Flowers/ thorny stems	Upright/ bushy	Moderate to sparing	Bright; some direct sun	60°–70°F/16°–21°C	Stems produce latex when damaged; this can be an irritant
Euphorbia pulcherrima	Poinsettia, Christmas star, Mexican flame leaf	Flowers (bracts)	Bushy	Moderate	Bright; some direct sun	60°–70°F/16°–21°C	Short days are necessary for the production of flower heads
Eurya japonica	Eurya	Foliage	Bushy	Moderate	Bright; some direct sun	50°–60°F/10°–16°C	Will tolerate light shade
Eustoma grandiflorum	Prairie gentian, lisianthus	Flowers	Bushy	Moderate	Bright; some direct sun	55°–65°F/13°–18°C	Discard after flowering
Exacum affine	German violet, Arabian violet, Persian violet	Scented flowers	Low, bushy	Plentiful to moderate	Bright; no strong direct sun	60°–70°F/16°–21°C	Deadhead to prolong flowering

F

PLANT	COMMON NAMES	FEATURES	SHAPE	WATERING	LIGHT	IDEAL INDOOR TEMPERATURE	SPECIAL POINTS
x *Fatshedera lizei*	Tree ivy	Foliage	Upright	Plentiful during growing season; otherwise, moderately to sparingly	Medium to bright	55°–60°F/13°–16°C	Provide a stake to support stem or similar support
Fatsia japonica	Japanese fatsia, Japanese aralia, false castor-oil plant	Foliage	Upright	Plentiful to moderate	Medium to bright	55°–60°F/13°–16°C	Prune hard to reduce the plant's size
Faucaria tigrina	Tiger jaws	Flowers and succulent foliage	Rosette-forming	Plentiful in spring and summer; sparingly in fall and winter	Full sun	60°–70°F/16°–21°C	Repot only when essential
Felicia amelloides (*Agathaea coelestis*)	Blue marguerite	Flowers	Bushy, rosette-forming	Moderate in active growth period; less in winter	Bright; some direct sun	50°–70°F/10°–21°C	Pinch off growing tips regularly. Discard when no longer attractive
Ferocactus latispinus	Barrel cactus, fish-hook cactus, devil's tongue	Succulent stem	Globular	Sparing	Full sun	60°–70°F/16°–21°C	Beware of the sharp, hooked spines
Ficus benjamina	Weeping fig	Foliage	Treelike	Moderate	Bright; some direct sun	60°–70°F/16°–21°C	Many named varieties exist
Ficus deltoidea var. *deversi folia*	Mistletoe fig	Foliage and fruit	Treelike	Moderate	Bright; some direct sun	60°–70°F/16°–21°C	Fruit is inedible
Ficus elastica 'Robusta'	Rubber plant	Foliage	Treelike	Moderate	Bright; some direct sun	60°–70°F/16°–21°C	Clean leaves regularly
Ficus lyrata	Fiddle leaf fig	Foliage	Treelike	Moderate	Bright; some direct sun	60°–70°F/16°–21°C	Pinch off the growing tips to encourage branching
Ficus pumila	Creeping fig	Foliage	Creeping/ trailing	Plentiful to moderate	Medium light or light shade	55°–70°F/13°–21°C	Never allow the potting mix to dry out
Fittonia verschaffeltii argyroneura	Silver net leaf, nerve plant	Foliage	Creeping	Plentiful to moderate	Bright light or light shade	65°–75°F/18°–24°C	High humidity essential; ideal for a terrarium

PLANT	COMMON NAMES	FEATURES	SHAPE	WATERING	LIGHT	IDEAL INDOOR TEMPERATURE	SPECIAL POINTS
Freesia spp.	Freesia	Scented flowers	Grassy	Plentiful while flowering; moderately before drying corms off completely	Bright; some direct sun	55°–65°F/13°–18°C	Support flowering stems with bamboo stakes
Fuchsia hybrid	Fuchsia	Flowers	Bushy	Moderate; sparingly in winter	Bright; some direct sun	60°F/16°C	Pinch off growing tips to encourage bushy growth

G

Gardenia augusta (*G. jasminoides*, *G. grandiflora*)	Gardenia	Scented flowers	Bushy/upright	Moderate; sparingly in winter	Bright; some direct sun in winter	60°–70°F/16°–21°C	Protect from drafts, especially when buds are forming
Genista x *spachiana*	Genista	Scented flowers	Upright/bushy	Plentiful while flowering; otherwise, moderately to sparingly	Bright	50°–60°F/10°–16°C	Stand the plant outdoors during the summer
Geogenanthus undatus (*G. poeppegii*)	Seersucker plant	Foliage	Low spreading	Moderate; sparingly in winter	Bright; no direct sun	70°F/21°C	High humidity essential
Gerbera jamesonii	African, Barberton, or Transvaal daisy	Flowers	Rosette-forming	Plentiful to moderate	Bright; some direct sun	50°–70°F/10°–21°C	Discard after flowering
Glechoma hederacea 'Variegata'	Ground ivy	Foliage	Trailing	Plentiful; sparingly in winter	Bright; no direct sun	55°–65°F/13°–18°C; 50°F/10°C in winter	Good for a hanging basket
Gloriosa superba 'Rothschildiana'	Gloriosa lily	Flowers	Climbing	Moderate; dry tubers off after flowering	Bright; no strong direct sun	60°–70°F/16°–21°C	Provide support for climbing stems
Gomphrena globosa	Globe amaranth, bachelor's button	Flowers	Bushy	Plentiful	Bright; some direct sun	55°–65°F/13°–18°C	Discard when no longer attractive
Graptophyllum pictum	Caricature plant	Foliage and flowers	Shrubby	Plentiful	Bright; some direct sun	65°–75°F/18°–24°C	Pinch off growing tips regularly to keep the plant compact
Grevillea robusta	Silk oak	Foliage	Treelike	Moderate	Bright; some direct sun	55°–60°F/13°–16°C	Large specimens are suitable for sunrooms
Guzmania dissitiflora	Guzmania	Foliage and flowers (bracts)	Rosette-forming	Moderate; keep the "vase" full of water	Bright; no direct sun	65°–75°F/18°–24°C	High humidity required
Guzmania lingulata	Scarlet star	Foliage and flowers (bracts)	Rosette-forming	Moderate; keep the "vase" full of water	Bright; no direct sun	65°–75°F/18°–24°C	High humidity required
Gymnocalycium mihanovichii 'Red Cap'	Gymnocalycium	Grafted stems; flowers	Upright	Plentiful in summer; sparingly in winter	Bright	65°–75°F/18°–24°C; 40°F/4°C in winter	Needs a cool winter rest to encourage flowering
Gynura 'Purple Passion'	Purple passion vine, velvet plant	Foliage	Trailing	Moderate; more sparingly in winter	Bright; some sun, but not summer sun	60°–70°F/16°–21°C	Remove flowers as they appear

H

Haemanthus humilis 'Wilsonii'	Haemanthus	Flowers	Grassy	Freely in summer; sparingly in winter	Bright; some direct sun	60°–70°F/16°–21°C	Repot only when essential
Haworthia pumila (*H. margaritifera*)	Pearl plant	Succulent leaves	Rosette-forming	Moderate; sparingly in winter	Medium to bright; no direct sun	60°–70°F/16°–21°C	Never allow the potting mix to dry out completely
Hebe x *andersonii*	Hebe	Flowers and foliage	Shrubby	Plentiful to moderate	Bright; no direct strong sun	55°–65°F/13°–18°C; cooler in winter	Stand plants outdoors in summer
Hedera helix	English ivy	Foliage	Climbing	Moderate	Bright; some direct sun	50°–55°F/10°–13°C	Provide supports for the climbing stems
Hedychium coronarium	Butterfly ginger, white ginger lily	Fragrant flowers	Upright/bushy	Moderate; sparingly in winter	Bright; no direct sun	65°–75°F/18°–24°C	Most suitable for a greenhouse

PLANT	COMMON NAMES	FEATURES	SHAPE	WATERING	LIGHT	IDEAL INDOOR TEMPERATURE	SPECIAL POINTS
Heliconia schiedeana	Lobster claws	Flowers and foliage	Upright/ bushy	Moderate	Semishade	65°–75°F/18°–24°C	High humidity required
Hemigraphis colorata (*H. alternata*)	Red ivy, red-flame ivy	Foliage	Creeping	Moderate	Bright; no direct sun	60°–70°F/16°–21°C	Free-draining potting mix and high humidity required
Hibiscus rosa-sinensis	Rose of China	Flowers	Shrubby	Plentiful in spring and summer; otherwise, moderately	Bright; some direct sun	60°–70°F/16°–21°C; 55°F/13°C in winter	Do not move the plant while buds are forming
Hippeastrum x acramannii (*H. x ackermannii*)	Amaryllis	Flowers	Grassy	Moderate; allow bulb to dry out in fall	Bright; some direct sun	55°–65°F/13°–18°C	A rest period is required to initiate flower buds
Hoffmannia regalis 'Roezlii'	Taffeta plant	Colored foliage	Bushy	Moderate to sparing	Bright, filtered	65°–75°F/18°–24°C	Protect from drafts
Howea belmoreana	Sentry palm, curly palm	Foliage	Bushy/ upright	Plentiful in growing season; sparingly in winter	Bright, filtered	60°–70°F/16°–21°C	Tolerates shade well
Hoya carnosa	Wax plant	Flowers	Trailing	Moderate; sparingly in winter	Bright; some direct sun	60°–70°F/16°–21°C	Stems can be trained around a wire hoop
Hoya lanceolata bella	Miniature wax plant	Flowers	Trailing	Moderate; sparingly in winter	Bright; some direct sun	70°–75°F/21°–24°C	Avoid moving plants while buds are forming
Hyacinthus orientalis	Hyacinth	Flowers	Bushy	Moderate	Bright	60°F/16°C while flowering	Bulbs require cool, dark forcing period
Hydrangea macrophylla (*H. hortensis*)	Hydrangea	Flowers	Shrubby	Plentiful in growing season; sparingly in winter	Bright; no direct sun	55°–60°F/13°–16°C	Ericaceous potting mix required for blue flowers
Hymenocallis littoralis	Spider lily	Scented flowers	Upright	Plentiful in growing season; otherwise, moderately	Bright; no direct sun	65°–80°F/18°–27°C	Best grown in a greenhouse and brought indoors for flowering
Hypoestes phyllostachya	Polka dot plant, freckle face	Colored foliage	Bushy	Moderate to sparing	Bright; some direct sun	60°–70°F/16°–21°C	Discard when leggy and replace with cuttings

I

PLANT	COMMON NAMES	FEATURES	SHAPE	WATERING	LIGHT	IDEAL INDOOR TEMPERATURE	SPECIAL POINTS
Impatiens walleriana	Impatiens, touch-me-not	Flowers	Bushy	Plentiful to moderate	Bright	60°–70°F/16°–21°C	Flowers carried all year if temperature is maintained above 60°F/16°C
Ipheion uniflorum	Spring star flower	Flowers	Grassy	Moderate; reduce after flowering until the leaves die down	Bright; some direct sun	50°–60°F/10°–16°C	Keep in a cold greenhouse and bring indoors for flowering
Ipomoea tricolor	Morning glory	Flowers	Climber	Moderate	Full sun or light shade	60°–70°F/16°–21°C	Discard after flowering
Iresine herbstii	Beefsteak plant, bloodleaf	Colored foliage	Bushy	Plentiful to moderate	Bright; no direct strong sun	60°–70°F/16°–21°C	Pinch off growing tips regularly to keep plants bushy
Ixora coccinea	Flame-of-the-woods	Flowers	Shrubby	Plentiful; sparingly in winter	Full sun	65°–75°F/18°–24°C	Protect plants from drafts

J

PLANT	COMMON NAMES	FEATURES	SHAPE	WATERING	LIGHT	IDEAL INDOOR TEMPERATURE	SPECIAL POINTS
Jacaranda mimosifolia	Jacaranda	Foliage	Treelike/ bushy	Moderate; sparingly in winter	Bright; no direct sun	60°–70°F/16°–21°C	Plants can be cut back hard when they become leggy
Jasminum mesnyi	Primrose jasmine	Flowers	Scrambling	Moderate	Bright; some direct sun	55°–65°F/13°–18°	Tie stems to a support
Jasminum polyanthum	Chinese jasmine	Scented flowers	Twining	Moderate; sparingly in winter	Bright; some direct sun	60°–65°F/16°–18°C	Can be trained around a wire hoop
Jatropha podagrica	Gout plant, tartogo	Swollen bottle-shaped stem, flowers	Upright	Very sparing, particularly in winter	Bright, filtered light or semi-shade	65°–75°F/18°–24°C	Good drainage essential

PLANT	COMMON NAMES	FEATURES	SHAPE	WATERING	LIGHT	IDEAL INDOOR TEMPERATURE	SPECIAL POINTS
Justicia carnea (*Jacobinia carnea*)	Brazilian plume, king's crown, pink acanthus	Flowers	Bushy	Moderate in summer; sparingly in winter	Bright; some direct sun	60°–70°F/16°–21°C; 55°F/13°C in winter	Cut back stems by half after flowering
Justicia pauciflora (*J. rizzinii*)	Justicia	Flowers	Bushy	Moderate to sparing in the rest period	Bright, filtered light; some direct sun	60°–70°F/16°–21°C; 55°F/13°C in the rest period	Pinch off growing tips to promote bushiness

K

PLANT	COMMON NAMES	FEATURES	SHAPE	WATERING	LIGHT	IDEAL INDOOR TEMPERATURE	SPECIAL POINTS
Kalanchoe blossfeldiana	Flaming Katy	Flowers	Bushy	Moderate to sparing	Bright; some direct sun	60°–70°F/16°–21°C	Flowers in short days
Kalanchoe manginii	–	Flowers	Semi-trailing	Moderate to sparing	Bright; some direct sun	60°–70°F/16°–21°C	Good for hanging baskets
Kalanchoe marmorata	Penwiper	Foliage	Upright	Moderate to sparing	Bright; some direct sun	60°–70°F/16°–21°C	Provide a winter rest at 50°F/10°C
Kalanchoe pumila	–	Foliage and flowers	Semi-trailing	Moderate to sparing	Bright; some direct sun	60°–70°F/16°–21°C	Good for hanging baskets
Kalanchoe tomentosa	Panda plant, pussy ears	Foliage	Upright	Moderate to sparing	Bright; some direct sun	60°–70°F/16°–21°C	Provide a winter rest at 50°F/10°C
Kohleria eriantha and hybrids	Kohleria	Flowers	Upright	Moderate; sparingly in winter	Bright, filtered	60°–70°F/16°–21°C	High humidity required, but do not mist the leaves directly

L

PLANT	COMMON NAMES	FEATURES	SHAPE	WATERING	LIGHT	IDEAL INDOOR TEMPERATURE	SPECIAL POINTS
Lachenalia aloides	Cape cowslip	Flowers	Grassy	Moderate; reduce after flowering, to allow bulbs to dry	Full sun or light shade	50°–60°F/10°–16°C	Plant bulbs in late summer
Lantana camara	Yellow sage	Flowers	Bushy	Moderate; sparingly in winter	Bright; some direct sun	60°–70°F/16°–21°C	Prone to infestation by whiteflies
Leea coccinea	West Indian holly	Foliage	Bushy/treelike	Moderate	Bright; no direct sun	65°–75°F/18°–24°C	Protect from drafts
Lilium spp.	Trumpet lily	Flowers	Upright	Plentiful in growth; reduce after flowering to allow bulbs to dry	Bright; no direct sun	50°–60°F/10°–16°C	Support the flowering stems with canes
Liriope muscari (*L. graminifolia densiflora*)	Big blue lilyturf	Flowers	Grassy	Moderate	Bright	60°–70°F/16°–21°C; 40°–50°F/4°–10°C in winter	Tolerant of shade; keep out of drafts
Lithops lesliei	Living stones	Flowers and succulent leaves	Pebble-shaped	Sparing in the growing season; keep dry through winter	Full sun	60°–70°F/16°–21°C	Old leaves die after flowering and are replaced by new ones

M

PLANT	COMMON NAMES	FEATURES	SHAPE	WATERING	LIGHT	IDEAL INDOOR TEMPERATURE	SPECIAL POINTS
Mammillaria bocasana	Powder-puff cactus	Hairy stems, flowers	Cylindrical	Moderate to sparing	Full sun	65°–70°F/18°–21°C	Mealybugs may be a problem
Mandevilla x *amoena* 'Alice du Pont'	Mandevilla	Flowers	Climbing	Moderate	Bright; no direct sun	60°–70°F/16°–21°C	Prune back stems after flowering
Manettia inflata	Firecracker vine	Flowers	Climbing/trailing	Moderate	Bright; some direct sun	60°–70°F/16°–21°C	Repot this vigorous plant as necessary
Maranta leuconeura	Prayer plant	Foliage	Bushy	Moderate	Medium; no direct sun	60°–65°F/16°–18°C	Requires high humidity
Medinilla magnifica	Rose grape	Flowers	Bushy	Moderate; sparingly in winter	Bright, filtered	70°F/21°C	Difficult to bring into flower
Mikania dentata (*M. ternata*)	Plush vine	Foliage	Trailing	Moderate	Bright; some direct sun	60°–70°F/16°–21°C	Do not mist the foliage directly
Miltonia	Pansy orchid	Flowers	Upright	Plentiful in spring and summer; sparingly in winter	Medium; full sun in winter	65°–70°F/18°–21°C	Protect from temperature fluctuations

PLANT	COMMON NAMES	FEATURES	SHAPE	WATERING	LIGHT	IDEAL INDOOR TEMPERATURE	SPECIAL POINTS
Mimosa pudica	Sensitive plant	Foliage and flowers	Bushy	Moderate	Bright; some direct sun	60°–70°F/16°–21°C	Leaflets fold up rapidly when they are touched
Monstera deliciosa	Swiss cheese plant, split leaf, window plant, Mexican breadfruit, fruit salad plant	Foliage	Climbing	Moderate	Medium to bright; no direct sun	65°–70°F/18°–21°C	Characteristic splits and holes develop on older leaves

N

PLANT	COMMON NAMES	FEATURES	SHAPE	WATERING	LIGHT	IDEAL INDOOR TEMPERATURE	SPECIAL POINTS
Narcissus spp.	Daffodil, narcissus	Flowers	Upright/grassy	Moderate; allow bulbs to dry out as leaves fade	Bright; no direct sun	50°–60°F/10°–16°C	Bulbs need a cool, dark forcing period after planting
Nematanthus gregarius (*Hypocyrta radicans*)	Nematanthus	Flowers	Bushy	Moderate; sparingly in winter	Bright; some direct sun	60°–70°F/16°–21°C; cooler in winter	Benefits from being placed outdoors in summer
Neoregelia carolinae 'Tricolor'	Blushing bromeliad	Foliage and flowers	Rosette-forming	Moderate to sparing	Bright; some direct sun	60°–70°F/16°–21°C	Keep the central "vase" filled with water
Neoregelia 'Meyendorffii'	Neoregelia	Foliage and flowers	Rosette-forming	Moderate to sparing; keep the "vase" full	Bright; some direct sun	60°–70°F/16°–21°C	An attractive cultivar
Nepenthes x hookeriana	Pitcher plant	Insect-catching traps	Climbing	Plentiful to moderate; use lime-free water	Medium; no direct sun	65°–75°F/18°–24°C	High humidity essential for pitchers to form
Nephrolepis exaltata 'Bostoniensis'	Boston fern, ladder fern, sword fern	Foliage	Bushy/pendant	Plentiful to moderate	Bright; no direct sun	60°–70°F/16°–21°C	Good for hanging baskets
Nerine bowdenii	Nerine	Flowers	Upright/grassy	Plentiful during growth; otherwise, not at all	Bright light; some sun	50°–60°F/10°–16°C	Can stand a temperature as low as 5°F/-15°C
Nerium oleander	Oleander	Flowers	Treelike	Plentiful to moderate	Bright; some direct sun	60°–70°F/16°–21°C; 55°F/13°C during the winter rest period	All parts of the plant are very poisonous
Nertera granadensis	Bead plant, coral moss	Berries	Creeping	Moderate	Full sun	50°–60°F/10°–16°C	Placing plants outdoors while flowering ensures a good set of berries
Nidularium billbergioides	Nidularium	Foliage and flowers	Upright rosette	Moderate; less in winter; keep the "vase" filled with water	Bright; no direct sun	60°–70°F/16°–21°C	Epiphytic bromeliad producing stolons
Nidularium innocentii 'Striatum'	Bird's-nest bromeliad	Foliage and flowers	Rosette-forming	Moderate; sparingly in winter	Bright; no direct sun	60°–70°F/16°–21°C	Keep the central "vase" filled with water

O

PLANT	COMMON NAMES	FEATURES	SHAPE	WATERING	LIGHT	IDEAL INDOOR TEMPERATURE	SPECIAL POINTS
Ocimum basilicum	Sweet basil	Aromatic foliage	Bushy	Moderate	Bright; no direct strong sunlight	60°–70°F/16°–21°C	Pinch off growing tips regularly
Odontoglossum grande	Tiger orchid	Flowers	Upright	Moderate; sparingly in winter rest period	Bright, filtered	60°F/16°C	Use special orchid potting mix
Olea europaea	Olive	Foliage	Shrubby	Moderate	Full sun	60°–75°F/16°–24°C	Benefits from a spell outdoors in summer
Oncidium spp.	Oncidium	Flowers, arching	Upright/arching	Sparing in period of active growth; keep almost dry in rest period	Direct sun, except midday summer sun	65°F/18°C; 55°F/13°C during rest period	Mist-spray and stand pot in a tray of moist pebbles when temperature is over 70°F/21°C
Ophiopogon jaburan	White lily-turf	Flowers and foliage	Grassy	Moderate	Bright; no direct sun	55°–65°F/13°–18°C	Tolerant of shade
Oplismenus hirtellus	Basket grass	Foliage	Trailing	Moderate	Bright; some direct winter sun	60°–70°F/16°–21°C	Best replaced every year or two
Opuntia microdasys	Prickly pear cactus, bunny ears	Succulent stems	Branching, flattened stems	Sparing	Full sun	60°–70°F/16°–21°C	Bristly spines can be irritating to the skin

PLANT	COMMON NAMES	FEATURES	SHAPE	WATERING	LIGHT	IDEAL INDOOR TEMPERATURE	SPECIAL POINTS
Osmanthus heterophyllus 'Variegatus'	Variegated false holly	Foliage	Shrubby	Moderate	Full sun	50°–55°F/10°–13°C	Pinch off growing points to encourage bushiness
Oxalis deppei	Lucky clover	Flowers and foliage	Spreading	Moderate to sparing	Bright; some direct sun	50°–65°F/10°–18°C	Discard when plants become too leggy

P

PLANT	COMMON NAMES	FEATURES	SHAPE	WATERING	LIGHT	IDEAL INDOOR TEMPERATURE	SPECIAL POINTS
Pachystachys lutea	Lollipop plant	Flowers (bracts)	Upright/ bushy	Plentiful to moderate	Bright; no direct sun	60°–70°F/16°–21°C	Prune stems by one-third in early spring
Pandanus veitchii	Veitch's screw pine	Foliage	Upright/ grassy	Moderate	Bright; some direct sun	65°–75°F/18°–24°C	High humidity required
Paphiopedilum **spp.**	Lady's slipper orchids	Flowers	Upright	Moderate to sparing	Bright; direct sun only in winter	65°–75°F/18°–24°C	High humidity essential
Passiflora caerulea	Common passion-flower	Flowers	Climber	Plentiful; sparingly in winter	Full sun	70°F/21°C; cooler in winter	Hardy down to 0°F/-18°C
Pelargonium x *hortorum*	Zonal geranium	Flowers	Bushy	Moderate; very sparingly in winter	Full sun	55°–65°F/13°–18°C	Prune stems back hard in early spring
Pelargonium peltatum	Ivy geranium	Flowers; foliage (some varieties)	Trailing	Moderate; very sparingly in winter	Full sun	55°–65°F/13°–18°C	Good for hanging baskets
Pelargonium **spp.**	Scented-leafed geraniums	Aromatic foliage	Mainly bushy	Moderate; sparingly in winter	Full sun	55°–65°F/13°–18°C	Many different species with different fragrances exist
Pellaea rotundifolia	Button fern	Foliage	Spreading	Moderate	Bright; no direct sun	60°–70°F/16°–21°C	Protect from fluctuating temperatures
Pellionia daveauana (*P. repens*)	Watermelon begonia	Foliage	Trailing	Plentiful to moderate	Bright or semishaded	70°–80°F/21°–27°C	High humidity and protection from drafts required
Pentas lanceolata (*P. carnea*)	Egyptian star cluster	Flowers and foliage	Bushy	Moderate; sparingly after flowering	Bright; some direct sun	65°–75°F/18°–24°C	Pinch off growing tips to keep plant bushy
Peperomia caperata	Emerald ripple	Foliage and flower spikes	Bushy	Sparing	Medium; no direct sun	60°–70°F/16°–21°C	Take care not to overwater in winter
Peperomia magnoliifolia	Desert privet	Foliage	Bushy	Sparing	Bright; no direct sun	60°–70°F/16°–21°C	High humidity required
Peperomia scandens	Cupid peperomia	Foliage	Trailing	Sparing to moderate	Bright; no direct strong sun	60°–70°F/16°–21°C	High humidity required
Phalaenopsis **spp.**	Moth orchid	Flowers	Upright	Moderate to plentiful	Light shade	70°F/21°C	Likes good air circulation
Philodendron bipinnatifidum	Tree philodendron	Foliage	Bushy	Moderate; sparingly in winter	Medium; no direct sun	60°–70°F/16°–21°C	Requires plenty of space
Philodendron erubescens	Blushing philodendron	Foliage	Climbing	Moderate	Medium; no direct sun	60°–70°F/16°–21°C	Provide a moss-covered pole or similar support
Philodendron scandens	Heartleaf philodendron, sweetheart plant	Foliage	Climbing/ trailing	Moderate	Bright; no direct sun	60°–70°F/16°–21°C	Tie stems to their support
Phoenix roebelenii	Pygmy date palm	Foliage	Bushy	Plentiful in growing season; sparingly in winter	Bright; some direct sun	60°–70°F/16°–21°C	High humidity required
Pilea cadierei	Aluminum plant	Foliage	Bushy	Moderate	Medium; no direct sun	60°–70°F/16°–21°C	Discard when leggy
Pilea peperomioides	Pilea	Foliage	Mound-forming	Moderate to sparing	Medium to bright; no direct sun	65°–75°F/18°–24°C	Pinch off growing tips regularly to keep plants compact. Keep out of drafts
Piper nigrum	Black pepper	Foliage	Climbing	Moderate	Bright; no direct strong sun	65°–75°F/18°–24°C	High humidity and even temperature essential

PLANT	COMMON NAMES	FEATURES	SHAPE	WATERING	LIGHT	IDEAL INDOOR TEMPERATURE	SPECIAL POINTS
Piper ornatum	Celebes pepper	Foliage	Climbing/creeping	Moderate	Bright; no direct sun	60°–70°F/16°–21°C	Cut out weak shoots in early spring. Provide a support for the plant to climb on
Pisonia umbellifera 'Variegata'	Bird-catcher tree	Foliage	Bushy	Moderate; sparingly in winter	Full sun or light shade	65°–75°F/18°–24°C	Prune to shape when repotting. Leaves lose color in poor light
Pittosporum tobira	Japanese pittosporum, Australian laurel	Foliage and flowers	Bushy	Moderate; sparingly in winter	Bright; no direct sunlight	50°–70°F/10°–21°C	Needs bright conditions to flower
Platycerium bifurcatum	Staghorn fern	Foliage	Spreading	Mist-spray or plunge as necessary	Bright; some direct sun	60°–80°F/16°–27°C	Epiphyte that is best in a slatted orchid basket or mounted on bark
Plectranthus coleoides 'Marginatus'	Candle plant	Foliage	Bushy	Plentiful; sparingly in winter	Bright; some direct sun	60°–70°F/16°–21°C	Best discarded at the end of the season and replaced with cuttings
Plumbago auriculata	Cape leadwort	Flowers	Semi-climbing	Moderate; sparingly in winter	Bright; some direct sun	50°–65°F/10°–18°C	Prune hard in spring. Provide supports or a wire hoop
Plumeria rubra (*P. acuminata*)	Frangipani, temple tree, nosegay, West Indian jasmine, pagoda tree	Scented flowers	Treelike	Plentiful in growing season; sparingly in winter	Bright; some direct sun	65°–75°F/18°–24°C	Needs plenty of space
Podocarpus macrophyllus	Buddhist pine, Japanese yew, Kusamaki	Foliage	Treelike	Moderate; sparingly in winter	Partial shade	50°–65°F/10°–18°C	Tolerates drafty conditions
Polyscias scutellaria 'Balfourii'	Ming aralia	Foliage	Bushy	Moderate; sparingly in winter	Bright; no direct sun	65°–75°F/18°–24°C	High humidity essential
Primula denticulata	Drumstick primula	Flowers	Bushy	Plentiful	Bright; some direct sun	50°–60°F/10°–16°C	Can be planted outdoors after flowering
Primula 'Kewensis'	Primula	Flowers	Bushy	Plentiful	Bright; some direct sun	50°–60°F/10°–16°C	Leaves and stems are covered with white meal
Primula malacoides	Fairy primrose	Flowers	Bushy	Plentiful	Bright	50°–60°F/10°–16°C	Best discarded after flowering
Primula obconica	Poison primrose	Flowers	Bushy	Plentiful while flowering; otherwise, moderate to sparing	Bright; some direct sun	50°–60°F/10°–16°C	Touching foliage can cause adverse skin reactions in some people
Primula sinensis	Chinese primrose	Flowers	Bushy	Plentiful to moderate	Bright	50°–60°F/10°–16°C	Plants benefit from spending summer outside
Primula vulgaris	Common primrose	Flowers	Bushy	Plentiful	Bright; some direct sun	50°–60°F/10°–16°C	Can be planted outdoors in the garden after flowering
Pseuderanthemum atropurpureum	Pseuderanthemum	Foliage, flowers	Upright	Moderate	Bright light to partial shade	65°–75°F/18°–24°C	High humidity essential
Pteris cretica	Table fern, Cretan brake, ribbon fern	Foliage	Rosette-forming	Moderate to plentiful	Bright; no direct sun	55°–70°F/13°–21°C	High humidity required
Punica granatum 'Nana'	Dwarf pomegranate	Flowers, fruit	Bushy	Moderate	Bright; some direct sun	60°–70°F/16°–21°C	Hand-pollinate flowers to encourage fruiting

R

PLANT	COMMON NAMES	FEATURES	SHAPE	WATERING	LIGHT	IDEAL INDOOR TEMPERATURE	SPECIAL POINTS
Radermachera sinica (*Stereospermum sinicum*)	Emerald tree, Asian bell tree	Foliage	Treelike/bushy	Moderate	Bright; no direct sun	60°–70°F/16°–21°C	Tolerates dry air well, but will not tolerate a smoky atmosphere
Rebutia minuscula	Red crown cactus, Mexican sunball	Flowers, succulent stems	Globular	Moderate in spring and summer; otherwise, sparingly	Full sun	50°–75°F/10°–24°C	A cool winter rest encourages flowering
Rhapis excelsa	Miniature fan palm, little lady palm	Foliage	Bushy	Moderate; sparingly in winter	Bright; some direct winter sun	60°–70°F/16°–21°C	High humidity required

PLANT	COMMON NAMES	FEATURES	SHAPE	WATERING	LIGHT	IDEAL INDOOR TEMPERATURE	SPECIAL POINTS
Rhipsalidopsis gaertneri	Easter cactus	Flowers	Trailing	Moderate while flowering; sparingly afterward	Bright; no direct sun	60°–70°F/16°–21°C	Give a short, cool rest period after flowering
Rhipsalis baccifera (*R. cassutha*)	Mistletoe cactus	Succulent stems, fruits	Trailing	Moderate; sparingly in winter	Bright; no direct sun	60°–75°F/16°–24°C	Provide a cool winter rest period
Rhipsalis cereuscula	Coral cactus	Succulent stems, fruits	Trailing	Moderate; less in winter	Bright; no direct midday summer sun	60°–75°F/16°–24°C	Needs a cool winter rest period
Rhododendron simsii and hybrids	Sim's azalea	Flowers	Shrubby	Plentiful	Bright; no direct sun	50°–55°F/10°–13°C	Use ericaceous (lime-free) potting mix
Rhoeo spathacea 'Variegata'	Boat lily, Moses-in-the-cradle	Foliage and flowers	Rosette-forming	Plentiful in growing season; sparingly in winter	Medium; no direct sun	60°–70°F/16°–21°C	High humidity required
Rochea coccinea (*Crassula coccinea*)	Rochea	Flowers and foliage	Upright	Moderate; sparingly in winter	Bright; some direct sun	45°–60°F/7°–16°C	Requires a well-ventilated location
Rosa spp.	Miniature rose	Flowers	Bushy	Moderate to plentiful	Full sun or light shade	55°–65°F/13°–18°	Move plants outdoors after flowering; bring in before the first hard frost
Ruellia makoyana	Monkey plant, trailing velvet plant	Flowers and foliage	Trailing	Moderate	Bright; no direct sun	60°–70°F/16°–21°C	A good plant for hanging baskets

S

PLANT	COMMON NAMES	FEATURES	SHAPE	WATERING	LIGHT	IDEAL INDOOR TEMPERATURE	SPECIAL POINTS
Saintpaulia spp.	African violet	Flowers, foliage (some varieties)	Rosette-forming	Moderate	Bright; no direct sun	65°–70°F/18°–21°C	Avoid splashing water on leaves
Salpiglossis sinuata	Painted tongue	Flowers	Bushy	Plentiful, but allow potting mix to dry out between waterings	Bright; some direct sun	50°–65°F/10°–18°C	Discard after flowering
Sanchezia speciosa (*S. nobilis*)	Sanchezia	Foliage and flowers	Shrubby	Plentiful in growing season; sparingly in winter	Bright; no direct summer sun	60°–70°F/16°–21°C	Prune in spring to maintain compact shape
Sansevieria trifasciata 'Laurentii'	Mother-in-law's tongue, snakeskin plant	Foliage	Tall, upright	Moderate; very sparingly in winter	Full sun	65°–70°F/18°–21°C	Use heavy clay pots to provide stability
Sarracenia flava	Yellow pitcher plant	Liquid-filled insect traps	Upright	Plentiful during the period of active growth	Bright; some direct sun	55°–60°F/13°–16°C	Needs some humidity
Saxifraga stolonifera	Strawberry begonia	Foliage and plantlets	Rosette-forming with trailing plantlets	Moderate; sparingly in winter	Bright; some direct sun	50°–60°F/10°–16°C	Good for hanging baskets
Schefflera arboricola	Umbrella tree	Foliage	Upright/treelike	Moderate	Bright; some direct sun	60°–70°F/16°–21°C	Pinch off the growing tips for a bushy plant; otherwise, provide a moss-covered pole for support
Schizanthus pinnatus	Poor man's orchid, butterfly flower	Flowers	Bushy	Moderate to plentiful	Full sun	55°–65°F/13°–18°C	Discard after flowering
Schlumbergera x buckleyi	Christmas cactus	Flowers	Trailing	Moderate; sparingly during rest period	Bright; some direct winter sun	60°–70°F/16°–21°C; cooler during rest period	Provide a cool, fairly dry rest period of eight weeks after flowering
Schlumbergera truncata	Crab cactus	Flowers	Trailing	Moderate; sparing in rest period	Bright; some direct winter sun	60°–70°F/16°–21°C; cooler in the rest period	Needs a fairly dry, cool rest period after flowering
Scilla siberica	Siberian squill	Flowers	Grassy	Moderate	Bright; no direct sun	40°–55°F/4°–13°C	Place newly potted bulbs outdoors until shoots develop
Sedum morganianum	Burro's tail	Foliage	Trailing	Moderate; sparingly in winter	Bright; some direct sun	60°–70°F/16°–21°C	Take care not to overwater

PLANT	COMMON NAMES	FEATURES	SHAPE	WATERING	LIGHT	IDEAL INDOOR TEMPERATURE	SPECIAL POINTS
Sedum sieboldii (*Hylotelephium siebodii*)	Stonecrop	Foliage and flowers	Trailing	Moderate to sparing	Full sun	50°–60°F/10°–16°C	Good for hanging baskets
Selaginella kraussiana	Spreading clubmoss	Foliage	Creeping	Plentiful	Medium light or light shade; no direct sun	60°–70°F/16°–21°C	High humidity essential; ideal for a terrarium
Senecio x *hybridus* (*Pericallis* x *hybridus*)	Cineraria	Flowers	Bushy	Moderate	Bright; some direct sun	50°–60°F/10°–16°C	Discard after flowering
Senecio rowleyanus	String-of-beads	Foliage	Trailing	Moderate to sparing	Bright; some direct sun	60°–70°F/16°–21°C	Discard when leggy and replace with cuttings
Setcreasea purpurea (*Tradescantia pallida*)	Purple heart	Foliage	Trailing, creeping	Moderate	Bright; some direct sun	60°–70°F/16°–21°C	Discard when leggy and replace with cuttings
Siderasis fuscata	Brown spiderwort	Foliage	Rosette-forming	Moderate	Medium to bright; no direct sun	70°F/21°C	Protect from fluctuating temperatures
Sinningia cardinalis	Cardinal flower, helmet flower	Flowers	Bushy	Plentiful while flowering, then reduce to allow tubers to dry out	Bright; no direct sun	70°F/21°C; under 50°F/10°C when dormant	Tubers become dormant shortly after flowering
Sinningia speciosa	Gloxinia	Flowers	Bushy	Plentiful to moderate; reduce after flowering and allow tubers to dry out	Bright; no direct sun	60°–70°F/16°–21°C	Tubers become dormant shortly after flowering
Smithiantha hybrids	Temple bells	Flowers	Bushy	Moderate; reduce after flowering and allow tubers to dry out	Light shade	70°F/21°C	Tubers become dormant shortly after flowering
Solanum capsicastrum	False Jerusalem cherry	Berries	Bushy	Moderate	Full sun	50°–60°F/10°–16°C	Place plants outdoors in summer to encourage formation of berries
Soleirolia soleirolii (*Helxine soleirolii*)	Mind-your-own-business, baby's tears	Foliage	Creeping	Plentiful to moderate	Medium to bright	60°–65°F/16°–18°C	Can be invasive
Sonerila margaritacea	Pearly sonerila	Foliage	Bushy	Moderate	Bright; no direct sun	70°F/21°C	High humidity essential
Sparmannia africana	African hemp, indoor linden, linden tree	Foliage and flowers	Treelike	Plentiful to moderate	Bright; no direct strong sun	55°–65°F/13°–18°C	Replace plants annually with cuttings
Spathiphyllum wallisii	Peace lily, white sails	Flowers and foliage	Bushy	Moderate; sparingly in winter	Bright light; no direct sun	60°–70°F/16°–21°C	High humidity required
Stapelia variegata (*Orebea variegata*)	Carrion flower	Flowers	Upright/spreading	Sparing to moderate	Full sun	60°–70°F/16°–21°C	Flowers have an unpleasant smell
Stenotaphrum secundatum 'Variegatum'	St. Augustine grass, buffalo grass	Foliage	Grassy	Plentiful in growing season; sparingly in winter	Bright; some direct sun	60°–70°F/16°–21°C	Good for hanging baskets
Stephanotis floribunda	Madagascar jasmine	Scented flowers	Climbing	Plentiful in growing season; sparingly in winter	Bright; no direct summer sun	65°–70°F/18°–21°C	Avoid fluctuating temperatures
Strelitzia nicolai	White bird-of-paradise	Flowers and foliage	Upright	Moderate to sparing	Bright; some direct sun	60°–70°F/16°–21°C; below 60°F/16°C in winter	Requires plenty of space
Strelitzia reginae	Bird-of-paradise, crane flower	Flowers and foliage	Upright	Moderate to sparing	Bright; some direct sun essential for flowering	60°–70°F/16°–21°C; about 55°F/13°C in winter	Plants from seed do not flower until they are about five years old
Streptocarpus x *hybridus*	Cape primrose	Flowers	Rosette-forming	Moderate	Bright; no direct sun	60°–70°F/16°–21°C	Remove faded flowers before seeds form
Streptosolen jamesonii	Marmalade bush, fire bush	Flowers	Scrambling	Plentiful to moderate in growing season; sparingly in winter	Bright; some direct sun	50°–70°F/10°–21°C	Best trained against a greenhouse wall
Strobilanthes dyeranus	Persian shield	Foliage	Upright	Moderate to sparing	Bright, filtered	60°–70°F/16°–21°C	Replace annually by cuttings

PLANT	COMMON NAMES	FEATURES	SHAPE	WATERING	LIGHT	IDEAL INDOOR TEMPERATURE	SPECIAL POINTS
Stromanthe amabilis (*Calathea amabilis*)	Stromanthe	Foliage	Bushy	Moderate	Medium to bright; no direct sun	65°–75°F/18°–24°C	High humidity required
Syagrus weddelliana	Weddel palm	Foliage	Bushy	Moderate	Bright; no direct sun	70°–75°F/21°–24°C	High humidity essential
Syngonium podophyllum	Arrowhead vine, goosefoot plant	Foliage	Climbing	Moderate	Bright; no direct sun	60°–80°F/16°–27°C	Leaves change shape as the plant matures; give support

T

PLANT	COMMON NAMES	FEATURES	SHAPE	WATERING	LIGHT	IDEAL INDOOR TEMPERATURE	SPECIAL POINTS
Tetrastigma voinieranum	Chestnut vine	Foliage	Climbing	Plentiful to moderate	Bright; no direct sun	60°–80°F/16°–27°C	Avoid fluctuating temperatures. Provide sturdy support
Thunbergia alata	Black-eyed Susan	Flowers	Climbing	Plentiful	Bright; sun direct sun	55°–65°F/13°–18°C	Annual, raised from seed in spring
Thymus vulgaris	Wild thyme	Aromatic foliage, flowers	Upright or spreading	Moderate	Bright; some direct sun	55°–65°F/13°–18°C	Place plants outdoors in summer
Tillandsia cyanea (*T. lindenii*)	Pink quill	Foliage and flowers	Grasslike	Mist-spray twice weekly in summer; less frequently in winter	Bright; no direct sun	60°–80°F/16°–27°C	Epiphyte, often mounted on wood, but also grown in potting mix
Tillandsia ionantha	Sky plant	Foliage and flowers	Rosette	Mist-spray twice weekly in summer; less frequently in winter	Bright; no direct sun	60°–70°F/16°–21°C	Epiphyte, usually mounted on wood
Tolmiea menziesii	Piggyback plant	Foliage	Bushy, semitrailing	Moderate	Bright; some direct sun	55°–65°F/13°–18°C	Plantlets are produced on the leaves
Trachycarpus fortunei	Windmill palm	Foliage	Bushy	Moderate; sparingly in winter	Full sun	40°–60°F/4°–16°C	Benefits from a spell outdoors in summer
Tradescantia fluminensis 'Variegata'	Wandering Jew, spiderwort, speeding Jenny	Foliage	Trailing	Plentiful in growing season; moderately in winter	Bright; some direct sun	60°–70°F/16°–21°C	Replace leggy plants with cuttings
Tulipa hybrids	Tulips	Flowers	Upright	Moderate	Bright	55°–60°F/13°–16°C	Bulbs require a cool, dark forcing period after planting

V

PLANT	COMMON NAMES	FEATURES	SHAPE	WATERING	LIGHT	IDEAL INDOOR TEMPERATURE	SPECIAL POINTS
Vallota speciosa (*Cyrtanthus elatus*)	Scarborough lily	Flowers	Grassy	Moderate; sparingly in winter and early spring	Bright; some direct sun	60°–70°F/16°–21°C; about 50°F/10°C in winter	Repot only when essential
Vriesea splendens	Flaming sword	Foliage and flowers	Vase-shaped	Sparing to moderate	Bright; some direct sun	60°–70°F/16°–21°C	Main vase dies after flowering

W

PLANT	COMMON NAMES	FEATURES	SHAPE	WATERING	LIGHT	IDEAL INDOOR TEMPERATURE	SPECIAL POINTS
Washingtonia filifera	Desert fan palm, petticoat palm	Foliage	Upright	Plentiful to moderate	Bright; plenty of direct sun	70°–75°F/21°–24°C; about 50°F/10°C in winter	Benefits from a spell outdoors in summer

Y

PLANT	COMMON NAMES	FEATURES	SHAPE	WATERING	LIGHT	IDEAL INDOOR TEMPERATURE	SPECIAL POINTS
Yucca elephantipes	Spineless yucca	Foliage	Treelike or rosette-forming	Moderate; very sparingly in winter	Full sun	60°–70°F/16°–21°C	Use clay pots for extra stability with tall plants

Z

PLANT	COMMON NAMES	FEATURES	SHAPE	WATERING	LIGHT	IDEAL INDOOR TEMPERATURE	SPECIAL POINTS
Zantedeschia aethiopica (*Z. africana*)	White calla lily, white arum lily	Flowers	Upright/bushy	Plentiful when flowering, then reduce to sparing as leaves begin to die back	Bright; some direct sun	55°–65°F/13°–18°C	Stand plants outdoors in summer
Zebrina pendula	Silvery inch plant, wandering Jew	Foliage	Trailing	Plentiful to moderate; sparingly in winter	Bright; some direct sun	60°–70°F/16°–21°C	Tolerant of shade, though leaf color will be reduced

GLOSSARY

*Some of the botanical terms used in this book are explained here. A word appearing in **bold italic** refers to another related entry, and the two entries should be read in conjunction.*

Acid Of soils and potting mix: below pH 7; containing no lime. (See *alkaline, ericaceous, pH*.)

Active growth period The time when a plant makes new growth, producing leaves and flowers. (See *dormant, resting*.)

Aerial roots Roots produced from the stems of a plant that can often absorb moisture from the air.

Alkaline Of soils and potting mixes: above pH 7; usually containing lime. (See *acid, pH*.)

Annual A plant that grows from seed, produces flowers and seeds, and dies in one growing season.

Anther The male, pollen-bearing part of a flower.

Architectural Refers to plants, usually with bold outlines, that are grown for their dramatic appearance.

Areole The part of the stem of cacti from which arise wool, spines, leaves (when present), lateral branches, and flowers.

Axil The angle between a leafstalk and the stem from which it grows.

Biennial A plant that grows from seed in one season, and produces flowers and seeds and dies the following season. (See *annual*.)

Biological control The deliberate use of natural enemies to control plant pests and diseases.

Blade The flat part of a leaf.

Bottom heat Warmth provided at the base of the growing medium in a propagator to encourage cuttings to root.

Bract A modified leaf that forms part of a flower; it may be brightly colored and decorative, as in bougainvillea. Bracts are sometimes confused with petals.

Bulb An underground storage organ that contains embryo leaves and/or flowers.

Bulbil A miniature bulb that develops around the base of mature bulbs or on the stem of plants such as lilies, often in the leaf *axil*.

Calyx The outer covering of a flower bud, consisting of modified leaves, or *sepals*. Calyxes are often green but are sometimes colorful and decorative.

Carnivorous Describes plants, also known as insectivorous, that capture and digest insects to obtain nutrients.

Chlorosis Yellowing of foliage due to loss of *chlorophyll*; often caused by nutrient *deficiency*. Chlorosis may cause distinctive patterns on the leaf.

Chlorophyll The green pigment in leaves that is important for *photosynthesis*.

Corm An underground storage organ, as in crocus, developed from the base of a stem.

Corolla The petals of a flower. They may be fused to form a tube, bell, or another shape, or they may be separate.

Crock Broken pieces of clay pot used as a layer in the bottom of a plant container to provide thorough drainage.

Crown The top of a tree including branches and leaves.

Cultivar A variety that has been bred in cultivation rather than arising in the wild. (See *variety*.)

Deadheading Removing faded flowers to prevent the production of seeds and improve a plant's appearance.

Deciduous Refers to plants that lose their leaves at the end of the *active growth period*.

Deficiency Shortage of a specific *nutrient*, which causes adverse symptoms in the plant.

Diffuse light Light that is screened and filtered, by a blind or curtain, for example.

Dormant Refers to a plant in a temporary period of inactivity, normally when top growth and roots die back. (See *resting*.)

Double Flowers with more than one layer of petals.

Entire Refers to leaf margins that are not divided.

Epiphytic Refers to a plant that in nature grows upon another plant, rather than in soil. Such plants absorb water and nutrients from the air and from rain, and use aerial roots for support.

Ericaceous Of plants: those that cannot tolerate lime in the growing medium; includes azaleas and heathers. Of *potting mix*: suitable for lime-hating plants.

Evergreen Refers to plants that retain their leaves year-round. (See *deciduous*.)

Family A botanical grouping of plants that share some of the same characteristics: e.g., Cactaceae, Bromeliaceae. Families are subdivided into *genus, species*, and *variety* (or *cultivar*): e.g., family Bromeliaceae, genus *Aechmea*, species *fasciata*, cultivar 'Variegata.'

Flower The reproductive, seed-forming organ of a plant.

Forcing Bringing plants into flower or growth earlier than their natural season by manipulating temperature, light, etc.

Frond The leaf of a fern or palm.

Genus A group of related *species*. (See *family*.)

Growing point The tip of a shoot where growth occurs.

Habit The overall shape and form of a plant, such as bushy, spreading, creeping, etc.

Hardy Describes a plant that can survive in the open without protection year-round, including periods of frost.

Heel A small strip of bark or older wood torn away with a side shoot when it is taken to form a cutting. Some plants root better when a heel is present.

Herbaceous Refers to plants that have no woody stems and die down in winter. (See *perennial*.)

Humidity The amount of water vapor present in the air.

Humus Rotted organic matter in the soil; it improves the soil's structure.

Hybrid A plant resulting from a cross between two nonidentical parents. Most hybrids are the result of crossing two different varieties, although some arise from crossing two different species (interspecific hybrids) or, more rarely, two different genera (bigeneric or intergeneric hybrids). Interspecific and bigeneric hybrids are indicated by an "×" in the botanical name—examples: *Schlumbergera* × *buckleyii* (interspecific hybrid between *S. russelliana* and *S. truncata*); × *Fatshedera lizei*, a bigeneric hybrid between *Fatsia japonica* 'Moseri' and *Hedera helix* var. *hibernica*.

Hydroponic cultivation A method of growing plants in water rather than soil by adding all nutrients to the water.

Larva The caterpillar stage in the life cycle of an insect. Since larvae are the feeding stage, they can be very damaging to plants.

Lateral A side shoot; a sublateral is a shoot arising from the side shoot.

Leaf Usually the main area of a plant in which *photosynthesis* takes place. Leaves occur in many shapes and sizes; a few plants, such as some cacti, have no leaves.

Leaflet A single segment of a compound (divided) leaf.

Loam Soil, originally from rotted-down turf. Good loam is a mixture of sand, clay, and humus and forms the basis of soil-based *potting mix*.

Lobe Section of a leaf, *bract*, or petal partly but not entirely separated from the whole.

Microclimate The atmospheric conditions created within a small area that differ from those of the general area around it: e.g., the relatively humid atmosphere immediately around a group of houseplants within a dry room.

Midrib The usually large, central vein of a leaf, generally raised on the underside of the leaf.

Mist A very fine spray of water applied to or around the foliage. The tiny droplets of water will not damage the leaves.

Node The part of a plant where the leaf joins the stem. Many cuttings root most readily from nodes.

Nutrients Minerals required by the plant and usually taken up in solution from the growing medium. Nitrogen, phosphorus, and potassium are the major nutrients (macronutrients), but plants need many others, some in tiny quantities (micronutrients). Plants that are not receiving enough nutrients will show *deficiency* symptoms.

Offset A small, new plant, usually produced at the base of the parent, which can be separated for propagation purposes. Several cacti, succulents, bulbs, and bromeliads produce offsets.

Ovate Of a leaf: broad and round at the bottom and tapering toward the tip.

Palmate Of a leaf: shaped like a spread hand, generally with five lobes.

Peat moss Decomposed vegetable matter, usually moss and sedges, used as a potting medium. Substitutes, such as coir, can often be used instead.

Pendant Applied to flowers that hang down, usually from slender flower stalks.

Perennial A plant that persists from year to year. (See *annual*.)

Petal A modified leaf that forms part of the *flower* and is often decorative and brightly colored.

Petiole The leafstalk.

pH The scale on which acidity and alkalinity of soil is measured. pH 7 is neutral; soil is alkaline above this point and acid below it.

Phloem The transportation system for nutrients in plants.

Photoperiodism The reaction of plants to variation in day length; often important in the initiation of flower buds.

Photosynthesis The process by which green-leafed plants convert light to usable energy. See *chlorophyll*.

Pinnate Refers to compound leaves with leaflets in opposite pairs on each side of the midrib.

Pistil The female part of a *flower*, consisting of *style*, *stigma*, and ovary.

Potting mix Growing medium specially prepared for plants in pots. Also waste organic matter rotted down in the garden.

Pricking out Moving small plants (usually seedlings) from one container to another where they can be spaced more widely.

Pseudobulb A thickened stem base on some orchids that acts as a storage organ and from which the leaves arise.

Rest period The time when plants make little or no growth but, unlike *dormant* plants, retain their leaves.

Rhizome A normally fleshy underground stem bearing shoots and roots.

Root ball The near-complete root system of a plant, with the potting mix that clings to the roots.

Rosette An arrangement of leaves that radiate in a circle from a single point.

Runner A long, slender stem bearing a new plant at intervals along it or at the tip.

Sepal A modified leaf that covers the flower bud. (See *calyx*.)

Shrub A plant that produces a permanent framework of woody stems, usually branching from the base.

Slow release Refers to fertilizers that break down gradually to release their nutrient content over an extended period.

Spadix A club-shaped, fleshy flower spike with small flowers on the surface; usually surrounded by a *spathe*.

Spathe A relatively large single *bract* surrounding a *spadix*. Often brightly colored.

Species Individuals that are alike and can cross-pollinate with each other. (See *family*.)

Spur A short branch carrying flowers; also a long, slender projection from some flowers.

Stamen The male part of a flower, consisting of a pollen-bearing *anther* on a filament.

Stigma The tip of the female part of the flower (the *pistil*) that receives pollen from the male.

Stolon A creeping stem that grows along the ground and roots where the *nodes* touch the soil.

Stopping Pinching off the growing tips to stimulate the production of side shoots.

Style The stem joining the *stigma* of a flower with the ovary.

Succulent A plant that stores water in its stems and/or leaves and is adapted to growing in a dry environment.

Sucker A shoot arising directly from the roots or stem of a plant.

Tender Of plants: damaged by frost or low temperature; not *hardy*.

Tendril A slender, threadlike shoot that twines around objects to support a climbing plant.

Terrarium A decorative miniature greenhouse that provides ideal conditions for plants requiring high humidity and protection from drafts.

Terrestrial Of orchids: species that grow in soil as opposed to being *epiphytic*.

Top-dress To apply potting mix and fertilizers on the soil surface of a potted plant. This usually entails removing the top 2–3in/ 5–8cm of old potting mix and replacing it with fresh. It is carried out instead of repotting when a plant is already in the largest convenient pot.

Trace elements Essential minerals needed in very small quantities by plants; also known as micronutrients. (See *nutrients*.)

Tuber An underground stem for food storage from which new plants can arise.

Tubercle A wartlike projection on a plant; common on the stems of cacti.

Undulate Of leaves or petals: wavy edged.

Variegation Different colored markings on green leaves; usually white, cream, or yellow, but other colors occur.

Variety A subdivision of a plant species; strictly applied to forms that arise in the wild. (See *cultivar*.)

Vein Conductive tissues used to transport food and water within plants.

Woody Applied to plant tissue and stems that become hardened and persist after leaf fall.

Xylem Water-conducting tissue within the plant. (See *phloem*.)

INDEX

The index should be used in conjunction with the Buyer's Guide and the Glossary.

A

Abutilon 16
  x hybridum 30
  —'Cannington Red' 30
  —'Kentish Belle' 30
  —'Pink Lady' 30
  —'Red Belle' 30
  —'Savitzii' 30
  pictum 'Thompsonii' 13, 19, 30
Acalypha
  hispida 31
  —'Alba' 31
  wilkesiana 31
  —'Can Can' 31
  —'Marginata' 31
Achimenes 32, 194
Acorus gramineus 146
Adiantum
  hispidulumm 26
  raddianum 13, 18, 26, 32
Adromischus festivus (A. cooperi) 146
Aechmea
  cylindrata 33
  fasciata 19, 33, 48
  —'Purpurea' 33
  —'Variegata' 33
Aeonium arboreum
  'Atropurpureum' 34
  'Schwartzkopf' 34
aerial roots 27, 204
Aeschynanthus
  lobbianus 34
  marmoratus 34
  speciosus 19, 34
African daisy 77, 90
African hemp 183
African lily 146
African violet 14, 20, 22, 23, 130, 206
Agapanthus africanus 146
  albus 146
  Headbourne hybrids 146
Agathaea coelestis see
  Felicia amelloides

Agave americana 35
Aglaonema
  commutatum 18
  'Silver Queen' (A. crispum) 35
air-layering 208
air plant 48, 49
Albizia julibrissin 147
Allamanda cathartica 19, 36
allergies 21
Alocasia sanderiana 36
Aloe
  barbadensis 37
  humilis 37
  —'Globosa' 37
  jucunda 37
  variegata 37, 38
  vera see A. barbadensis
aluminum plant 13, 122
amaryllis 95
Amaryllis belladonna 95, 147
Amazon lily 161
Ananas
  bracteatus var. tricolor 38
  comosus 22, 38
angel's trumpet 21, 158
angel wings 13, 51
annuals 191
anthers 190
Anthurium
  andraeanum 39
  crystallinum 148
  scherzerianum 19, 39
  —'Rothschildeanum' 39
  —'Wardii' 39
Aphelandra squarrosa 15, 40, 193
aphids 212
Aporocactus flagelliformis 40
apple geranium 118
Arabian coffee plant 155
Arabian violet 84
Aralia elegantissima see Dizygotheca
  elegantissima
Araucaria heterophylla (A. excelsa) 41
architectural plants 11, 20
Ardisia crenata 41
Areca lutescens (areca palm) see
  Chrysalidocarpus lutescens
areoles 140
Argyranthemum frutescens see
  Chrysanthemum frutescens
Aristolochia
  clematis 148
  elegans (A. littoralis) 148
arrowhead vine 12, 142
Arundinaria viridistriata (Pleioblastus
  auricoma) 148
Asclepias curassavica 148–9
Asian bell tree 178
Asparagus densiflorus (asparagus fern)
  'Myers' 42
  'Sprengeri' 12, 22, 42
Aspidistra
  elatior 18, 42, 194
  lurida 42, 194
Asplenium
  australasicum 43
  bulbiferum 149, 209
  nidus 18, 43
Astrophytum myriostigma 149
Aucuba japonica 150, 193
  'Crotonifolia' 150
  'Fructu-albo' 150
  'Variegata' 150
Australian laurel 175

B

baby's tears 172, 182
bachelor's button 164
Bacillus thuringiensis 213

bamboo 17, 148
bamboo palm 128
banyan tree 86
Barberton daisy 90
barrel cactus 162–3
basal rot 212
basket grass 172
basket plant 34
bead plant 12, 172
Beaucarnea recurvata 43
beefsteak plant see Acalypha wilkesiana;
  Iresine herbstii
Begonia 44–5
  bowerii 26
  'Corallina de Lucerna' 44
  x hiemalis Elatior
    'Heidi' 44–5
  masoniana 45
  rex 12, 13, 19, 45, 61
  sutherlandii 44
  x tuberhybrida 44
Belgian evergreen 79
belladonna lily 147
bellflower 54, 195
Beloperone guttata 46
Bertolonia marmorata 150
  'Bruxellensis' 150
  'Mosaica' 150
big blue lilyturf 170
bigeneric hybrids 84
Billbergia
  nutans 46
  rhodocyanea see Aechmea fasciata
biological control 212
bird-catcher tree 175
bird-of-paradise 184
bird's-nest bromeliad 111
bird's-nest fern 43
birthwort 148
bishop's cap/miter cactus 149
black-eyed Susan 186
black pepper 175
bleeding-heart vine 62
blood flower 148–9
bloodleaf 13, 100
blue echeveria 160
blue marguerite 162
blue passion flower 174
blushing bromeliad 110
blushing philodendron 121
boat lily 129
Boston fern 110
botrytis 212, 215
bottle gardens 26–7
bottle palm 43
Bougainvillea 15
  x buttiana 47
  —'Amethyst' 47
  —'Golden Glow'/'Hawaiian Gold' 47
  —'Jamaica Red' 47
  —'Killie Campbell' 47
  —'Orange King' 47
  —'Surprise'/'Mary Palmer' 47
  glabra 19, 47
  —'Alexandra' 47
  —'Variegata' 47
Bouvardia
  longiflora 150
  ternifolia 150
Bowiea volubilis 151
Brassaia actinophylla see Schefflera
  actinophylla
Brazilian firecracker 106
Brazilian plume 101
Breynia nivosa (B. disticha) 151
  'Rosea-Picta' 151
Brodiaea laxa (Triteleia laxa) 151
  'Queen Fabiola' 151
bromeliads 17, 48–9, 194–5, 203

bronze inch plant 145
Browallia speciosa
  'Blue Troll' 50
  'Major' 50
  'White Troll' 50
brown spiderwort 181
Brugmansia x candida see Datura x
  candida
Brunfelsia pauciflora (B. calycina) 50
Buddhist pine 176
Buddleia madagascariensis (Nicodemia
  madagascariensis) 152
buffalo grass 183
bunny ears 140–1
Burmese fishtail palm 153
burn plant 37
burro's tail 134
bush violet 50
bushy plants 11
butterfly flower 180–1
butterfly ginger 165
butterfly palm 59
button fern 26, 174

C

cabbage tree 67
cacti 23, 24, 140–1, 191, 193, 194–5
  repotting 200
Caladium x hortulanum 13, 19, 51, 191
  'Carolyn Morton' 51
  'Frieda Hempel' 51
  'Pink Beauty' 51
  'White Queen' 51
calamondin 62
Calathea
  amabilis see Stromanthe amabilis
  makoyana 18, 52
Calceolaria x herbeohybrida 15, 52
calico flower 148
California pitcher plant 158
Calliandra
  haematocephala (C. inaequilatera) 152
  tweedii 152
Callisia
  elegans (Setcreasea striata) 53
  repens 53
Callistemon citrinus 53, 194
Camellia japonica 12, 54, 194
Campanula isophylla 16, 22, 54, 195
  'Stella Blue' 54
  'Stella White' 54
candle plant see Plectranthus coleoides
  'Marginatus'; P. oertendahlii
Cape cowslip 169
Cape jasmine 90
Cape leadwort 125
Cape primrose 139
capillary matting 196
Capsicum annuum 21, 55
  'Fireball' 55
  'Holiday Cheer' 55
  'Red Missile' 55
cardinal flower 182
Carex morrowii 'Variegata' 18, 56
Carica papaya 152–3
  'Solo' 152
caricature plant 164
Carludovica palmata 153
carnation tortrix moth 213
carnivorous plants 191
carrion flower 183
Caryota mitis 153
cast-iron plant 42
caterpillars 213
Catharanthus roseus 56
cathedral windows 52
Cattleya 57, 114
  Bob Betts 'White Wings' 57
  'Guatamalensis' 57

intermedia 57
labiata 57
Nigritian 'King of Kings' 57
'Violacea' 57
Celebes pepper 123
century plant 35
Cephalocereus senilis (Pilocereus senilis) 21, 153
Ceropegia woodii (C. linearis ssp. *woodii)* 154
Cestrum
aurantiacum 154
elegans 'Smithii' 154
nocturnum 154
chain of hearts 154
Chamaedorea elegans 12, 18, 20, 58, 185
Chamaerops humilis 11, 58, 195
chenille plant 31
chestnut vine 185
chilli pepper 55
Chinese evergreen 35
Chinese jade plant 68
Chinese jasmine 101
Chinese primrose 127
chlorophyll 13
Chlorophytum 208
comosum 'Vittatum' 11, 18, 59
Christmas cactus 133
Christmas pepper 55
Christmas star 83
Chrysalidocarpus lutescens 59
Chrysanthemum 193, 194
frutescens 60
—'Etoile d'Or' 60
—'Mary Wootton' 60
x *morifolium* 19, 60
cigar/cigarette flower 71
cineraria 14, 135
Cissus
antarctica 18, 61, 185, 204
—'Minima' 61
discolor 61
rhombifolia 61
—'Ellen Danica' 61
x *Citrofortunella microcarpus* (x *C. mitis)* 19, 62
Clerodendrum thomsoniae 62
—'Variegatum' 62
Clianthus
formosus 7, 154
puniceus 154
climbing fig 86
climbing onion 151
climbing plants 11, 27, 204
Clivia miniata 13, 15, 18, 63
'Striata' 63
clown orchid 112
cobra lily 158
Coccoloba uvifera 155
Cocos weddelliana see *Syagrus weddelliana*
Codiaeum variegatum pictum 13, 19, 64
'Aucubifolium' 64
'Bravo' 64
'Craigii' 64
'Golden Bell' 64
'Reidii' 64
Coelogyne cristata 65
Coffea arabica 155
'Nana' 155
coir 201
Coleus blumei 13, 19, 22, 65
Columnea 193
x *banksii* 66,
gloriosa 22, 66
—'Alpha' 66
—'Chanticleer' 66
—'Mary Ann' 66
—'Purpurea' 66
—'Stavanger' 66

common passion flower 174
common primrose 127, 195
common sundew 159
common thyme 142
containers 21, 24–5
Convallaria majalis 155
'Fortin's Giant' 155
'Prolificans' 155
'Rosea' 155
copper leaf 31
coral berry 41
coral moss 172
Cordyline 22, 193
australis 67
—'Atropurpurea' 67
—'Purpurea' 67
terminalis 67
—'Baptistii' 67
—'Kiwi' 67
—'Rededge' 67
corm 191
corn plant 78
Costus
igneus (C. cuspidatus) 156
pulverulentus (C. sanguineus) 156
speciosus 156
spiralis 156
Cotyledon
orbiculata 156
undulata 156
cowslip 126
crab cactus 133, 140
crane flower 19, 184
Crassula
arborescens 68
—'Variegata' 68
coccinea see *Rochea coccinea*
cotyledon see *Crassula arborescens*
muscosa 140
ovata (C. portulacea) 68
creeping Charlie 26
creeping fig 11, 86
creeping thyme 142
crepe ginger 156
crested fishtail palm 153
Cretan brake 177
crimson bottle brush 53
Crinum
bulbispermum 156
moorei 156
x *powellii* 156
—'Album' 156
cristate table fern 177
Crocus hybrids 7, 15, 69, 194
'Little Dorrit' 69
'Pickwick' 69
'Queen on the Blues' 69
Crossandra
infundibuliformis 69
—'Mona Walhead' 69
pungens 69
undulifolia see *C. infundibuliformis*
croton 64
crown of thorns 82
Cryptanthus 26, 48
acaulis 70
—'Roseo-pictus' 70
—'Roseus' 70
—'Ruber' 70
bivittatus 48
crystal anthurium 148
Ctenanthe
amabilis see *Stromanthe amabilis*
oppenheimiana 'Tricolor' 70
Cuphea hysiopifolia 71
Cuphea ignea (C. platycentra) 71
Cupid peperomia 120

Cupid's bower 32
curly palm 12, 20, 96
cuttings 206–7
Cyanotis
kewensis 157
somaliensis 157
Cycas revoluta 71
cyclamen 14, 20, 72–3, 193, 194
cyclamen mites 213
Cyclamen persicum 12, 18, 72–3
Cymbidium 74, 114
'Mem Rosl Greer' 74
'Minuet' 74
'Peter Pan' 74
'Western Rose' 74
Cyperus
alternifolius 18, 75
—'Variegatus' 75
isocladus see *C. prolifer*
papyrus 157
—'Nanus' 157
prolifer 157
Cyrtanthus elatus see *Vallota speciosa*
Cyrtomium falcatum 157
'Rochfordianum' 157
Cytisus fragrans see *Genista* x *spachiana*
x *spachianus* see *Genista* x *spachiana*

D
daffodil 109
Darlingtonia californica 158
Datura aurea 158
x *candida* 19, 21, 158
—'Plena' (*D.* 'Knightii') 158
versicolor 158
Davallia fejeensis 75
day length 83, 211
deadheading 205
deciduous plants 191
Delairea odorata see *Senecio mikanioides*
delta maidenhair fern 13, 26, 32
Dendranthema x *grandiflorum* see *Chrysanthemum* x *morifolium*
Dendrobium 114
desert fan palm 187
desert privet 119
devil's ivy 81
devil's tongue 162–3
Dichorisandra
reginae 159
thyrsiflora 159

Dicksonia antarctica 159
Dieffenbachia 21
x *bausei* 76
maculata (D. picta) 11, 19, 76
—'Camilla' 76
—'Exotica' 76
—'Rudolph Roehrs' 76
—'Tropic Snow' 76
seguine 76
Dimorphotheca sinuata (*D. aurantiaca)* 77
'Giant Orange'/'Goliath' 77
'Glistening White' 77
'Salmon Queen' 77
Dionaea muscipula 77
Dipladenia 106
diseases 212–15
displaying plants 20–1
division 208
Dizygotheca elegantissima 12, 78
Dracaena 22
fragrans 'Massangeana' 13, 78
indivisa 67
marginata 19, 20, 79
—'Colorama' 79
—'Tricolor' 12, 13, 79
sanderiana 13, 79
terminalis 67
Drosera rotundifolia 159
drumstick primula 126
dumb cane 11, 21, 76
Dutch crocus 69
dwarf fan palm 58
dwarf mountain palm 58
dwarf pomegranate 177
Dyckia fosteriana 48, 160

E
Easter cactus 128
east walls 192, 193
Echeveria secunda var. *glauca* 160
Echinocactus grusonii 141
Echinocereus eyriesii see *Echinopsis eyriesii*
pectinatus 80
Echinopsis eyriesii 160
Egyptian star cluster 174–5
elephant foot 43
elephant's-ear see *Alocasia sanderiana*; *caladium* x *hortulanum*
elfin herb 71

elkhorn fern 124
emerald-feather fern 42
emerald ripple 26, 119
emerald tree 178
English ivy see *Hedera helix*
Epiphyllum ackermannii 80
epiphytes 48–9, 140, 175, 191, 196, 203
Epipremnum aureum 18, 19, 20, 81
  'Marble Queen' 81
  'Tricolor' 81
Episcia cupreata 82
Eranthemum atropurpureum see
  Pseuderanthemum atropurpureum
Erica carnea 160
  x *hiemalis* 160–1
Eriobotrya japonica 161
Eucharis x *grandiflora* (Eucharist lily) 161
Euphorbia
  milii
   —*lutea* 82
   —var. *splendens* 82
  pulcherrima 15, 19, 21, 83, 194, 211
   —'Diva' 83
   —'Ecke's White' 83
   —'Hot Pink' 83
   —'Lemon Drop' 83
   —'Pink Peppermint' 83
   —'Rosea' 83
   —'Top White' 83
European fan palm 11, 58, 195
Eurya japonica 162
  —'Winter Wine' 162
Eustoma grandiflorum 162
  'Echo' 162
  'Yodel' 162
evergreen plants 191, 194
Exacum affine 84, 191
  'Rococo' 84

F

fairy primrose 126
falling stars 54
false aralia 78
false castor-oil plant 85
false heather 71
false Jerusalem cherry 15, 21, 137
false palm 67
x *Fatshedera lizei* 18, 84
Fatsia japonica 12, 18, 85
  'Moseri' 84
Faucaria tigrina 85
feeding 198–9
Felicia amelloides (*Agathaea coelestis*) 162
fern spores 209
Ferocactus latispinus 162–3
fertilisers 198–9
Ficus 86–7
  benghalensis 86
  benjamina 11, 13, 19, 20, 86, 87
   —'Starlight' 22, 87
  deltoidea var. *diversifolia* 86
  elastica 13, 20, 86, 208
   —'Black Prince' 13
   —'Decora' 86
   —'Robusta' 19, 86–7
  lyrata 12, 19, 20, 86
  microcarpa (*F. retusa*) 86
   —'Hawaii' 86
  pumila (*F. repens*) 11, 18, 86
  pumila minima 26
  rubiginosa 86
fiddle leaf fig 12, 20, 86
fiery costus 156
filament 190
finger aralia 78
fire bush 184
firecracker flower 69
firecracker vine 106
fire dragon plant 31

fish-hook cactus 162–3, 195
Fittonia verschaffeltii 26
  argyroneura 26, 88
flame nettle 13, 22, 65
flame-of-the-woods 167
flame violet 82
flaming Katy 102
flamingo flower 39
flaming sword 144
florists' chrysanthemum 11, 22, 60, 193
florists' cyclamen 72–3
flowering and day length 83, 211
flowering plants 14–15
foliage plants 12–13, 17, 24, 191
foliar feed 198, 199
fountain dracaena 67
foxtail fern 42
frangipani 176
freckle face 99
Freesia 88
  'Super Giant' 88
French heather 160–1
friendship plant 46
fruit salad plant 108
Fuchsia 18, 89, 193
  'Cascade' 89
  'Checkerboard' 89
  'Display' 89
  'Dollar Princess' 89
  'Falling Stars' 89
  'Golden Marinka' 89
  'Little Charmer' 89
  'Swingtime' 89
fungicides 215
fungus gnats 214

G

Gardenia augusta (*G. grandiflora/*
  G. jasminoides) 15, 90, 193
garland flower 165
Genista x *spachiana* 163
Geogenanthus undatus (*G. poeppegii*) 163
geranium 117
Gerbera jamesonii 90
German ivy 136
German violet 84
Glechoma hederacea 'Variegata' 164
globe amaranth 164
Gloriosa superba 'Rothschildiana'
  (gloriosa lily) 19, 91, 204
glory pea 7, 154
gloxinia 137, 182
gold dust tree 150
golden barrel cactus 141
golden feather palm 59
golden pothos 81
golden trumpet 36
goldfish plant 66
Gomphrena globosa 164
  'Buddy' 164
  'Nana' 164
good luck palm 58
good luck plant 67
goosefoot plant 12, 142
gout plant 168
grape ivy 61, 185
Graptophyllum pictum 164
grass nut 151
grass palm 67
gray mold 212, 215
green earth star 70
greenfly 212
Grevillea robusta 91, 194
ground ivy 164
grouping plants 22–3
Guzmania
  dissitiflora 164–5
  lingulata 48
Gymnocalycium mihanovichii 'Red Cap' 141

Gynura aurantiaca 92
  procumbens 92
  'Purple Passion' 12, 13, 22, 92

H

Haemanthus humilis
  'Wilsonii' 92
  katherinae 92
hair palm 58
harmful plants 21
Hatiora gaertneri see
  Rhipsalidopsis
  gaertneri
Haworthia pumila
  (*H. margaritifera*) 165
heartleaf philodendron 12, 121
hearts entangled 154
hearts on a string 154
Hebe x *andersonii* 165
  'Variegata' 165

Hedera
  algeriensis 'Gloire de Marengo' 13, 93
  helix 13, 18, 19, 93, 195, 204
   —'Glacier' 93
   —'Goldheart' 93
   —'Ivalace' 93
   —'Little Diamond' 13
   —'Sagittifolia' 93
  var. *hibernica* 84
hedgehog cactus 80
Hedychium coronarium 165
Heliconia schiedeana 166
helmet flower 182
Helxine soleirolii see *Soleirolia soleirolii*
Hemigraphis colorata (*H. alternata*) 166
  'Exotica' 166
  repanda 166
hen-and-chickens fern 149
Heptapleurum arboricolum see *Schefflera*
  arboricola
herbaceous plants 191
herringbone plant 13, 107
Hibiscus rosa-sinensis 94, 193
  —'Golden Belle' 94
  —'Koenig' 94
  —'Paramaribo' 94
  —'Rosalie' 94
  —'Surfrider' 94
  schizopetalus 94
Hippeastrum x *acramannii*
  (*H.* x *ackermannii*) 95, 194
  'Appleblossom' 95
  'Bijou' 95
  'Lady Jane' 95
  'Picotee' 95
  'Red Lion' 95
Hoffmannia
  ghiesbreghtii 96
  —'Variegata' 96
  refulgens 96
  —'Vittata' 96
  regalis 'Roezlii' 96
holly fern 157
holly-leafed osmanthus 173
honey plant 97
hormone rooting powder 206
horsehead philodendron 120
hot-water plant 32
Howea belmoreana 12, 20, 96
  forsteriana 96
Hoya australis 97

Hoya carnosa 97
  —'Variegata' 97
  lanceolata ssp. *bella* 97
humidity 194–5
huntsman's horn 180
Hyacinthus orientalis (hyacinth)15, 25, 98
  'Anna Marie' 98
  'City of Haarlem' 98
  'Delft Blue' 98
Hydrangea macrophylla (*H. hortensis*)
  19, 98
  'Blue Prince' 98
  'Garten-Baudirektor Kuhnert' 98
  'Holstein' 98
  'Maréchal Foch' 98
  'Queen Elizabeth' 98
hydroponics (hydroculture) 210–11
Hylotelephium sieboldii see *Sedum*
  sieboldii
Hymenocallis littoralis 166
Hypocyrta radicans see *Nematanthus*
  gregarius
Hypoestes phyllostachya 13, 99
  'Pink Splash' 99
  'Rose Splash' 99
  'White Splash' 99

I

Impatiens walleriana 12, 19, 99
Indian laurel 86
indoor linden 183
insecticides 212–15
Ipheion uniflorum 167
  'Froyle Mill' 167
Ipomoea tricolor 167, 191
  'Heavenly Blue' 167
Iresine herbstii 13, 100
  'Aureo-reticulata' 100
  'Brilliantissima' 100
Irish ivy 84
irrigator 196
Ithuriel's spear 151
ivy geranium 118
Ixora coccinea 167

J

Jacaranda mimosifolia 168
Jacobinia carnea see *Justicia carnea*

'Nelsonii' 169
'Pearsonii' 169
ladder fern 110
Lady's slipper orchids 173
Lantana camara 104
 'Chelsea Gem' 104
 'Sundancer' 104
layering 208
leaf cuttings 206–7
leaf embryos 209
leaf flower 151
leaf miners 213
leaf vein cuttings 206–7
leaves 190–1
 color, shape texture 12–13
 Leca 210
 Leea coccinea 169
 'Burgundy' 169
 'Green' 169
lemon geranium 118
lemon-scented thyme 142
leopard lily 76
light 20, 192–3, 211
Lilium 169
 'Chinook' 169
 'Cinnabar' 169
 'Connecticut King' 169
 'Destiny' 169
 'Pixie' 169
 'Prosperity' 169
lily of the valley 155
linden tree 183
lipstick plant 34
Liriope muscari (*L. graminifolia densiflora*) 170
 'Gold-banded' 170
 'Silvery Midget' 170
Lisianthus russellianus see *Eustoma grandiflorum*
Lithops lesliei 104, 194
little lady palm 128
living stones 104
lobster claw 154
lobster claws 166
lobster plant 83
lollipop plant 116
loquat 161
lucky clover 116
Lycaste 114

M

macronutrients 198
Madagascar dragon tree 20, 79
Madagascar jasmine 138
Madagascar periwinkle 56
Malay ginger 156
Mammillaria
 bocasana 105
 zeilmanniana 105
Mandevilla
 amabilis 106
 x *amoena* 'Alice du Pont' 106
 splendens 106
Manettia inflata (*M. bicolor/M. luteo-rubra*) 106
Maranta 185
 leuconeura 12–13, 107
 erythroneura (*M. tricolor*) 13, 18, 107
 kerchoveana 107
 leuconeura (*M. l. massangeana*) 107
marlberry 41
marmalade bush 184
match-me-if-you-can 31
mealybugs 213
medicine aloe 37
Medinilla magnifica 108
Mexican breadfruit 108
Mexican flame leaf 83

Mexican sunball 178
Microcoelium weddellianum see *Syagrus weddelliana*
micronutrients 198
Mikania dentata (*M. ternata*) 170
Miltonia 114, 170
 candida 170
 regnellii 170
Mimosa pudica 170–1
mind-your-own-business 182
Ming aralia 176
miniature agave 160
miniature creeping fig 26
miniature eyelash begonia 26
miniature fan palm 128
miniature rose 179
miniature wax plant 97
mistletoe cactus 178–9
mistletoe fig 86
money tree 68
monkey plant 179
monk's hood cactus 149
Monstera deliciosa 11, 12, 19, 20, 27, 108
morning glory 167
Moses-in-the-cradle 129
moss pole 27, 204
mother-in-law's tongue 11, 131
mother-of-thousands 143
mother spleenwort 149
moth orchid 114–15, 175

N

Narcissus 15, 109, 194
 'Baby Moon' 109
 'Carlton' 109
 'February Gold' 109
 'February Silver' 109
 'Fortune' 109
 'Ice Follies' 109
 'King Alfred' 109
 'Minnow' 109
 'Paperwhite' 15, 109
 'Soleil d'Or' 109
 'Tête-à-Tête' 109
Neanthe elegans see *Chamaedorea elegans*
Nematanthus gregarius (*N. radicans/Hypocyrta radicans*) 171
Neoregelia
 carolinae 'Tricolor' 110
 'Meyendorffii' 49
 tristis 49
Nepenthes x *hookeriana* 171
Nephrolepis exaltata 'Bostoniensis' 18, 110, 193
Nerine bowdenii 171
 'Alba' 171
 'Fenwick's Variety' 171
 'Zeal Giant' 171
Nerium oleander 12, 21, 111
Nertera granadensis 12, 172
nerve plant 88
never-never plant 70
New Zealand cabbage palm 67
Nicodemia madagascariensis see *Buddleja madagascariensis*
Nidularium
 billbergioides 48
 innocentii
 —'Lineatum' 111
 —'Striatum' 111
night-blooming jasmine 154
Nolina recurvata see *Beaucarnea recurvata*
Nopalxochia ackermannii see *Epiphyllum ackermannii*
Norfolk Island pine 41
north walls 192, 193
nosegay 176

O

oak-leafed geranium 118
Ocimum basilicum 18, 112
 'Crispum' 112
 'Dark Opal' 112
 'Purple Ruffles' 112
 'Ruffles' 112
Odontoglossum 114
 grande 112
offsets 207
old-man cactus 153
Olea europaea 172
oleander 21, 111, 195
olive 172
Oncidium 115
Ophiopogon
 jaburan 113
 —'Vittatus'/'Variegatus'/'Argenteo-variegatus'/'Aureo-variegatus'/'Javanensis' 113
 planiscapus 'Nigrescens' 113
Oplismenus hirtellus 172
 'Variegatus' 172
Opuntia microdasys 140–1
orchid cactus 80
orchids 14, 15, 16, 17, 19, 22, 114–15
Orebea variegata see *Stapelia variegata*
ornamental chilli pepper 21, 55
ornamental pepper 21, 55, 123
Osmanthus heterophyllus 'Variegatus' (*O. ilicifolius*) 173
Oxalis deppei (*O. tetraphylla*) 116

P

Pachystachys lutea 116, 193
pagoda tree 176
painted drop tongue 35
painted-leaf begonia 12
painted net leaf 26
painted nettle 65
painted tongue 180
palm lily 67
Panama-hat plant 153
Pandanus veitchii 173
panda plant 102
pansy orchid 114, 170
papaya 152–3
paper flower 47
Paphiopedilum 115, 173
 callosum 173
 sukhakulii 173
papyrus 157
para-para 175
parlor palm 20, 58
parlor plant 42
parrot's beak 154
parsley fern 149
partridge-breast aloe 23, 38
Passiflora caerulea 19, 174
pawpaw 152–3
peace lily 138
peacock plant 52
pearl plant 165
pearly sonerila 182
peat and peat moss 201
pebble plant 104
Pelargonium 17, 193
 abrotanifolium 118
 capitatum 118
 crispum 12, 118
 x *domesticum* 117
 —'Grand Slam' 117
 graveolens 118
 x *hortorum* 18, 117
 —'Mrs Henry Cox' 117
 —'Robert Fish' 117
 odoratissimum 118
 peltatum 118

Jacob's coat 31
jade tree 68
Japanese aralia/fatsia 12, 84, 85
Japanese hibiscus lantern 94
Japanese laurel 150
Japanese pittosporum 175
Japanese sago palm 71
Japanese sedge grass 56
Japanese yew 176
jasmine 14, 15, 27
Jasminum
 mesnyi 100
 polyanthum 12, 18, 101
 primulinum see *J. mesnyi*
Jatropha podagrica 168
Jerusalem cherry 137
Jew, wandering see wandering Jew
Joseph's coat 13, 64
Justicia
 brandegeana see *Beloperone guttata carnea* 101
 pauciflora (*J. rizzinii*) 25, 168

K

kaka beak 154
Kalanchoe 22, 102–3
 beharensis 102
 blossfeldiana 12, 19, 102–3
 —'Calypso' 102
 diagremontiana 209
 manginii 'Tessa' 102
 marmorata 102, 103
 pumila 103
 tomentosa 102
kangaroo vine 61, 185
kanniedood aloe 38
kentia palm 96
king's crown 101
Kohleria eriantha 168–9
Kusamaki 176

L

Lachenalia aloides 169
 'Aurea' 169

—'L'Elégante' 118
—'Rouletta' 118
—'Summer Showers' 118
quercifolium 118
tomentosum 118
Pellaea rotundifolia 26, 174
Pellionia daveauana (*P. repens*)174
pulchra 174
Pentas lanceolata (*P. carnea*) 174–5
penwiper 102, 103
Peperomia 13, 22
caperata 13, 119
—'Emerald Ripple' 119
—'Little Fantasy' 26
—'Variegata' 119
magnoliifolia 119
—'Green and Gold' 119
—'Variegata' 119
obtusifolia 119
scandens (*P. serpens*) 18, 19, 120
—'Variegata' 120
peppermint geranium 118
perennials 191
Pericallis
cruentus see *Senecio* x *hybridus*
x *hybridus* see *Senecio* x *hybridus*
Persian shield 185
Persian violet 84
pesticides 212–15
pests 212–15
petticoat palm 187
Phalaenopsis spp. 114–15, 175
pheasant's wings 38
Philodendron 194
bipennifolium 120
bipinnatifidum 19, 120
erubescens 121
—'Burgundy' 121
—'Red Emerald' 121
scandens 12, 18, 19, 20, 121, 193
phloem 190, 191
Phoenix roebelenii 122
phosphorus 198
photoperiodism 211
photosynthesis 192
piggyback plant 143
Pilea 22
cadierei 13, 122
—'Minima' 122
involucrata 123
'Moon Valley' (*P. mollis*) 123
nummularifolia 26
peperomioides 123
spruceana see *P. involucrata*
Pilocereus senilis see *Cephalocereus senilis*
pinching out 205, 212
pineapple 38, 48
pink acanthus 101
pinkquill 49
Piper
crocatum see *P. ornatum*
nigrum 175
ornatum 123, 193
Pisonia umbellifera 'Variegata' 175
pistil 190
pitcher plant 171
pith 190, 191
Pittosporum tobira 175
'Variegatum' 175
plant anatomy 190–1
plant care 189–215
plant shapes 11
plant types 191
Platycerium bifurcatum (*P. alcicorne*)
124
Plectranthus
australis 124
coleoides 'Marginatus' (*P. forsteri*) 124
oertendahlii 124

Pleioblastus auricoma see *Arundinaria viridistriata*
Plumbago auriculata (*P. capensis*) 125
'Alba' 125
indica 125
Plumeria rubra (*P. acuminata*) 176
plush vine 170
pocketbook plant 52
Podocarpus macrophyllus 176
'Maki' 176
poinsettia 15, 21, 22, 83, 194, 211
poisonous plants 21
poison primrose 21, 126, 127
polka dot plant 99
polyanthus 126
Polyscias scutellaria 'Balfourii'
(*P. balfouriana*) 176
pomegranate 177
ponytail plant 43
poor man's orchid 180–1
Port Jackson fig 86
positioning, plants 16–19
potassium 198
Pothos aureus see *Epipremnum aureum*
potting mixes 201
potting on 202
powder-puff cactus 105
powder-puff plant 152
powdery mildew 215
prairie gentian 162
prayer plant 12–13, 107
prickly pear cactus 140–1
primrose jasmine 100
primroses/primulas 14, 25, 126–7
Primula
denticulata 126
'Kewensis' 126
malacoides 126
obconica 21, 25, 126–7
—'Ariane' series 126
—'Libre' series 126
sinensis 126, 127
x *tommasinii* 126
veris 126
vulgaris 126, 127, 195
propagation 206–9
pruning 205
Pseuderanthemum atropurpureum 177
'Tricolor' 177
'Variegatum' 177
pseudobulbs 57

Pteris cretica 177
'Albolineata' 177
'Alexandrae' 177
Punica granatum 'Nana' 177
purple heart 136
purple passion vine 12, 92
purple tree aeonium 34
pussy ears see *Cyanotis somaliensis*;
Kalanchoe tomentosa
pygmy date palm 122

Q, R
queen's spiderwort 159
queen's tears 46
rabbit's-foot fern 75
rabbit tracks 107
Radermachera sinica (*Stereospermum sinicum*) 178
rainbow plant 79
rat's-tail cactus 40
Rebutia minuscula 178
red crown cactus 178
red dracaena 67
red-flame ivy 166
red-hot cat's-tail 31
red ivy 166
red pineapple 38
red spider mites 212, 214
regal geranium 117
repotting 200–3
rest periods 211
resurrection plant 134
Rhapis excelsa 128
Rhipsalidopsis gaertneri 128
Rhipsalis
baccifera (*R. cassutha*) 178–9
cereuscula 140
rhizome 32, 44, 45, 75, 191
Rhododendron simsii 19, 129
Rhoeo spathacea 'Variegata'
(*R. discolor*) 129
Rhoicissus rhomboidea see *Cissus rhombifolia*
ribbon fern 177
ribbon plant see *Chlorophytum comosum*
'Vittatum'; *Dracaena sanderiana*

Rochea coccinea (*Crassula coccinea*) 179
'Alba' 179
'Bicolor' 179
roots 27, 190, 191, 204
Rosa 179
chinensis 'Minima' 179
rosary vine 154
rose bay 111
rose geranium 118
rose grape 108
rose of China 94
rose pincushion 105
rose-scented geranium 118
Rossioglossum grande see *Odontoglossum grande*
rubber plant 13, 20, 86
Ruellia makoyana 179
rust 215
rusty fig 86

S
saffron spike 40
St. Augustine grass 183
Saintpaulia 12, 18, 19, 22, 130, 193, 206
'Chimera' 130
'Little Delight' 130
'Love Bug' 130
'Marguerite' 130
'Pip Squeak' 130
'Wee Hope' 130
Salpiglossis sinuata 180
Sanchezia speciosa (*S. nobilis*) 180
Sansevieria trifasciata 11, 193
'Craigii' 131
'Golden Hahnii' 131
'Hahnii' 131
'Laurentii' 131
'Silver Hahnii' 131
sapphire flower 50
Sarracenia flava 180
satin pellionia 174
Saxifraga stolonifera 132
—'Tricolor' 132
Scadoxus multiflora ssp. *katherinae* 92
scale insects 214
Scarborough lily 186
scarlet leadwort 125
scarlet star 48
scarlet trompetilla 150
scent 15
scented-leafed geraniums 118
Schefflera
actinophylla 132
arboricola 12, 132
elegantissima see *Dizygotheca elegantissima*
Schizanthus pinnatus 180–1, 191
Schlumbergera x *buckleyi* (*S. bridgesii*) 13, 133
russelliana 133
truncata 133, 140
sciarid flies 214
Scilla siberica 181
'Alba' 181
'Spring Beauty' 181
Scindapsus aureus see *Epipremnum aureum*
sea grape 155
sea urchin cactus 160
Sedum
burrito 134
morganianum 134
sieboldii (*Hylotelephium sieboldii*) 81
—'Medio-variegatum' 181
seeds 208–9
seersucker plant 163
Selaginella
kraussiana 26, 134
lepidophylla 134
martensii 26

Senecio
  × *hybridus* (*S. cruentus*) 135
  —'Brilliant' 135
  —'Chloe' 135
  —'Cindy' 135
  macroglossus 136
  —'Variegatus' 136
  mikanioides 136
  rowleyanus 136
sensitive plant 170–1
sentry palm 96
Setcreasea purpurea 136
  striata see *Callisia elegans*
shamrock plant 116
shrimp plant 46
shrubby plants 191
Siberian squill 181
Siderasis fuscata 181
silk oak 91
silk tree 147
silver crown 156
silver jade plant 68
silver net leaf 26, 88
silver vase plant 33
silvery inch plant 145
Sim's azalea 129
Sinningia
  cardinalis 182
  speciosa 137
  —'Brocade' 137
  —'Glory' 137
  —'Princess Elizabeth' 137
  —'Waterloo' 137
siting plants 16–19, 192, 193
sky plant 143
slipper flower 15, 52
slipper orchids 115, 173
slipperwort 52
Smithiantha hybrids 182
snakeskin/snake plant 131
snow bush 151
Solanum
  capsicastrum 15, 21, 55, 137
  pseudocapsicum 137
soldier boys 169
Soleirolia soleirolii 172, 182
  'Argentea' 182
  'Aurea' 182
Solenostemon scutellarioides see *Coleus blumei*
Sonerila margaritacea 182
south walls 192, 193
Spanish bayonet 145
Sparmannia africana 183
Spathiphyllum wallisii 12, 18, 138
  'Cupido' 138
  'Illusion' 138
  'Mauna Loa' 138
  'Petite' 138
  'Sensation' 138
specimen plants 20
speeding Jenny 144
spiceberry 41
spider lily see *Crinum* × *powellii*;
  Hymenocallis littoralis
spider plant 11, 59
spiderwort 144
spineless yucca 12, 145
split leaf plant 108
spotted dumb cane 76
spotted flowering maple 30
spreading clubmoss 26, 134
spring star flower 167
staghorn fern 124
Stapelia variegata 183
starfish plant 70
star of Bethlehem see *Campanula isophylla*; *Eucharis* × *grandiflora*
star of the veldt 77
stem cuttings 206
stems 190, 191
Stenotaphrum secundatum 'Variegatum' 183

Stephanotis floribunda 15, 138
Stereospermum sinicum see *Radermachera sinica*
stonecrop 181
stone plant 104
stopping 205
strap flower 148
strawberry begonia geranium 132
strawberry mites 213
Strelitzia
  nicolai 184
  reginae 19, 184
Streptocarpus × *hybridus* 139, 194
  'Constant Nymph' 139
  'Falling Stars' 139
  'John Innes' 139
  'Wiesmoor' 139
Streptosolen jamesonii 184
string-of-beads 136
striped inch plant 53
Strobilanthes dyeranus 185
Stromanthe amabilis (*Ctenanthe amabilis*) 185
Sturt's desert pea 7, 154
succulents 140–1, 191, 193
sunrooms 17, 19
supports 27, 204–5
Swedish ivy see *Plectranthus australis*; *P. oertendahlii*
sweet basil 112
sweet bouvardia 150
sweet flag 146
sweetheart plant 121
Swiss cheese plant 12, 27, 108
sword fern 110
Syagrus weddelliana (*Microcoelium weddellianum*/*Cocos weddelliana*) 185
Syngonium podophyllum 12, 142
  'Butterfly' 142
  'Pixie' 142
  'White Butterfly' 142

T
table fern 177
taffeta plant 96
tailflower 39
taro vine 81
tarsonemid mites 213
tartogo 168
Tasmanian tree fern 159
teddy bear vine 157
temperature 194–5
temple bells 182
temple tree 176
tendrils 204
terraria 26–7
Tetrastigma voinieranum 185
Thanksgiving cactus 133
thrips 214
Thunbergia alata 186
thunderflies 214
Thymus
  × *citriodorus* 142
  —'Doone Valley' 142
  serpyllum 142
  —'Aureus' 142
  vulgaris 142
  —'Silver Posie' 142
tiger aloe 38
tiger jaws 85
tiger orchid 112
Tillandsia 48
  cyanea 49
  ionantha 143
ti tree/plant 67
Tolmiea menziesii 143, 209
  'Variegata'/'Taff's Gold' 143
top-dressing 203
touch-me-not 99
trace elements 198
Trachycarpus fortunei 186

Tradescantia
  fluminensis 18, 193
  —'Quicksilver' 144
  —'Variegata' 19, 144
  pallida 'Purple Heart' see *Setcreasea purpurea*
  spathacea see *Rhoeo spathacea*
  zebrina see *Zebrina pendula*
trailing plants 11, 204–5
trailing velvet plant 179
training 204–5
transpiration 196
Transvaal daisy 90
tree ivy 84
tree philodendron 120
Triteleia laxa see *Brodiaea laxa*
trumpet lilies 169
tuber 191
tufted fishtail palm 153
Tulipa
  'Apricot Beauty' 186
  'Bellona' 186
  'Christmas Marvel' 186
  'Flair' 186
  greigii 186
  kaufmanniana 186
  'Maréchal Niel' 186
  'Peach Blossom' 186
  'Schoonoord' 186

U, V
umbrella plant 75
umbrella tree 12, 132
upright plants 11
urn plant 33, 48
Vallota speciosa (*Cyrtanthus elatus*) 186
Vanda 114
variegated false holly 173
variegated table fern 177
vascular bundle 190, 191
Veitch's screw pine 173
velvet-leaf 102
velvet plant 12, 92
Venus's-flytrap 77
Vinca 56
vine weevils 214–15
Vriesea × *poelmannii*
  —'Margot' 144
  —'Marjan' 144
  —'White Line' 144
Vriesea splendens 144

W
wandering Jew see *Callisia elegans*; *Tradescantia fluminensis* 'Variegata'; *Zebrina pendula*

Washingtonia filifera 187
watering 196–7
water-lily tulip 186
watermelon begonia 174
watermelon pilea 122
wax flower 138
wax plant 97
wax vine 136
Weddel palm 185
weeping fig 11, 20, 87
West Indian holly 169
West Indian jasmine 176
west walls 192, 193
white arum lily 187
white bird-of-paradise 184
white calla lily 187
whiteflies 215
white ginger lily 165
white lily-turf 113
white marguerite 60
white sails 138
wild thyme 142
windmill palm 186
window plant 108
winter cherry 137
winter heath 160

X, Y, Z
xylem 190, 191
yellow palm 59
yellow pitcher plant 180
yellow sage 104
yesterday-today-and-tomorrow 50
youth-on-age 143
Yucca aloifolia 145
Yucca elephantipes 12, 19, 145
  —'Jewel' 145
  —'Silver Star' 145
  —'Variegata' 145
Zantedeschia
  aethiopica (*Z. africana*) 187
  —'Childsiana' 187
  —'Green Goddess' 187
  —'Little Suzie' 187
  elliotiana 187
  rehmannii 187
zebra plant 40
Zebrina pendula 11, 19, 145
  'Purpusii' 145
  'Quadricolor' 145
zonal geranium 117
zygocactus 133

Acknowledgments

PHOTOGRAPHIC CREDITS

B=BOTTOM; C=CENTER; L=LEFT; R=RIGHT; T=TOP

10 The Interior Archive; 11–13 Chas Wilder; 14–15L Spike Powell; 15TR Spike Powell; 15BR Chas Wilder; 16L Elizabeth Whiting & Associates; 16R Robert Harding Picture Library; 17T Elizabeth Whiting & Associates; 17B Camera Press; 20 Robert Harding Picture Library; 21 Elizabeth Whiting & Associates; 22 Spike Powell; 23T Linda Burgess/The Garden Picture Library; 23B Spike Powell; 24 Linda Burgess/The Garden Picture Library; 25 Spike Powell; 26T Chas Wilder; 26B Spike Powell; 30 Chas Wilder; 31L John Freeman/Lorenz Books; 31R Harry Smith Collection; 32L Photos Horticultural; 32R Chas Wilder; 33T Harry Smith Collection; 33B–35 Chas Wilder; 36 Robert Harding Syndication; 37L Chas Wilder; 37R Peter McHoy; 38 Chas Wilder; 39T Flower Council of Holland; 39B Chas Wilder; 40L A–Z Botanical Collection; 40R–41L Chas Wilder; 41R Peter McHoy; 42–43 Chas Wilder; 44L–44CL Andrew Payne; 44CR–44R Peter Rauter; 45 Harry Smith Collection, 46–47T Chas Wilder; 47B Andrew Payne; 48L Photos Horticultural; 48CL Chas Wilder; 48CR Harry Smith Collection; 48R Chas Wilder; 49–50L Andrew Payne; 50R Peter McHoy; 51T Chas Wilder; 51B Andrew Payne; 52L Chas Wilder; 52R Myer/Le Scanff/The Garden Picture Library; 53L Robert Harding Syndication; 53R Andrew Payne; 54 Chas Wilder; 55 Harry Smith Collection; 56L Peter McHoy; 56R Andrew Payne; 57L Chas Wilder; 57R Harry Smith Collection; 58–59L Chas Wilder; 59R Jacqui Hurst/Kyle Cathie; 60L Peter Rauter; 60R–61T Chas Wilder; 61B Peter Rauter; 62L Chas Wilder; 62R Andrew Payne; 63L Chas Wilder; 63R Andrew Payne; 64T Peter Rauter; 64B Chas Wilder; 65 Harry Smith Collection; 66T John Freeman/Lorenz Books; 66B Peter Rauter; 67–68 Chas Wilder; 69L Harry Smith Collection; 69R A–Z Botanical Collection; 70L Harry Smith Collection; 70R Chas Wilder; 71L Andrew Payne; 71R–72CL Chas Wilder; 72CR Harry Smith Collection; 72R Chas Wilder; 73L Harry Smith Collection; 73R–74L Chas Wilder; 74R Elizabeth Whiting & Associates; 75L John Freeman/Lorenz Books; 75R–76 Chas Wilder; 77 Harry Smith Collection; 78–79 Chas Wilder; 80L Andrew Payne; 80R Mark Gatehouse; 81 Chas Wilder; 82L Harry Smith Collection; 82R–83 Chas Wilder; 84L Andrew Payne; 84R–85L Chas Wilder; 85R Andrew Payne; 86L Harry Smith Collection; 86CL Chas Wilder; 86CR Peter H. Hallett/A–Z Botanical Collection; 86R–87L Chas Wilder; 87R Harry Smith Collection; 88L Chas Wilder; 88R Peter McHoy; 89L John Freeman/Lorenz Books; 89R Andrew Payne; 90 Chas Wilder; 91L A–Z Botanical Collection; 91R Harry Smith Collection; 92L Chas Wilder; 92R Harry Smith Collection; 93 Chas Wilder; 94L John Freeman/Lorenz Books; 94R Mark Gatehouse; 95T John Glover/The Garden Picture Library; 95B Chas Wilder; 96L Charles Marden Fitch; 96R Chas Wilder; 97L Harry Smith Collection; 97R Peter McHoy; 98–99L Chas Wilder; 99R Andrew Payne; 100L Harry Smith Collection; 100R–101L Chas Wilder; 101R Andrew Payne; 102L–102CL Chas Wilder; 102CR Christopher Fairweather/The Garden Picture Library; 102R–103 Chas Wilder; 104L Andrew Payne; 104R Chas Wilder; 105L Harry Smith Collection; 105R Andrew Payne; 106 Andrew Payne; 107–109 Chas Wilder; 110L Andrew Payne; 110R Chas Wilder; 110L Andrew Payne; 110R John Freeman/Lorenz Books; 112L Andrew Payne; 112R–113T Harry Smith Collection; 113B Andrew Payne; 114L Peter McHoy; 114CL–115 Chas Wilder; 116 Andrew Payne; 117T Chas Wilder; 117B Andrew Payne; 118–119 Chas Wilder; 120L Andrew Payne; 120R Harry Smith Collection; 121L Robert Harding Syndication; 121R–122 Chas Wilder; 123L Robert Harding Picture Library; 123R Harry Smith Collection; 124L Chas Wilder; 124R John Freeman/Lorenz Books; 125L Peter McHoy; 125R Andrew Payne; 126L–126CL Chas Wilder; 126CR Elizabeth Whiting & Associates; 126R Mark Gatehouse; 127L Harry Smith Collection; 127R Chas Wilder; 128L Harry Smith Collection; 128R Mark Gatehouse; 129L Chas Wilder; 129R Peter McHoy; 130–133L Chas Wilder; 133R Andrew Payne; 134–135 Chas Wilder; 136L Robert Harding Syndication; 136R–138 Chas Wilder; 139 Andrew Payne; 140L–140CL Chas Wilder; 140CR Andrew Payne; 140R–141L Chas Wilder; 141R Andrew Payne; 142L Chas Wilder; 142R Andrew Payne; 143 Chas Wilder; 144R Jacqui Hurst/Kyle Cathie; 145L Chas Wilder; 145R John Freeman/Lorenz Books; 146L Peter McHoy; 146R–148 Harry Smith Collection; 149L Chas Wilder; 149R Peter McHoy; 150L Chas Wilder; 150R Steven Wooster/The Garden Picture Library; 151 Peter McHoy; 152T Pam Collins/A–Z Botanical Collection; 153T John Freeman/Lorenz Books; 153B Peter McHoy; 154L–154C Chas Wilder; 154R–155L Robert Harding Syndication; 155R–156L Harry Smith Collection; 156R Peter McHoy; 157 Chas Wilder; 158L Photos Horticultural; 158R Derek Fell; 159L Harry Smith Collection; 159R–161T Chas Wilder; 161B Mark Gatehouse; 162 Chas Wilder; 163 John Freeman/Lorenz Books; 163R–164 Chas Wilder; 165T Bjorn Svensson/A–Z Botanical Collection; 165B Chas Wilder; 166L Charles Marden Fitch; 166C Brigitte Thomas/The Garden Picture Library; 166R–167T Harry Smith Collection; 167B–168L Peter McHoy; 168R Chas Wilder; 169 Harry Smith Collection; 170T Derek Fell; 170B Charles Marden Fitch; 171 Derek Fell; 172–173L Chas Wilder; 173R Gary Rogers/The Garden Picture Library; 174–176L Chas Wilder; 176R–177L Peter McHoy; 177C Chas Wilder; 177R Peter McHoy; 178L Chas Wilder; 178R Harry Smith Collection; 179 Mark Gatehouse; 180L Chas Wilder; 180R Harry Smith Collection, 181 Neil Davies/A–Z Botanical Collection; 182–183T Chas Wilder; 183B–185 Harry Smith Collection; 186–187T Chas Wilder; 187B Flower Council of Holland; 188–191 Chas Wilder; 194 Robert Harding Picture Library; 195T Stan Osolinski/Oxford Scientific Films; 195C Mr P. Clement/Bruce Coleman; 195B M.P.L. Fogden/Bruce Coleman; 198–240 Chas Wilder.

ARTWORK CREDITS

David Ashby 210–211
Lynn Chadwick 114–115, 126–127, 190
Chris Forsey Endpapers, 18–19, 192–193
Roger Kent 44–45, 48–49, 72–73, 86–87, 102–103, 140–141
Kuo Kang Chen 27, 196–197, 198–199, 204–205, 206–207, 208–209, 210–211, 212–213, 214–215.

The publishers wish to thank the following for providing plants for photography. Their kind cooperation is much appreciated.
Alexandra Palace Garden Centre
Architectural Plants
Arnott & Mason
Europlants
Holly Gate Cactus Nursery
McBeans Orchids
Palm Centre
The Conservatory
The Dutch Nursery

The publishers also wish to thank **Snapdragon Ltd** for the loan of the pots used in the photographs on pages 14 and 25.